Out of Bounds

Out of Bounds

Racism and the Black Athlete

LORI LATRICE MARTIN, EDITOR

Racism in American Institutions
Brian D. Behnken, Series Editor

 PRAEGER

AN IMPRINT OF ABC-CLIO, LLC
Santa Barbara, California • Denver, Colorado • Oxford, England

Library of Congress Cataloging-in-Publication Data

Martin, Lori Latrice.
  Out of bounds : racism and the Black athlete / Lori Latrice Martin.
    pages cm. — (Racism in American institutions)
  Includes bibliographical references and index.
  ISBN 978–0–313–39937–4 (hardback) — ISBN 978–0–313–39938–1 (ebook)
1. Racism in sports—United States. 2. African American athletes. I. Title.
GV706.32.M38   2014
796.089′96073—dc23   2013046467

ISBN: 978–0–313–39937–4
EISBN: 978–0–313–39938–1

18 17 16 15 14   2 3 4 5

This book is also available on the World Wide Web as an eBook.
Visit www.abc-clio.com for details.

Praeger
An Imprint of ABC-CLIO, LLC

ABC-CLIO, LLC
130 Cremona Drive, P.O. Box 1911
Santa Barbara, California 93116-1911

This book is printed on acid-free paper ∞

Manufactured in the United States of America

To
Emily Ann Thornton

Contents

Series Foreword

Brian D. Behnken

Out of Bounds is the third book to be published in Praeger/ABC-CLIO's new series, Racism in American Institutions (RAI). The RAI series examines the ways in which racism has become, and remains, a part of the fabric of many American institutions. For example, while the United States may have done away with overtly racist policies such as disfranchisement laws, racism still affects many of America's established institutions from the local voting registrar to political advertisements that marginalize communities of color. Schools may not be legally segregated, and yet many districts are not integrated. Recent 21st-century examples of racism in sports, from mascots that caricature Native American figures to sportscasters who argue that African Americans make superior athletes because of the legacy of slavery, also abound. This open-ended series examines the problem of racism in established American institutions. Each book in the RAI series traces the prevalence of racism within a particular institution throughout the history of the United States and explores the problem in that institution today, looking at ways in which the institution has attempted to rectify racism, but also the ways in which it has not.

Out of Bounds is the first collection of essays to be published in the RAI series. Volume editor Lori Latrice Martin has assembled an all-star cast of scholars and researchers to probe the institutional racism present in popular sports. Despite the increasing diversity visible in a variety of heretofore all-white sports, from golf to NASCAR, race and racial bias continue to be significant issues in American sports. And sports remain in many ways a microcosm of American cultural and societal beliefs. This collection offers both a long historical examination of racism in sports, as well as a more contemporary sociological and cultural exploration of institutionalized racism. The essayists elucidate how racial ideologies are discursive and socially constructed aspects of American life, especially in sports. They address a wide range of sports, from baseball to hockey, as well as how specific subsets within the African-American community, especially black female athletes, complicate our understanding of institutionalized racism in sports.

Lori Latrice Martin, a sociologist by training, has published widely in the fields of income inequality and race studies. The contributors are all respected experts in their fields. *Out of Bounds* highlights numerous controversies involving racism in sports, as well as policies and practices that structure racial disparities in sports in the United States today. Despite the increasing presence of black athletes, racism in sports endures because it has become institutionalized over time. *Out of Bounds* helps to explain how that institutionalization happened.

Brian D. Behnken
Iowa State University
Ames, Iowa

Acknowledgments

I wish to express my deepest appreciation to the contributors to this volume, *Out of Bounds: Racism and the Black Athlete.* I also would like to express my sincerest gratitude to one of my mentors, Kwando M. Kinshasha, the driving force behind the project, and to C. Keith Harrison for his words of support and encouragement throughout the development of this important work. I also wish to acknowledge Melissa Kong, Peter Massenat, Joseph Adams, and Donovan Smile for their assistance. I am forever indebted to a group of loyal family members and friends who support me in all that I do. Words cannot adequately express how grateful I am to the following people for their continued love and support of me and my work: Lee and Edith Burns, John Thornton, Sonji Thornton, Rachel Nichols, Lee Burns Jr., Mahima Christian, Walter Martin, Leroy Evans, David I. Rudder, Sonya Williams, Dione Cooper Footman, Donna Footman, McKinley and Sue Johnson, Dorothea Swann, Kelly Norman Ellis, Angeline Butler, Imani Kinshasa, Jannette Domingo, Carmen Solis, Reggie and LaDonna Sanders, Win and Betty Perry, James Hershberger, Theodore Burgett, Natasha Scott-Daniels, Cheryl Ellis, Carolyn Slaughter, Delores Jones-Brown, Katie Gentile, Kate Szur, Teresa A. Booker, Ernest Lee, Keith L.T. Wright, Henry Louis Taylor, Mark Naison, Hayward Derrick Horton, Murray Martin, Bill Batson, Derrick Martin, Sidney Jerome Rand, Barbara Ann Johnson, Leola Graham, Vivian Rand, Doris Graham, Ebrima Gaye, Michael Jerome Thornton, and Emir Sykes.

Introduction

Lori Latrice Martin

Out of Bounds: Racism and the Black Athlete is a collection of essays that trace racial controversy and conflict in sports in the United States. Contributors provide solutions and/or plans of action that address the problems of racism in sports. To place their work into an appropriate context, it is imperative that we understand the significance of sports in our society, and to do so, we must understand sports as a reflection of American culture.

Culture is defined as material, and even nonmaterial, objects that are passed from one generation to the next. Cultures often vary across space and time. While cultures may be diverse, they also share some similarities. Scholarly research has identified several cultural universals, that is, cultural attributes that may be found wherever people occupy a territory. These cultural universals, according to anthropologist George Murdock, include approved mating arrangements, family, religion, language, medicine, and games. Games are an important part of every culture, including American culture. Sports, or games, involve physical competitive activities that are well established and officially governed, and in which participants are motivated by both internal and external rewards. Sports are perhaps more American than apple pie.[1] Sports are socially constructed. They are politically contested. Sporting arenas, both at the amateur and the professional level, are sites where individuals, groups, and institutions meet. Sports do not operate in a vacuum. They influence society while simultaneously being influenced by it. The same social ills that have haunted American society—namely, classism, sexism, and racism—are evidenced at all levels of the sporting world. However, the dominant narrative is quite the opposite.

For many, sports are regarded as one of the few places in American society where the playing field is level. There is, of course, the acknowledgment that this was not always the case. Many Americans today know of Jackie Robinson and his role in breaking the color barrier in modern-day Major League Baseball, and many Americans today believe that race is either no longer a factor or has declined in significance. This assessment of the state of race relations in America applies not only to the world of sports, but to the society at large. The election of President Barack Hussein Obama and the multimillion-dollar athletic contracts and product endorsement deals are often cited as evidence that the United States is a postracial society.

Throughout the years, many debates have surrounded the topic of sports and race, debates that can be heard countrywide, from all sections of society: fans, players, coaches, commentators, educators, and so on. Although these issues may seem to be limited to the playing field or the ring, the issues surrounding racism in sports impact people in every realm of life, as they are often representative of problems that have not been addressed in society as a whole. The challenges our country faces in addressing these issues are not going to go away anytime soon. The purpose of this unique volume is to bring about an awareness of the issues, to aid readers in making the links between sports and society as a whole, and to encourage readers to think about solutions to the problems presented.

Contributors to this volume are engaged in active research agendas showing, empirically, that racism continues to exist in many American institutions, including sports. The volume is comprised of three parts. The first part looks at racism and sports in a theoretical perspective. The second examines evidence of racism in college and professional sports. In the first chapter, I both lay out and debunk the myth that we in the United States are living in a postracial society. Despite claims that sports are race neutral, I argue that contemporary sports serve as a classic example of the institutionalization of racism. In making the argument, I review the sociological literature on race and racism, and on race and sports. I begin by operationalizing racism. The term is often used but rarely defined and appropriately measured. I also explore the process by which black athletes come to be associated with selected sports and white athletes with other sports. I use golf as a case study.

In Chapter 2, Michael Regan, Akilah R. Carter-Francique, and Joe R. Feagin use the systematic racism theoretical framework to help us better understand the dominant positioning of whites and the lack of advancement of blacks in leadership positions in college sports. Systematic racism theory highlights the ideals, hierarchies, and problems that are characteristic of sports in American society in contemporary times and in historical context. It also uses empirical facts to provide a deeper understanding of the multilevel and multidimensional nature of racial oppression.

John A. Fortunato and Jerome D. Williams, in Chapter 3, use marketing theory to understand an issue that is apparent to many, whether you are a fan of professional baseball or not. Specifically, the researchers explore the disappearance of black athletes in Major League Baseball. While socio-economic status, competition from other sports, and the globalization of American baseball explain part of the decline of black participation in pro-fessional baseball, Fortunato and Williams focus instead on marketing. Marketing, argue the researchers, is the one variable within the control of league officials. Social identity theory and relationship marketing are useful frameworks for understanding and addressing the problem.

Social identity theory is also at the heart of Chapter 4, by Joshua B. Dickhaus and Lance Kinney. The authors examine the roles of race and in-group bias on perceptions of same-race and different-race controversial athletes. More precisely, Dickhaus and Kinney collect data from black and white participants at two southern universities to explore the roles of race and racism in credibility and character ratings for controversial athletes Brett Favre, Ben Roethlisberger, Michael Vick, and Tiger Woods.

In Chapter 5, Hayward Derrick Horton and I introduce a perspective called the critical demography of athletic destinations. The perspective draws from critical race theory, the colorism perspective, the population and structural change thesis, and the critical demography paradigm to aid in our understanding of athletic destinations for black and white athletes. The overrepresentation of blacks in selected sports may best be understood as a manifestation of racism heightened by population and structural changes in society at large.

David Naze has a provocative piece on racism in professional baseball involving Jackie Robinson. While Robinson is recognized by the league as an iconic figure who endured mistreatment by participants and spectators, Naze contends in Chapter 6 that Major League Baseball, due in large part to the persistence of racism, has done Robinson's legacy a great disservice. Major League Baseball, along with American society as a whole, has virtu-ally ignored Robinson's political voice and the negative implications of Robinson's acceptance into Major League Baseball for many within the black community. The narrative surrounding Robinson, argues Naze, has been purposefully constructed from a largely white male perspective.

To aid in our understanding of the existence and persistence of racism in sports in contemporary America, Wade P. Smith, Eric Primm, and Valerie

R. Stackman empirically analyze the devaluation of sport card values for black athletes in the National Basketball Association over the past few decades in Chapter 7. An athlete's race has been shown to impact how sports cards are valued over times. The researchers found evidence of a long-lived social construction of race, signified by the evaluation of players by the color of their skin.

The second part of this volume on racism and sports ends with an article by C. Keith Harrison. In Chapter 8, Harrison, examines black athletes in higher education. He explores and empirically assesses the reality in which students can be assessed as athletes and athletes as students. A situation such as this involves the efforts of individuals and groups who engage with one another and value both academic and athletic prowess. Specifically, a case study and snapshot for this investigation examines the Ashe Sports Scholars. Harrison contends that athletics in American higher education is a unique entity. Collegiate athletics provides an opportunity to analyze racism and sports.

The third part of this book, which focuses on race, gender, and media representations, opens with a chapter by noted cultural scholar David J. Leonard. In enhancing our understanding of racism and sports, Leonard focuses on a population that is arguably understudied, black female athletes. Leonard contends in Chapter 9 that while Title IX increased opportunities for women to participate in sports, opportunities for women have not been expanded universally. Although female athletes are not well represented in media coverage, white female athletes are disproportionately covered, rendering black female athletes undesirable and virtually invisible.

In Chapter 10, scholar Tiffany E. Barber examines the co-opting of black sports bodies and streetball in advertising campaigns in the 1990s. Barber focuses on the construction and commodification of blackness and masculinity. Exploring Pope.L's artistic intervention framework, she also addresses the black male body as a site of desire and consumption.

Chapter 11, written by Jennifer Greer and Christopher Murray, weighs in on the role that racism continues to play in sports in their analysis of the media's coverage of two highly controversial athletes. Murray and Greer perform a content analysis of framing and race in newspapers in America based upon the treatment of athletes Barry Bonds and Lance Armstrong.

C. Keith Harrison and his team of researchers address cultural myths and stereotypes about black male athleticism in Chapter 12. Using contact hypothesis theory and labeling theory, the scholars study racial knowledge about sport and place their findings within the context of the continuing significance of race in America. Their study includes a survey of over 300 university students' attitudes at a predominately white institution in the Midwest. Using quantitative and qualitative research methods, the researchers found significant differences between black and white respondents on whether black athleticism was the result of nature (genetic predisposition) or nurture (environmental forces).

In short, the chapters in this volume are meant to highlight controversies surrounding racism in sports and to present the policies and practices that both shape and perpetuate racial disparities in American sports today. While several of the chapters are of historical nature, the focus of the volume is on sports in America today with an emphasis on possible solutions to the problems presented that will encourage readers to think about changes that could be made to discourage racist policies and practices going forward.

Note

1. Coakley, Jay. (2009). *Sports and Society.* New York: McGraw-Hill.

Part I

Racism and Sports: Theoretical Perspectives

Chapter 1

The Black Athlete and the Postracial Myth

Lori Latrice Martin

Race as a Social Construction

Individuals who share similar physical characteristics such as skin color are said to have membership in the same racial group. However, race is not simply about biology. Race is considered a social construct because of the meanings we attach to certain groups. In American society, being white has historically come with far more privileges than having membership in any other racial group, thus race has meant access to certain rights and privileges for some and the exclusion from the same for others. It does not take much to search through American history for examples of people of color receiving unequal treatment when compared with members of the dominant racial group, whites.

Asians, blacks, Native Americans, and some white ethnic groups have felt the brunt of America's racialized social system. People of Chinese ancestry, for example, were excluded from becoming citizens. People of Japanese ancestry were forced into internment camps. Blacks were forced to labor as chattel slaves and then to live in a separate and unequal society. Native American tribes saw their population sizes decline rapidly over time, following their first encounter with early European settlers. Native Americans were not permitted to govern themselves; rather, various efforts were made to force upon them a foreign system of governance that would lead to the assimilation of that group and a transfer of millions of acres into European ownership. Thousands of Native Americans were not permitted to pursue happiness; instead, they were expelled from their land and forced to take up residence in unfamiliar territory. Even some white ethnic groups, upon their arrival into the United States, were considered to be separate races. They were considered nonwhite and as a result were excluded from certain jobs and even persecuted for their religious beliefs. Racial minority groups throughout American history have been excluded from owning land and/or have had restrictions placed on their ability to acquire such assets, while similar restrictions were not put upon members of the dominant group.

Racial minorities do not only receive unequal treatment relative to the dominant group, says Schaefer,[1] but they have a host of other characteristics that distinguish them from members of the dominant group. Racial minorities have physical and/or cultural characteristics such as skin color, hair texture, and language that are the bases upon which those with membership in racial minority groups are treated. Individuals with darker skin tone, for example, are often not considered as desirable as individuals with lighter skin tones. Darker-skinned individuals may be more closely associated with negative characteristics, while lighter-skinned may be more closely associated with positive characteristics. Prospective employees, for example, may favor lighter-skinned applicants over darker-skinned applicants.

In addition to receiving unequal treatment and having distinguishing physical and cultural characteristics, racial minority groups in America also share a sense of solidarity, their membership in their group is involuntary, and within-group membership is the norm. Individuals with membership in a racial group often feel a sense of connectedness between themselves and with other group members, even if the group members have not met personally. The shared experience of oppression, direct or indirect, historical or contemporary, is the tie that binds. It is the reason individuals with membership in the same racial group and in different gender, religious, social class, and ethnic groups can come together in a show of support around important issues. The George Zimmerman verdict is a great example. Many blacks disagreed with the jury's verdict. A week after the verdict was announced, protests were scheduled in 100 cities and featured blacks on the Fortune 500 list working alongside other blacks. Throughout the ordeal, we witnessed expressions of support for the family of the 17-year-old, Trayvon Martin.

Individuals with membership in a racial minority group do not sign up. There are no drives, campaigns, or sign-up bonuses; rather, individuals are members, willingly or reluctantly, by virtue of their birth. Individuals with membership in a minority group tend to marry others with membership in the same group.

Although the number of individuals identifying themselves as multiracial has increased over time, it is still the case that most often, blacks marry other blacks. A number of explanations have been offered to explain why this might be the case. Anecdotally, some say people tend to marry individuals with similar interest. Others say it is only "natural" that one would prefer someone with membership in one's own racial group. Empirical inquiries have led to other conclusions.

Sex imbalance ratios and a shortage of black males with the economic means to support a household have been the two dominant themes in the literature on the decline in black marriages over time. The mass incarceration of black males over the past few decades has also contributed to a decline in marriage rates for blacks. Although some black women may be willing to marry a black man with a criminal past, data show that "There is a significant shortage of Black men relative to Black women in the United States, and many of the men who are available for marriage are burdened with criminal records and limited economic resources."[2]

It should be noted that interracial marriage, particularly by black males, exists. Some scholars contend that interracial marriage involving blacks is understudied in contemporary times, particularly as it relates to explanations of the decline of black marriages. While "racial endogamy is still the rule for the black population, rates of marriage between black grooms and non-black brides have reached a substantial magnitude and, most important, greatly outnumber marriages involving black brides and non-black grooms."[3]

The general tendency of blacks to marry other blacks is undoubtedly a consequence of perceptions about beauty and desirability wherein European features are favored over Afrocentric features. Quinlan, Bates, and Webb provide a nice summary of media stereotypes of black women, for example.[4] Quinlan and colleagues argue that black women are often portrayed negatively in the media. Black women can regularly be seen as "criminals, buffoons, or hypersexual individuals." Black men are often portrayed in a similar manner.

Harkening back to earlier comments about the killing of Trayvon Martin, some have argued that these negative stereotypes of black people portrayed in the media existed long before the now infamous shooting in February 2012. Such stereotypes preceded the Martin case and have led to tragic consequences, for athletes and nonathletes alike.

Sadly, the Zimmerman verdict is not news; rather, it is history repeating itself. I am reminded of the documentary *Scottsboro: An American Tragedy*, which included a still image of Stanley Lebowitz, the Jewish lawyer from New York who was paid by the Communist Party to defend nine black males against charges that they raped two white women on a train headed for Chattanooga, Tennessee. The photo shows a stunned Lebowitz who had just heard that his clients had been sentenced to the death chamber. He, along with a multiracial coalition of individuals and organizations from across the globe, fought long and hard against a system that was designed to protect and serve some and control and oppress all others.

Despite the odds, and history being stacked against them, they kept the faith; the substance of things hoped for but not seen. They deeply and passionately believed in the set of principles upon which this nation was founded, principles and core values that like their ancestors, they fought not only to preserve, but to expand to others. They fought within a system that had historically fought against the very people whose lives they were trying to save. Far too many did not fully understand the depth of hatred, disdain, and animosity that the gatekeepers of the racial social order had not only for the defendants, but for what they represented—a group that had long been considered property. People of African ancestry had historically been considered a subrace of individuals who lacked civilization and had a propensity toward violence along with an insatiable thirst for white women.

Despite the facts of the case and the evidence presented, the Scottsboro defendants were found guilty and Lebowitz, the press, family, friends, and supporters worldwide were stunned. They were stunned not because they were unaware of what they were up against, but because they had believed that the system—with all of its imperfections—had structures in place that could bring about a different outcome. The defendants, most of whom did not receive official pardons until 2013, more than 70 years later, led tragic lives as a result of their lengthy and harsh incarceration.

The case of the Scottsboro defendants would not be the last time the justice system would shatter the hopes of a nation and help the world see how blind justice can really be. Many have compared the lynching of Emmett Till and the killing of Trayvon Martin. We must understand that there are some among us who do not understand the connections because they know very little about Till other than passing references to his name in musical lyrics. Yes, both young boys went to the store to buy candy before their lives ended and before the lives of their families, and many in the nation, were turned upside down. But the similarities go much deeper.

Like the Scottsboro defendants, Till and Martin were born in a world that refused to see each young man as a total person. In the documentary *Unforgivable Blackness*, James Earl Jones made the same observation about America's first black heavyweight champion, Jack Johnson. Emmett "Bo" Till was not seen through the eyes of the residents of Money, Mississippi, as a fun-loving 14-year-old boy with his whole life ahead of him; instead, he was criminalized, dehumanized, and made to serve as a lesson for blacks as to what would happen if they decided to defy the racial social norms of the day. Ultimately, the trial of Roy Bryant and J. W. Milam, the confessed killers of Till, was not about them; it was about preserving a way of life.

Similarly, the killing of Trayvon Martin, and the trial that followed, was not just about the taking of a young man's life before it even really got started. It was not just about two devoted parents humbly, gracefully, and courageously seeking justice for their son. It was about much more than that. No matter how many times people say it was not about race, the fact remains that like many cases before it, race was at the core. Trayvon Martin had the audacity to invade whitespace. Just as other African Americans who had managed to get beyond the gates that were supposed to keep whites safe, Martin had to be stopped and just like in days gone by, some ordinary white citizens have taken that to mean that it is their civic and patriotic duty to protect their women and children from the Trayvon Martins of the world. After all, it was the white woman home alone with her child who was the victim of a home invasion that led Zimmerman to start the Neighborhood Watch program to begin with.

Many had hoped that this time justice would be different. Over 2 million Americans of many different racial and ethnic groups signed a petition calling for the arrest of Zimmerman. Hundreds of thousands broke out their hoodies in a show of solidarity. They watched each person's testimony with bated breath. They watched the news that a verdict had been reached. As the verdict was announced, many were stunned, left without speech. Gifted writers, journalists, academicians, elected officials, mothers, fathers, sons, and daughters suddenly had no words. Soon anger turned to action, peaceful protests sprouted across the nation, and editorials began flowing again. Much has—and will—be written about the verdict, including missteps on both sides, and like far too many tragedies, the furor surrounding the Zimmerman case may lessen, but one thing we cannot forget is that this trial, this verdict, this episode in history, despite the 24-hour coverage and use of social media, was not "news"; instead, it was history repeating itself.

And the only way to bring about real change is to demythologize the idea that we are living in a postracial society, the idea that race no longer matters. Some—blacks and whites alike—have tried to argue over the past few decades that race has declined in significance, while others of us have argued the contrary. Oh how we wish we were wrong, but the killing of Trayvon Martin is just one of the many contemporary examples of the widening gap between what society is and how it should be.

The case against Jack Johnson notwithstanding, many continue to believe that sports provide the best evidence that we are living in a postracial society. It can be shown that sports serve as a classic textbook example of the existence and persistence of racism in America in the 21st century. Scholars and laypersons alike often find the aforementioned statement hard to believe due to a number of factors, including the overrepresentation of blacks in high–revenue generating sports; however, blacks are underrepresented in far more sports, such as in golf. Two other important reasons include a lack of understanding of what racism is and is not and the failure on the part of scholars to link the sociological literature on racial socialization with sports and the literature on sports with racial socialization. In this chapter, I define racism and its relationship to racial socialization and the identification of selected sports as "white sports" or "black sports." I use the treatment of blacks in golf in historical and in contemporary times to illustrate the continuing significance of race in general—and race in sports in particular—to debunk the myth that we are living in a postracial era.

Racism Defined

The term "racism" is often used in scholarly literature and in everyday conversations; however, there appears to be some confusion or misunderstanding about what racism is and is not. The terms "racism" and "prejudice" are sometimes used interchangeably. For example, Berg describes symbolic racism as a kinder and gentler form of racial prejudice than that experienced in the past.[5] Racism is often treated as a medical condition, as a psychological problem afflicting small pockets within the population. One need only conduct a search of academic journal articles with the term "racism" in the title to see observe just how many recent publications can be found in psychological journals and how many define racism as a belief, feeling, or negative attitude.[6] For instance, Tarman and Sears define racism as a "latent psychological belief system that disfavors minorities and then emerges in dominant group members when they are confronted with certain political symbols, resulting in oppression to various race-targeted policies."[7] Not only do the authors see racism as largely a psychological phenomenon, racism mysteriously appears and disappears in response to representations of material and nonmaterial objects to which we attach shared meaning, as opposed to a system that is the foundation of our social structure and racialized social system.

Horton and Sykes provide a more accurate understanding of not only how best to define, but also how best to measure, racism.[8] The definition and operationalization of racism by Horton and Sykes shows how society is structured such that public policies and private actions privilege whites and disadvantages others, including blacks.[9] Horton and Sykes define racism as "a multilevel and multidimensional system of dominant group oppression that scapegoats the race and/or ethnicity of one or more subordinate groups."[10] From the definition provided, we can see that racism occurs not only at the micro level, but at the macro level as well. The operationalization of racism as both a multilevel and multidimensional phenomena points to the fact that manifestations of racism are many, and they vary across place and time. In other words, racism is not stagnant or constant; rather, it is ever-changing. One manifestation of racism in the 21st century is the perception of selected sports as black sports or white sports, which occurs as a result of a process of racial socialization (Figure 1.1).

Horton and Sykes are not the only scholars to understand racism in this manner. In their work on the racial formation perspective from nearly two decades ago, Omi and Winant describe race as a social construct and discuss the extent to which it is politically contested. The scholars argue, among other things, that racial categories are "created, inhabited, transformed, and destroyed."[11] As a society undergoes demographic, economic, and structural changes, the ways in which we define what it means to be of a particular racial group also change. And yet the fact that some groups remain privileged at the expense of others remains the same.

Bonilla-Silva's work on color-blind racism is also critical in understanding the historic and contemporary significance and centrality of race, and of racism, in our society. Bonilla-Silva describes four frameworks that help us understand how many people in our society attempt to explain away clear disparities, particularly racial disparities, by ignoring or skirting around central causes like race. This is particularly significant in the world of sports, where the assumption of far too many is that the playing field is leveled and has been for decades.

FIGURE 1.1   Racism and Athletic Destinations: The Role of Racial Socialization.

Bonilla-Silva contends that legislative changes necessitated a shift from what he calls Jim Crow racism toward color-blind racism. Tactics under Jim Crow racism were more overt, while tactics under the new racism are more covert.[12] Not only are the tactics more covert, but much of the language and principles used in the struggle for justice and human dignity at the height of the modern day civil rights movement have been co-opted and used to justify the persistent and growing disparities that have come to characterize American life. Bonilla-Silva describes four frameworks, which are essential to understanding color-blind racism: abstract liberalism, naturalization, cultural racism, and minimization. White liberals, in short, may support equality in principle and see evidence of racial inequality but explain away such differences as evidence of personal misfortunes or personal failures, not the consequence of historic, or even contemporary, institutional policies and procedures of which they are among the chief beneficiaries. Racial socialization describes a set of processes by which the dominant racial ideology is communicated, and contrary to popular scholarly opinion, these processes are not confined to black families but are evidenced throughout society, including throughout the sports world.[13]

A Sociology of Racial Socialization in America

The literature on racial socialization has grown over time to reflect changes in society and changes in the way we think about and deal with race and ethnicity in this country.[14] Writing in the 1980s, Peters and Massey described racial socialization as including the dual task of giving children a positive black identity and teaching children how to live in a hostile world.[15] The definition is similar to the one posited by Hill and others.[16] How those messages were communicated involved cultural socialization, or taking into account historical or cultural figures. In the 1990s, greater emphasis was placed on socialization that was context specific.[17] In more recent years, racial socialization has been modified within the new context of an assimilation-based theory of adult black identity. This new context is called the investment in blackness hypothesis.

The investment in blackness hypothesis, according to Shelton, focuses on who teaches what during racial socialization. Who teaches what may impact whether the message is one that promotes mistrust of nonblacks and/or one based upon one's social class position. Friendship networks and cultural communication, claims Shelton, may also influence what black parents teach their children about race relations.[18] A number of strategies have been identified within the context of this hypothesis, including race-conscious, race-neutral, race-avoidant and class consciousness.[19] The most recent developments surrounding racial socialization also recognize growing cultural complexity among blacks.[20] Within this context, it is suggested that blacks who are more committed to black social heritage are more likely to discuss race matters with their children.[21]

However, much of the focus of the research on racial socialization remains on the family.[22] Little, if any, attention is devoted specifically to spaces such as the world of sports as an agent of racial socialization. Most studies that do explore race and sports do not examine the set of processes by which members of the dominant group and members of racial minority groups come to "know" their place in the social structure in general and their place in sports in particular. Through sports, messages are communicated as to what is acceptable participation, and behavior, for selected racial groups.

To be clear, there is a great deal of research on race and sports.[23] However, the research on race and sports is missing, in my view, a unified theory for understanding how sports participation, performance, observance, and media representations are differentiated based upon one's socially constructed racial classification.[24] Racial socialization does that, but it is underutilized in the literature. Much of the research on racial socialization treats the process as one that occurs almost exclusively within the context of the parent-child relationship, when racial socialization—at its best and at its worst—is much more complex than that. Racial socialization can best be understood as the process by which we learn the ways of society as they have been prescribed for us based upon the racial groups to which we belong. After all, it is through social experiences that we learn culture, the material and nonmaterial objects that are passed from one generation to the next.[25] Agents of socialization play important roles, but the family is not the only one, and it is not always the most influence in certain contexts.[26] Sports—"well-established, officially governed competitive physical activities in which participants are motivated by internal and external rewards"[27]— may play more of a role than the family, peer groups, religion, politics, the economy, or even education.

The significance and influence of sports in our lives cannot be underestimated. Even people who claim to detest the violence and brutality some associate with boxing, hockey, and football, for example, are in line with the rest of us in the days leading up to Super Bowl Sunday buying food, drinks, televisions, and so on, if only for the commercials. They are at the local Catholic Church, often regardless of their religious affiliation, signing their children up to play on the Catholic Youth Organization (CYO) team. They are peddling raffle tickets to support the Pop Warner cheerleading squad or Junior Midget team to help defray the cost of going to the championship tournament. Their taxes go to building a stadium for the professional team or constructing a new athletic complex in the community that is said to generate jobs and revenue for their local towns. The children they have loved and nurtured can often recite the stats for their favorite team or player more fluently than they can each of these 50 United States. Sports are an important agent of socialization, particularly racial socialization.

So, what is the core theoretical and methodological issue surrounding racial socialization and sports? The issue is that the literature on race and sports tends to ignore socialization, and the literature on socialization tends to ignore issues of race and sports. Coakley correctly observes that over the past half-century, the literature on socialization has focused primarily on three areas: "the process of becoming involved and staying involved in sports; the process of changing or ending sport participation; and the impact of being involved in sports."[28] Matters of race are not viewed as central to these processes. "The meanings given to sport experiences vary from one person to another because social relationships are influenced by social definitions, which may or may not, include race." This understanding of socialization, and the prevailing understanding of racial socialization in particular, is based upon the micro-level interactionists perspective, which focuses on face-to-face interactions and small group relationships and has replaced models based on structural theories that, according to Coakley, dominated the literature prior to the 1980s.[29]

There is a need for scholars interested in studying race and sports to revisit the overreliance on socialization from a micro-level perspective; instead, scholars must explore the methodological and theoretical implications of understanding the multilevel and multidimensional nature of racial socialization in sports. This will allow scholars to adequately account for the centrality of race in our society and the centrality of race in sports. An examination of two sports in which blacks have historically been underrepresented shows the many manifestations of racism over time, the role of racial socialization, and sports as an agent of socialization in determining athletic destinations.

Racial Socialization and Golf: The Early Years

While the amateur and professional basketball courts and football fields may be filled with black athletes, American golf courses surely are not.[30] Nevertheless, most Americans, whether they are fans of golf or not, know the name Tiger Woods. Woods was a household name even before his very public split with his wife. Few Americans know that he is the latest in a long legacy of golf participation among blacks that dates back to the late 1800s.[31] Charlie Sifford and Lee Elder were among the better-known golfers of their day; others like Teddy Rhodes, Bill Spiller, Nathaniel Starks, James Black, and Joe Roach were less well known.[32]

Until the mid-20th century blacks were excluded from participating in the Professional Golf Association of America (PGA).[33] On the official PGA website, the organization is described as the largest working sports organization, with more 27,000 members. Established in 1916 in New York City, its purpose was to increase equipment sales. During the organization's first year, the first ever PGA championship was held. The championship was cancelled in 1917 and 1918 due to World War I. The PGA Championship resumed in 1919. The fee for entry in the championship was $5, and membership in the organization was over 1,300. Dues increased in $10 in 1928 and $50 in 1929.

In 1940, the PGA established a fund to support members who were unable to work. The association paid out over $4,600. A year later, the group celebrated its twenty-fifth anniversary with over 2,000 members. The Golf Hall of Fame was also established at this time. The PGA Championship was again cancelled due to war. About a decade later, membership had almost doubled and shortly thereafter, a major television network purchased the broadcasting rights for PGA Championships that would last for four years. As a result, PGA membership had reached almost 10,000 members by the mid-1980s. Missing from the rich history of the PGA is information about important dates and events involving people of color. This is because for much of the organization's history, blacks were excluded altogether or were placed in very restrictive roles.

Like blacks had done in so many other cases, both inside and outside of the sports world, they created their own association. The black professional golfers played throughout Florida. Blacks made other important contributions to the game. The African American Registry tells about Dr. George F. Grant. Grant was one of the first black dentists and one the first black golfers. Using his dental skills, he invented an improved golf tee that is the basis for golf tees in use today.

John M. Shippen Jr., according to the Registry, also made an important contribution to the sport of golf even though the message that was clearly being sent was that golf was a white sport. Shippen, at the age of 16, became the first professional American golfer. In 1896, he was one of two nonwhite players in the second U.S. Open. The other nonwhite player was Oscar Bunn, who lived on the Shinnecock Reservation. The Shinnecock Hills Golf Club was established in 1891 on 80 acres of land purchased by local residents, according to the club's official website. Shippen learned the game from Willie Dunn. Dunn was a Scottish golfer who was responsible for expanding the course from 12 to 18 holes. Shippen quickly picked up the game while helping construct the course.

Shippen's role in the history of golf was chronicled in an episode of the PBS series *History Detectives*. Investigators took on the case of a golf club bearing the name J. M. Shippen. The club was donated to a foundation named after Shippen. The purpose of the foundation is to teach minority children the game of golf. Upon receipt of the golf club, Shippen's grandson wondered if the club had been used in the U.S. Open back in 1896. The history detectives showed that golf was a relatively new game in 1896.

Moreover, Gwendolyn Wright of the *History Detectives* show pointed out that "golf was a game for America's wealthy elite and the first American country clubs were for whites only."[34] The investigators provided more information about Shippen's background based on interviews with a host of people in the know.

The first professional American golfer was born in Washington, DC. His father was a Presbyterian minister who went to Shinnecock Indian Reservations to minister to the Shinnecock Indians. He was hired in 1890 to clear land for a new golf course on Long Island. Many Shinnecock Indians were also hired to clear land. By the time the course opened in 1892, say the investigators, Shippen was working as a caddy and even taught the club's new white members the game. It was the club members who entered Shippen and Dunn in the U.S. Open. Shippen's European opponents did not like the idea of playing nonwhite opponents and walked out. When informed by officials that the competition would proceed with or with them, the European opponents returned. Although Shippen finished fifth, he led on day one and received national attention.

The investigators were also able to uncover information from Shippen's last caddy, Ralph Wise. He was a caddy at a golf club formerly known as Shady Rest, which was established in 1921. Shady Rest was built to "cater to the area's growing African American middle class."[35] It was considered the first black country club in America. After 1896, Shippen was prohibited from participating in many professional golf competitions due to his race, but he continued to play professionally on mostly black courses. He went on to run a business, as many golf professionals did at that time, making and selling golf clubs. The golf club donated to the foundation bearing his name one of the very first clubs Shippen made.

John Bartholomew was a black architect who was well known for his abilities as a greens keeper, but he could not even play on the very courses he designed because he was black. Troubled by the lack of opportunity for black golfers, they formed the Colored Golfers Association of America. The organization held a tournament in Stow, Massachusetts, in 1926 that was very successful. "The tournament was a proving ground for gifted minorities and a place where Black golfers came together in a show of strength and harmony in a segregated America," says the African American Registry.

The African American Registry, in its brief history of blacks and golf, found that most blacks learned to play the game of golf while they were caddies. It was estimated that there were over 5,000 golf facilities in the late

1930s and fewer than 10 allowed black players. However, wealthy blacks in places such as Polk County, Florida, created their own spaces to enjoy the game of golf. Wealthy blacks purchased land in places like American Beach, near Amelia Island. Prior to the purchase of the land, it was not uncommon for whites playing on segregated courses, such as the Cleveland Heights Golf Course and the Carpenter's Home Golf Course, to pull local children out of classes at nearby high schools to serve as caddies. Caddies could play on the segregated courses once a week and were allowed to use inadequate equipment. LaFrancine Burton, writing for the *Ledger* (Lakeland, FL), said that "learning how to play golf under such circumstances led to the remarkable skills possessed by some of the early golfers."[36] Many black golfers enjoyed much success professionally playing against other professional black golfers. The black association, however, folded due to a lack of adequate funding and by the 1980s, it ceased hosting tournaments. Like in other sports, once blacks moved toward the predominately white league, the predominately black league folded.

In *Unlevel Playing Field*, Wiggins and Miller go into great depth about the legacy of racism in golf. The authors note that legal battles in sports increased following World War II and that his was the case for golf, too. Lawsuits related to golf were the result of the popularity of the sport in the black community, an increase in black militancy, and the lack of private and public golf courses that were available to blacks. Wiggins and Miller describe one of the more publicized cases involving black golfers William Spiller, Ted Rhodes, and Madison Gunter.[37]

Spiller, according to sports writer Jimmie Tramel, was a native of Tulsa, Oklahoma, and one of its most famous residents. Spiller was born in 1913 in Tishomingo. He was a good athlete in high school and went on to earn a degree at Wiley College in Texas. Spiller eventually made his way to Los Angeles, where he developed a love and expertise for the game of golf. Tramel, in an effort to increase awareness about Spiller's legacy, tells us that in 1948, Spiller played in the Los Angeles Open, which was one of only a handful of tournaments that permitted blacks to compete.

"Many black golfers of that era took a pacifist approach and were willing to embrace equal rights in increments. Not Spiller," says Peter McDaniel, author of *Uneven Lies*. "Not only was he radical by nature, he was also intelligent. So he could argue pretty much his own case and he knew his rights and he knew his rights were being broken. That was unbearable for him. He was a civil rights activist long before it was fashionable simply through the game of golf and the game he was determined to play no matter what."[38]

Ted Rhodes was another highly skilled golfer, but he was limited in what he could accomplish because of the bold seemingly impenetrable colorline drawn by the PGA and many private and public clubs. In honor of Black History Month in 2007, Rhonda Glenn of the U.S. Golf Association (USGA), told the story of Rhodes's trials and triumphs. Born in Nashville, Tennessee, when he was young, Rhodes worked as a caddy at Belle Meade County Club and Richland County Club, which Glenn describes as exclusive. Blacks were prohibited from playing there. He honed his skills, says Glenn, using a 2-iron someone had thrown away. Rhodes did not play on the plush greens that many wealthy and middle-class whites had access to; instead, he practiced at local baseball fields.

In addition to working as a caddy, Rhodes worked as part of the Civilian Conservation Corp before joining the navy. A World War II veteran, Rhodes settled in Chicago, where he became friends with another legend in American competitive sports, Joe Louis. Glenn said the relationship between Rhodes and Louis had a profound impact on Rhodes's life. Louis loved the game of golf and hired Rhodes to be his player partner and his personal instructor. Rhodes and Louis were quite the team.

Louis sponsored Rhodes and assisted him in networking with individuals who could help take him to the next level. Ray Magrum, brother of Lloyd Mangrum, a U.S. Open Champion of the mid-1940s, did just that. The challenge was finding a place where Rhodes could play. Rhodes played in tournaments sponsored by the U.S. Colored Golf Association, but the purses paled in comparison to what one could win in PGA-sponsored tournaments. Glenn reported that the United Golf Association (UGA), as the United States Colored Golf Association is now called, had awards "that often provided as little as $100 to the winner."[39]

Between 1946 and 1947, Rhodes was victorious in six UGA tournaments, including the Joe Louis Open in Detroit. His best year, according to Glenn, was in 1948. In that year, Rhodes competed in the LA Open at Riviera Country Club. Spiller also competed there. Both golfers finished high enough to qualify for the Richmond Open that was to be held in California.

Rhodes, along with Spiller and Madison Gunther, attempted to gain entry into the event but were turned away by the clause excluding non-whites. The three, with the help of Jonathan Rowell, filed a lawsuit. Wiggins and Miller published a copy of a letter written by Rowell seeking support in the case from Thurgood Marshall, who was then at the National Association for the Advancement of Colored People (NAACP). In the letter, Rowell established that he has fought for many social justice issues, including a case surrounding the bombing of a black person's house. He also stressed his association with one of the local branch of the NAACP in San Francisco.[40]

Rowell provided Marshall with the facts of the case and insight as to how he was planning to proceed. The lawyer for the three black golfers reported that he filed a complaint in superior court for the county of Contra Costa, where the Richmond Golf Club was located. He identified the following code: "All citizens within the jurisdiction of this state are entitled to the full and equal accommodations, advantages, facilities, and privileges of . . . places of public accommodation or amusement."[41] Rowell let Marshall know that he argued that the three black golfers were trying to gain entrance into a professional tournament, which was in keeping with the spirit of the code. On their behalf, Rowell reported that he would be seeking $5,000 in damages—$2,000 would be for actual damages, and the rest would be for humiliation, stress, and anguish.

A suit would also be brought against the PGA in the amount of $100,000 each for Rhodes, Spiller, and Gunther because the PGA essentially operated as a monopoly and provided economic opportunities for golfers, which these three men were denied the right to earn. Rowell believed there was a precedent for this in *James v. Marinship* (25 Cal. 2nd 721, 1944). According to the opinion of the court, this case dealt with:

> an appeal from an order of the Superior Court in Marin County awarding a preliminary injunction which, among other things, restrained defendants from discharging or causing the discharge of plaintiff and [25 Cal.2d 725] other Negro employees because they are not members of a labor union with which their employer has a closed shop agreement, but which will not grant Negroes full membership privileges. The basic question presented is whether a closed shop may be enforced by a labor union together with an arbitrarily closed or partially closed union membership.

The judgment was affirmed.

Just before the case was to come to court, the PGA vowed to do away with its discriminatory policy, and the three men dropped their lawsuit. A year later, after enjoying much success playing against black golfers,

Rhodes attempted to enter a PGA tournament in Iowa but was denied. Rhodes left his mark on the game. He was a mentor to Lee Elder, a native of Dallas, Texas, and the first black person to play in the Masters (in 1975).

Racial Socialization and the Reluctant Black Golfer

Few people have had the kind of impact on a professional sport that Tiger Woods, who publically had acknowledged the sacrifices of black athletes before him, has. Few who follow the sport can forget seeing Woods on the course with his dad by his side. Julia Wang of *People Magazine* edited a piece on Woods and notes that he began his golf training at the young age of 10 months in the late 1970s.[42] He did what most kids did, imitating what he saw someone else doing—in this case, his dad. Seeing that his son was taking an interest in the game, his father taught him about it. By 1990, Tiger Woods was on the Junior Amateur circuit, winning world title after world title. As a tenth grader, he became the youngest person ever to play in a PGA tour event. A few years later, he entered Stanford University but left after two years to play golf professionally. Within no time, he had million-dollar endorsement deals with major companies such as Nike. He was winning awards and gracing the covers of sports magazines. In 1997, he was the youngest person ever to win the Masters. Woods continues to be a dominant player but suffered the tragic loss of his father in 2006. Within about three years, Woods was making the headlines for all the wrong reasons. He was accused of cheating on his wife with multiple women after a very public incident near his home. After some time away from the game, Woods started staging a comeback.

An examination of the scholarly literature on Woods speaks less to his skills on the golf course than to how he is identified racially and how he identifies himself. Nishime discussed how his refusal to identify solely as black in favor of a more multicultural identity gained him support from many other multiracial individuals. However, he did lose support from blacks, some of whom believed he was attempting to distance himself from the racial group.

Comparing Woods and Homer Plessy from the historic *Plessy v. Ferguson* Supreme Court case (1896), Nishime observes that Asians were used in both situations to promote color-blind rhetoric. "Asians are used to turn our attention away from the debate over racial categorization and to preemptively stabilize racial categories."[43] Cashmore is another scholar who tackled this issue but from a very different perspective.

Cashmore sees Tiger Woods as a "colorfree emblem of a new America in which racism is dead and there are no barriers to progress for any member of its citizenry—a new racial order." Cashmore goes as far as to define Woods as "a new kind of white person." Said another way, Cashmore contends:

> Woods effectively invites consumers not to challenge racism directly, but to buy commodities that externalize success and in this way avoid confronting the racism that continues to bedevil most of America's black population.[44]

So it is not Woods the individual here, it is the representation of Woods to the media. He becomes a "personalized reproduction of America. It is a place where the racism that was such a source of torment throughout the 20th century has now almost disappeared."[45] Cashmore's reference to "niggas" in the article is inappropriate, and his claim that racism is dead contradicts statements and data presented in the article about persistent racial and ethnic inequality. Tiger Woods's declaration concerning how he plans to identify himself racially informs the ongoing debate in communications and in other social sciences regarding whether to consider racial categories as an imagined social construct or as a material reality. At the same time, his experiences with some golfers on the tour serve as a reminder that many of his counterparts still see him as a black golfer. He is still seen as an outsider.

One golfer recently caved to pressure and issued an apology to Woods after making a "fried chicken" comment, according to an article appearing in the *Washington Times* on May 22, 2013. This was not the first time Woods was on the receiving end of a "joke" that was heavily laden with racist overtones. In the same article, readers are reminded of a comment made in the late 1990s by Fuzzy Zoeller, who said of Woods's Masters victory, "You pat him on the pack and say congratulations and enjoy it and tell him not to serve fried chicken next year. Got it? Or collard greens or whatever the hell they serve."[46] Although Woods—and any other person of color—has the right to identify himself any way he sees fit, it is important to note that society has its own way of reminding one, at least for some, that race still matters.

Although Cashmore and Woods both seem to think that American society has entered a postracial era in which people of color can identify with the racial or ethnic group of their choice despite highly visible racial markers such as skin color, the PGA has identified ways to address what it continues to see as a race problem in the sport, targeting children, college students, and even minority business owners.

PGA Plans for Diversity

The PGA publishes a document outlining diversity goals related to increasing participation and employment opportunities for women and people of color.

The National Golf Foundation found that participation rates were lowest among blacks for each of the years under study and that there has been a decline in participation rates over time for blacks and whites. At the same time more Asians and Hispanics are participating.

The National Golf Foundation found a connection between household income and minority participation in golf for 2010. For each group, participation rates increased as income increased. Incomes and participation rates were higher for whites, Asians, and Hispanics at all income levels when compared with the black population. Continued discrimination in the sport or lack of interest among golfers and nongolfers may be to blame.

A number of strategies were outlined to increase the number of nonwhites. The PGA said it raises awareness about careers in golf at junior golf tournaments that feature minority players and at historically black colleges and universities (HBCUs). Additionally, the PGA says its partners provide scholarships to minorities through the PGA Minority Collegiate Golf Championship in an effort to defray the cost of attending the PGA Professional Golf Management Program, which includes an internship opportunity.

The golf association boasts that it has provided over $10 million in funding to youth development programs across the country that include minority youth. These programs include Midnight Golf and Urban League Youth Golf. Scholarships have also been provided for minority students interested in attending an institution of higher learning that offers the PGA Golf Management University Program. Recently, according to the PGA, the University of Maryland Eastern Shore became the first HBCU in the nation to offer the management program.

A commitment to increasing minority representation among vendors at PGA-sponsored events is also underway. The association aims to have 25 percent of vendors/suppliers at major championships be certified as minority- and women-owned companies.

Conclusion

The prevailing wisdom is that blacks have taken over sports and that the overrepresentation of blacks in selected sports is evidence that we are living in a postracial society where race no longer matters. It is said that black athletes earning million-dollar salaries is evidence that sports and society at large are color blind. While black participation in selected sports has increased, particularly since World War II, it has declined and/or is virtually nonexistent in other sports. Golf is but one sport that historically has been considered a white endeavor but to which black players make important contributions, from creating equipment to winning integrated championships, even without the benefit of the training and facilities, open to their white counterparts. The reasons for the underrepresentation and the overrepresentation of blacks in an array of sports are multifaceted. The common thread, however, is that whatever sport professional black athletes are engaged in, they are subject to the same racialized social hierarchy that has existed throughout the globe for centuries and in this county before the War of Independence and after the Civil War.

Black athletes sometimes experience symbolic inclusion, as blacks in other areas of social life do, but each eventually encounters a personal experience, or learns of the experience of others, that serves as a reminder that the individuals who have less power and control over their lives than members of a dominant group are still considered subordinate and receive unequal treatment as a result. The underrepresentation of blacks in most sports at the amateur and professional levels is a powerful reminder that racism is not dead, nor is it dying. It is a reminder that we live in a racialized social system from which no social institution is immune, not even the great wide world of sports. It is important, therefore, that scholars interested in race and sports understand the role of racial socialization in athletic destinations. It is equally important that scholars interested in race understand the important role that sports play in communicating and perpetuating the postracial myth.

Notes

1. Shaefer, R. (2010). *Racial and ethnic groups.* Upper Saddle River, NJ: Pearson.

2. King, A. O., & Allen, T. T. (2009). Personal characteristics of the ideal African American marriage partner: A survey of adult black men and women. *Journal of Black Studies, 4,* 570.

3. Crowder, K. D., & Tolnay, S. E. (2000). A new marriage squeeze for black women: The role of racial intermarriage by black men. *Journal of Marriage & Family*, 62(3), 792.

4. Quinlan, M. M., Bates, B. R., & Webb, J. B. (2012). Michelle Obama "got back": (re)defining (counter)stereotypes of black females. *Women & Language*, 35(1), 119–126.

5. Berg, J. A. (2013). Opposition to pro-immigration public policy: Symbolic racism and group threat. *Sociological Inquiry*, 83(1), 1–31.

6. Horton, H. D. & Sykes, L. L. (2008). Critical demography and the measurement of racism: A reproduction of wealth, status, and power. In *White logic, white methods: Racism and methodology*, edited by Tukufu Zuberi and Eduardo Bonilla-Silva. Lanham, MD: Rowman & Littlefield, 239–250.

7. Tarman, C., & Sears, D. O. (2005). The conceptualization and measurement of symbolic racism. *Journal of Politics*, 67, 731–761.

8. Horton & Sykes. Critical demography and the measurement of racism.

9. Leonard, D. (2012). Joe Paterno: White patriarchy and privilege; Nostalgia and the football-media complex. *Cultural Studies Cultural Methodologies*, 12, 373–376.

Rothenberg, P.S. (2008). *White privilege*. New York: Worth Publishers.

10. Horton & Sykes. Critical demography and the measurement of racism, 241.

11. Omi, M., & Winant, H. (1994). *Racial formation in the United States*. New York: Routledge, 55.

12. Collins, P. H. (2006). *From black power to hip hop*. Philadelphia: Temple University Press.

13. Bonilla-Silva, E. (2010). *Racism without racists: Color-blind racism and the persistence of racial inequality in America*. New York: Rowland and Littlefield.

14. Bennett, M. D. (2006). Culture and context. *Journal of Black Psychology*, 32(4), 479–500.

15. Peters, M., & Massey, G. (1983). Mundane extreme environmental stress in family stress theories: The case of black families in white America. *Marriage and Family Review*, 6(1), 193–218.

16. Hill, S. (1999). *African American children: Socialization and development in families*. Thousand Oaks, CA: Sage.

17. Harris, J. R. (1995). Where is the child's environment? A group socialization theory of development. *Psychology Review*, 102(3), 458–489.

18. Shelton, J. E. (2008). The investment in blackness hypothesis. *Du Bois Review: Social Science Research on Race*, 5(2), 235–257.

19. Burt, C. H., Simons, R. L., & Gibbons, F. X. (2012). Racial discrimination, ethnic-racial socialization, and crime. *American Sociological Review*, 77(4), 648–677.

20. Caughy, M., Nettles, S. M., O'Campo P., & Lohrfink, K. F. (2006). Neighborhood matters: Racial socialization of African American children. *Child Development*, 77(5), 1220–1236.

21. Lacy, K. *Blue chip black*. (2007). Berkeley: University of California Press.

22. Banerjee, M., Zaje A. T. H., & Johnson, D. J. (2011). Racial/ethnic socialization and parental involvement in education as predictors of cognitive ability and achievement in African American children. *Journal of Youth and Adolescence*, 40(5), 595–605.

23. Abdul-Jabbar, Kareem. (2007). *On the shoulders of giants*. New York: Simon & Schuster.

24. Coventry, B. T. (2004). On the sidelines: Sex and racial segregation in television sports broadcasting. *Sociology of Sport Journal*, 21(3), 322–341.

25. Benokraitis, N. (2011). *SOC*. Belmont, CA: Cengage Learning.

26. Maconis, J. (2011). *Sociology: The basics*. Upper Saddle River, NJ: Pearson.

27. Coakley, J. (2008). *Sports and Society*. New York: McGraw-Hill, 9.

28. Ibid.

29. Ibid.

30. Brown, D. L., & Tylka, T. L. (2011). Racial discrimination and resilience in African American young adults: Examining racial socialization as a moderator. *Journal of Black Psychology*, 37(3), 259–285.

31. Sinnette, C. (1998). *Forbidden fairways*. Ann Arbor, MI: Sleeping Bear Press.

32. Dawkins, M. P. (2004). Race relations and the sport of golf. *Western Journal of Black Studies*, 23(1), 327–331.

33. Ibid., Sinnette, C. (1998). *Forbidden fairways*. Ann Arbor: Sleeping Bear Press.

34. Episode 12, 2004: Shippen Golf Club Southampton, Long Island. History Detectives. http://www-tc.pbs.org/opb/historydetectives/static/media/transcripts/2011-04-22/212_golf.pdf

35. Ibid.

36. Burton, L. (January 4, 2003). Despite no local course, Polk players made golf hall of fame. *Ledger. Lakeland, Florida*. http://www.theledger.com/article/20030104/COLUMNISTS0303/301040443.

37. Wiggins, D. K. & Miller, P. (2003). *The unlevel playing field: A documentary of the African American experience in sport*. Chicago: University of Illinois Press.

38. McDaniel, P. (2000). *Uneven lies*. Greenwich, CT: American Golfer.

39. Ibid.

40. Wiggins, & Miller, *Unlevel playing field*.

41. Ibid., 241.

42. "Celebrity Central. Tiger Woods Biography." *People Magazine*. http://www.people.com/people/tiger_woods/biography/.

43. Nishime, L. (2012). The case for Cablinasian: Multiracial naming from Plessy to Tiger Woods. *Communication Theory*, 22(1), 92-111.

44. Cashmore, E. (2008). Tiger Woods and the new racial order. *Current Sociology*, 56(4), 621–634, 621.

45. Ibid., 623.

46. Boren, C. (May 22, 2013). Sergio Garcia apologies for "fried chicken" remark about Tiger Woods. *Washington Post*. http://www.washingtonpost.com/blogs/early-lead/wp/2013/05/22/sergio-garcia-apologizes-for-fried-chicken-remark-about-tiger-woods/.

Bibliography

Abdul-Jabbar, K. (2007). *On the shoulders of giants*. New York: Simon & Schuster.

Banerjee, M., Zaje, A. T. H., & Johnson, D. J. (2011). Racial/ethnic socialization and parental involvement in education as predictors of cognitive ability and achievement in African American children. *Journal of Youth and Adolescence*, 40(5), 595–605.

Barr, S. C., & Neville, H. (2008). Examination of the link between parental racial socialization messages and racial ideology among black college students. *Journal of Black Psychology*, 34(2), 131–155.

Benedict, J. (2004). *Out of bounds: Inside the NBA's culture of rape, violence, and crime*. New York: Harper Collins.

Bennett, M. D. (2006). Culture and context. *Journal of Black Psychology*, 32(4), 479–500.

Benokraitis, N. (2011). *SOC*. Belmont: Cengage Learning.

Berg, J. A. (2013). Opposition to pro-immigration public policy: Symbolic racism and group threat. *Sociological Inquiry*, 83(1), 1–31.

Bonilla-Silva, E. (2010). *Racism without racists: Color-blind racism and the persistence of racial inequality in America*. New York: Rowland and Littlefield.

Bowen, R. T. (1982). Race, home town and experience as factors in deep south major college football. *International Review for Sociology*, 17, 41–53.

Braddock, J. H., Smith, E., & Dawkins, M. P. (2012). Race and pathways to power in the National Football League. *American Behavioral Scientist*, 56(5), 711–727.

Brown, D. L., & Tylka, T. L. (2011). Racial discrimination and resilience in African American young adults: Examining racial socialization as a moderator. *Journal of Black Psychology*, 37(3), 259–285.

Brown, T. L., & Krishnakumar, A. (2007). Development and validation of the adolescent racial and ethnic socialization scale (ARESS) in African American families. *Journal of Youth and Adolescence*, 36(8), 1072–1085.

Brown, T. L., Linver, M. R., & Evans, M. (2010). The role of gender in the racial and ethnic socialization of African American adolescents. *Youth & Society*, 41(3), 357–381.

Brown, T. L., Linver, M. R., Evans, M., & Degennaro, D. (2009). African-American parents' racial and ethnic socialization and adolescent academic grades: Teasing out the role of gender. *Journal of Youth and Adolescence*, 38(2), 214–227.

Buffington, D., & Fraley, T. (2011). Racetalk and sport. *Sociological Inquiry*, 81(3), 333–352.

Buford M., &, Reuben, A. (2009). The good and bad of it all: Professional black male basketball players as role models for young black male basketball players. *Sociology of Sport Journal*, 26(3), 443–461.

Burt, C. H., Simons, R. L., & Gibbons, F. X. (2012). Racial discrimination, ethnic-racial socialization, and crime. *American Sociological Review*, 77(4), 648–677.

Cashmore, E. (2008). Tiger Woods and the new racial order. *Current Sociology*, 56(4), 621–634.

Caughy, M., Nettles, S. M., O'Campo, P., & Lohrfink, K. F. (2006). Neighborhood matters: Racial socialization of African American children. *Child Development*, 77(5), 1220–1236.

Coakley, J. (2009). *Sports in society*. Colorado Springs: McGraw Hill.

Collins, P. H. (2006). *From black power to hip hop*. Philadelphia: Temple University Press.

Cooper, S. M., & McLoyd, V. C. (2011). Racial barrier socialization and the well-being of African American adolescents: The moderating role of mother-adolescent relationship quality. *Journal of Research on Adolescence*, 21(4), 895–903.

Coventry, B. T. (2004). On the sidelines: Sex and racial segregation in television sports broadcasting. *Sociology of Sport Journal*, 21(3), 322–341.

Crouter, A. C., Baril, M. E., Davis, K. D., & McHale, S. M. (2008). Processes linking social class and racial socialization in African American dual-earner families. *Journal of Marriage and Family*, 70(5), 1311–1325.

Dawkins, M. P. (2004). Race relations and the sport of golf. *Western Journal of Black Studies*, 23(1), 327–331.

Day, J. C., & McDonald, S. (2010). Not so fast, my friend: Social capital and the race disparity in promotions among college football coaches. *Sociological Spectrum*, 30(2), 138–158.

Denham, B. E., Billings, A. C., & Halone, K. K. (2002). Differential accounts of race in broadcast commentary of the 2000 NCAA men's and women's final four basketball tournaments. *Sociology of Sport Journal*, 19(3), 315–332.

Dyson, M. Eric. (1993). *Reflecting black*. Minneapolis: University of Minnesota Press.

Edwards, H. (1969). *Revolt of the black athlete*. New York: Free Press.

Ferguson, T. (2009). Combating unseen strategies: The African American male football player. *Journal of the Indiana University Student Personnel Association*, 52–64.

Follis, C. (2001). *Outside the lines: African Americans and the integration of the National Football League*. New York: New York University Press.

Gaines, S. O., Bagha, S., Barrie, M., Bhattacharjee, T., Boateng, Y., Briggs, J., Ghezai, H., Gunnoo, K., Hoque, S., Merchant, D., Mehra, K., Noorkhan, N., & Rodriques, L. (2012). Impact of experiences with racism on African-descent persons' susceptibility to stereotype threat within the United Kingdom. *Journal of Black Psychology*, 38(2), 135–152.

Gerdin, S. (1999). *Jackie Robinson: Race, sports, and the American dream.* Armonk, NY: M. E. Sharpe.

Giardina, M., & McCarthy, C. (2005). The popular racial order of urban America. *Cultural Studies/Critical Methodologies*, 5(2), 145–173.

Harris, J. R. (1995). Where is the child's environment? A group socialization theory of development. *Psychology Review*, 102(3), 458–489.

Hill, S. (1999). *African American children: Socialization and development in families.* Thousand Oaks, CA: Sage.

Horton, H. D. & Martin, L. L. (2008). Critical demography and the measurement of racism. In *White logic, white methods: Racism and methodology,* edited by Tukufu Zuberi and Eduardo Bonilla-Silva. Latham, MD: Rowman & Littlefield, 239–250.

Joseph, N., & Hunter, C. D. (2011). Ethnic-racial socialization messages in the identity development of second-generation Haitians. *Journal of Adolescent Research*, 26(3), 344–380.

Kooistra, P., Mahoney, J. S., & Bridges, L. (1993). The unequal opportunity for equal ability hypothesis: Racism in the National Football League? *Sociology of Sport Journal*, 10(3), 241–255.

Lacy, K. (2007). *Blue chip black.* Berkeley: University of California Press.

Lee, E. A., Soto, J.A., Swim, J. K., & Bernstein, M. J. (2012). Bitter reproach or sweet revenge? Cultural differences in response to racism. *Personality and Social Psychology Bulletin*, 38(7), 920–932.

Leonard, D. (2012). Joe Paterno: White patriarchy and privilege; Nostalgia and the football-media complex. *Cultural Studies Cultural Methodologies*, 12, 373–376.

Lipsitz, G. (2011). *How racism takes place.* Philadelphia: Temple University Press.

Maconis, J. (2011). *Sociology: The basics.* Upper Saddle River, NJ: Pearson.

Margolis, B., & Piliavin, J. A. (1999). Stacking in Major League Baseball: A multivariate analysis. *Sociology of Sport Journal*, 16(1), 16–34.

McDaniel, P. (2000). *Uneven lies.* Greenwich, CT: American Golfer.

Nishime, L. (2012). The case for Cablinasian: Multiracial naming from Plessy to Tiger Woods. *Communication Theory*, 22(1), 92–111.

Ogden, D., & Rose, R.A. (2005). Using Giddens's structuration theory to examine the waning participation of African Americans in baseball. *Journal of Black Studies*, 35(4), 225–245.

Omi, M., & Winant, H. (1994). *Racial formation in the United States.* New York: Routledge.

Pendry, N. (2012). Race, racism and systemic supervision. *Journal of Family Therapy*, 34(4), 403–418.

Perry, B. L., Pullen, E. L., & Oser, C. B. (2012). Too much of a good thing? Psycho-social resources, gendered racism, and suicidal ideation among low socioeconomic status African American women. *Social Psychology Quarterly*, 75(4), 334–359.

Peters, M., & Massey, G. (1983). Mundane extreme environmental stress in family stress theories: The case of black families in white America. *Marriage and Family Review*, 6(1), 193–218.

Powell, S. (2008). *Souled out? How blacks are winning and losing in sports*. Champaign, IL: Human Kinetics.

Rhoden, W. (2007). *Forty million dollar slaves*. New York: Broadway.

Ross, C. (2004). *Race and Sport: The Struggle for Equality on and off the Field*. Jackson, MS: University Press of Mississippi.

Rothenberg, P. S. (2008). *White privilege*. New York: Worth.

Shelton, J. E. (2008). The investment in blackness hypothesis. *Du Bois Review: Social Science Research on Race*, 5(2), 235–257.

Sinnette, C. (1998). *Forbidden fairways*. Ann Arbor, MI: Sleeping Bear Press.

Stevens-Watkins, D., Perry, B., Harp, K. L., & Oser, C. B. (2012). Racism and illicit drug use among African American women. *Journal of Black Psychology*, 38(4), 471–496.

Tarman, C., & Sears, D. O. (2005). The conceptualization and measurement of symbolic racism. *Journal of Politics*, 67, 731–761.

Trail, T. E., Goff, P. A., Bradbury, T. N., & Karney, B. R. (2012). The costs of racism for marriage. *Personality and Social Psychology Bulletin*, 38(4), 454–465.

Wiggins, D. K., & Miller, P. (2003). *The unlevel playing field: A documentary of the African American experience in sport*. Chicago: University of Illinois Press.

Williams, L. (2008). The constraint of race. In Paula S. Rothenberg, *White privilege: Essential readings on the other side of racism*. New York: Worth, 91–96.

Zirin, D. (2008). *A people's history of sports in the United States*. New York: New Press.

Chapter 2

Systemic Racism Theory: Critically Examining College Sport Leadership

Michael Regan, Akilah R. Carter-Francique, and Joe R. Feagin

According to Carter, "Understanding how our knowledge is cultivated impacts how we see the world, and thus, understand our social realities. It is these social realities, or phenomena, which can then be explained by theory."[1] Therefore, the sociologist who attends to sport from a scholarly perspective, as in any investigation of social phenomena, according to Eitzen,[2] is directed by a theoretical perspective; thus, the focus of interest, the questions generated, the connections sought, the interpretations submitted, and the insights untangled are grounded in a theoretical base. Considering that sport represents a microcosm of society, reflecting its ideals, hierarchies, and problems,[3] the use of theory serves as a means to analyze the social and cultural meanings of sport.

The purpose of this chapter is to introduce the *systemic racism* theoretical framework[4] to college sport to better facilitate analysis of both the dominant positioning of whites and the lack of advancement of blacks in leadership positions (e.g., assistant coach, head coach, athletic director). This dissection will be followed by the offering of solutions geared to making relevant changes. As a sociological theory, systemic racism employs a critical theoretical perspective. This seems fitting, given that "critical theorists challenge the view of those in positions of power by making changes in the oppressive and exploitive behavior within sporting contexts, to include providing opportunities for diverse populations,"[5] which in essence is the aim of the current chapter. Several sociological theories concerning race relations have surfaced over the years (e.g., race relations cycle, racial formation theory, social distance, symbolic racism), but they are not with-out limitations.[6] Conversely, the systemic racism framework makes up for these deficiencies. More specifically, systemic racism theory strategically and critically illustrates historical-to-contemporary, deep-to-surface level, and society-wide links of racial oppression, through empirical facts and the application of its six primary tenets, to indicate that racism is not just tacked onto an otherwise already healthy system. Furthermore, a funda-mental strength of the theory of systemic racism is its deliberate elucidation and interrogation of white economic domination, a necessity when exam-ining power dynamics in the United States. Moreover, systemic racism theory attends to the necessity of giving voice to those who have been tradi-tionally voiceless (e.g., racial and ethnic minorities) and those belonging to the dominant group (i.e., whites), a comparative approach that has the potential to uncover the perceptual gaps in the existence and/or intensity of racial oppression, which can be utilized in strengthening change efforts.

The systemic racism perspective has been used as a comprehensive tool to elucidate the black American experience in the United States.[7] Because systemic racism theory has been employed to uncover the racial oppressive realities within the United States, this essay will appropriately focus on American collegiate athletics. To achieve this objective the discussion will be organized to: (a) detail the assumptions of the systemic racism theoreti-cal framework and how the suppositions underlining the theory are situ-ated to thoroughly explain the lack of advancement by black Americans in collegiate athletic leadership; (b) illustrate the significance of positioning *racism* in the sporting context if real change is to occur; and (c) offer prac-tical directions for change.

Assumptions of Systemic Racism Theory

As its name implies, systemic racism theory centers its attention on a sys-tem of racism that has historically affected black Americans and other peo-ple of color (e.g., Latinos, Asians) within the United States, and is entrenched in all major institutions in society (e.g., political, economic, educational, legal). The overwhelming marginalization of people of color must be deeply understood if changes are to be made. As Cornell West argued, *race* must be the central topic of dialogue when attempting to pro-foundly comprehend the negative position of racial and ethnic groups in the United States.[8] To realize the systemic racist nature of U.S. society, ascertaining black Americans' history in this country is a good place to start.

Historically, a racial hierarchy was established by white elites toward black Americans in the seventeenth century when Africans were stolen from their homelands and enslaved in what we now call the United States; it was a barbaric system that economically benefited a majority of whites then, and its foundation continues to favor whites today.[9] Because of this hierarchal creation and maintenance, Singer asserted, to accurately explore the problem of racism in the United States, *whiteness* must be understood as the most favorable status criterion—encompassing power and privilege—in this society.[10] This domination by whites, according to Morris,[11] has created an ideological framework that allows the continuation of oppression toward people of color, which enables whites to maintain power and privilege within this society. Therefore, it becomes very difficult to challenge the position of whites (or enhance the position of people of color) because of the long, deep-rooted history of planting the "normal" way of doing things in U.S. society. It is important to recognize that systemic racism is a unique framework geared to grasp the systemic racism issue, in order to make realistic approaches to solving the inequitable position faced by black Americans. This is significant when considering the historic and contemporary marginalized position faced by black Americans in the context of sport.

Racism and Sport

The mid-nineteenth century was a period marked by a national acceptance of black sport participation (e.g., baseball, boxing, golf, hockey, horseracing, tennis).[12] Unfortunately, this reception was short lived. One primary reason for the opposition to black American sport involvement was due to an inferior framing toward blacks by white decision makers, a period marked by a rise in worldwide imperialism, social Darwinism, and the spread of scientific racism in the academic community.[13] Wiggins emphasizes that the inferior complex directed toward black Americans was so widespread that even northern white Republicans reneged on their postwar commitments to support constitutional rights for blacks.[14] Among other things, the demise of black Americans in sport resulted in an economic shift in favor of whites. This was especially the case for black Americans as jockeys, a role blacks have filled and numerically dominated for many years but that was taken over by whites.[15] Eventually, though, black Americans found a way to thrive in sport.

Even with the exclusion from most organized sport by white decision makers, the first half of the twentieth century was a period in which some outstanding black American athletes participated and succeeded in professional boxing, Olympic competition, and athletics in predominantly white institutions of higher education (PWIHE); black Americans also thrived in their own all-black leagues in professional sport (e.g., football, baseball, basketball), and in all-black colleges and universities and high schools. However, according to Wiggins with the extensive racial integration of professional, college, and high school sport by the mid-twentieth century, economically prosperous all-black athletic leagues had crumbled.[16] While racial integration enhanced opportunities for blacks on a large scale to participate in athletics, this was not the case for black American leaders in sport (e.g., owners, managers, athletic directors, coaches). Regrettably, this continues to be a pertinent issue in sport today.

Although this pattern exists at different levels of sport (e.g., professional, college), collegiate athletics show a much slower progression in equitable positioning of black Americans. Lapchick, Hoff, and Kaiser's *Racial and Gender Report Card* for college athletics elucidates this reality. According to the latest report card, blacks continue to be marginally represented in all decision-making positions in both white-run National Collegiate Athletic Association (NCAA) offices and collegiate athletic departments on PWIHE campuses. This is especially illuminated in key decision-making positions closely linked to the playing field (i.e., athletic director, head coach, assistance coach) in NCAA Division I athletic programs. For instance, blacks in these positions are marginally represented at 6.7 percent, 6.3 percent, and 16.7 percent, respectively.[17]

If these numbers were not problematic enough, they appear even more troubling when considering the two sports (men's basketball and football) not only where black student-athletes are overly represented, but where the most revenue is generated. For instance, black student-athletes comprise 60.9 percent and 45.8 percent of Division I men's basketball and football, respectively; however, black head coaches for men's basketball and football are represented at 21 percent and 5.1 percent, respectively, and assistant coaches at 39.5 percent and 17.6 percent, respectively.[18] These figures demonstrate that blacks are overrepresented on the fields and courts of play and excessively underrepresented in positions of leadership. The authors of this chapter contend that the fundamental elements of systemic racism theory will assist in exposing and explaining the underrepresentation of black Americans in sport leadership from an array of perspectives, while clearly exemplifying the existence of white-on-black oppression.[19]

The remainder of this section will outline systemic racism theory through the use of the following tenets: (a) whites' unjust enrichment and black Americans' unjust impoverishment; (b) racial hierarchy with divergent group interests; (c) the white racial frame; (d) social reproduction and alienation; (e) extraordinary costs and burdens of racism; and (f) resisting systemic racism. For comparative purposes, an explanation of each principle will be followed by its relevance to college sport to exemplify a more in-depth understanding of the underrepresentation of black Americans in collegiate sport leadership.

Whites' Unjust Enrichment and Black Americans' Unjust Impoverishment

The first tenet of systemic racism theory, *whites' unjust enrichment and black Americans' unjust impoverishment*, identifies that from the outset of establishing U.S. society, black Americans' life chances of fair advancement were already dictated by their enslavement and later Jim Crow segregation. Within the institution of slavery (1619–1865), blacks were not considered complete human beings by whites; rather, they were seen as property. However, as a compromise between northern and southern states, slaves were counted as three-fifths of a person for purposes of taxation and appointment of the members to the U.S. House of Representatives (i.e., 3/5 compromise; U.S. Constitution, 1787). This status not only allowed whites to obtain undeserved wealth, but it also ensured that blacks would remain at the bottom of the status hierarchy. Eventually, the Civil War ended slavery, at which point, systemic racism took the form of segregation from 1876 to 1965.[20]

The period of Jim Crow guaranteed black Americans' unjust treatment and access to employment, education, housing, justice system, and politics (and unjust enrichment for whites).[21] When racial segregation was outlawed, according to Bobo and Smith, contemporary institutionalized racism took the form of covert racism.[22] This contemporary form of racism is not only recognized by the continued struggle by black Americans for equality throughout U.S. society, but it is also evident where blacks are accorded access and are overly represented (e.g., college sport participation) for nothing more than the economic benefits white elites gain from their presence (i.e., the interest-convergence principle).[23] Hence, college athletics offers an ideal arena to illustrate this inequitable reality.

Similar to how whites historically functioned as colonizers of the Americas by enslaving Africans for labor, the power structure of NCAA Division I PWIHE "operate as colonizers who prey on the athletic prowess of young black males, recruit them from black communities, exploit their athletic talents, and discard them once they are injured or their eligibility is exhausted." Hawkins suggests when considering the notion of colonization (i.e., political, economic, racial exploitation), it becomes clearer that such a model is fitting. For instance, (a) little has been done in terms of policy to ensure a better life for black American athletes during their college experience and once their college athletics careers are complete[24] (e.g., inadequate academic preparation/guidance, mentorship[25]); (b) most attention by the NCAA has been geared toward increasing revenues from the labor of student-athletes, while simultaneously refusing to compensate them;[26] and (c) those who have been most adversely affected by the college athletic experience have been black student-athletes (e.g., racist stereotypes, coaches and athletic departments, unacceptable graduation rates[27]). Therefore, the many unchanged adverse conditions faced by black student-athletes have led many researchers to conclude that the economic benefits gained by whites are the only reason blacks are recruited for athletics at PWIHE.[28]

Racial Hierarchy with Divergent Group Interests

A second tenet of systemic racism theory is *racial hierarchy with divergent group interests*. From the inception of slavery, white economic elites forcefully developed a system of racial oppression. While historically this system was developed and supported by those with financial interests (e.g., slaveholders, traders, merchants) and was later maintained by industrialists and political elites (e.g., drafters of the U.S. Constitution), it was different classes of whites who assisted in the reproduction and maintenance of the oppressive scheme.[29]

According to Allen, there was a historical period in which white elites feared a massive rebellion due to the oppressive nature of society over all lower socioeconomic classes; however, this potential threat was appeased by persuading lower-class whites that they had more social, cultural, and economic opportunity than people of color.[30] Thus, the creation of a white racial hierarchy was born. After the Civil War, there were points in time when lower-class white men and women joined forces with people of color to fight injustice and economic inequality. However, most whites were able to be financially and ideologically persuaded to recognize their white privilege and even violently turn against black Americans.[31] These latter critical phases were turning points that could have potentially deflated a racialized society, but the continued aggressive nature of the economic elites diffused this opportunity, just as it did throughout the founding of this nation. McDowell suggests the white-created dual subordinated social class and racial classification experienced by black Americans in the United States is carried over to sport.[32]

This deemed inferior condition experienced by black Americans is illuminated in collegiate athletics and is perpetuated by an overrepresented white hierarchal structure of both men and women. As highlighted previously, black male student-athletes are overly represented in both men's NCAA Division I basketball and football but are remarkably outnumbered by whites in coaching positions (i.e., assistant coach, head coach). Interestingly, black American females experience the same numerical marginalization at the hands of both white males and females in the leadership structure (i.e., assistant coach, head coach) of sport where black female student-athletes are numerically dominant, namely women's basketball.

For instance, according to Lapchick and colleagues, black female student-athletes (51 percent) outnumber white female student-athletes (40.2 percent) in women's NCAA Division I basketball; however, as assistant coaches, white females (40.7 percent) outnumber black females (26.8 percent), and the gap increases at the head coaching position (53.9 percent and 11.4 percent, respectively).[33] It appears women as a whole continue to be numerically marginalized in the leadership ranks (e.g., assistant coach, head coach) by white men in women's sports.[34] Simultaneously, white women are overrepresented in coaching positions that black females seem to be, at least numerically, in a better position to fill.

One final statistic should explicate a white hierarchy within the collegiate athletic setting, in the position at the highest rank of leadership, the athletic director. According to Lapchick and colleagues within NCAA Division I athletic departments, white males currently hold a numerical majority of the athletic director roles (81.8 percent), followed by white females (7 percent), then black males (6.7 percent), and finally black females (0.7 percent). These numbers indicate that while white males hold a majority of the leadership posts, and white males and females are concentrated at the top of the leadership ladder, a dominate arrangement exists that can make it more difficult for blacks to maneuver upward.[35]

The White Racial Frame

A third tenet of systemic racism theory is the *white racial frame*. "Frame," from this perspective, is what contemporary scientists (e.g., cognitive, neurological, social) refer to as "a perspectival frame that gets embedded in individual minds (brains), as well as in collective memories and histories, and helps people make sense out of everyday situations."[36] The white racial frame accentuates a strong pro-white subframe, or a shared belief that whites are virtuous and superior in every important way compared to people of color, and a strong antiblack and antiothers (e.g., Latino) subframe (e.g., racist stereotypes and prejudices, racial narratives, racial images, racial emotions, racial ideologies) established over centuries and used to explain and rationalize extensive white power and privilege along with institutionalized oppression targeting people of color.

The late nineteenth century illuminates the white racial framing, for it was known as a time when scientific racism was in full force, in which black Americans were seen and treated as a biologically and intellectually inferior race in all aspects compared to whites.[37] These racialized images grow to be part of the consciousness of many whites at an early age, and eventually develop as part of the unconscious mind,[38] which has been confirmed in multiple "unconscious stereotyping" psychological tests (e.g., implicit association test[39]). Other tests have revealed that regardless of what region of the country whites live in, they all share similar positive images and stereotypes about whites, and negative images and stereotypes regarding Americans of color.[40] And even with the long and recent history of unjustified treatment toward people of color, many whites believe the reason whites are more advantaged in the United States is that they work harder than nonwhites. Therefore, the white racial frame is a powerful reinforcer of systemic racism because of the shared negativity toward people of color, whether conscious, unconscious, or misinformed. In the context of sport, the framing of black Americans by whites has been clearly evident and has served as a means to stagnate the progression of black Americans beyond the playing field.

As highlighted previously, black American acceptance in several sports (e.g., baseball, boxing, golf, hockey, horseracing, tennis[41]) during the mid- to latter half of the nineteenth century was short lived due to an inferior framing toward blacks that took hold throughout society (e.g., scientific racism[42]). Scientific racism is one useful perspective in comprehending the lack of black Americans in sport leadership.

When black and white Americans began to discredit scientific thought of physical inferiority, whites again utilized pseudoscientific practices to explain this prowess. Several researchers have illustrated that many whites, to explain black Americans' athletic excellence, have embraced a belief that blacks are born with supreme athletic ability.[43] While this belief was and is an act by whites to explain why black Americans are surpassing them in athletics and to discredit their work ethic, it also serves to position black Americans as athletic, short of any other positive characteristics (e.g., intellectual). Such framing has led to this notion of stacking, or positioning of players to central or noncentral position on the field based on race and/or ethnicity.[44]

Whites have traditionally placed themselves in more central positions, positions associated with greater interaction, leadership, and intelligence; while black Americans have been situated in more peripheral positions linked to less leadership, minimal interaction, and greater athletic ability. For example, Brooks and Althouse indicate that there is a correlation between those higher up in the leadership ranks (e.g., head coach, athletic director) and past playing position.[45] In particular, prestigious sport jobs are generally acquired by those who have played more central positions (e.g., quarterback in football, pitcher in baseball); thus, because black Americans more often are relegated to peripheral positions (e.g., wide receiver in football, outfield in baseball) that supposedly require less intelligence, leadership, and interaction, blacks are often framed as less qualified to enter leadership positions beyond the playing field. While the status of black Americans in sport leadership positions can be explained by comprehending the athletic ability–intellect framework, which is persistently perpetuated by the sport media,[46] the negative framing goes much deeper. As such, researchers have examined and continue to examine the internal stereotypes and discriminatory framing held by whites toward black American males and females in sport on a broader scale.[47] Thus, the white racial frame is a powerful force that plays a key role in the continued marginalization of black Americans. When white decision makers consistently concentrate themselves in leadership roles, as the previous section indicated, their negative framing toward black Americans can serve as a mechanism to hinder black advancement, while improving the position of whites because they view themselves more positively.

Social Reproduction and Alienation

A fourth tenet of systemic racism theory, *social reproduction and aliena-tion*, explains how wealth and privilege historically is transferred to wealth and privilege in later generations. To understand how the social system of racial inequity is reproduced, according to Feagin, "an inter-temporal per-spective on racial discrimination and related oppression is critical to a comprehensive understanding of the development and structure of US society."[48] Social reproduction is evident when tracking the routine pat-terns of control over economic resources, along with police, political, and ideological power, which establishes an alienated relationship between the oppressors (i.e., whites) and the oppressed (i.e., people of color). Alienation establishes and maintains a clear hierarchy of difference that is passed down from generation to generation in close networks (e.g., family, friends, co-workers), communities, and all major institutions.

Therefore, the system of inequality is so embedded in society that most whites miscalculate the extent the United States is a racist society, and they underestimate the racial and social inheritance (e.g., privilege, resources) that was passed down from their ancestors. Though class and gender differ-ences exist among whites, which have hampered some whites from access-ing substantial wealth, all whites have gained psychological benefits and other societal advantages (e.g., education, jobs, health care). When consid-ering contemporary white numerical dominance in college sport leader-ship, it becomes apparent that such control has come about through white social reproduction.

Using college football as an example, Hill paints a vivid picture of the reproductive nature of whites over time. For instance, Hill reveals while there have been 381 vacancies in NCAA Division IA head football coaching positions since 1982, blacks have been hired for a mere 19 (4 percent) of these positions.[49] Several other studies[50] show that black American coach-ing opportunities may have been thwarted due to the tendency of white decision makers to choose white candidates (qualified and unqualified) over qualified blacks. Powerful and older whites' use of their white social networks allows for the continuation of passing along socioeconomic capital, and various other forms of social capital, to younger whites, which manages to keep people of color in their place. What makes the black American struggle to gain an equal footing in sport leadership even more troubling is that many of those who make the final hiring decisions (i.e., athletic directors) perceive employment opportunities to be equal for blacks.[51] Such blinded awareness, along with a prevalent white coaching culture, has resulted in an alienation effect on black Americans.

Brooks and Althouse assert the coaching opportunities and persistent white advancement in sport leadership lead to blacks feeling a lack of belonging. They also argue that blacks' perception of not fitting in results in decreased social interaction, mentoring, and overall networking, which are key ingredients for entering and enhancing maneuverability beyond the lower ranks of sport leadership.[52]

Extraordinary Costs and Burdens of Racism

A fifth tenet is the importance of considering the life experiences and experiential intelligence of Americans of color when taking theoretical approaches to understanding the costs of racial oppression. After all, it makes sense that black Americans (and other people of color) would understand their past and present experiences dealing with racism better than anyone else. Moreover, this tenet of systemic racism theory, the *extraordinary costs and burdens of racism*, is indicative of the underserved impoverishment of black Americans, past and present, which is directly connected to the unwarranted wealth and privilege garnered by whites. This tenet is illuminated by many patterns such as reduced life expectancy and economic net worth of black families compared to those of whites; a lack of cultural capital, such as education and job skills; and reduced ability to catch up to whites economically due to limited access to employment and education. These patterns have been recognized from slavery through legal segregation and in extensive present-day discrimination.[53] In many cases, the extraordinary costs are not readily visible, and the voices of those who suffer these disparities may be the only way to fully understand racial oppression. This has especially proved to be the case in understanding the black American perspective on the oppressive nature of sport.

The extraordinary cost and burdens of racism can have debilitating effects on both black Americans in college coaching and those wishing to enter (i.e., student-athletes). For instance, Cunningham and Sagas found the continued presence of discriminatory treatment in coaching is a leading cause of black Americans choosing to leave the profession.[54] Additionally, they found that when racial minorities in the collegiate coaching profession felt their perceived opportunity for advancement was low, their level of career satisfaction was low, and their occupational turnover intent was high.[55] Similarly, Cunningham, Bruening, and Straub found that both perceived access and treatment discrimination felt by black American collegiate basketball and football assistant coaches led to greater occupational turnover intent.[56] Furthermore, Cunningham, Sagas, and Ashley found that although black coaches' occupational commitment was high, their occupational turnover intent was also high. They suggest the presence of discriminatory perceptions may have potentially mediated this outcome. These burdens are shared by black student-athletes as well.[57]

In an attempt to understand the dearth of minorities in the coaching profession, Kamphoff and Gill found that black athletes were more likely than white athletes to agree that coaches are treated differently in sport based on their race/ethnicity.[58] Moreover, Cunningham found that although black student-athletes intended to join the coaching ranks as a career path, they perceived less opportunity for career advancement than did their white counterparts.[59] Similarly, Cunningham and Singer found that when compared to whites, racial minorities expected to encounter negative stereotypes and discrimination once in their coaching careers.[60] As the preceding examples accentuate, discrimination is so profound that it is felt by both current and potential black leaders in sport. However, while difficult to attend to, pervasive discriminatory actions in sport leadership have led to black Americans finding ways to strategically maneuver through the injustice.

Resisting Systemic Racism

A sixth and final tenet of the systemic racism perspective is *resisting systemic racism*. Feagin contends that not only is resistance the most important element of the systemic racism theoretical framework, but it is the only obvious and logical way to end racial oppression.[61] To end racial oppression, aggressive activism must take place. With the end of slavery and Jim Crow segregation, history has demonstrated aggressive collectiveness to be the only solution. Because racial oppression is evident in all major institutions, the demand for change should not be limited to individual institutions; rather, reaching across boundaries and working together with others experiencing similar shortcomings can strengthen the demand for change. Whereas black Americans, and other people of color, must be the strongholds in the movement, white allies may strengthen the thrust in the process for demanding social change. This endeavor is no different within the institution of sport. Resistance to racial inequity over time in sport is indicative of this.

During the civil rights movement (1955–1968), many black student-athletes spoke out against racism. These athletes advocated for change to benefit themselves and all blacks throughout U.S. society. This included advocating to change the underrepresentation of black coaches and administrators in college athletics.[62] A key historical account that speaks to this was the black protests at the 1968 Mexico City Olympics, which received intense white backlash. While there have been many positive societal benefits gained by black Americans due to activism, Lapchick and colleagues' statistics indicate that progress for black Americans in college sport beyond the playing field is sluggish.[63] This does not signify that blacks are not concerned about their slow headway in college sport leadership positions, but perhaps methods of advancement have become more strategic. For instance, Cunningham and Sagas found while investigating 191 NCAA Division I men's basketball programs that although the proportion of black assistant coaches was significantly lower than the proportion of potential black coaches, black head coaches were more likely to have a greater number of black assistant coaches on staff than did white head coaches.[64] These findings demonstrate that black Americans are utilizing their roles as decision makers to increase overall black numbers in collegiate sport leadership positions. At least from this perspective, it appears that as black Americans continue to elevate their decision-making authority by status and numbers, they are also resisting the systemic nature of racism by placing more blacks in positions of power.

Thus, based on the six primary tenets of systemic racism and the abstract nature of theory, it will be beneficial to examine a visual depiction to aid in the interpretation and understanding of the theory. Considering that several researchers have demonstrated that sport represents a microcosm of society,[65] Figure 2.1 portrays the interworking of white domination (e.g., power, privilege, wealth) and black American marginalization in sport.

Acknowledging the Existence of Racism in Sport

As the information presented earlier in this chapter illustrates, racism is evident in sport. What is also apparent is that in sport, as in the broader U.S. society, the historical racist disposition of many whites is firmly grounded, ensuring the advancement of blacks is dictated by and limited to the interests of whites. In outlining the six primary tenets of systemic racism theory, it is indubitable the systemic nature of racism in college sport leadership has served as a mechanism to guarantee whites persist in controlling this institution, while blacks remain marginalized in power and numbers. What is even

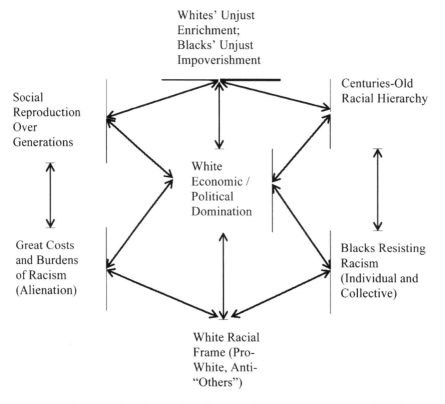

FIGURE 2.1   The six primary tenets of systemic racism theory, the simultaneous interaction of the tenets with one another and with the root cause and maintenance of systemic racism: white economic domination.

more troubling is that some 40 years ago, Edwards doggedly articulated the realities of the race problem in sport, and today we are still trying to come to grips with its existence, which suggests that racism is not just tacked onto an otherwise already healthy system.[66]

In 1993, Anderson exposed the realities of institutional racism in NCAA Division I athletics, and she indicated the pattern of underrepresented blacks in leadership positions (i.e., athletic directors, head coaches, assistant coaches, coordinators) would continue unless intervened upon. Sport management researchers have stepped up to the plate and made their appeals to the inequities in sport.[67] For instance, Frisby suggested that for researchers to challenge the dominant (i.e., white) ways of thinking, sport organizations should be viewed as operating as part of the larger cultural, economic, and political environments, in which the power structure is widespread and historically grounded.[68] Singer stressed this to be especially important "when studying and conducting research with individuals from racial and ethnic groups that have historically been marginalized (e.g., blacks) in Western civilization" because the system has historically and systemically adversely affected these individuals most. However, to succeed in equalizing the leadership structure, whites will have to play a significant role.[69]

Oglesby and Schrader contend that the primary barrier to equalizing the sport leadership structure is the reluctance of the dominant group (i.e., whites) within the institution of sport to admit a race problem exists. They argue that white privilege plays a role in some whites' color-blind mentality or obliviousness to the level of inequality faced by nonwhite groups, while others recognize racial inequity but refuse to depreciate their position of power to elevate others'. Oglesby and Schrader further argue that when some whites do recognize and decide to attend to discriminatory practices against racial and ethnic minorities, the tendency is to not identify the severity and/ or depth of the problem. For instance, whites tend to reduce the race problem to an individual matter and to negative judgments toward nonwhites (i.e., prejudice), instead of recognizing that the problems racial and ethnic groups face move beyond prejudice and should be identified as individual and institutional power structures that work to maintain the inferior status of nonwhites (i.e., racism).[70] Therefore, when attending to the race problem in sport leadership, whether from a research or organizational perspective, there must first be a clear understanding of the comprehensiveness of the race issue, which will facilitate offering appropriate and necessary solutions.[71]

Practical Directions for Change

Given the substantial evidence of systemic racism in the NCAA Division I collegiate athletic setting, the data confirming the existence of systemic racism in the NCAA have the potential to influence policy. Similar to suggestions put forward by Regan and Cunningham related to increasing the representation of women in athletic leadership roles are comparable proposals for increasing the number of blacks.[72] For instance, if the head coaching positions of the two black-dominated collegiate sports of men's basketball and football are controlled by white head coaches (77.3 percent and 93.1 percent, respectively), and these hiring decisions are made by the athletic director, a position also overwhelmingly held by whites (88.8 percent), then one potential way to increase the proportion of black head coaches is to increase the proportion of black athletic directors. Specifically, blacks represent just 7.4 percent of athletic directors in Division I athletics, but as the numbers increase, so too should the number of black head coaches. Because of the potential for structural changes to be limiting, as an additive and alternative, providing awareness and training to acknowledge racial biases in the selection process should be considered. Identification of personal biases, whether implicit or explicit, can help people take remedial actions and decrease the occurrence of their discriminatory behavior.[73]

Additionally, to help promote a fair selection process, it is beneficial for search committees to include persons who are not athletic administrators or coaches, as well as racially diverse members. A diverse hiring committee that assists and advises the athletic director and coaches could function as an essential step in a just direction. The university's president should also be engaged in the discourse. Because most institutions have a mission statement that addresses the significance of inclusivity, if this is not apparent in the athletic department, it is essential to have the mission conveyed directly by the president.

Furthermore, because final hiring decisions are made by the athletic director, there should be some discussion with the university's affirmative action officer before the final decision. Because athletic departments appear to be exempt from affirmative action policies, unjust hiring practices have been clandestinely carried out for years. Perhaps there should be more cooperation between the two entities (i.e., a connection between the Affirmative Action and Athletic Departments). Such an alliance can serve as a driving force in fairness of representation.

Given these propositions, it is evident that systemic racism requires systemic change, coalitions working for real liberty and justice for all. These proposals are merely the first step in the diversification process. Once change has taken hold, it will take both dedicated and determined leaders in order to manage diverse organizations.

Summary

The purpose of this chapter was to introduce the systemic racism theoretical framework to college sport to better facilitate analyzing both the dominant positioning of whites and the lack of advancement of blacks in leadership positions. As a critical sociological theory, the systemic racism framework has effectively been utilized to critically examine the black experience throughout the United States, as the preceding information indicated. The current chapter has demonstrated the black condition in college sport leadership is similar to the black condition in society as a whole. Because of this resemblance, as well as the calls to recognize the institutional racism realities in sport, systemic racism theory has the potential to scrutinize and guide change efforts in sport as well. However, the message must be received by decision makers who have the ability to make changes within college athletic departments. With that, there are practical suggestions for equitable change within these structures. The hope is that in time, sport will offer an equal playing field for all those who participate.[74]

Notes

1. Carter, A. R. (2010). Using social theories to understand sport. In G. Cunningham and J. Singer (Eds.), *Sociology of Sport and Physical Activity* (pp. 23–46). College Station, TX: Center for Sport Management Research and Education, p. 23.

2. Eitzen, D. S. (1988). Conflict theory and deviance in sport. *International Review for the Sociology of Sport, 23*, 193–204.

3. Edwards, H. (1973). *Sociology of sport*. Homewood, IL: Dorsey; Eitzen D. S., & Sage, G. H. (1997). *Sociology of North American sport*. Dubuque, IA: Brown & Bechmark; Sage, G. H. (1998). *Power and ideology in American sport: A critical perspective* (2nd ed.). Champaign, IL: Human Kinetics.

4. Feagin, J. R. (2006). *Systemic racism: A theory of oppression*. New York: Routledge.

5. Carter, A. R. (2010). Using social theories to understand sport. In G. Cunningham and J. Singer (Eds.), *Sociology of Sport and Physical Activity* (pp. 23-46). College Station, TX: Center for Sport Management Research and Education, p. 31.

6. See Smith, E., & Henderson, D. (2000). Stacking in the team sport of intercollegiate baseball. In D. Brooks and R. Althouse (Eds.), *Racism in college athletics: The African American athlete's experience* (2nd ed., pp. 65–84). West Virginia University: Fitness Information Technology, Inc.

7. Feagin, J. R. (2006). *Systemic racism: A theory of oppression*. New York: Routledge; Feagin, J. R. (2010). *Racist America: Roots, current realities, and future reparations*. New York: Routledge; Feagin, J. R. (2010b). *The white racial frame: Centuries of racial framing and counter-framing*. New York: Routledge.

8. West, Cornell. (1994). *Race matters*. New York: Vintage.

9. Feagin, *Systemic racism*; Feagin, *Racist America*.

10. Singer, J. N. (2005). Addressing epistemological racism in sport management research. *Journal of Sport Management, 19*, 464–479.

11. Morris, A. (1993). Centuries of black protest: Its significance for America and the world. In H. Hill & J. Jones Jr. (Eds), *Race in America: The struggles for equality* (pp. 19–69). Madison: University of Wisconsin Press.

12. Wiggins, D. (2007). Climbing the racial mountain: A history of the African American experience in sport. In D. Brooks and R. Althouse (Eds.), *Diversity and social justice of college sports: Sport management and the student athlete* (pp. 21–47). West Virginia University: Fitness Information Technology, Inc.

13. See, for example, Feagin, J. R. (2010). *The white racial frame: Centuries of racial framing and counter-framing.* New York: Routledge; Miller, P. B. (1998). The anatomy of scientific racism: Racialized responses to black athletic achievement. *Journal of Sport History, 25*(1), 119–151; Wiggins, Climbing the racial mountain.

14. Wiggins, Climbing the racial mountain.

15. Rhoden, W. C. (2006). *Forty million dollar slaves: The rise, fall, and redemption of the black athlete.*, New York: Three Rivers.

16. Wiggins, Climbing the racial mountain.

17. Lapchick, R., Hoff, B., & Kaiser, C. (2011, March 3). *The 2010 racial and gender report card: College sport.* Orlando, FL: Institute for Diversity and Ethics in Sport, University of Central Florida.

18. Ibid.

19. Feagin, *Systemic racism.*

20. See Robinson, A. L. (2005). Full of faith, full of hope: African-American experience from emancipation to segregation. In W.Scott (Ed.), *African-American reader: Essays on African-American history, culture, and society* (pp. 105–123). Washington, DC: U.S. Department of State.

21. See Alexander, M. (2010). *The new Jim Crow: Mass incarceration in the age of colorblindness.* New York: New Press.

22. Bobo, L., & Smith, R. (1998). From Jim Crow racism to laissez-faire racism: The transformation of racial attitudes. In W. Katkin, N. Landsman & A. Tyree (Eds.), *Beyond pluralism: The conception of groups and group identities in America* (pp. 182–220). Urbana: University of Illinois Press.

23. See Bell, D. (1992) *Race, racism and American law.* Boston: Little Brown.

24. Hawkins, B. (2001). *The new plantation: The internal colonization of black student athletes.* Winterville, GA: Sadiki.

25. See Eitzen, D. S. (2000). Racism in big-time college sport: Prospects for the year 2020 and proposals for change. In D. Brooks and R. Althouse (Eds.), *Racism in college athletics: The African American athlete's experience* (2nd ed., pp. 293–306). West Virginia University: Fitness Information Technology, Inc.

26. Eitzen, Racism in big-time college sport; Hawkins, *New plantation;* Lapchick, R. (2003). Race and college sport: A long way to go. In J. Boxhill (Ed.), *Sport and ethics: An anthology* (pp. 304–309). Malden, MA: Blackwell.

27. Eitzen, Racism in big-time college sport; Hawkins, *New plantation.*

28. See Donner, J. K. (2005). Towards an interest-convergence in education of African American football student athletes in major college sports. *Race, Ethnicity and Education, 8*(1), 45–67; Edwards, H. (1973). *Sociology of sport.* Homewood, IL: Dorsey Press.

29. Feagin, *Systemic racism*; Feagin, *White racial frame*.

30. Allen, T. (1994). *The invention of the white race: Racial oppression and control*. London: Verso.

31. Du Bois, W. E. B. (1992). *Black reconstruction in America, 1860–1880*. New York: Atheneum. (Original work published 1934).

32. McDowell, J. (2010). Social class and stratification. In G. Cunningham and J. Singer (Eds.), *Sociology of sport and physical activity* (pp. 321–346). College Station, TX: Center for Sport Management Research and Education.

33. Lapchick et al.. *2010 racial and gender report card*.

34. See Acosta, R. V., & Carpenter, L. J. (2010). *Women in intercollegiate sport: A longitudinal study thirty-three year update, 1977–2010*. Manuscript, Brooklyn, NY: Brooklyn College; Lapchick et al.. *2010 racial and gender report card*.

35. Lapchick et al.. *2010 racial and gender report card*.

36. Feagin, *White racial frame*, 10.

37. See Feagin, *White racial frame*; Miller, P. B. (1998). The anatomy of scientific racism: Racialized responses to black athletic achievement. *Journal of Sport History*, *25*(1), 119–151; Wiggins, Climbing the racial mountain.

38. Lawrence, C. R. (1987). The id, the ego, and equal protection. *Stanford Law Review*, *39*, 323–324.

39. Vedantam, S. (2005, January 23). Many Americans believe they are not prejudiced. Now a new test provides powerful evidence that a majority of us really are. *Washington Post*. Retrieved from http://www.beliefnet.com/story/156/story_15664_1.html.

40. Feagin, J. R., & O'Brien, E. (2003). *White men on race: Power, privilege, and the shaping of the culture consciousness*. Boston: Beacon.

41. Wiggins, Climbing the racial mountain.

42. See Feagin, *White racial frame*; Miller, Anatomy of scientific racism; Mosely, A. (2003). Racial differences in sports: What's ethics got to do with it? In J. Boxhill (Ed.), *Sports and ethics: An anthology* (pp. 297–303). Malden, MA: Blackwell.

43. See Marquesee, M. (2003). Sports and stereotype: From role model to Muhammad Ali. In J. Boxhill (Ed.), *Sports and ethics: An anthology* (pp. 310–332). Malden, MA: Blackwell;

Mosely, Racial differences in sports.

44. See Smith, E., & Henderson, D. (2000). Stacking in the team sport of intercollegiate baseball. In D. Brooks and R. Althouse (Eds.), *Racism in college athletics: The African American athlete's experience, 2nd edition* (pp. 65-84). West Virginia University: Fitness Information Technology, Inc.

45. Brooks, D. & Althouse, R. (2000). African American head coaches and administrators. In D. Brooks and R. Althouse (Eds.), *Racism in college athletics: The African American athlete's experience* (2nd ed., pp. 85–117). West Virginia University: Fitness Information Technology, Inc.

46. See Sailes, G. (2000). The African American athlete: Social myths and stereotypes. In R. Althouse & D. Brooks (Eds.), *Racism in college athletics: The African American athlete's experience* (pp. 53–64). West Virginia University: Fitness Information Technology, Inc.

47. See Ferber, A. L. (2007). The construction of black masculinity: White supremacy now and then. *Journal of Sport & Social Issues, 31*(1), 11–24; McKay, J., & Johnson, H. (2008). Pornographic eroticism and sexual grotesquerie in representation of African American sportswomen. *Social Identities, 14*(4), 491–504.

48. Feagin, *White racial frame*, 18.

49. Hill, F. (2004). Shattering the glass ceiling: Blacks in coaching. *Black Issues in Higher Education, 21*(4), 36–37.

50. See Cunningham, G. B., & Sagas, M. (2005). Access discrimination in intercollegiate athletics. *Journal of Sport and Social Issues, 29*, 148–163; Sagas, M., & Cunningham, G. B. (2005). Racial differences in the career success of assistant football coaches: The role of discrimination, human capital, and social capital. *Journal of Applied Social Psychology, 35*, 773–797; Sartore, M. L., & Cunningham, G. B. (2006). Stereotypes, race, and coaching. *Journal of African American Studies, 10*(2), 69–83.

51. Tabron, M. (2004). An examination of athletic directors' perception of barriers to employment opportunities. Unpublished master's thesis, Washington, DC: Howard University.

52. Brooks, D., & Althouse, R. (2000). African American head coaches and administrators. In D. Brooks and R. Althouse (Eds.), *Racism in college athletics: The African American athlete's experience* (2nd ed., pp. 85–117). West Virginia University: Fitness Information Technology, Inc.

53. Oliver, M., & Shapiro, T. (2006). *Black wealth/white wealth: A new perspective on racial inequality.* New York: Routledge.

54. Cunningham, G. B., & Sagas, M. (2007). Perceived treatment discrimination among coaches: The influence of race and sport coached. *International Journal of Sport Management, 8*, 1–20.

55. Cunningham, G. B., & Sagas, M. (2004). Racial differences in occupational turnover intent among NCAA Division IA assistant football coaches. *Sociology of Sport Journal, 21*, 84–92.

56. Cunningham, G. B., Bruening, J. E., & Straub, T. (2006). Examining the under-representation of African Americans in NCAA Division I head-coaching positions. *Journal of Sport Management, 20*, 387–417.

57. Cunningham, G. B., Sagas, M., & Ashley, F. B. (2001). Occupational commitment and intent to leave the coaching profession: Differences according to race. *International Review for the Sociology of Sport, 16*, 131–148.

58. Kamphoff, C., & Gill, D. (2008). Collegiate athletes' perceptions of the coaching profession. *International Journal of Sports Science & Coaching, 3*, 55–71.

59. Cunningham, G. B. (2003). Already aware of the glass Ceiling: Race-related effects of perceived opportunity on the career choices of college athletes. *Journal of African American Studies, 7*(1), 57–71.

60. Cunningham, G. B., & Singer, J. N. (2010). "You'll face discrimination wherever you go": Student athletes' intentions to enter the coaching profession. *Journal of Applied Social Psychology, 40*(7), 1708–1727.

61. Feagin, *Systemic racism.*

62. Edwards, H. (1970). *The revolt of the black athlete.* New York: Free Press.

63. Lapchick et al. *2010 racial and gender report card.*

64. Cunningham, G. B., & Sagas, M. (2005). Access discrimination in intercollegiate athletics. *Journal of Sport and Social Issues, 29*, 148–163.

65. See Edwards, H. (1973). *Sociology of sport.* Homewood, IL: Dorsey Press; Eitzen D. S., & Sage, G. H. (1997). *Sociology of North American sport.* Dubuque, IA: Brown & Bechmark; Sage, G. H. (1998). *Power and ideology in American sport: A critical perspective* (2nd ed.). Champaign, IL: Human Kinetics.

66. Edwards, *Sociology of sport.*

67. See Frisby, W. (2005). The good, the bad, and the ugly: Critical sport management research. *Journal of Sport Management, 19*(1), 1–12; Singer, J. N. (2005). Addressing epistemological racism in sport management research. *Journal of Sport Management, 19*, 464–479.

68. Frisby, Good, the bad, and the ugly.

69. Singer, J. N. (2005). Addressing epistemological racism in sport management research. *Journal of Sport Management, 19*, 464–479, 464.

70. Oglesby, C. & Schrader, D. (2000). Where is the white in the rainbow coalition? In D. Brooks and R. Althouse (Eds.), *Racism in college athletics: The African American athlete's experience*, (2nd ed., pp. 279–291). West Virginia University: Fitness Information Technology, Inc.

71. See Brooks, D. Althouse, R., & Tucker, D. (2007). African American coaching mobility models and the global marketplace. In D. Brooks and R. Althouse (Eds.), *Diversity and social justice of college sports: Sport management and the student athlete* (pp. 117–138). West Virginia University: Fitness Information Technology, Inc.; Cunningham, G. B. (2010). Understanding the under-representation of African American coaches: A multilevel perspective. *Sport Management Review, 13*, 395–406; Oglesby, & Schrader, Where is the white in the rainbow coalition?

72. Regan, M. R., & Cunningham, G. B. (2012). Analysis of homologous reproduction in community college athletics. *Journal for the Study of Sports and Athletes in Education, 6*(2), 159–170.

73. See Kulik, C. T., & Roberson, L. (2008). Common goals and golden opportunities: Evaluations of diversity education in academic and organizational settings. *Academy of Management Learning & Education, 7*, 309–331; Wentling, R. M., & Palma-Rivas, N. (1999). Components of effective diversity training programmes. *International Journal of Training and Development, 3*, 215–226.

74. See Anderson, D. (1993). Cultural diversity on campus: A look at intercollegiate football coaches. *Journal of Sport and Social Issues, 17*, 61–66; Edwards, *Sociology of sport;* Oglesby & Schrader, Where is the white in the rainbow coalition?; Singer, Addressing epistemological racism in sport management research.

Bibliography

Acosta, R. V., & Carpenter, L. J. (2010). *Women in intercollegiate sport: A longitudinal study thirty-three year update, 1977–2010.* Manuscript, Brooklyn, NY: Brooklyn College.

Alexander, M. (2010). *The new Jim Crow: Mass incarceration in the age of colorblindness.* New York: New Press.

Allen, T. (1994). *The invention of the white race: Racial oppression and control.* London: Verso.

Anderson, D. (1993). Cultural diversity on campus: A look at intercollegiate football coaches. *Journal of Sport and Social Issues, 17*, 61–66.

Bell, D. (1992). *Race, racism and American law.* Boston: Little Brown.

Bobo, L., & Smith, R. (1998). From Jim Crow racism to laissez-faire racism: The transformation of racial attitudes. In W. Katkin, N. Landsman & A. Tyree (Eds.), *Beyond pluralism: The conception of groups and group identities in America* (pp. 182–220). Urbana: University of Illinois Press.

Brooks, D., & Althouse, R. (2000). African American head coaches and administrators. In D. Brooks and R. Althouse (Eds.), *Racism in college athletics: The African American athlete's experience* (2nd ed., pp. 85–117). West Virginia University: Fitness Information Technology, Inc.

Brooks, D. Althouse, R., & Tucker, D. (2007). African American coaching mobility models and the global marketplace. In D. Brooks and R. Althouse (Eds.), *Diversity and social justice of college sports: Sport management and the student athlete* (pp. 117–138). West Virginia University: Fitness Information Technology, Inc.

Carter, A. R. (2010). Using social theories to understand sport. In G. Cunningham and J. Singer (Eds.), *Sociology of Sport and Physical Activity* (pp. 23–46). College Station, TX: Center for Sport Management Research and Education.

Cunningham, G. B. (2003). Already aware of the glass ceiling: Race-related effects of perceived opportunity on the career choices of college athletes. *Journal of African American Studies, 7*(1), 57–71.

Cunningham, G. B. (2010). Understanding the under-representation of African American coaches: A multilevel perspective. *Sport Management Review, 13*, 395–406.

Cunningham, G. B., Bruening, J. E., & Straub, T. (2006). Examining the under-representation of African Americans in NCAA Division I head-coaching positions. *Journal of Sport Management, 20*, 387–417.

Cunningham, G. B., & Sagas, M. (2004). Racial differences in occupational turn-over intent among NCAA Division IA assistant football coaches. *Sociology of Sport Journal, 21*, 84–92.

Cunningham, G. B., & Sagas, M. (2005). Access discrimination in intercollegiate athletics. *Journal of Sport and Social Issues, 29*, 148–163.

Cunningham, G. B., & Sagas, M. (2007). Perceived treatment discrimination among coaches: The influence of race and sport coached. *International Journal of Sport Management, 8*, 1–20.

Cunningham, G. B., Sagas, M., & Ashley, F. B. (2001). Occupational commitment and intent to leave the coaching profession: Differences according to race. *International Review for the Sociology of Sport, 16*, 131–148.

Cunningham, G. B., & Singer, J. N. (2010). "You'll face discrimination wherever you go": Student athletes' intentions to enter the coaching profession. *Journal of Applied Social Psychology, 40*(7), 1708–1727.

Donner, J. K. (2005). Towards an interest-convergence in education of African American football student athletes in major college sports. *Race, Ethnicity and Education, 8*(1), 45–67.

Du Bois, W. E. B. (1992). *Black reconstruction in America, 1860–1880*. New York: Atheneum. (Original work published 1934).

Edwards, H. (1970). *The revolt of the black athlete*. New York: Free Press.

Edwards, H. (1973). *Sociology of sport*. Homewood, IL: Dorsey Press.

Eitzen, D. S. (1988). Conflict theory and deviance in sport. *International Review for the Sociology of Sport, 23*, 193–204.

Eitzen, D. S. (2000). Racism in big-time college sport: Prospects for the year 2020 and proposals for change. In D. Brooks and R. Althouse (Eds.), *Racism in college athletics: The African American athlete's experience* (2nd ed., pp. 293–306). West Virginia University: Fitness Information Technology, Inc.

Eitzen, D. S., & Sage, G. H. (1997). *Sociology of North American sport*. Dubuque, IA: Brown & Bechmark.

Feagin, J. R. (2006). *Systemic racism: A theory of oppression*. New York: Routledge.

Feagin, J. R. (2010). *Racist America: Roots, current realities, and future reparations*. New York: Routledge.

Feagin, J. R. (2010). *The white racial frame: Centuries of racial framing and counter-framing*. New York: Routledge.

Feagin, J. R., & O'Brien, E. (2003). *White men on race: Power, privilege, and the shaping of the culture consciousness*. Boston: Beacon.

Ferber, A. L. (2007). The construction of black masculinity: White supremacy now and then. *Journal of Sport & Social Issues, 31*(1), 11–24.

Frisby, W. (2005). The good, the bad, and the ugly: Critical sport management research. *Journal of Sport Management, 19*(1), 1–12.

Hawkins, B. (2001). *The new plantation: The internal colonization of black student athletes*. Winterville, GA: Sadiki.

Hill, F. (2004). Shattering the glass ceiling: Blacks in coaching. *Black Issues in Higher Education, 21*(4), 36–37.

Kamphoff, C., & Gill, D. (2008). Collegiate athletes' perceptions of the coaching profession. *International Journal of Sports Science & Coaching, 3,* 55–71.

Kulik, C. T., & Roberson, L. (2008). Common goals and golden opportunities: Evaluations of diversity education in academic and organizational settings. *Academy of Management Learning & Education, 7,* 309–331.

Lapchick, R. (2003). Race and college sport: A long way to go. In J. Boxhill (Ed.), *Sport and ethics: An anthology* (pp. 304–309). Malden, MA: Blackwell.

Lapchick, R., Hoff, B., & Kaiser, C. (2011, March 3). *The 2010 racial and gender report card: College sport.* Orlando, FL: Institute for Diversity and Ethics in Sport, University of Central Florida.

Lawrence, C. R. (1987). The id, the ego, and equal protection. *Stanford Law Review, 39,* 323–324.

Marquesee, M. (2003). Sports and stereotype: From role model to Muhammad Ali. In J. Boxhill (Ed.), *Sports and ethics: An anthology* (pp. 310–332). Malden, MA: Blackwell.

McDowell, J. (2010). Social class and stratification. In G. Cunningham and J. Singer (Eds.), *Sociology of sport and physical activity* (pp. 321–346). College Station, TX: Center for Sport Management Research and Education.

McKay, J., & Johnson, H. (2008). Pornographic eroticism and sexual grotesquerie in representation of African American sportswomen. *Social Identities, 14*(4), 491–504.

Miller, P. B. (1998). The anatomy of scientific racism: Racialized responses to black athletic achievement. *Journal of Sport History, 25*(1), 119–151.

Morris, A. (1993). Centuries of black protest: Its significance for America and the world. In H. Hill & J. Jones Jr. (Eds.), *Race in America: The struggles for equality* (pp. 19–69). Madison: University of Wisconsin Press.

Mosely, A. (2003). Racial differences in sports: What's ethics got to do with it? In J. Boxhill (Ed.), *Sports and ethics: An anthology* (pp. 297–303). Malden, MA: Blackwell.

Oglesby, C. & Schrader, D. (2000). Where is the white in the rainbow coalition? In D. Brooks and R. Althouse (Eds.), *Racism in college athletics: The African American athlete's experience* (2nd ed., pp. 279–291). West Virginia University: Fitness Information Technology, Inc.

Oliver, M., & Shapiro, T. (2006). *Black wealth/white wealth: A new perspective on racial inequality.* New York: Routledge.

Regan, M. R., & Cunningham, G. B. (2012). Analysis of homologous reproduction in community college athletics. *Journal for the Study of Sports and Athletes in Education, 6*(2), 159–170.

Rhoden, W. C. (2006). *Forty million dollar slaves: The rise, fall, and redemption of the black athlete.* New York: Three Rivers.

Robinson, A. L. (2005). Full of faith, full of hope: African-American experience from emancipation to segregation. In W. Scott (Ed.), *African-American reader: Essays on African-American history, culture, and society* (pp. 105–123). Washington: U.S. Department of State.

Sagas, M., & Cunningham, G. B. (2005). Racial differences in the career success of assistant football coaches: The role of discrimination, human capital, and social capital. *Journal of Applied Social Psychology, 35*, 773–797.

Sage, G. H. (1998). *Power and ideology in American sport: A critical perspective* (2nd ed.). Champaign, IL: Human Kinetics.

Sailes, G. (2000). The African American athlete: Social myths and stereotypes. In R. Althouse & D. Brooks (Eds.), *Racism in college athletics: The African American athlete's experience* (pp. 53–64). West Virginia University: Fitness Information Technology, Inc.

Sartore, M. L., & Cunningham, G. B. (2006). Stereotypes, race, and coaching. *Journal of African American Studies, 10*(2), 69–83.

Singer, J. N. (2005). Addressing epistemological racism in sport management research. *Journal of Sport Management, 19*, 464–479.

Smith, E., & Hattery, A. (2011). Race relations theories: Implications for sport management. *Journal of Sport Management, 25*, 107–117.

Smith, E., & Henderson, D. (2000). Stacking in the team sport of intercollegiate baseball. In D. Brooks and R. Althouse (Eds.), *Racism in college athletics: The African American athlete's experience* (2nd ed., pp. 65–84). West Virginia University: Fitness Information Technology, Inc.

Tabron, M. (2004). An examination of athletic directors' perception of barriers to employment opportunities. Unpublished master's thesis, Washington, DC: Howard University.

U.S. Constitution (1787). Retrieved from http://www.archives.gov/exhibits/charters/constitution.html

Vedantam, S. (2005, January 23). Many Americans believe they are not prejudiced. Now a new test provides powerful evidence that a majority of us really are. *Washington Post*. Retrieved from http://www.beliefnet.com/story/156/story_15664_1.html.

Wentling, R. M., & Palma-Rivas, N. (1999). Components of effective diversity training programmes. *International Journal of Training and Development, 3*, 215–226.

West, C. (1994). *Race matters*. New York: Vintage.

Wiggins, D. (2007). Climbing the racial mountain. A history of the African American experience in sport. In D. Brooks and R. Althouse (Eds.), *Diversity and social justice of college sports: Sport management and the student athlete* (pp. 21–47). West Virginia University: Fitness Information Technology, Inc.

Chapter 3

Using Marketing Theory to Increase African-American Participation with Major League Baseball

John A. Fortunato and Jerome D. Williams

Introduction

The date April 15, 2013, marked the sixty-sixth anniversary of Jackie Robinson's breaking the color barrier in Major League Baseball. The day was celebrated for the fifth consecutive year with all players and coaches wearing the number 42 to honor the American hero. The celebration was, however, set against a backdrop of only 8.3 percent of the players on Major League Baseball rosters at the beginning of the 2013 season being African American, a decrease of more than half from the 1995 season when African Americans accounted for 19 percent of major league players.[1] The challenge for Major League Baseball is trying to address the lack of African-American players in a sports environment with increasing competition for talent and spectators.

Determining the reasons is the beginning step for finding solutions. Several authors point out the lack of African-American players can be attributed to many root causes, including socio-economics, the rise in popularity of football and basketball, competition from cultures where baseball is more popular, collegiate scholarship allocation for baseball, the African-American cultural experience, and how Major League Baseball markets its sport.[2]

Of all the variables hindering the appeal to the African-American community, Major League Baseball has the most control over how it markets its sport. Researchers in the fields of sports marketing, marketing communications, and ethnic studies have established an understanding of marketing best practices in a variety of scenarios that can be applied to this particular situation and provide insight into how Major League Baseball can best proceed in addressing the lack of African-American participation.

This chapter does not intend to propose solutions for every variable causing the lack of African-American participation in the sport of baseball. The general purpose of this chapter is to demonstrate that there are marketing communications strategies that can provide potential solutions for Major League Baseball in increasing African-American participation. Applying theoretical claims to Major League Baseball's current strategy will demonstrate flaws in its approach as well as provide some suggestions and opportunities in developing future strategies. This chapter specifically identifies social identity theory and relationship marketing as two theoretical models that Major League Baseball can use as guides for developing and implementing the communication strategies that could address the situation. The chapter concludes that while Major League Baseball is developing programs to get African-American youths to play baseball, providing the totality of the experience is needed: playing the sport, watching on television, and attending games. In particular, to better build the relationship with the African-American community, Major League Baseball should seek opportunities for increased exposure with more games on free, over-the-air television.

The Lack of African-American Participation in Baseball: The Root Causes

Before examining marketing theory and addressing any potential marketing opportunities for Major League Baseball, some discussion of the root causes of the lack of African-American participation is needed to better depict the gravity of the situation. From a socio-economic perspective, it has been suggested that the shrinking number of baseball diamonds in inner cities over several decades, equipment expense, and the lack of people to supervise leagues and coach teams have contributed to the lack of African-American players.[3]

The socio-economic variables of a lack of equipment and the necessary fields and facilities are compounded by the competition that African Americans face in baseball. In any professional sport there is a limited work supply, and African-American players are competing against players from cultures where baseball is arguably the most popular sport. Latino players accounted for 28.2 percent of Major League Baseball rosters in 2013, Asian players 2.1 percent, and Caucasian players 61.2 percent. The number of Caucasian players remained consistently between 59 and 61.6 percent from 1998 to 2013, with the exception of 2004, when it reached 63 percent.[4] In his book *Growing the Game: The Globalization of Major League Baseball* (2006), Alan Klein begins by arguing, "Major League Baseball's efforts at globalization are not only provident for the future of the sport but also critical to its prosperity. The ability of the game to rely upon its domestic base of fans and players has receded to the point where globalizing is imperative."[5] Klein, however, also acknowledges, "By far, MLB's biggest marketing failure and cultural oversight has been the loss of the African-American community."[6]

Another explanation for African Americans having strayed from baseball is because the sport lacks a firm place in their culture. Powell argues, "Decades of racism and the barring of blacks from the Major Leagues proved far more powerful than Robinson" (referring to the positive impact of Jackie Robinson).[7] He states, "Black America, as a whole, doesn't care deeply about baseball and never will, no matter how hard baseball tries to seduce the race."[8]

This cultural disconnect can be embodied in the concept of baseball being "street credible." Although writing about hip-hop music, researchers offer insight into the "street cred" concept. The implication is that being street credible means having gained approval from inner-city blacks from within their own region.[9] Balaji defines "street credible" as an individual being able to "Relate to a specific experience or locale, and more importantly, tie his/her identity with the ghetto and its presumed norms." Balaji adds that being street credible is an important aspect of "Cultural production and commodification."[10] At the press conference to recognize his winning the 2007 National League MVP award, Jimmy Rollins, the Philadelphia Phillies shortstop, commented on that theme, stating, "I know how black kids feel about baseball. I really do. They don't think it's street credible."[11]

The African-American cultural experience is even more relevant considering that baseball competes with football and basketball for talent. Many youths may see football and basketball as easier stepping-stones to college scholarships and pro careers—partly because baseball requires a long apprenticeship in the minor leagues, and many collegiate baseball scholarships are only partial scholarships.[12] In comparison to Major League

Baseball having less than 9 percent participation, 78 percent of National Basketball Association players are African American,[13] and 67 percent of National Football League players are African American.[14] While other generations might have looked to Willie Mays or Henry Aaron as their athletic heroes, the popularity of football and basketball and the marketing of African-American stars in the National Football League (e.g., Adrian Peterson or Robert Griffin III) or in the National Basketball Association (e.g., Lebron James or Kobe Bryant) are contributing factors depressing African-American interest in baseball.

In comparison to football and basketball, other variables should be noted. First, the pace of a baseball game might be a factor in its lack of appeal. The preference for a faster-paced game of football or basketball, of course, might not only be racial, but a generational preference for younger fans. Second, the nature of participation is a factor in viewing the game. In basketball, the star plays almost the entire game. In football, the quarterback is involved in every offensive play. In baseball, the star player has an at bat but then might not get the chance to hit again for a long period of time.

Moving forward, Major League Baseball could either consider the lack of African-American participation a problem that does not need to be addressed, or it can try to improve the current situation. Bud Selig, Major League Baseball commissioner, acknowledged the issue, stating, "Somewhere we lost a generation or two of African-Americans. I don't know why that happened."[15] So is there an opportunity for Major League Baseball to adapt to the competitive cultural environment and encourage increased African-American participation in baseball? Marketing theory does begin to provide a guide for Major League Baseball in developing and implementing the communication strategies that could address the situation.

Literature Review

Marketing communication goals are defined as trying to "inform, persuade, incite, and remind customers, directly or indirectly, about the brands they sell."[16] Specific marketing communications strategies must be implemented to achieve these goals. Determining the specific communication strategies is a challenge for all marketers in achieving marketing goals and overall business success. These marketing communication strategies often involve obtaining brand exposure and a positive portrayal of the brand so as to build a relationship with the targeted publics.

Social Identity Theory

The challenge for Major League Baseball in trying to increase African-American participation is explicated through an examination of social identity theory, which posits that people value group membership of a social category.[17] Social identity is defined as "the individual's knowledge that he (or she) belongs to certain social groups together with some emotional and value significance to him (or her) of the group membership."[18] Parsimoniously stated, people want to have some form of group association. Sherif, however, provides an important variable to consider in this group association dynamic, pointing out that people tend to view positively groups with which they can identify.[19]

Researchers document that sports play a significant role in creating these social identities.[20] Sapolsky argues that sport spectators have a natural attraction and even a preference for athletes who are of the same race.[21] In that light, basketball as a competitor with baseball is a major factor in this situation. Appiah refers to a collective identity, the incorporation of cultural traits helping to form an individual's self-image and self-identity.[22] Ogden and Hilt claim that basketball has surpassed baseball with the African-American community through this collective identity process. They identify several factors that contribute to the African-American youth preference for basketball, such as the encouragement by authority figures to pursue basketball, basketball being a form of expression and empowerment, the perception of basketball's influence on social mobility, and there being several black role models in basketball.[23] Through applying these factors as described by Ogden and Hilt, fans in Detroit might, for example, have a greater collective identity and more civic pride with the National Basketball Association's Pistons rather than the Major League Baseball's Tigers. Andrew McCutchen, a Pittsburgh Pirates center fielder, commented, "It's what you grow up around. For the African-American community, it's more basketball, it's more football." He added, "Growing up I really loved baseball and it's something I flourished at as a child."[24]

The role of the media as an element of marketing communication in helping develop a social identity is also undeniable. Exposure to and positive portrayal of sports figures through the media are important in the social identification process. Eagleman highlights differences in how Major League Baseball players were depicted in *Sports Illustrated* and *ESPN: The Magazine* from 2000 to 2007. Eagleman not only found black players were portrayed more negatively, she found that these depictions enhanced stereotypes in the minds of the audience. She states, "When sport communication professionals use race and/or nationality to inappropriately construct and deconstruct realities of athletes of differing race and nationality, they contribute to the danger of creating and reinforcing a discriminating culture for individuals who may identify with the race or ethnicity of the offended athlete." Eagleman argues, "Sport communication professionals have the opportunity and the obligation to educate sport media consumers accurately and responsibly, and thus promote greater racial and nationalistic understanding, tolerance, and goodwill."[25]

It is this social identification that can translate in behavior. Jones and colleagues claim, "While individuals maintain many identities, some roles are more salient than others, and these identities influence consumption decisions."[26] Similar to social identity theory, theories of the "self" focus on how self-image influences consumer behavior with a need to purchase the right products from the right stores.[27] These purchase decisions become extensions of and help define the self.[28]

Race obviously becomes a factor in developing the self-concept, thus making the racial and cultural experience a factor in making purchase or other behavior decisions.[29] Researchers claim that the consumption of "black culture" helps define, assert, and affirm membership as black.[30] In one study of cultural participation, Banks details how middle-class African Americans demonstrate racial unity and community advancement by patronizing black cultural institutions and purchasing the works of black artists. Nadeau and colleagues apply the self-concept to sport consumption. Sports fans develop a self-concept and self-consistency that impact their sport consumption decisions. These decisions range from the purchase of tickets to sporting events, to the purchase of sporting apparel.

Extending the idea of the racial-ethnic self-concept to the fan of a professional sports club is based on the idea that racial-ethnic congruency between fans and the players contributes to the particular fan's self-concept (i.e., those players represent me) and self-consistency (i.e., I am part of the community that team represents), which, in turn, impact their sport consumption decisions (e.g., purchase tickets, watch on television, buy merchandise, support sponsor products).[31]

So behaviors such as playing baseball or even watching baseball can have identity repercussions if seen as acceptable or unacceptable behavior to the other members of the group in which the individual is trying to identify.

It is incumbent upon the organization trying to influence the desired behavior to develop strategies that foster the social identity. The process of developing a social identity with the audience in a sports context begins with and is the responsibility of the league and its teams. With the literature pointing out that a developed social identity with an organization can potentially translate into consumer behavior, the lack of African-American players is a problem for Major League Baseball in communicating with the African-American population. From a simple business perspective, the application of social identity theory and theories of the self explain that enhancing this association and potentially influencing consumer behavior with the African-American community offers Major League Baseball an economic opportunity.

Relationship Marketing

In the challenge of getting African Americans to identify with the sport of baseball and the Major League Baseball brand, the opportunity for Major League Baseball is explicated through relationship marketing. Relationship marketing is described as activities directed toward establishing, developing, and maintaining successful relationship exchanges.[32] Relationship marketing entails ongoing cooperative behavior between the marketer and the consumer.[33] Bee and Kahle claim that all sports marketing transactions involve some form of relationship marketing. They comment, "Teams, leagues, athletes, marketing corporations, and fans have relationships with one another that depend on successful relationship enactment," and "relationship marketing is characterized by the attraction, development, and retention of customers."[34]

Researchers consistently identify that the critical variable in reaching out to and building a relationship with the sports audience is personal experience. Connections to a team, and for that matter an entire sport, are created through direct experiences.[35] Without prior experience, sports consumers would not have a strong connection to a team or a sport.[36] The sports experience at a young age largely comes through playing the game, attending games, and watching the sport on television or through other media coverage.

From a promotional communication perspective in terms of providing an experience to a large audience, the most important marketing strategy for any sport and all sports leagues is television presence. With only a small number of fans having access game tickets, watching on television remains the dominant method for the mass audience to visually experience the sport live.[37] Television networks provide sports leagues with a substantial source of revenue and their greatest source of exposure.[38] McChesney focuses on the amount of exposure that television networks can provide a sports league, claiming that "Virtually every surge in the popularity of sport has been accompanied by a dramatic increase in the coverage provided by the media."[39]

Exposure is ascertained through the league's placement in the television programming schedule (the network on which the game is televised and the day and time that the game is played). The signing of a broadcast contract creates a partnership between a sports league and a television network so that both now have a vested interest in increasing the audience watching the games. In addition to game placement, determining which teams and league stars will play in these televised games is very much part of a league's exposure strategy. The selection of which teams, and therefore which players, will appear on nationally televised games is the first step in setting up the entire schedule of games for a league. The general objective is to provide the audience with games involving the best teams and players at the best placement within the programming schedule. Offering the games with the best teams and players at the best placement in the programming schedule allows the best assets of the brand to receive exposure to the largest possible audience.

In terms of attendance at Major League Baseball games, attracting the African-American community is another challenge. One survey by Scarborough Marketing Research reported that only 9 percent of fans who attended a Major League Baseball game in 2011 were African American.[40] Armstrong contends that the racial and ethnic composition of a team's players is among the many factors that African Americans take into consideration when deciding to attend sporting events.[41] Nadeau and colleagues explain, "The motivation to attend a game is broader than the game itself. The cultural identity that African-Americans experience in relation to the team and the feeling that it is an event that will be attended by others of similar ethnic background influence their decision to attend." They questioned if a team's player composition reflects the diversity of its community and if that reflection (or as they term it "congruency") could influence the business success of that sports franchise. They claim, "Higher attendance might be achieved in MLB (and perhaps the other professional sports leagues) by including athletes on the team to better reflect the racial-ethnic composition of the home market." They even go so far as to suggest that if there are players of similar skill, the team could benefit from selecting the player that better reflects the community's racial and ethnic composition. However, in selecting players, St. Louis Cardinals general manager John Mozeliak contends, "We're all about talent. It doesn't matter if you're white, black, brown, or green."[42] It is also important to note that it is simplistic to conclude that a team's racial and ethnic composition is the only factor influencing a decision to attend a sporting event, as several factors ultimately influence that decision.

The final necessary experiential behavior is getting kids to play baseball. Fans can relate to sports because they are watching people participate in sports they have often played.[43] The connection people have with sports stems from personal encounters with athletics and the observation of contests where we have been able to witness exceptional performances (e.g., seeing Michael Jordan, Peyton Manning, or Tiger Woods play).[44] When combining these two behaviors, playing the sport can work in tandem with being able to watch its games on television for a more significant influence (e.g., the child comes home from baseball practice, then watches the local team play its game that night on television). This totality of the experience helps to better achieve the characteristic of relationship marketing as being an ongoing endeavor.[45]

By providing the totality of the experience (playing the sport, watching on television, and attending games) a theoretical progression can be established where relationship marketing efforts help produce the social identity, which could potentially help produce the participation behavior. If Major League Baseball can improve its relationship with the African-American population, and perhaps the youth in particular, so as to enhance the identification with baseball players, there will be more of a desire by African Americans to associate themselves with those players and, in essence, the sport of baseball.

The Major League Baseball Outreach Strategy

Major League Baseball has implemented several outreach programs to the African-American community to try to give youths the experience of playing baseball. Its most extensive program is Reviving Baseball in Inner Cities (RBI). RBI is designed "to increase participation and interest in baseball and softball among underserved youth populations, encourage academic participation and achievement, increase the number of talented athletes prepared to play in college and minor leagues, promote greater inclusion of minorities into the mainstream of the game, and teach the value of teamwork."[46]

The RBI program was started by John Young, a former Major League Baseball player and scout, in South Central Los Angeles in 1989. Young found that the majority of kids stopped playing baseball between the ages of 13 and 16 due to a lack of organization, a lack of funding for youth baseball, and the deterioration of communities. He wanted to offer disadvantaged youths an opportunity to learn and experience the game of baseball. Young believed the best way to revive baseball in Los Angeles was through a comprehensive program that would encourage participation in baseball as well as provide youths with a positive, team-oriented activity that would keep them off the streets while challenging them physically and mentally.

RBI leagues now exist in more than 200 cities worldwide and have more than 200,000 participants between the ages of 13 and 18. Major League Baseball teams have drafted more than 170 RBI participants, including current major leaguer players Carl Crawford, Yovanni Gallardo, James Loney, Jimmy Rollins, C. C. Sabathia, and Justin Upton. In 2010, the Jr. RBI program was launched for kids ages five through 12, with more than 90,000 participants annually.

Since the program's inception, Major League Baseball and its teams have donated more than $30 million of resources to the program. In 2007, Major League Baseball Charities began a scholarship program for youths who participated in the RBI program and were pursuing college. Annual scholarships of $5,000 are provided for 12 RBI participants who have achieved academically, have demonstrated leadership qualities, and have financial need.

Another academic component is that RBI programs are provided with a version of the educational curriculum Breaking Barriers: In Sports, In Life, which is designed to teach students how to deal with barriers, obstacles, and challenges in their lives. Information is also provided to RBI programs about alcohol and substance abuse, including performance-enhancing drugs.

Two other outreach programs of Major League Baseball that target youths are the Baseball Tomorrow Fund and the Urban Baseball Academy. The Baseball Tomorrow Fund is "A joint initiative between Major League Baseball and the Major League Baseball Players Association. The fund awards grants to organizations involved in the operation of youth baseball and softball programs and facilities."[47] As of May 2012, the program had funded more than 600 grants totaling more than $22 million in the United States, Canada, Latin America, the Caribbean, Europe, and Asia to help more than 300,000 youth players participate.

In 2006, Major League Baseball established the Urban Baseball Academy, a nonprofit entity located at Compton College in California that partners with local and national youth support programs to promote youth baseball and softball. The mission statement of the Urban Baseball Academy is "To set the standard for instruction, teaching and education in Urban America through the strength of the National Pastime and to enhance the quality of life in the surrounding communities."[48] The objective of the academy is more than teaching the game of baseball. Instruction includes all areas of the sport, such as field maintenance, umpiring, coaching, journalism, statistics, and interpersonal development. Major League Baseball has helped construct four academies in Philadelphia, three in Houston, and one in New Orleans. Bud Selig, Major League Baseball commissioner, stated, "My ultimate goal is to have an academy in every major league city. I really believe we're a social institution with important social responsibilities, and we're making progress."[49]

On a corporate level, the Major League Baseball Diverse Business Partners program was created in 1998 with a mission to "Promote efficiency and profitability for Major League Baseball and its Clubs while extending Baseball's ability to contribute to the economic growth, strength and well-being of diverse communities." The program specifically seeks to "Cultivate new and existing partnerships with minority- and women-owned businesses."[50]

Major League Baseball has created several events to highlight the role that African Americans have played in the history of the sport. Events can be successful in appealing to racial and ethnic minority communities. First, there are Jackie Robinson Day celebrations across Major League Baseball. In 2007, Major League Baseball began an annual Civil Rights game to raise awareness and demonstrate it is tying to deal with the lack of African-American participation. The first two Civil Rights games were exhibition games played in Memphis, Tennessee, on the weekend before the regular season opened. The Civil Rights game is now a regular season game that has been played at different times during the season with Chicago, Cincinnati, and Atlanta having served as host cities.

Marketing through Television

While Major League Baseball continues its efforts to get kids to play baseball and has events at its ballparks, television presence in an attempt to provide the totality of the baseball experience is important to consider. From a communication perspective in terms of providing an experience to a large audience, the most important marketing strategy for any sport and all sports leagues is presence on television. The trend in sports programming is for games to be broadcast on cable television, with those networks acquiring the rights to many prominent sporting events because they have the dual revenue source of advertising income and monthly subscription fees. ESPN is the most expensive cable network. Cable providers pay more than an estimated $5.54 per subscriber per month to have ESPN as part of the package of channels that they offer to customers.[51] The New York Yankee–owned Yankees Entertainment and Sports (YES) Network televises the majority of the Yankees' games and gets approximately $3.20 per subscriber per month.[52]

Major League Baseball has its most prominent national exposure through its free, over-the-air television game of the week on Saturday on Fox. In television contracts that will extend beyond the 2013 season, Fox televises the Saturday game of the week, the All-Star Game, one of the League Championship Series, and the World Series. Major League Baseball's other two national television partners are both cable networks: ESPN and TBS. ESPN televises the Sunday night game of the week and games on Monday and Wednesday. TBS has a Sunday afternoon national game, exclusively carries the entire Division Series round of the playoffs, and one of the League Championship Series.

The Fox Saturday game of the week accounts for only 26 total games on free, over-the-air television. The rights for games not televised on the Fox Saturday or the ESPN Sunday night game of the week broadcasts revert back to the individual teams to sell on a local basis. These games air primarily on cable television, with only a handful of games sold to a free, over-the-air channel in the local area. For example, in New York where there are two teams, aside from the games on Fox, only another 40 to 45 games over the course of the season are scheduled for broadcast on free, over-the-air television. Cable television contracts on a local level are very lucrative for Major League Baseball teams. One estimate claimed that the YES Network earned over $435 million in 2010.[53] In other major league cable television rights contracts, in December 2011, the Los Angeles Angels agreed to a 20-year contract with Fox Sports West valued at more than $3 billion, and the Texas Rangers in August 2010 reached an agreement with Fox Sports Southwest valued at $3 billion over 20 years.[54] More recently, the Los Angeles Dodgers reached an agreement with Time

Warner Cable that will pay the team an estimated $8 billion over 25 years.[55]

With new national television contracts beginning in 2014 and extending through 2021, Major League Baseball will have even less exposure on free television. Fox will televise only 12 regular season games on its over-the-air network, with another 40 games to be televised on one of its cable channels. Fox is paying Major League Baseball an annual average of $525 million to acquire these broadcast rights.[56]

When considering statistics regarding cable television ownership in the African-American community, this majority of baseball exposure on cable is problematic. In the top 30 African-American television markets, only 87.8 percent of all African-American television households have cable television. There are several Major League Baseball cities in which the percentage of African-American cable television households is less than the 87.8 percentage total of African-American television households. In Houston, for example, only 82.7 percent of African-American television households have cable television. This simply means that over 17 percent of the African-American community has virtually no chance of seeing the vast majority of Astros games. The percentage statistics for African-American households having cable television are similar for other cities: Chicago, 84.2 percent; Detroit, 84.1 percent; Philadelphia, 86.2 percent; Baltimore, 86.3 percent; Cleveland, 83.6 percent; and Dallas-Fort Worth, 78.7 percent. In several other major league cities, the percentage of African-American cable television households is just over 90 percent of the total number of African-American television households: New York, 91.9 percent; St. Louis, 91.8 percent; San Francisco–Oakland, 91.8 percent; and Atlanta, 92.3 percent. Los Angeles has a percentage of 89.1 percent of African-American television households with cable.

Currently, the lack of baseball's free, over-the-air television exposure in comparison to football and baseball is significant. The National Football League is the only league to provide all of its games involving a particular city's team to be on free television in that city. Even if the game is on ESPN or the NFL Network, the National Football League mandates that it is provided on an over-the-air channel in the two cities of the competing teams. In fact, the only time fans do not see their local team on television is if they live in a city in which the game does not sell out 72 hours before kickoff. In the instance of a local team blackout on a Sunday afternoon, a different National Football League game is televised into that city. One of the variables contributing to the National Football League being viewed as the most successful professional sports league is certainly its constant availability on free, over-the-air television. The National Basketball Association is more similar to Major League Baseball in that much of its programming is broadcast on cable television. The only over-the-air televising of National Basketball Association games is the Sunday afternoon game of the week, some playoff games, and the National Basketball Association finals on ABC. Even the National Basketball Association All-Star Game is televised on cable.

In addition to the National Football League and National Basketball Association, football and basketball receive exposure through collegiate athletics constantly being on free, over-the-air television, an exposure characteristic that baseball does not have. Autumn Saturdays are littered with college football games potentially airing on ABC, CBS, Fox, and NBC. In the winter, the weekend features many college basketball games on free television and much of the NCAA college basketball tournament is also on free television (it should be noted that portions of the NCAA college basketball tournament are on cable television as CBS and Turner in a joint bid are now the broadcast rights holders). This television exposure allows the audience to begin to build a relationship with the stars who will soon be playing in the National Basketball Association and National Football League.

Discussion

In 2012, Major League Baseball revenues climbed to more than $7.5 billion. In the same year, Major League Baseball games had more than 74 million people in attendance, and the final game of the World Series was watched on television by more than 15 million people. With this evidence of business success, Major League Baseball could consider the lack of African-American participation a problem that does not need to be addressed, or it can try to improve the current situation, recognizing that from a social and an economic perspective, there is value in having increased African-American participation in its sport. As has been demonstrated, Major League Baseball has undertaken several initiatives and investments to try to build its relationship with the African-American community and should be applauded for these efforts. It can, however, be easily concluded that there is still more that Major League baseball can do. Indeed, there are certainly variables beyond Major League Baseball's control that have led to the current lack of African-American participation. Major League Baseball does, however, control how it markets its games, and several promotional communication opportunities do exist.

Marketing theory provides valuable insight into developing a potentially successful strategy for Major League Baseball. Social identity theory posits that people view positively groups with which they can identify.[57] Relationship marketing is categorized as an ongoing endeavor with the ultimate goal of fan retention.[58] A theoretical progression can thus be established where relationship marketing efforts help produce the social identity, which could potentially help produce the result of African-American participation behavior in the sport of baseball. In addressing this question of how Major League Baseball might build this relationship with the African-America community, researchers have identified that experiencing the sport (playing the sport, watching on television, and attendance at games) is essential.[59] While Major League Baseball is developing programs to get African-American youths to play baseball, providing the totality of the experience is needed.

Major League Baseball is demonstrating in some ways that it cares about the lack of African-American participation, but it is neglecting the most obvious exposure strategy. Marketing a sport in terms of attaining wide exposure begins with having games on television. The availability of few Major League Baseball games on free television is exacerbated by significant percentages of African-American television households not having cable television.[60] With over 15 percent of the African-American television households without cable television in Major League Baseball cities such as Chicago, Cleveland, Dallas, Detroit, and Houston, large segments of the African-American community have the ability to see only a relatively small number of baseball games on television in a given year. Major League Baseball could simply decide to put more games on free, over-the-air television if it is trying to reach a larger population as a whole and the African-American community in particular. The dilemma for Major League Baseball and its teams with their lucrative cable television contracts is that it is not in their economic interests to put more games on free television. At the very least, games on the national cable channels, such as ESPN and Turner, could also be aired on a local channel as the NFL does for its cable telecasts.

Currently, the relatively few African-American players means that there is a limited number of African-American role models in the game for African-American youths to look up too. The underrepresentation of

African-American athletes in Major League Baseball will ultimately influence the number of African-American major leaguers in the future. To break that cycle, African-American youths have to want to be identified as baseball players before they make a commitment to participate in the sport as players or even fans. For that to happen, they have to see the sport being played by major leaguers. This exposure could help increase their desire to play baseball. It is having both experiences, playing and watching excellence in a sport, that have been found by scholars as contributing to why people become fans of a particular sport.[61] Dusty Baker, who had a 19-year playing career and has been named Manager of the Year on three occasions in his 20-year managerial career, stated that "exposure is the key. You see a lot of guys in baseball whose fathers were ballplayers. They were introduced to the sport at a very, very young age. Once you fall in love with baseball, most times you remain in love with baseball. The hard part is falling in love with baseball at an older age. Then it appears slow."[62]

In obtaining exposure through television, Major League Baseball could also make a more concerted effort to market its African-American stars through that communication vehicle. While African Americans make up less than 9 percent of Major League Baseball players in 2013, there are many talented African-American players, such as Ryan Howard, Philadelphia Phillies first baseman and former National League MVP; David Price, Tampa Bay Rays pitcher and Cy Young Award winner in 2012; C. C. Sabathia, New York Yankees pitcher and former American League Cy Young Award winner; Jimmy Rollins, Philadelphia Phillies shortstop and former National League MVP; as well as emerging stars Matt Kemp, Los Angeles Dodgers center fielder; Andrew McCutchen, Pittsburgh Pirates center fielder; and Adam Jones, Baltimore Orioles center fielder.

Perhaps showcasing these players prominently in games on free television can increase their profile and arouse the social identification process of assisting African-American youths wanting to identify with them and the game of baseball. Dontrelle Willis, major league pitcher and 2003 National League Rookie of the Year, commented that when he was 11 years old, he was influenced by seeing Dave Stewart, former Oakland Athletics pitcher, have the first of his four consecutive 20-win seasons in 1987. Willis stated, "The reason I picked up a baseball is because of Dave Stewart. Being an African-American pitcher and seeing him do what he was doing with the talent he had, I said that's who I want to emulate my game after."[63] In trying to serve as a role model for African-American youths, Los Angeles Dodgers center fielder Matt Kemp added, "I'm trying to make baseball cool for African-Americans and let African-American kids know that baseball can give you the same opportunities as football, basketball or any of the other sports. You get paid just as much, get to drive those nice cars and do all of that stuff that all the other NBA guys get to do."[64]

Currently it can be argued that Major League Baseball is not providing the totality of the experience through television. If putting significantly more games on free television is not economically feasible due to the lucrative cable contracts, perhaps placing a couple of games with relevant African-American themes on free television is more practical. Having a game on the April 15 anniversary of Jackie Robinson breaking the color barrier is one possibility. Another possible idea is to have the Civil Rights game on the Thursday after the Major League Baseball All-Star Game (played on a Tuesday) in the city of the All-Star Game and televised by Fox on its free, over-the-air network. The Civil Rights game might be attractive for the network because it would be a stand-alone game as opposed to it currently being played on a night when it receives competition from all other major league teams playing games. The production of the game for Fox would also be simple and cost-effective because the cameras and other equipment would already be in place for the All-Star Game. The Civil Rights game can be promoted throughout the broadcast of the All-Star Game. Other media covering the All-Star Game would also already be in the city to now report on the Civil Rights game. Finally, the game could involve a team that has an African-American star. For example, in 2013, the All-Star Game was played at Citi Field, home of the New York Mets. On that Thursday after the All-Star Game, the Mets could have hosted the Los Angeles Dodgers and Matt Kemp or the Philadelphia Phillies with Ryan Howard and Jimmy Rollins. With it being the only major league game being played that night and having the greater attention of the sports media and the audience, the challenge of African-American participation in baseball can be better highlighted throughout the broadcast.

Another option to the free television dilemma is using Internet technologies. Major League Baseball does provide games over the Internet, however, also on a pay basis. Major League Baseball, or a collection of its players, could make this subscription service free and available to any youths who participate in an RBI league. There could even be an academic requirement of having good grades to receive the Major League games on the Internet. In terms of attendance at games, and once again adding an academic component, teams could offer a free ticket to any students in their respective city who graduate high school. Through this offering recognizing an academic achievement, other paying customers will not be devalued. Major League Baseball and its teams might also attract sponsors to invest in these programs, as they too are often interested in corporate social responsibility initiatives and have used the established programs of sports leagues as part of their own charitable profile.

If a segment of the community is not obtaining the experience of baseball, it is incumbent upon Major League Baseball to facilitate providing that experience and foster the critical social identity. The process of developing a social identity with the audience in a sports context begins with and is the responsibility of the league and its teams. Investments in providing the totality of the baseball experience (playing baseball, attending a Major League Baseball game, and having the opportunity to watch Major League Baseball on television) might be the only chance of demonstrable change for Major League Baseball in establishing a relationship and creating an identity with the African-American community. Owners make large amounts of revenue from their cable television contracts, and players earn high salaries. A substantial joint investment in providing these necessary experiences could address some of the marketing root causes of the lack of African-American participation that Major League Baseball can control. As Jimmy Rollins, former RBI participant and Philadelphia Phillies shortstop stated, "It would be a sad day if one day we are—quote, unquote—extinct from this game."[65]

Notes

1. Lapchick, Richard. 2013. University of Central Florida's Institute for Diversity and Ethics in Sports, http://www.tidesport.org/RGRC/2013/2013_MLB_RGRC_Final_Correction.pdf

2. Cousens, Laura, and Trevor Slack. 2005. "Field-Level Change: The case of North American Major League Professional Sport." *Journal of Sport Management* 19, no. 1: 13–42; Lapchick, Richard. 2013. University of Central Florida's Institute for Diversity and Ethics in Sports, http://www.tidesport.org/RGRC/2013/2013_MLB_RGRC_Final_Correction.pdf; Nightengale, Bob. 2012, April 16. "African American' MLB Presence Wanes: Percentage Dips to 8% of Rosters, Down from 27% in 1975." *USA Today*, 1C. Powell, Shaun. 2008. *Souled Out? How Blacks are Winning and Losing in Sports*. Chicago: Human Kinetics; Sack, Allen L., Parbuyal Singh, and Robert Thiel. 2005. "Occupational Segregation on the Playing Field: The Case of Major League Baseball." *Journal of Sport Management* 19, no. 3: 300–318; Snyder, Deron. 2011, August 19. "Decline in Black Players Should Concern All Who Love Baseball." *Washington Times*, 1. Winfield, Dave.

2007. *Dropping the Ball: Baseball's Troubles & How We Can & Must Solve Them.* New York: Scribner.

3. Nightengale, "African American' MLB Presence Wanes"; Powell, *Souled Out?*; Winfield, *Dropping the Ball.*

4. Lapchick, University of Central Florida's Institute for Diversity and Ethics in Sports.

5. Klein, Alan M. 2006. *Growing the Game: The Globalization of Major League Baseball.* New Haven, CT: Yale University Press, 1.

6. Klein, Alan M. 2006. *Growing the Game: The Globalization of Major League Baseball.* New Haven, CT: Yale University Press, 18.

7. Powell, Shaun. 2007. *Souled Out? How Blacks are Winning and Losing in Sports.* Champaign, IL: Human Kinetics, 127.

8. Powell, Shaun. 2007. *Souled Out? How Blacks are Winning and Losing in Sports.* Champaign, IL: Human Kinetics, 128.

9. Watkins, S. Craig. 2005. *Hip Hop Matters: Politics, Popular Culture and the Struggle for the Soul of a Movement.* Boston: Beacon.

10. Balaji, Murali. 2012. "The Construction of 'Street Credibility' in Atlanta's Hip-Hop Music Scene: Analyzing the Role of Cultural Gatekeepers." *Critical Studies in Media Communication* 29, no. 4: 313–330, 317.

11. Associated Press. 2007, November 21. "Rollins, Who Spurred Phils into Playoffs, Wins MVP." http://sports.espn.go.com/mlb/news/story?id=3120573

12. Nightengale, Bob. 2012b, April 16. "African American' MLB Presence Wanes: Percentage Dips to 8% of Rosters, Down from 27% in 1975." *USA Today*: 1C.

13. Lapchick, Richard. 2012b. University of Central Florida's Institute for Diversity and Ethics in Sports, http://www.tidesport.org/RGRC/2012/2012_NBA _RGRC[1].pdf

14. Lapchick, Richard. 2012a. University of Central Florida's Institute for Diversity and Ethics in Sports, http://www.tidesport.org/RGRC/2012/2012_NFL _RGRC.pdf

15. O'Connor, Ian. 2010, April 15. "The Commissioner and His Quest: Bud Selig's Legacy Depends on Bringing African-Americans Back to Baseball." http:// sports.espn.go.com/new-york/mlb/columns/story?id=5095255

16. Keller, Kevin, 2001. "Mastering the Marketing Communications Mix: Micro and Macro Perspectives on Integrated Marketing Communication Programs." *Journal of Marketing Management* 17: 819–847, 819.

17. Hickman, Thomas M., Katherine E. Lawrence, and James C. Ward. 2005. "A Social Identities Perspective on the Effects of Corporate Sport Sponsorship on Employees." *Sport Marketing Quarterly* 14, no. 3: 148–157; Kahle, Lynn R. 1996. "Social Values and Consumer Behavior: Research from a List of Values." In *The Psychology of Values: The Ontario Symposium Vol. 8*, edited by Clive Seligman, James M. Olson, and Mark P. Zanna, 135–151. Mahwah, NJ: Lawrence Erlbaum

Associates; Mael, Fred A., and Blake E. Ashforth. 2001. "Identification in Work, War, Sports, and Religion: Contrasting the Benefits and Risks." *Journal for the Theory of Social Behavior* 31, no. 2: 197–222; Stryker, Sheldon. 1980. *Symbolic Interactionism: A Socio-Structural Version.* Menlo Park, CA: Benjamin/ Cummings; Tajfel, Henri. 1982. *Social Identity and Intergroup Relations.* New York, NY: Cambridge University Press.

18. Tajfel, *Social Identity and Intergroup Relations*, 31.

19. Sherif, Muzafer. 2001. "Superordinate Goals in the Reduction on Intergroup Conflict." In *Intergroup Relations: Essential Readings; Key Readings in Social Psychology*, edited by Michael A. Hogg and Dominic Abrams, 64–70. New York: Psychology Press.

20. Hartmann, Douglas. 2000. "Rethinking the Relationship between Sport and Race in American Culture: Golden Ghettos and Contested Terrain." *Sociology of Sport Journal* 17, no. 3: 229–253; Ogden, David C., and Michael L. Hilt. 2003. "Collective Identity and Basketball: An Explanation for the Decreasing Number of African-Americans on America's Baseball Diamonds." *Journal of Leisure Research* 35, no. 2: 213–227.

21. Sapolsky, Barry S. 1980. "The Effect of Spectator Disposition and Suspense on the Enjoyment of Sport Contests." *International Journal of Sport Psychology* 11: 1-10.

22. Appiah, K. Anthony. 2000. "Racial Identity and Racial Identification." In *Theories of Race and Racism*, edited by Les Back and John Solomos, 607–615. London: Routledge.

23. Ogden and Hilt, "Collective Identity and Basketball."

24. Nightengale, "African American' MLB Presence Wanes."

25. Eagleman, Andrea N. 2011. "Stereotypes of Race and Nationality: A Qualitative Analysis of Sport Magazine Coverage of MLB Players." *Journal of Sport Management* 25: 156–168, 166.

26. Jones et al., "Affinity Credit Cards as Relationship Marketing Tools," 139.

27. Malholtra, Naresh. 1988. "Self Concept and Product Choice: An Integrated Perspective." *Journal of Economic Psychology* 9, no. 1: 1-28; Onkvisit, Sak, and John Shaw. 1987. "Self-Concept and Image Congruence: Some Research and Managerial Implications." *Journal of Consumer Marketing* 4, no. 1: 13–23.

28. Belk, Russell. 1988. "Possessions and the Extended Self." *Journal of Consumer Research* 15: 139–168; Sirgy, M. Joseph, Dhruv Grewal, and Tamara Mangleburge. 2000. "Retail Environment, Self-Congruity, and Retail Patronage: An Integrative Model and a Research Agenda." *Journal of Business Research* 49, no. 2: 127–138.

29. Armstrong, Ketra L. 2002. "Race and Sport Consumption Motivations: A Preliminary Investigation of Black Consumers' Sport Motivation Scale." *Journal of Sport Behavior* 25, no. 4: 309–331; Armstrong, Ketra L. 2002. "An Examination of the Social Psychology of Blacks' Consumption of Sport." *Journal of Sport Management* 16, no. 4: 267–289; Nadeau, John, D. Floyd Jones, Ann Pegoraro, Norm

O'Reilly, and Paulo Carvalho. 2011. "Racial-Ethnic Team-Market Congruency in Professional Sport." *Journal of Sport Management* 25, no. 2: 169–180.

30. Banks, Patricia A. 2010. "Black Cultural Advancement: Racial Identity and Participation in the Arts among the Black Middle Class." *Ethnic and Racial Studies* 33 no. 2: 272–289; Lamont, Michele, and Virag Molnar. 2001. "How Blacks Use Consumption to Shape Their Collective Identity: Evidence from African-American Marketing Specialists." *Journal of Consumer Culture* 1, no. 1: 31–45.

31. Nadeau et al., "Racial-Ethnic Team-Market Congruency."

32. Arnold, Kara A., and Constanza Bianchi. 2001. "Relationship Marketing, Gender, and Culture: Implications for Consumer Behavior." *Advances in Consumer Research* 28: 100–105; Morgan, Robert M., and Shelby D. Hunt. 1994. "The Commitment-Trust Theory of Relationship Marketing." *Journal of Marketing* 58: 20–38; Peterson, Richard A. 1995. "Relationship Marketing and the Consumer." *Journal of the Academy of Marketing Science* 23: 278–281.

33. Sheth, Jagdish N., and Atul Parvatiyar. 2000. *Handbook of Relationship Marketing*. Thousand Oaks, CA: Sage.

34. Bee, Colleen C., and Lynn R. Kahle. 2006. "Relationship Marketing in Sports: A Functional Approach." *Sport Marketing Quarterly* 15, no. 2: 102–110, 102, 103.

35. James, Jeffrey D., Richard D. Kolbe, and Galen T. Trail. 2002. "Psychological Connection to a New Sport Team: Building or Maintaining the Consumer Base?" *Sport Marketing Quarterly* 11, no. 4: 215–225.

36. Mullin, Bernard J., Stephen Hardy, and William A. Sutton. 2007. *Sport Marketing*, 3rd ed. Champaign, IL: Human Kinetics.

37. Lever, Janet, and Stanton Wheeler. 1993. "Mass Media and the Experience of Sport." *Communication Research* 20, no. 1: 125–143; Wenner, Lawrence A. 1989. "Media, Sports, and Society: The Research Agenda." In *Media, Sports, and Society*, edited by Lawrence A. Wenner, 13–48. Newbury Park, CA: Sage.

38. Fortunato, John A. 2001. *The Ultimate Assist: The Relationship and Broadcast Strategies of the NBA and Television Networks*. Cresskill, NJ: Hampton; Fortunato, John A. 2008. "The NFL Programming Schedule: A Study of Agenda-Setting." *Journal of Sports Media* 3, no. 1: 27–49.

39. McChesney, Robert W. 1989. "Media Made Sport: A History of Sports Coverage in the United States." In *Media, Sports, and Society*, edited by Lawrence A. Wenner, 49–69. Newbury Park, CA: Sage, 49.

40. Nightengale, "African American' MLB Presence Wanes."

41. Armstrong, Ketra L. 2008. "Consumers of Color and 'Culture' of Sport Attendance: Exploratory Insights." *Sport Marketing Quarterly* 17, no. 4: 218–231.

42. Nadeau et al., "Racial-ethnic Team-market Congruency"; Nightengale, "African American' MLB Presence Wanes."

43. Zillmann, Dolf, Jennings Bryant, and Barry S. Sapolsky. 1989. "Enjoyment from Sports Spectatorship." In *Sports, Games, and Play: Social and Psychological*

Viewpoints, edited by Jeffrey H. Goldstein, 241–278. Hillsdale, NJ: Lawrence Erlbaum.

44. Tutko, Thomas A. 1989. "Personality Change in the American Sport Scene." In *Sports, Games, and Play: Social and Psychological Viewpoints*, edited by Jeffrey H. Goldstein, 111–127. Hillsdale, NJ: Lawrence Erlbaum.

45. Sheth, Jagdish N., and Atul Parvatiyar. 2000. *Handbook of Relationship Marketing*. Thousand Oaks, CA: Sage.

46. Reviving Baseball in Inner Cities (RBI) Program. http://minnesota.twins .mlb.com/min/community/twins_rbi.jsp.

47. Baseball Tomorrow Fund: About the Fund. www.mlbcommunity.org/ programs/baseball_tomorrow_fund.jsp

48. MLB Urban Youth Academy: About Us. http://mlb.mlb.com/news/ press-releases.

49. O'Connor, "The Commissioner and His Quest."

50. Diverse Business Partners: About DBP. http://mlb.mlb.com/mlb/official _info/mlb_official_info_diverse.jsp?content=about

51. Deitsch, Richard. 2013, March 18. "A Shot at the Champ: Fox Promises to Come Out Swinging with a New 24/7 Channel, but Can FS1 Really Challenge ESPN?" *Sports Illustrated* 118, no. 12: 16.

52. Ourand, John. 2013, February 11–17. "Deal with Dodgers Shifts Attention to Local Team Rights." *Street and Smith's Sports Business Journal* 15, no. 41: 12.

53. Sandomir, Richard. 2011, August 20. "Regional Sports Networks Show the Money." *New York Times*, D1.

54. Nightengale, "African American' MLB Presence Wanes."

55. Ourand, "Deal with Dodgers Shifts Attention."

56. Ourand, John. 2013, January 7-13. "Deal Could Make Yanks a Fixture on Fox." *Street and Smith's Sports Business Journal* 15, no. 36: 3.

57. Sherif, Muzafer. 2001. "Superordinate Goals in the Reduction on Intergroup Conflict." In *Intergroup Relations: Essential Readings; Key Readings in Social Psychology*, edited by Michael A. Hogg and Dominic Abrams, 64–70. New York: Psychology Press.

58. Bee, Colleen C., and Lynn R. Kahle. 2006. "Relationship Marketing in Sports: A Functional Approach." *Sport Marketing Quarterly* 15, no. 2: 102–110; Sheth, Jagdish N., and Atul Parvatiyar. 2000. *Handbook of Relationship Marketing*. Thousand Oaks, CA: Sage.

59. James, Jeffrey D., Richard D. Kolbe, and Galen T. Trail. 2002. "Psychological Connection to a New Sport Team: Building or Maintaining the Consumer Base?" *Sport Marketing Quarterly* 11, no. 4: 215–225; Mullin et al., *Sport Marketing*.

60. Fortunato, *Ultimate Assist*; Fortunato, "NFL Programming Schedule."

61. Tutko, "Personality Change in the American Sport Scene"; Zillmann, Dolf, Jennings Bryant, and Barry S. Sapolsky. 1989. "Enjoyment from Sports

Spectatorship." In *Sports, Games, and Play: Social and Psychological Viewpoints*, edited by Jeffrey H. Goldstein, 241–278. Hillsdale, NJ: Lawrence Erlbaum.

62. Snyder, "Decline in Black Players."

63. Snyder, "Decline in Black Players."

64. Nightengale, "African American' MLB Presence Wanes."

65. Associated Press. 2007, November 21. "Rollins, Who Spurred Phils into Playoffs, Wins MVP." http://sports.espn.go.com/mlb/news/story?id=3120573

Bibliography

Appiah, K. A. (2000). Racial identity and racial identification. In L. Back & J. Solomos (Eds.), *Theories of race and racism* (pp. 607–615). London: Routledge.

Armstrong, K. L. (2002). Race and sport consumption motivations: A preliminary investigation of black consumers' sport motivation scale. *Journal of Sport Behavior, 25*(4), 309–331.

Armstrong, K. L. (2002). An examination of the social psychology of blacks' consumption of sport. *Journal of Sport Management, 16*(4), 267–289.

Armstrong, K. L. (2008). Consumers of color and "culture" of sport attendance: Exploratory insights. *Sport Marketing Quarterly, 17*(4), 218–231.

Arnold, K. A., & Bianchi, C. (2001). Relationship marketing, gender, and culture: Implications for consumer behavior. *Advances in Consumer Research, 28*, 100–105.

Balaji, M. (2012). The construction of "street credibility" in Atlanta's hip-hop music scene: Analyzing the role of cultural gatekeepers. *Critical Studies in Media Communication, 29*(4), 313–330.

Banks, P. A. (2010). Black cultural advancement: Racial identity and participation in the arts among the black middle class. *Ethnic and Racial Studies, 33*(2), 272–289.

Bee, C. C., & Kahle, L. R. (2006). Relationship marketing in sports: A functional approach. *Sport Marketing Quarterly, 15*(2), 102–110.

Belk, R. (1988). Possessions and the extended self. *Journal of Consumer Research, 15*, 139–168.

Cousens, L., & Slack, T. (2005). Field-level change: The case of North American major league professional sport. *Journal of Sport Management, 19*(1), 13–42.

Deitsch, R. (2013, March 18). A shot at the champ: Fox promises to come out swinging with a new 24/7 channel, but can FS1 really challenge ESPN? *Sports Illustrated, 118*(12), 16.

Eagleman, A. M. (2011). Stereotypes of race and nationality: A qualitative analysis of sport magazine coverage of MLB players. *Journal of Sport Management, 25*, 156–168.

Fortunato, J. A. (2001). *The ultimate assist: The relationship and broadcast strategies of the NBA and television networks*. Cresskill, NJ: Hampton.

Fortunato, J. A. (2008). The NFL programming schedule: A study of agenda-setting. *Journal of Sports Media, 3*(1), 27–49.

Hartmann, D. (2000). Rethinking the relationship between sport and race in American culture: Golden ghettos and contested terrain. *Sociology of Sport Journal, 17*(3), 229–253.

Hickman, T. M., Lawrence, K. E., & Ward, J. C. (2005). A social identities perspective on the effects of corporate sport sponsorship on employees. *Sport Marketing Quarterly, 14*(3), 148–157.

James, J. D., Kolbe, R. H., & Trail, G. T. (2002). Psychological connection to a new sport team: Building or maintaining the consumer base? *Sport Marketing Quarterly, 11*(4), 215–225.

Jones, S. A., Suter, T. A., & Koch, E. (2006). Affinity credit cards as relationship marketing tools: A conjoint analytic exploration of combined product attributes. *Sport Marketing Quarterly, 15*(3), 138–146.

Kahle, L. R. (1996). Social values and consumer behavior: Research from a list of values. In C. Seligman, J. M. Olson, & M. P. Zanna (Eds.), *The psychology of values: The Ontario symposium* (Vol. 8, pp. 135–151). Mahwah, NJ: Lawrence Erlbaum Associates.

Keller, K. (2001). Mastering the marketing communications mix: Micro and macro perspectives on integrated marketing communication programs. *Journal of Marketing Management, 17*, 819–847.

Klein, A. M. (2006). *Growing the Game: The Globalization of Major League Baseball.* New Haven, CT: Yale University Press.

Lamont, M., & Molnar, V. (2001). How blacks use consumption to shape their collective identity: Evidence from African-American marketing specialists. *Journal of Consumer Culture, 1*(1), 31–45.

Lapchick, R. (2012). University of Central Florida's Institute for Diversity and Ethics in Sports, http://web.bus.ucf.edu/documents/sport/2012-MLB-RGRC.pdf.

Lever, J., & Wheeler, S. (1993). Mass media and the experience of sport. *Communication Research, 20*(1), 125–143.

Mael, F. A., & Ashforth, B. E. (2001). Identification in work, war, sports, and religion: Contrasting the benefits and risks. *Journal for the Theory of Social Behavior, 31*(2), 197–222.

Malholtra, N. (1988). Self concept and product choice: An integrated perspective. *Journal of Economic Psychology, 9*(1), 1–28.

McChesney, R. W. (1989). Media made sport: A history of sports coverage in the United States. In L.A. Wenner (Ed.), *Media, sports, and society* (pp. 49–69). Newbury Park, CA: Sage.

Morgan, R. M., & Hunt, S. D. (1994). The commitment-trust theory of relationship marketing. *Journal of Marketing, 58*, 20–38.

Mullin, B. J., Hardy, S., & Sutton, W. A. (2007). *Sport marketing* (3rd ed.). Champaign, IL: Human Kinetics.

Nadeau, J., Jones, D. F., Pegoraro, A., O'Reilly, N., & Carvalho, P. (2011). Racial-ethnic team-market congruency in professional sport. *Journal of Sport Management, 25*(2), 169–180.

Nightengale, B. (2012, February 10). Cash flows through MLB cable outlets: Local TV deals add revenue, alter landscape. *USA Today*, 1C.

Nightengale, B. (2012, April 16). African American' MLB presence wanes: Percentage dips to 8% of rosters, down from 27% in 1975. *USA Today*, 1C.

O'Connor, I. (2010, April 15). The commissioner and his quest: Bud Selig's legacy depends on bringing African-Americans back to baseball. http://sports.espn.go.com/new-york/mlb/columns/story?id=5095255

Ogden, D. C., & Hilt, M. L. (2003). Collective identity and basketball: An explanation for the decreasing number of African-Americans on America's baseball diamonds. *Journal of Leisure Research, 35*(2), 213–227.

Onkvisit, S., & Shaw, J. (1987). Self-concept and image congruence: Some research and managerial implications. *Journal of Consumer Marketing, 4*(1), 13–23.

O'Reilly, N., & Nadeau, J. (2006). Revenue generation in professional sport: A diagnostic analysis. *International Journal of Sport Management and Marketing, 1*(4), 311–330.

Ourand, J. (2013, January 7–13). Deal could make Yanks a fixture on Fox. *Street and Smith's Sports Business Journal, 15*(36), 3.

Ourand, J. (2013, February 11–17). Deal with Dodgers shifts attention to local team rights. *Street and Smith's Sports Business Journal, 15*(41), 12.

Peterson, R. A. (1995). Relationship marketing and the consumer. *Journal of the Academy of Marketing Science, 23*, 278–281.

Powell, S. (2008). *Souled out? How blacks are winning and losing in sports*. Chicago: Human Kinetics.

Sack, A. L., Singh, P., & Thiel, R. (2005). Occupational segregation on the playing field: The case of Major League Baseball. *Journal of Sport Management, 19*(3), 300–318.

Sandomir, R. (2011, August 20). Regional sports networks show the money. *New York Times*, D1.

Sapolsky, B. S. (1980). The effect of spectator disposition and suspense on the enjoyment of sport contests. *International Journal of Sport Psychology, 11*, 1–10.

Sherif, M. (2001). Superordinate goals in the reduction on intergroup conflict. In M.A. Hogg & D. Abrams (Eds.), *Intergroup relations: Essential readings; Key readings in social psychology*. New York: Psychology Press.

Sheth, J. N., & Parvatiyar, A. (Eds.). (2000). *Handbook of relationship marketing*. Thousand Oaks, CA: Sage.

Sirgy, M. J., Grewalb, D., & Mangleburge, T. (2000). Retail environment, self-congruity, and retail patronage: An integrative model and a research agenda. *Journal of Business Research, 49*(2), 127–138.

Snyder, D. (2011, August 19). Decline in black players should concern all who love baseball. *Washington Times,* 1.

Stryker, S. (1980). *Symbolic interactionism: A socio-structural version.* Menlo Park, CA: Benajamin/Cummings.

Tajfel, H. (1982). *Social identity and intergroup relations.* New York: Cambridge University Press.

Tutko, T. A. (1989). Personality change in the American sport scene. In J.H. Goldstein (Ed.), *Sports, games, and play: Social and psychological viewpoints* (pp. 111–127). Hillsdale, NJ: Erlbaum.

Watkins, S. C. (2005). *Hip hop matters: Politics, popular culture and the struggle for the soul of a movement.* Boston: Beacon.

Wenner, L. A. (1989). Media, sports, and society: The research agenda. In L.A. Wenner (Ed.), *Media, sports, and society* (pp. 13–48). Newbury Park, CA: Sage.

Winfield, D. (2007). *Dropping the ball: Baseball's troubles & how we can & must solve them.* New York: Scribner.

Zillmann, D., Bryant, J., & Sapolsky, B. S. (1989). Enjoyment from sports spectatorship. In J.H. Goldstein (Ed.), *Sports, games, and play: Social and psychological viewpoints* (pp. 241–278). Hillsdale, NJ: Lawrence Erlbaum.

Chapter 4

Race, In-Group Bias, and Their Influence on Perceptions of Controversial Same-Race and Different-Race Athletes

Joshua B. Dickhaus and Lance Kinney

Sports are often viewed as reflecting the race relations of nations and communities. While separate but equal was still the law, heavyweight champion Joe Louis was the country's biggest celebrity. Before the U.S. Supreme Court required public schools to integrate, Jackie Robinson broke Major League Baseball's color barrier. Jim Plunkett became the first Mexican American to win the Heisman Trophy in 1970, while Tom Flores became the NFL's first Mexican-American head coach in 1979. Doug Williams became the first black quarterback to play in and win the Super Bowl in 1988. Art Shell became the first black NFL modern-era head coach in 1989 when the Los Angeles (now Oakland) Raiders' white owner, Al Davis, promoted Shell to the position 14 years before the NFL's Rooney Rule requiring all NFL teams to consider and interview at least one black candidate for each available head coaching position. In 2004, black NBA stars Carmelo Anthony and Lebron James said race is no longer an issue in the NBA. However, this does not mean there are no serious race issues in sports.[1]

Politically conservative radio broadcaster Rush Limbaugh, then serving as a professional football analyst for ESPN, suggested the black quarterback of the Philadelphia Eagles, Donovan McNabb, received less critical coverage for his performance than would a white quarterback with similar statistics. Limbaugh claimed McNabb's favorable coverage resulted from sports media's desire for a successful black quarterback. Limbaugh's remarks generated enough critical media reaction for ESPN to relieve Limbaugh of his duties.[2] More recently, black ESPN sports analyst Rob Parker received a 30-day suspension from ESPN for calling Washington Redskins quarterback Robert Griffin III a "cornball brother."[3] Parker asserted that Griffin's only expression of blackness was his cornrow hairstyle. Parker specifically referred to Griffin's white fiancé and Parker's suspicion that Griffin preferred Republican political stances. Parker's contract, which expired at the end of 2012, was not renewed by ESPN.

Following the arrest and eventual imprisonment of black NFL quarterback Michael Vick in 2007, racism (considered only in terms of white and black) became the most hotly debated topic in sports media.[4] Warren Moon, the first black quarterback selected for the NFL Hall of Fame, called Vick's punishment excessive relative to what a white quarterback could expect. On HBO's *Real Sports with Bryant Gumbel*, Gumbel claimed it was time for people to stop piling on Vick. ESPN's *First Take* commentary program's white host, Skip Bayless, openly criticized Vick. Many of the show's black guests defended Vick, claiming his punishment was harsher than a white athlete could expect under similar circumstances.[5]

Two public opinion polls released in 2010 identifying the public's most-hated sports personalities fueled racial debates. The *Forbes* magazine list of the top 10 most disliked sports people consisted of five blacks, four whites, and one Latino. Michael Vick topped the *Forbes* list. Mixed-race golfer Tiger Woods was the fourth most hated athlete.[6] A second poll received the attention of ESPN's commentary programs. Marketing Evaluation, Inc., conducts public opinion surveys to determine how popular public figures are with the American public, resulting in the subject's Q Score. If respondents recognize the athlete, they rate the athlete on a scale ranging from "poor" to "one of my favorites." The number of people rating the athlete positively is divided by the number of people who recognize the athlete.[7] A negative Q Score, indicating that an athlete is disliked, could cost the athlete millions of dollars in the endorsement market.

In the Q Score poll of the most disliked athletes, all six athletes were black. In order, the Q Score list included Michael Vick, Tiger Woods, Terrell Owens, Chad Ochocinco, Kobe Bryant and Lebron James. To black commentators, this poll was evidence of pervasive racism in America.[8] While Vick was convicted of a crime in 2007 and Bryant tried for sexual assault in 2003, the other black athletes on this list were not involved in criminal activity. This led a black columnist to write, "We are not living in a post-racial society, we are living in denial."[9] Another black sports ana-lyst questioned how white athletes Brett Favre and Ben Roethlisberger did not make the negative Q Score list, concluding that a racial component must be present. Rob Parker also agreed with a question posed to him on ESPN's *1st and 10*: black people do not like white quarterback Brett Favre and do not believe a black athlete behaving like Favre would be treated the same way.[10]

The research reported here assesses perceptions of black and white ath-letes among black and white sports fans. The next section addresses rel-evant literature on how people develop racial identity. Hypotheses pertaining to the racial attitudes of sports fans are presented. Research methods used to test the hypotheses are described, followed by hypothesis tests. This research concludes with a discussion of the results, along with recommendations for future research areas concerning sports and race.

Social identity theory, specifically in-group bias, and source credibility are the major theories used to investigate subject responses in this research. Social identity theory's in-group versus out-group propositions explain how individuals identify themselves along racial lines and how respondents might perceive same-race and different-race athletes. In-group bias result-ing in same-race preference, in turn, may impact credibility perceptions for same-race and different-race athletes.

Tajfel and Turner proposed social identity theory to explain intergroup discrimination.[11,12] The core assumptions of social identity theory are that individuals are motivated to develop and protect a sense of personal and collective self-esteem, different social groups are associated with values and/or characteristics that can be perceived positively or negatively, and individuals view themselves in relationship to these value-laden associa-tions.[13] In-group membership also lowers levels of alienation and loneli-ness.[14,15] Social in-groups are those groups to which one feels connection and membership, while feeling distinct from, opposed to, or competitive with out-groups. People are disposed to protect self-esteem via in-group association; therefore, intergroup discrimination is a self-esteem protection strategy bolstering one's social identity.[16] However, each person is a member of many different in-groups (ethnic, occupational, sports fandom, martial status, etc.). Social contexts provide cues as to which in-group iden-tity is most salient at any time.[17] When one is confronted with a situation requiring him or her to select and assert a social identity from among these alternatives, he or she will select the in-group identity offering the most positive self-concept in that particular context.[18] In-groups that cause people to feel negatively about themselves will be mitigated, if possible, in the person's mind. People want to belong to groups that make them feel good about themselves and raise their self-esteem, even at the expense of other people or groups.[19]

Tajfel and Turner identified categorization, identification, comparison, and psychological distinctiveness as key processes in social identity formation.[20] Via categorization, individuals place themselves and others into distinct social categories based upon perceived or actual differences. For example, noting that someone is a basketball fan, a Muslim, or a teacher categorizes that person by sports preference, religious affiliation, and occupation. Similarly, people often refer to themselves by their race or sex (e.g., white male). Identification helps a person discern a preferred in-group status from those identified with out-groups. Identification with the preferred in-group generates the strongest feelings of self-esteem.[21] When comparing one's in-group status to a competing out-group's status, individuals look for the best possible comparison. Categorization, identification, and comparison all bolster the psychological need for self-esteem by providing an in-group identity perceived as superior to that of the out-group.[22] An overly strong in-group identity can produce hostility and hatred toward out-groups.[23] Research demonstrates that strong group identification, along with stereotypical portrayals of other ethnicities, strengthens racial biases and hatred levels toward ethnic out-groups.[24] Strong ethnic attitudes correlate with increased negative feelings toward other ethnicities.[25] Viewing different out-groups positively mitigate, but do not dispel, hateful feelings: Subjects may be less prejudiced toward different ethnicities, but those different ethnicities are still perceived as out-groups. [26]

Demographic factors are the primary bases for social identities. Sex, race, and religious beliefs are examples of characteristics driving strong in-group affiliations.[27] Ethnic group membership has proved to be the most salient in-group factor for most people, especially members of ethnic minorities.[28] while whites are less likely to indicate race as their most salient in-group membership, this is not the case for blacks and Latinos. College students tend to select professional role models from their ethnic in-group.[29] Ethnic identity is also influential when celebrity status is considered. Subjects were more likely to defend the perceived negative actions of celebrities of their race while condemning negative actions of different-race celebrities.[30]

Similar in-group versus out-group results are reported in sports contexts. Fans feel a strong connection to preferred teams and feel part of the fanship group.[31] Team in-group identification can be so strong that fans take losses harder than actual team members do.[32] Since members want their preferred in-groups to reflect positively on them, it is common for people to deliberately support successful, winning teams. This creates a bandwagon effect: Fans share in the team's success, commonly called basking in reflected glory, aka BIRGing,[33] whereas fans of losing teams feel embarrassed when their preferred team loses. The losing team's fans mitigate the effects of the loss by casting off reflected failure, aka CORFing.[34] People may abandon a team that constantly loses to support a winning team. Loyalty toward individual athletes tends to be stronger. However, fans will mitigate or end their connection to an athlete if the athlete's actions become unacceptable.

Credibility is commonly defined as a person's believability.[36] Three specific credibility elements have been identified.[37] Competence is the perception of being adequately or well qualified, or as having a specific domain of skill, knowledge, or ability. Competence is positively correlated to perceptions of a source's expertise on a specific topic.[38] Competence in one domain does not necessarily transfer to other domains unless the individual is also perceived as competent in the other domain. Trustworthiness is defined as a source's perceived honesty or how confident people are that they can believe what a source tells them.[39, 40] A source's trustworthiness is often derived from the source's background. Once trust is established, the source will continue to build upon that trust, maintain an even level, or undermine it by actions or words. Confidence in a message is positively correlated with the receiver's perceived trust in the source. If the speaker is perceived as untrustworthy or unbelievable, the message may be perceived as untrustworthy or unbelievable.[41]

Previous credibility researchers theorized that trustworthiness alone was the most important element in source credibility; however, other researchers identified perceived character as the most important source credibility component.[42] Speaking style can impact source credibility. Researchers translated a Jesse Jackson speech from standard English to Ebonics then played each audio recording for research subjects. Subjects were not informed of the speaker's race in either instance. Subjects rated the standard English speaker as more credible, intelligent, and educated.[43] When considering issues with social or political implications, people look for heuristics to aid attitude formation. The source's race, perceived membership in the receiver's in-group, or beliefs about the source's expertise supply heuristic cues.[44] When a public racial dispute occurs, people are more likely to support a position favorable to their racial identity. People will seek a highly credible spokesperson as their race's public advocate while they distance themselves from a low-credibility source that could hurt them publicly or challenge the collective identity of the group.[45, 46]

These source credibility factors also apply to athletes. Character and attractiveness are important influences on an athlete's popularity and perceived endorsement value.[47] Prior to revelations of his sexual indiscretions, Tiger Woods was one of most visible and popular athletes in the world. His perceived good character and charisma were sought by business partners, and Woods was lavishly compensated.[48] Female athletes are rapidly gaining popularity and attracting brand endorsements. Attractiveness and sex appeal exert more influence for female endorsers than for male endorsers. Because of her attractiveness, Danica Patrick has been more successful at gaining fans and commercial endorsements than previous female auto racers.[49] Professional tennis player Anna Kournikova made millions of dollars in endorsements without ever winning a significant tennis tournament.[50]

There are relationships between perceived in-group membership and source credibility between races when applied to perceptions of media events. In-group bias produces a "tendency to favor the in-group over the out-group in evaluations and behavior."[51] People hold in-group members in higher esteem than they do members of perceived out-groups, even to the point of racial bias[52] and ethnocentrism, defined as a belief that one's own race, religion, gender or culture are superior to all others.[53, 54]

Blacks and whites interpret events differently based on racial perspective.[55] Blacks perceive the criminal justice system as routinely unfair to ethnic minorities, especially blacks.[56] Differing interpretations between blacks and whites were observed following Hurricane Katrina in 2005. Whites attributed the federal government's lackluster response to incompetence and a lack of committed presidential leadership,[57] while blacks believed the president's actions were evidence of a racist agenda.[58] One researcher described media depictions of events following Hurricane Katrina as decidedly racist against blacks. Media presented whites as rational, civilized, community-based people who knew leaving was the obvious response to the pending disaster. Blacks were portrayed as outsiders who violated the norms of proper decision making by remaining in New Orleans.[59]

In a sports context, a 2008 *Vogue* magazine cover featuring black NBA star Lebron James with white model Gisele Bundchen sparked controversy regarding black media imagery generally and black athlete imagery specifically.[60] James has his arm around Bundchen while yelling, his face contorted. James contended he was showing emotion, and he liked the photo.

ESPN's black commentator Jamele Hill said the cover was memorable for "all the wrong reasons"[61] but also claimed the image was typical: "White athletes are generally portrayed smiling or laughing while Black sports figures are given a beastly sort of vibe."[62] Black columnist Bryan Burwell agreed, remarking that the *Vogue* cover and other media images present black athletes in an animalistic or subhuman way.[63] A magazine analyst said the image of James suggested the racial stereotype of a beastly black man desiring a white woman.[64]

Research investigating news coverage of black male athletes accused of domestic violence concluded that media accounts present black male athletes as naturally aggressive. Black athletes' aggression was attributed to "black rage," suggesting that black men are inherently violent. White athletes were not classified as aggressive because of sports training, nor was the concept of white rage suggested when white athletes were accused of crimes.[65] Sports commentary has been deemed racially biased. Success for black athletes is attributed to their high skill level; white athletic success is attributed to superior intellect.[66] Sports commentary frames black athletes as outsiders, while white athletes are framed as insiders or more normal.[67] Journalists refer to and write about black and white athletes differently. Journalists of both races are more comfortable referring to athletes of the same race and use cautious language when referring to athletes of another race.[68] The racial characterizations presented in sports commentary can also affect audiences. White subjects believed blacks were inherently better athletes and whites were at a physical disadvantage. White subjects believed the way to make up for this difference was by using intelligence. Black subjects did not contend white athletes were more intelligent but did believe blacks were better athletes.[69]

Social identity theory suggests that in-group bias is established to protect and enhance personal self-esteem. Among the most firmly rooted in-group identities held by a person is the person's allegiance to his or her racial group. Source credibility theory asserts that a source's background influences the source's perceived credibility. This background could include the source's race, along with perceived similarity of experiences between the source and the receiver based upon the source's race. This intersection of social identity theory and source credibility theory suggests the following hypotheses.

H1: Black subjects self-reporting higher levels of racial identity are more likely than other subjects to perceive controversial black athletes as credible ($p \leq .05$).

H2: White subjects self-reporting higher levels of racial identity are more likely than other subjects to perceive controversial white athletes as credible (p ≤ .05).

However, as noted in this literature review, high levels of racial identity can result in ethnocentrism, defined as a feeling that one's own culture is more valuable than all others. This ethnocentrism can result in hostility, animosity, or even extreme hatred for other races. While H1 and H2 suggest a predisposition to ascribe credibility to same-race sources, strong in-group bias based upon racial identity may motivate subjects to rate different-race sources as low credibility sources with poor character associations.

H3: There will be a positive relationship between black and white racial identity and low credibility ratings for controversial athletes of other races (p ≤ .05).

Undergraduate students at two universities in the southeastern United States provided their assessments of the source credibility of six professional athletes (two white and two black). Two other athletes were used as foils. The white athletes were professional football players Ben Roethlisberger and Brett Favre. The black athletes were professional golfer Tiger Woods and professional football player Michael Vick. The foils were Manny Ramirez (Latino) and Ichiro Suzuki (Asian). The white and black athletes were purposefully selected because each has received extensive media coverage for offensive behavior. It was assumed that using athletes with controversial histories would be a more valid test of in-group bias. If in-group bias was observed despite the athlete's controversial reputation, it would clearly demonstrate that subjects were likely using their own racial in-group bias to protect their personal self-esteem despite an onslaught of negative publicity about the athlete.

Roethlisberger has been twice accused of criminal sexual assault in two different states. Despite the allegations, law enforcement ruled both times that there was too little evidence to proceed with a criminal case. Roethlisberger was subsequently suspended from his duties as quarterback of the Pittsburgh Steelers by NFL commissioner Roger Goodell.[70] Vick was convicted of a felony and sentenced to prison. Woods and Favre have no criminal history, but both have received negative publicity regarding sexual escapades (Woods and Favre) as well as drug abuse (Favre). The black athletes analyzed here were identified as two of the most hated athletes, while the white athletes were not part of that list.[71] Ramirez and Suzuki have not been accused of criminal behavior or significant off-the-field antics and were not part of *Forbes*'s most hated athletes list.

At the time of this research, Favre was a quarterback in the NFL. Controversy has centered on his admission of addiction to a prescription pain-killer.[72] Media reports also claim Favre inappropriately texted sexual content to a female sports reporter and left her sexually inappropriate voice mails.[73] Sports media commentators label Favre a diva, implying an elevated sense of self-importance coupled with disregard and disdain for other competitors, even teammates. Favre's unwillingness to commit to retirement or continued competition leaves teams unable to make player decisions for upcoming seasons.[74, 75] Analysts like ESPN.com's Rob Parker (black) have argued that Favre holds teams hostage, a move unacceptable for black players.

In November 2009, stories alleging extensive extramarital relations between Woods and various women were published.[76] Media also reported that Woods crashed his automobile near his home. Rumors swirled that the accident was caused by a domestic incident between Woods and his then wife.[77] In a carefully scripted, tightly controlled press conference in 2010, Woods admitted marital infidelity. Woods's status with the general public suffered, and he was listed as the second most disliked athlete on the Q Score list.[78]

Vick is currently the starting quarterback for the Philadelphia Eagles of the NFL and has been involved in several controversial incidents. Two men were arrested for distributing marijuana in a truck Vick owned. A woman filed a civil lawsuit against Vick claiming she contracted genital herpes from him.[79] He was charged by federal authorities with operating an interstate dog-fighting ring and was sentenced to 23 months in prison.[80] Released from prison in 2009, his NFL eligibility was restored in week three of the 2009 season.[81]

Ramirez and Suzuki were included for reliability purposes but not for statistical analysis. They were selected because they were of a different ethnicity from one another and neither is black or white. Both are accomplished professional baseball players with no record of negative publicity. These two athletes are present merely as distracters to aid in the reliability of subject response and to limit the possibility of demand effects in subject responses.

The racial identity scale is an established measure used in similar research assessing self-reported racial identity. Previous research in social

identity reported the items as reliable, with both face and criterion valid-
ities.[82, 83] Eleven items assess the subject's comfort with same-race and
different-race people, as well as perceived respect for and trustworthiness
of same-race and different-race people. The Cronbach alpha score for the
racial identity scale in this research was .96.

Subjects were provided the athlete's name, sports association and race,
for example, "Ben Roethlisberger is a white quarterback in the National
Football League." The respondent was asked to provide a familiarity level
with the source's athletic accomplishments on a seven-point scale ranging
from very unfamiliar to very familiar. Subjects were next provided a neutral
description of the athlete's controversial behavior and asked to indicate
familiarity with the athlete in this area, for example, "Roethlisberger has a
history of behavior some describe as offensive. How familiar are you with
his offensive behavior?" Responses again ranged from very unfamiliar to
very familiar scored on a seven-point scale. Each subject assessed the athlete for perceived credibility with the McCroskey Source Credibility Scale,
a semantic differential scale with five categorical factors. Each factor is
assessed with three items rated on a seven-point scale. This scale has been
used multiple times to measure perceived source credibility.[84, 85, 86, 87, 88]
Reliability for the McCroskey scale has ranged from .79 to .96, which offers
sufficient levels of internal consistency. Research demonstrates both face
and criterion validity.[89, 90] Cronbach alpha scores for this research ranged
from .94 to .96. The final section of the survey asked subjects to report year
of birth (used to compute age), race, and sex.

Eight different questionnaires were developed, each with one black and
one white athlete, along with Ramirez and Suzuki. Questionnaire one
assessed Roethlisberger and Vick. The second questionnaire included Favre
and Woods. Order of presentation effect was controlled by rotating each
athlete through the four positions. Data were collected from undergraduate
students in a classroom setting at two southeastern universities. Some students were offered course extra credit in exchange for participation. No
other incentive was offered. Effort was undertaken to ensure a sufficient
number of black respondents to permit valid, reliable statistical analysis.
In an effort to defeat demand effects or other face-saving responses, subjects were reminded several times that they were completing an anonymous
survey. The researcher had no method for connecting specific respondents
to survey responses.

A total of 324 subjects participated. For questionnaire one (Roethlisberger and Vick), 177 (55 percent) respondents completed the

questionnaire, while 147 (45 percent) respondents completed questionnaire two (Favre and Woods). In terms of racial breakdown, 191 (56 percent) of the subjects indicated their race as white, while 117 (36 percent) subjects indicated their race as black. The other 16 subjects (8 percent) who reported a race other than black or white were excluded from the analysis. Chi-square tests were used to check for significant differences between race and survey set. No significant differences were observed ($x^2 = 5.43$, df = 5, p ≤ .134). The subject population was majority female (66 percent), while 34 percent of subjects were male. A significant difference was found for the respondent's sex ($x^2 = 8.45$, df = 1, p ≤ .004). In terms of race-by-gender, 39 percent of subjects were white females and 27 percent were black females. For the male subjects, 23 percent were white, and 11 percent were black. Prior to hypothesis testing, normality tests were completed analyzing the skewness and kurtosis of the continuous data distributions, the ratings of all the athletes in this research, as well as all the appropriate continuous measures (both individual and composite scores). The data, for the most part, was non-normally distributed; therefore, nonparametric statistical tests were calculated to test the hypotheses. Power analysis was conducted to determine the ability of the statistical tests to identify significant differences. Power analysis indicated a 70 percent mark for the sample size in this study, which falls into the acceptable range.

H1 predicted that blacks strongly identifying with their race would be more likely than whites to rate black athletes as highly credible. Support for H1 is observed: black subjects are significantly more likely to rate black athletes as credible ($r_s = -.190$, p ≤ .001). Black subjects rated Woods as having higher character than did white subjects ($r_s = .272$, p ≤ .001). Significance was also observed for Vick's credibility score and subject race ($r_s = .312$, p ≤ .001), Vick's character average and subject race ($r_s = .367$, p ≤ .001), and black racial identity and Vick's character average ($r_s = -.180$, p ≤ .017).

H2 predicted that whites strongly identifying with their race would be more likely than blacks to perceive white athletes as highly credible. The correlation for subject race and white racial identity was found to be significant ($r_s = -.280$, p ≤ .001), demonstrating support for H2. Significance was also found for Favre's credibility average and white racial identity ($r_s = .238$, p ≤ .004). Similar results were observed for Roethlisberger's character average and white racial identity ($r_s = -.178$, p ≤ .021). Significant correlations were also found for Favre's credibility average and Favre's character average (r_s = .706, p ≤ .001), and the same was found for Roeth-lisberger's credibility and character averages (r_s = .598, p ≤ .001).

H3 predicted a significant relationship between strength of racial iden-tity and hostility toward controversial athletes of the opposite race. A stat-istically significant difference was observed for black and white subject perceptions of Roethlisberger's character (r_s = −.188, p ≤ .015); however, black subjects held Roethlisberger in higher esteem than did white subjects. The correlation for Favre's credibility average and black racial identity was significant (r_s = .227, p ≤ .007), as was Favre's character average and black racial identity (r_s = .168, p ≤ .046). The correlation between white racial identity and Vick's character average was significant (r_s = −.251, p ≤ .001), as was the correlation between white racial identity and Vick's credibility average (r_s = .010, p ≤ .01). Also, the correlation between white racial identity and Woods's character average was significant (r_s = −.167, p ≤ .044). Tables 3 and 4 contain the correlation matrices for this hypoth-esis. H3 is supported, as there are significant differences for strength of racial identity and hostility towards controversial athletes of the opposite race.

The first two hypotheses explored the impact the subject's race would have on credibility ratings of athletes of the same race, despite the athlete's controversial behavior. More specifically, H1 hypothesized that blacks with high racial identity would be more likely than whites to rate black athletes as highly credible. Previous research indicated that race was one of the most likely in-group associations for people.[91, 92] Additionally, previous research had shown that a strong racial identity increased a sense of belonging to that race and hostility toward people of other races.[93, 94] There was a significant correlation between black subjects' race and black racial identity, as well as the character and credibility ratings of the black athletes assessed here (Vick and Woods). H2 hypothesized that whites with high racial identity would rate white athletes significantly higher on credibility variables. Subject race and white racial identity were significantly corre-lated, as were Favre's credibility average and white racial identity, and Roethlisberger's character average and white racial identity. Previous social identity research indicated that strong in-group racial connections are prevalent for the majority of people but are most significant for blacks.[95] While both white and black subjects in this study displayed significant racial connections, the racial connection was actually stronger for whites. This presents a break from previous findings. There are many possible rea-sons for this; however, one reason may be that few studies focus on white racial identity. The majority of social identity studies dealing with race have focused on blacks or other minorities.

The stronger a person's racial identity, the stronger his or her negative stereotypes and even hatred for people of different races.[96, 97, 98] H3 hypothesized a positive relationship between racial identity and hostility toward athletes of the opposite race. Whites rated Vick's credibility and character significantly lower than did blacks, along with Woods's character. Blacks rated Favre's credibility and character significantly lower than did whites. The only anomalous finding was the significant correlation between black racial identity and Roethlisberger's character average: blacks rated Roethlisberger's character more positively than did whites. While Roethlisberger has been accused of sexual assault, he has never been indicted or convicted of a crime. It has been proposed that blacks are more skeptical of the criminal justice system than whites.[99] Because of this skepticism, blacks may have been more willing to give Roethlisberger the benefit of the doubt.

This study, like all research, must be interpreted through its methodological limitations. The relatively limited subject demographic profile prevents broad generalizability of the results. Subjects were southern university students with a mean age of 21.2 years. The preponderance of female subjects is noted. This is especially important since Farve, Woods, and Roethlisberger have all been associated with callous sexual treatment of females. White subjects outnumbered black subjects in this research. A more balanced ratio would be preferable. Only 16 subjects self-identified as a race other than black or white. Future research should include a broader array of demographic variables, including more age groups, ethnicities other than black and white, and more geographic diversity. While the results are not called into question with a 70 percent power rating, a larger subject pool would increase the power of the statistical tests to reveal significant differences.

A possible lack of detailed sports knowledge is another possible limitation. Athlete knowledge was evaluated on a Likert-type scale. However, what one subject considers high athlete knowledge would not necessarily be considered high athlete knowledge by another subject. A more in-depth subject selection process could gauge a subject's knowledge about the athletes reviewed in this research. A high knowledge level would give more credence to character and credibility evaluations. Survey research of the type reported here also has limitations. While surveys can demonstrate correlations between variables, causation cannot be assumed. Experiments manipulating the variables investigated here might demonstrate causal relationships between these variables.

Athletes rated in this research all received recent negative press coverage for controversial behavior; however, the infamy level was not equivalent. Vick committed a felony, including the death of animals and perjury, and was sentenced to prison. Woods committed adultery resulting in a divorce that was widely covered in the media. Favre was accused of sexual harassment against a female reporter, drug addiction, and self-centered professional behavior. Transgression level could be a heuristic used to assess these athletes. Subjects might consider crimes against people or animals to be more serious than crimes against property, theft, drug use, and so on. While this research did not consider the severity of the athlete's behavior, future research in this area should control for this variable.

This research investigated racial identity and credibility ratings of selected controversial professional athletes. Social identity theory has been used in sporting contexts to understand team fanship, but there has been little research done in this area to understand how subjects perceive individual athletes. The first area in which this research can be expanded is through the use of image restoration. Image restoration, a subset of apologia, is the process by which a maligned figure does not just apologize for misdeeds but attempts to restore a favorable public image. Also, how the athlete goes about rebuilding that image is important to analyze. For example, Vick conducts charity work with the American Society for the Prevention of Cruelty to Animals. He also agreed to participate in a reality television show aired on Black Entertainment Television showing his attempts to rehabilitate his image. Image restoration takes time, and the feelings subjects have toward athletes are affected by this process. Since the actions of the athletes used in this project occurred at different times, it would be beneficial to add in the image restoration factor, as credibility and character ratings of these athletes could be affected by image restoration strategies.

Image restoration strategies and tactics leading to more favorable public ratings suggest a research question with strong managerial impact for brands considering endorsement deals with athletes: Can an athlete that falls from public favor regain value in the endorsement market? Ray Lewis, linebacker for the Baltimore Ravens, was charged with murder in 2000. He eventually pleaded guilty to obstruction of justice and received probation. For years afterward, he was not a major product endorser. Recently, Lewis became a paid endorser of Old Spice male grooming products.

Conventional wisdom would suggest enough time has passed for consumers and companies to trust Lewis. Future research should focus on the time constraint, risk-reward for companies, and what types of products are most suitably endorsed by controversial athletes. Future theory-based research could investigate which of the credibility and character factors are most impacted by controversial behavior.

A final direction for future research is methodological. While experiments manipulating variables could demonstrate causation, qualitative methodologies could offer more in-depth analysis of specific feelings of personal racial identity and perceptions. For example, if a black subject gave Roethlisberger very low character ratings but did not do so for Vick, it could be beneficial to discuss the subject's thought processes and perceptions of each athlete.

Notes

1. Murry Nelson, "Sports History as a Vehicle for Social and Cultural Understanding in American History," *Social Studies* 96 (May–June 2005): 118–26.

2. Peter King, "Open Mouth, Insert Foot: Limbaugh's Comments on McNabb Aren't Racist, but They Are Boneheaded," http://sportsillustrated.cnn.com/2003/ writers /peter_king/09/30/mcnabb_limbaugh/ (accessed December 10, 2010).

3. Michael D. Smith, "ESPN Fires Rob Parker," http://profootballtalk.nbcsports .com /2013/01/08/espn-fires-rob-parker (accessed January 8, 2013).

4. Pierre Thomas, Jason Ryan, Jack Date, and Theresa Cook, "Atlanta QB Michael Vick Indicted in Dogfight Probe," http://abcnews.go.com/ TheLaw/ story?id=3387333 &page=1#.UcxiX-Cf—8 (accessed June 27, 2013).

5. Colin Campbell, "Quarterback Warren Moon on Michael Vick, Racism, and Why He Wouldn't Trade His Five Grey Cups for One Super Bowl Win," http:// www2.macleans.ca/2009/07/23/macleans-interview-warren-moon/ (accessed June 27, 2013).

6. Chelsea Cook, "Michael Vick Tops *Forbes'* List of Most-Hated Athletes," *AJC.com*, http://www.ajc.com/sports/michael-vick-tops-forbes-554412.html (accessed June 27, 2013).

7. Ethan Trex, "How Are Q Scores Calculated?" http://www.mentalfloss.com/ blogs/ archives/84935 (accessed June 27, 2013).

8. Dexter Rogers, "Why Do African-Americans Top the Most Hated People in America List?" *Bleecherreport.com*, http://bleacherreport.com/articles/470582-q -score-why-do-african-american-athletes-top-the-most-hated-list (accessed June 27, 2013).

9. Rogers, "Why Do African-Americans."

10. Rogers, "Why Do African-Americans."

11. Henri Tajfel and John Turner, "The Social Identity of Intergroup Behavior," in *Psychology of Intergroup Relations*, ed. Stephen Worchel and William V. Austin (Chicago: Nelson Hall, 1986), 276–93.

12. Kitty Dumont and Johann Louw, "A Citation Analysis of Henri Tajfel's Work on Intergroup Relations," *International Journal of Psychology* 44 (February 2009): 46–59.

13. Tajfel and Turner, "Social Identity of Intergroup Behavior."

14. Sheldon Cohen and Thomas Wills, "Stress, Social Support and the Buffering Hypothesis," *Psychological Bulletin* 98 (September 1985): 310–57.

15. John Rowe and Robert Kahn, *Successful Aging* (New York: Pantheon, 1998).

16. Henri Tajfel, "Social Psychology of Intergroup Relations," *Annual Review of Psychology* 33 (1989), 1–39.

17. Marilyn B. Brewer, "Ingroup Bias in the Minimal Ingroup Situation: A Cognitive Motivational Analysis," *Psychological Bulletin* 86 (March 1979): 307–24.

18. Rachel Shinnar, "Coping with Negative Social Identity: The Case of Mexican Immigrants," *Journal of Social Psychology* 148 (October 2008): 553–76.

19. Brewer, "Ingroup Bias."

20. Tajfel and Turner, "Social Identity of Intergroup Behavior."

21. Tajfel and Turner, "Social Identity of Intergroup Behavior."

22. Tajfel and Turner, "Social Identity of Intergroup Behavior."

23. Evan Harrington, "The Social Psychology of Hatred," *Journal of Hate Studies* 3 (2003/2004), 49–82.

24. Howard Giles and Jake Harwood, "A Self-Categorization Perspective on Intergroup Communication Processes," in *Intergroup Communication: Multiple Perspectives*, ed. Jake Harwood and Howard Giles (New York: Peter Lang, 2005), 241–64.

25. Maykel Verkuyten, "Ethnic Attitudes among Minority and Majority Children: The Role of Ethnic Identification, Peer Group Victimization, and Parents," *Social Development* 11 (November 2002): 558–70.

26. Omotayo Banjo, "What Are You Laughing At? Examining White Racial Identity and Enjoyment of Black Entertainment," *Journal of Broadcasting and Electronic Media* 55 (April 2011): 137–59.

27. Dumont and Louw, "Citation Analysis."

28. Shinnar, "Coping with Negative Social Identity."

29. Danesh Karunanayake and Margaret Nauta, "The Relationship between Race and Students' Identified Career Role Models and Perceived Role Model Influence," *Career Development Quarterly*, 53 (March 2004): 225–34.

30. Jennifer L. Knight, Traci A. Giuliano, and Monica G. Sanchez-Ross, "Famous or Infamous? The Influence of Celebrity Status and Race on Perceptions of Responsibility for Rape," *Basic and Applied Social Psychology* 23 (September 2001): 183–90.

31. Christian End, Beth Dietz-Uhler, Elizabeth Harrick, and Lindy Jacquemotte, "Identifying with Winners: A Reexamination of Sports Fans' Tendency to BIRG," *Journal of Applied Social Psychology* 32 (May 2002): 1017–30.

32. Janet Fink, Heidi Parker, Martin Brett, and Julie Higgins, "Off-Field Behavior of Athletes and Team Identification: Using Social Identity Theory and Balance Theory to Explain Fan Reactions," *Journal of Sport Management* 23 (March 2009): 142–55.

33. Robert B. Cialdini, Richard J. Borden, Avril Thorne, Marcus R. Walker, Stephen Freeman, and L. R. Sloan, "Basking in Reflected Glory: Three Football (Field) Studies," *Journal of Personality and Social Psychology* 34 (September 1976): 366–75.

34. C. R. Snyder, Mary Anne Lassegard, and Carol E. Ford, "Distancing after Group Success and Failure: Basking in Reflected Glory and Cutting Off Reflected Failure," *Journal of Personality and Social Psychology* 51 (August 1986): 382–88.

35. Dietz et al., "Identifying with Winners."

36. Stephen Lucas, *The Art of Public Speaking* (New York: McGraw-Hill, 2004).

37. Steven Beebe and Susan Beebe, *Public Speaking: An Audience Centered Approach* (Columbus, OH: Allyn & Bacon, 2003).

38. Kak Yoon, Hyun-Kim Choong, and Min-Sun Moon, "A Cross-Cultural Comparison of the Effects of Source Credibility on Attitudes and Behavioral Intentions," *Mass Communication and Society* 1 (1998): 153–73.

39. Beebe and Beebe, *Public Speaking.*

40. John Cole and James McCroskey, "The Association of Perceived Communication Apprehension, Shyness, and Verbal Aggression with Perceptions of Source Credibility and Affect in Organizational and Interpersonal Contexts," *Communication Quarterly* 51 (Winter 2003), 101–10.

41. Brian K. Arbour, "One Thing I've Learned: An Experimental Test of Background Appeals," paper presented at the 65th Annual National Conference of the Midwestern Political Science Association, Chicago, IL, 2007.

42. J. W. Wanzenreid and F. C. Powell, "Source Credibility and Dimensional Stability: A Test of the Leathers Personal Credibility Scale Using Perceptions of Three Presidential Candidates," *Perceptual and Motor Skills* 77 (October 1993): 403.

43. Kay Payne and Joe Downing, "Speaking Ebonics in a Professional Context: The Role of Ethos/Source Credibility and Perceived Sociability of the Speaker," *Journal of Technical Writing and Communication* 30, no. 4 (2000): 367.

44. David Domke, Taso Lagos, Mark Lapointe, Melissa Meade, and Michael Xenos, "Elite Messages and Source Cues: Moving beyond Partisanship," *Political Communication* 17 (October–December 2000): 395–402.

45. Nyla R. Branscombe and Daniel L. Wann, "Collective Self-Esteem Consequences of Outgroup Derogation when a Valued Social Identity Is on Trial," *European Journal of Social Psychology* 24 (November 1994): 641–57.

46. Branscombe and Wann, "Collective Self-Esteem."

47. Sally R. Ross, Lynn Ridinger, and Jacquelyn Cuneen, "Drivers to Divas: Advertising Images of Women in Motorsport," *International Journal of Sports Marketing and Sponsorship* 10 (April 2009): 204–14.

48. Rich Thomaselli, "Dream Endorser: Tiger Woods as a Giant of Marketing ROI," http://adage.com/article/news/dream-endorser-tiger-woods-a-giant-marketing-roi/ 112039 (accessed February 19, 2013).

49. Ross et al., "Drivers to Divas."

50. David Goetzl, "The Buzz." *Advertising Age,* July 15, 2002, 23.

51. Tajfel and Turner, "Social Identity of Intergroup Behavior."

52. Brewer, "Ingroup Bias."

53. Beebe and Beebe, *Public Speaking.*

54. Harrington, "Social Psychology of Hatred."

55. Marjorie R. Hershey and David B. Hill, "Is Pollution a 'White Thing'? Racial Differences in Preadults' Attitudes," *Public Opinion Quarterly* 41 (Winter 1977): 439–58.

56. Robert D. McFadden, "5 Inquiries Focus on Suspect in Slaying Who Died in Police Custody," http://www.newyorktimes.com/1988/05/03/nyregion/5-inquiries-focus-on-suspect-in-slaying-who-died-in-police-custody.html (accessed June 27, 2013).

57. Stephanie Kelly-Romano and Victoria Westgate, "Blaming Bush," *Journalism Studies* 8 (October 2007): 755–73.

58. Terry Jones, "Bush's Ratings Disaster," *St. Louis Journalism Review* 35 (October 2005): 7.

59. Hemant Shah, "Legitimizing Neglect: Race and Nationality in Conservative News Commentary about Hurricane Katrina," *Howard Journal of Communications* 20 (January–March 2009): 1–17.

60. Katherine Zaleski, "Lebron James *Vogue* Cover Criticized for Perpetuating Racial Stereotypes," *HuffingtonPost.com,* http://www.huffingtonpost.com/2008/03/25/lebron-james-vogue-cover-_n_93252.html (accessed June 27, 2013).

61. Jamele Hill, "Lebron Should Be More Careful with His Image," http://sports.espn.go. com/espn/page2/story?page=hill/080320&sportCat=nba (accessed June 27, 2013).

62. Zaleski, "Lebron James *Vogue* Cover."

63. Hill, "Lebron Should Be More Careful."

64. Zaleski, "Lebron James *Vogue* Cover."

65. Suzanne Enck-Wanzer, "All's Fair in Love and Sport: Black Masculinity and Domestic Violence in the News," *Communication & Critical Studies* 6 (March 2009): 1–18.

66. Andrew Billings, "Depicting the Quarterback in Black and White: A Content Analysis of College and Professional Football Broadcast Commentary," *Howard Journal of Communications* 15 (October–December 2004): 201–10.

67. Toni Bruce, "Marking the Boundaries of the 'Normal' in Televised Sports: The Play-by-Play of Race," *Media, Culture and Society* 26 (November 2004): 861–79.

68. Marie Hardin and Erin Whiteside, "Maybe It's Not a 'Generational Thing': Values and Beliefs of Aspiring Sports Journalists about Race and Gender," *Media Report to Women* 36 (Spring 2008): 8–15.

69. Daniel Buffington and Todd Fraley, "Skill in Black and White: Negotiating Media Images of Race in a Sporting Context," *Journal of Communication Inquiry* 32 (July 2008): 292–310.

70. Barry Wilner, "Roethlisberger Banned Six Games," http://www .csnwashington.com/ 04/21/10/Steelers-Roethislberger-Banned-Six-Games/landing_ reskins.html?blockID= 220473 (accessed June 25, 2013).

71. Cook, "Michael Vick Tops *Forbes*' List."

72. Gary D'Amato, "Dependence on Painkillers Brings Favre to New Low," http://www.jsoline.com/sport/packers/45266162.html (accessed February 9, 2013).

73. "Sterger May Speak with NFL Officials about Favre," http://www.cbssports .com/ nfl/story/14174192/sterger-may-speak-with-nfl-officials-about-favre/cbsnews (accessed February 9, 2013).

74. Tim Graham, "Jets Release Favre, Clear Way for Possible Return," http:// espn.go. com/blogafceast/post/_/id/1705/jets-release-favre-clear-way-for-possible -return (accessed November 22, 2010).

75. Chris Mortensen, "Favre Has 'Itch' to Ditch Retirement, Report to Camp," http://sports.espn.go.com/nfl/news/story?id=3471189 (accessed December 6, 2010).

76. Larry Dorman and Stuart Elliot, "Woods Apologizes and Gets Support," http://nytimes.com/2009/12/03/sports/golf/03woods.html?r=0 (accessed February 10, 2013).

77. Tim Dahlberg, "Two Weeks That Shattered the Legend of Tiger Woods," http://www.foxnews.com/wires/2009Dec12/0,4670,GLFTigerapossTerribleTime,00 .html (accessed February 9, 2013).

78. Cook, "Michael Vick Tops *Forbes*' List."

79. "Settlement Reached in Michael Vick Case," http://nbcsports.msnbc.com/id/ 12468203 (accessed February 9, 2013).

80. Gary Mihoces, "Vick's Status Uncertain as Jail Term Begins," http://usato day30.com/sports/football/nfl/falcons/2007-11-19-vick-surrender_N.htm (accessed February 9, 2013).

81. Bob Ford, "McNabb in Search of Redemption Too," http://articles.philly .com/2009-12-08/sports/24988423_1_donovan-mcnabb-brian-westbrook-redemption (accessed June 27, 2013).

82. Robert T. Carter, "Racial Identity Attitudes and Psychological Functioning," *Journal of Multicultural Counseling* 19 (July 1991): 105–14.

83. Anita J. Thomas and Suzette L. Speight, "Racial Identity and Racial Socialization Attitudes of African-American Parents," *Journal of Black Psychology* 25 (May 1999): 152–70.

84. Raymond L. Falcione, "The Factor Structure for Source Credibility Scales for Immediate Superiors in the Organizational Context," *Central States Speech Journal* 25 (March 1974): 63–66.

85. James McCroskey, Thomas Young, and Michael Scott, "The Effects of Message Sidedness and Evidence on Inoculation against Counter-Persuasion in Small Group Communication," *Speech Monographs* 37 (August 1972): 47–52.

86. McCroskey et al., "The Effects of Message Sidedness."

87. David B. Buller and R. Kelly Aune, "The Effects of Vocalics and Nonverbal Sensitivity on Compliance: A Replication and Extension," *Human Communication Research* 14 (March 1988): 301–22.

88. R. E. Bassett, "Effects of Source Attire on Judgments of Credibility," *Central States Speech Journal* 30 (September 1979): 282–85.

89. Lawrence Wheeless, "Some Effects of Time-Compressed Speech on Persuasion," *Journal of Broadcasting* 15 (Fall 1971): 415–20.

90. Craig Johnson and Larry Vinson, "Placement and Frequency of Powerless Talk and Impression Formation," *Communication Quarterly* 38 (Fall 1990): 325–33.

91. Thomas and Speight, "Racial Identity."

92. Jacob Cohen, *Statistical Power Analysis for the Behavioral Sciences* (Hillsdale, NJ: Erlbaum Associates, 1988).

93. Giles and Harwood, "Self-Categorization Perspective."

94. Verkuyten, "Ethnic Attitudes among Minority."

95. Shinnar, "Coping with Negative Social Identity."

96. Giles and Harwood, "Self-Categorization Perspective."

97. Harrington, "Social Psychology of Hatred."

98. Verkuyten, "Ethnic Attitudes Among Minority."

99. McFadden, "5 Inquiries Focus on Suspect."

Bibliography

Arbour, Brian K. "One Thing I've Learned: An Experimental Test of Background Appeals." Paper presented at the 65th Annual National Conference of the Midwestern Political Science Association, Chicago, IL, 2007.

Banjo, Omotayo. "What Are You Laughing At? Examining White Racial Identity and Enjoyment of Black Entertainment," *Journal of Broadcasting and Electronic Media* 55 (April 2011): 137–59.

Bassett, R. E. "Effects of Source Attire on Judgments of Credibility," *Central States Speech Journal* 30 (September 1979): 282–85.

Benoit, William L. *Accounts, Excuses and Apologies: A Theory of Image Restoration Strategies*. Albany, NY: SUNY Press, 1995.

Billings, Andrew. "Depicting the Quarterback in Black and White: A Content Analysis of College and Professional Football Broadcast Commentary," *Howard Journal of Communications* 15 (October–December 2004): 201–10.

Branscombe, Nyla R., and Daniel L. Wann. "Collective Self-Esteem Consequences of Outgroup Derogation when a Valued Social Identity Is on Trial," *European Journal of Social Psychology* 24 (November 1994): 641–57.

Brewer, Marilyn B. "Ingroup Bias in the Minimal Ingroup Situation: A Cognitive Motivational Analysis," *Psychological Bulletin* 86 (March 1979): 307–24.

Bruce, Toni. "Marking the Boundaries of the 'Normal' in Televised Sports: The Play-by-Play of Race," *Media, Culture and Society* 26 (November 2004): 861–79.

Buffington, Daniel, and Todd Fraley. "Skill in Black and White: Negotiating Media Images of Race in a Sporting Context," *Journal of Communication Inquiry* 32 (July 2008): 292–310.

Buller, David B., and R. Kelly Aune. "The Effects of Vocalics and Nonverbal Sensitivity on Compliance: A Replication and Extension," *Human Communication Research* 14 (March 1988): 301–22.

Campbell, Colin. "Quarterback Warren Moon on Michael Vick, Racism, and Why He Wouldn't Trade His Five Grey Cups for One Super Bowl Win," http://www2.macleans.ca/2009/07/23/macleans-interview-warren-moon/ (accessed June 27, 2013).

Carter, Robert T. "Racial Identity Attitudes and Psychological Functioning," *Journal of Multicultural Counseling* 19 (July 1991): 105–14.

Cialdini, Robert B., Richard J. Borden, Avril Thorne, Marcus R. Walker, Stephen Freeman, and L. R. Sloan. "Basking in Reflected Glory: Three Football (Field) Studies," *Journal of Personality and Social Psychology* 34 (September 1976): 366–75.

Cohen, Jacob. *Statistical Power Analysis for the Behavioral Sciences*. Hillsdale, NJ: Erlbaum Associates, 1988.

Cohen, Sheldon, and Thomas Wills. "Stress, Social Support and the Buffering Hypothesis," *Psychological Bulletin* 98 (September 1985): 310–57.

Cole, John, and James McCroskey. "The Association of Perceived Communication Apprehension, Shyness, and Verbal Aggression with Perceptions of Source Credibility and Affect in Organizational and Interpersonal Contexts," *Communication Quarterly* 51 (Winter 2003):101–10.

Cook, Chelsea. "Michael Vick Tops *Forbes'* List of Most-Hated Athletes," *AJC.com*, http://www.ajc.com/sports/michael-vick-tops-forbes-554412.html (accessed June 27, 2013).

D'Amato, Gary. "Dependence on Painkillers Brings Favre to New Low," http://www.jsoline.com/sport/packers/45266162.html (accessed February 9, 2013).

Domke, David, Taso Lagos, Mark Lapointe, Melissa Meade, and Michael Xenos. "Elite Messages and Source Cues: Moving beyond Partisanship," *Political Communication* 17 (October–December 2000): 395–402.

Dumont, Kitty, and Johann Louw. "A Citation Analysis of Henri Tajfel's Work on Intergroup Relations," *International Journal of Psychology* 44 (February 2009): 46–59.

Enck-Wanzer, Suzanne. "All's Fair in Love and Sport: Black Masculinity and Domestic Violence in the News," *Communication & Critical Studies* 6 (March 2009): 1–18.

End, Christian, Beth Dietz-Uhler, Elizabeth Harrick and Lindy Jacquemotte. "Identifying with Winners: A Reexamination of Sports Fans' Tendency to BIRG," *Journal of Applied Social Psychology* 32 (May 2002): 1017–30.

Falcione, Raymond L. "The Factor Structure for Source Credibility Scales for Immediate Superiors in the Organizational Context," *Central States Speech Journal* 25 (March 1974): 63–66.

Fink, Janet, Heidi Parker, Martin Brett, and Julie Higgins, "Off-Field Behavior of Athletes and Team Identification: Using Social Identity Theory and Balance Theory to Explain Fan Reactions," *Journal of Sport Management* 23 (March 2009): 142–55

Giles, Howard, and Jake Harwood. "A Self-Categorization Perspective on Intergroup Communication Processes," in *Intergroup Communication: Multiple Perspectives*, ed. Jake Harwood and Howard Giles (New York: Peter Lang, 2005), 241–64.

Graham, Tim. "Jets Release Favre, Clear Way for Possible Return," http://espn.go .com/blogafceast/post/_/id/1705/jets-release-favre-clear-way-for-possible -return (accessed November 22, 2010).

Hardin, Marie and Erin Whiteside, "Maybe It's Not a 'Generational Thing': Values and Beliefs of Aspiring Sports Journalists about Race and Gender," *Media Report to Women* 36 (Spring 2008): 8–15.

Harrington, Evan. "The Social Psychology of Hatred," *Journal of Hate Studies* 3 (2003/2004), 49–82.

Hershey, Marjorie R., and David B. Hill. "Is Pollution a 'White Thing'? Racial Differences in Preadults' Attitudes," *Public Opinion Quarterly* 41 (Winter 1977): 439–58.

Hill, Jamele. "Lebron Should Be More Careful with His Image," http://sports.espn .go.com/espn/page2/story?page=hill/080320&sportCat=nba (accessed June 27, 2013).

Johnson, Craig, and Larry Vinson. "Placement and Frequency of Powerless Talk and Impression Formation," *Communication Quarterly* 38 (Fall 1990): 325–33.

Jones, Terry. "Bush's Ratings Disaster," *St. Louis Journalism Review* 35 (October 2005): 7.

Karunanayake, Danesh, and Margaret Nauta. "The Relationship between Race and Students' Identified Career Role Models and Perceived Role Model Influence," *Career Development Quarterly* 53 (March 2004): 225–34.

Kelly-Romano, Stephanie, and Victoria Westgate, "Blaming Bush," *Journalism Studies* 8 (October 2007): 755–73.

King, Peter. "Open Mouth, Insert Foot: Limbaugh's Comments on McNabb Aren't Racist, but They Are Boneheaded," http://sportsillustrated.cnn.com/2003/ writers /peter_king/09/30/mcnabb_limbaugh/ (accessed December 10, 2010).

Knight, Jennifer L., Traci A. Giuliano, and Monica G. Sanchez-Ross. "Famous or Infamous? The Influence of Celebrity Status and Race on Perceptions of Responsibility for Rape," *Basic and Applied Social Psychology* 23 (September 2001): 183–90.

Lucas, Stephen. *The Art of Public Speaking.* New York: McGraw-Hill, 2004.

McCroskey, James, Thomas Young, and Michael Scott. "The Effects of Message Sidedness and Evidence on Inoculation against Counter-Persuasion in Small Group Communication," *Speech Monographs* 37 (August 1972): 47–52.

McFadden, Robert D. "5 Inquiries Focus on Suspect in Slaying Who Died in Police Custody," http://www.newyorktimes.com/1988/05/03/nyregion/5-inquiries -focus-on-suspect-in-slaying-who-died-in-police-custody.html (accessed June 27, 2013).

Nelson, Murray. "Sports History as a Vehicle for Social and Cultural Understanding in American History," *Social Studies* 96 (May–June 2005): 118–26.

Payne, Kay, and Joe Downing. "Speaking Ebonics in a Professional Context: The Role of Ethos/Source Credibility and Perceived Sociability of the Speaker," *Journal of Technical Writing and Communication* 30, no. 4 (2000): 367.

Rogers, Dexter. "Why Do African-Americans Top the Most Hated People in America List?" *Bleacherreport.com*, http://bleacherreport.com/articles/ 470582-q-score-why-do-african-american-athletes-top-the-most-hated-list (accessed June 27, 2013).

Ross, Sally R., Lynn Ridinger, and Jacquelyn Cuneen. "Drivers to Divas: Advertising Images of Women in Motorsport," *International Journal of Sports Marketing and Sponsorship* 10 (April 2009): 204–14.

Rowe, John, and Robert Kahn, *Successful Aging.* New York: Pantheon, 1998.

Shah, Hemant. "Legitimizing Neglect: Race and Nationality in Conservative News Commentary about Hurricane Katrina," *Howard Journal of Communications* 20 (January–March 2009): 1–17.

Shinnar, Rachel. "Coping with Negative Social Identity: The Case of Mexican Immigrants," *Journal of Social Psychology* 148 (October 2008): 553–76.

Smith, Michael D. "ESPN Fires Rob Parker," http://profootballtalk.nbcsports.com/ 2013/01/08/espn-fires-rob-parker (accessed January 8, 2013).

Snyder, C. R., Mary Anne Lassegard, and Carol E. Ford, "Distancing after Group Success and Failure: Basking in Reflected Glory and Cutting Off Reflected

Failure," *Journal of Personality and Social Psychology* 51 (August 1986): 382–88.

Tajfel, Henri. "Social Psychology of Intergroup Relations," *Annual Review of Psychology* 33 (1989), 1–39.

Tajfel, Henri, and John Turner."The Social Identity of Intergroup Behavior," in *Psychology of Intergroup Relations*, ed. Stephen Worchel and William V. Austin. Chicago: Nelson Hall, 1986, 276–93.

Thomas, Anita J., and Suzette L. Speight. "Racial Identity and Racial Socialization Attitudes of African-American Parents," *Journal of Black Psychology* 25 (May 1999): 152–70.

Thomas, Pierre, Jason Ryan, Jack Date, and Theresa Cook. "Atlanta QB Michael Vick Indicted in Dogfight Probe," http://abcnews.go.com/ TheLaw/story ?id=3387333 &page=1#.UcxiX-Cf—8 (accessed June 27, 2013).

Thomaselli, Rich. "Dream Endorser: Tiger Woods as a Giant of Marketing ROI," http://adage.com/article/news/dream-endorser-tiger-woods-a-giant-marketing -roi/112039 (accessed February 19, 2013).

Trex, Ethan. "How Are Q Scores Calculated?" http://www.mentalfloss.com/blogs/ archives/84935 (accessed June 27, 2013).

Verkuyten, Maykel. "Ethnic Attitudes among Minority and Majority Children: The Role of Ethnic Identification, Peer Group Victimization, and Parents," *Social Development* 11 (November 2002): 558–70.

Wanzenreid, J. W., and F. C. Powell. "Source Credibility and Dimensional Stability: A Test of the Leathers Personal Credibility Scale Using Perceptions of Three Presidential Candidates," *Perceptual and Motor Skills* 77 (October 1993): 403.

Wheeless, Lawrence. "Some Effects of Time-Compressed Speech on Persuasion," *Journal of Broadcasting* 15 (Fall 1971): 415–20.

Wilner, Barry. "Roethlisberger Banned Six Games," http://www.wfmj.com/story/ 12350007/updated-roethlisberger-banned-six-games?redirected=true (accessed June 25, 2013).

Yoon, Kak, Hyun-Kim Choong, and Min-Sun Moon, "A Cross-Cultural Comparison of the Effects of Source Credibility on Attitudes and Behavioral Intentions," *Mass Communication and Society* 1 (1998): 153–73.

Zaleski, Katherine. "Lebron James *Vogue* Cover Criticized for Perpetuating Racial Stereotypes," *HuffingtonPost.com*, http://www.huffingtonpost.com/2008/03/ 25/lebron-james-vogue-cover-_n_93252.html (accessed June 27, 2013).

Chapter 5

Racism Front and Center: Introducing the Critical Demography of Athletic Destinations

Lori Latrice Martin and Hayward Derrick Horton

In the modern era, certain sports have come to be associated with certain racial and ethnic groups. Some maintain the belief that biology equals destiny. Phenotype, bone density, muscle dexterity, and so on are thought to determine one's athletic destination, with race serving as one of the main filters.[1] One would think that such claims, which have been disproven time and time again, would fade into the deep recesses of our collective consciousness; sadly, they have not. Often cloaked in new raiment, the idea that blacks and whites are predisposed to participation and success in different sports remains with us still.[2] While there are a host of theories, perspectives, and paradigms in the social sciences, particularly in sociology, arguing for the continuing significance of race in our society,[3] few have found their way into scholarly discussions about sports.[4] Race-based theories that have been used to explain various phenomena have been limited in important ways, including the failure to place racism front and center. What is needed is an overarching, unifying framework that will aid in our understanding of not just the continuing significance of race in sports, but also the significance of racism in sports. Within the suggested framework, the multilevel and multidimensional roles of race and racism in determining athletic participation and destinations can best be understood.

In this chapter, the *critical demography of athletic destinations* is introduced. This new framework draws from the strengths of critical race theory,[5] the colorism perspective,[6] the population structural change thesis,[7] and critical demography paradigm[8]—namely, the centrality of race—while also addressing the observed weaknesses. Although critical race theory and colorism place the focus squarely on race and skin complexion, neither places racism at the forefront. Moreover, neither critical race theory nor colorism substantively takes into consideration the impact of population size on intergroup relations. Further, to date, neither the population structural change thesis nor the critical demography paradigm have been used to help us understand the unleveled playing field that characterizes American sports.

Critical Race Theory

Although it has its origins among legal scholars,[9] critical race theory is used to examine the linkages between race and education,[10] the family,[11] immigration,[12] public health,[13] and sports.[14] Critical race theory, like other social theories, theses, and perspectives, has supporters and critics. To fully understand the continued debates surrounding critical race theory, it is important to examine more closely its origins, development, and use over time.

Derrick Bell is among the scholars credited with institutionalizing the interest in systematically studying the lived reality of race. The purpose for introducing critical race theory was to draw attention to society as it is and society as it ought to be. Bell felt it necessary to address the gap between the real and the imagined, and to do so in a way that was at once a radical critique of the law and a radical emancipation by the law. Critical race theory was developed to address the aforementioned tension head-on.[15]

Many legal scholars quickly gravitated to critical race theory, due in large part to the key principles outlined. First, critical race theory holds that society is organized around race. Second, people of color receive unequal treatment when compared with members of the dominant racial group. The unequal treatment experienced by people of color occurs not only on a personal level; more important, it is institutionalized. Moreover, critical race theory explains how individuals within a given social system participate in the perpetuation of racialized social systems through social practices. Finally, critical race theory enhances our understanding of racial and ethnic identities as variable, social constructions that change across place and time.[16]

Critical race theory was intended to not only assist legal scholars in explaining various phenomena, but to be inclusive and transformative. Critical race theory was to bring to the center—from the margins—scholars of color, whom Bell argued were often silenced, discredited, or altogether ignored. He said, "We seek to empower and include traditionally excluded views and see all-inclusiveness as the ideal because of our belief and collective wisdom."[17]

As important as the work of Bell and others is, and has been, it was not the first to address such concerns about the law or about society in general.[18] However, their desire to "fight the silence about the intersection of race, racism, and the law"[19] ushered in a wave of scholarly research that moved concepts such as intersectionality,[20] antiessentialism,[21] normality of race, social construction, and differential racialization[22] toward forefront of progressive thinking and scholarship. Through the use of personal narratives, among other techniques, critical race theorists also raised awareness about bias—conscious and unconscious—in America's social institutions, including in the criminal justice system.[23]

In the end, critical race theory was to be the driving force behind efforts to bring about a more just society in which people of color would be regarded in the same manner as members of the dominant group and not perpetually regarded as "others," which had historically been the case.

Scholars see merit in applying critical race theory to the sports world because "racial thinking in sports is perpetuated by four weak theoretical propositions: 1. Sports are based on theoretical principals of equality; 2. The results of sport competition are unequal; 3. This inequality of results has a racial bias; and 4. Therefore, given the equality of access and opportunity; the explanation of the unequal results lies in racial physicality."[24] Critical race theory has the power to address the identified weak propositions with its emphasis on race and racism. It also has the power to challenge the notion of color-blindness. Critical race theory has many other positive attributes, including a commitment to social justice and its ability to transcend disciplinary boundaries.[25]

Moreover, critical race theory has the potential to enhance our understanding of the processes involved in the formation of power and ideologies by race.[26] Critical race theory has the power to inform leisure studies theory and "generate a useful theoretical vocabulary for the practice of progressive racial politics in sport."[27]

Despite the contributions of critical race theory to legal studies and beyond, there are identified weaknesses. Scholars call into question whether critical race theory is a theory.[28] Critical race theory "lacks the articulation of a set of precisely stated and logically related propositions that explain a relationship between concepts, to the formation of a structured conceptual scheme that provides a general interpretation or critique of social reality."[29] At best, critical race theory—say the scholars—is an intellectual movement.

Additionally, the use of narratives or storytelling, while a central feature in the application of critical race theory, is problematic, particularly for social scientists with a quantitative orientation. The narratives, while informative and illustrative of important concepts and themes, fail to meet the robust standards expected by many in the social sciences. One cannot in good faith generalize the findings to a known population.

Colorism

Still others argue that critical race theory does not devote adequate attention to colorism. "Colorism is the discriminatory treatment of individuals falling within the same 'racial' group on the basis of skin color. It operates both intraracially and interracially."[30] Colorism "is historically contingent on supremacist assumptions. In the United States color preferences are typically measured against putative European (i.e., White) standards."[31]

Until recently, critical race theory had been used almost exclusively to understand the black/white dichotomy that has dominated U.S. history since the foundation of the nation. The problem, as identified by scholars, is that although blacks may be disadvantaged relative to whites, all blacks may not be equally disadvantaged. There is a substantial body of literature that points to the advantages afforded light-skinned individuals relative to darker-skinned individuals.[32]

Colorism affects socialization practices within racial groups.[33] Moreover, colorism holds, "a person's skin will take on more importance in determining how she is treated by others than her ancestry."[34] Colorism is the result of a shift in the demographic composition of the nation as well as a change in racial ideologies.[35] It is an indication that racism is not dead; rather, discussions surrounding racism are muted. Dr. Angela Harris views colorism as the next stage in the continuum of racialized social systems in America. Harris further argues that colorism and racism are related, yet distinct.[36]

There is much to disagree with in the assertions made by Harris about colorism. First, the implication is that colorism is a relatively new phenomenon. We know that skin tone was used in the antebellum period as a mechanism for creating discord and disharmony among enslaved and free black people.[37] Colorism can best be understood, as Dr. Cedric Herring conceptualizes it, as a manifestation of racism, not a replacement of it. Moreover, Harris represents scholars who understand colorism to be an intragroup phenomenon. Some even refer to colorism as intragroup discrimination because it is devoid of any relationship to the larger set of processes by which racial groups are systematically oppressed and scapegoated by the dominant group. Herring correctly defines colorism as intra- and interracial. Claims such as those levied by Harris seek to equate tensions within groups with racism between whites and racial minority groups.

Despite differing views on what it is and is not, colorism is an underutilized perspective in the social sciences. It is particularly underutilized in the analysis of race and sports. Robst, VanGilder, Coates, and Berri conducted one of the few studies linking colorism and sports.[38] The researchers examined the effects of skin tone on wages for free agents in the National Basketball Association. They employed the use of computer software to objectively determine the skin tone of the subjects. The researchers argued that this methodological approach represents a departure from other studies on colorism that rely on the interviewer's judgment to determine where a respondent falls on the skin tone spectrum.[39]

Robst and colleagues did not find evidence of a statistically significant relationship between skin tone and wages.[40] Other recent studies have reported declines in the significance of skin tone as a predictor on a host of outcomes.[41] The Robst and colleagues study, like many others, is not without limitations. The researchers acknowledge the relatively small sample size as potentially problematic.

Another issue is the use of existing photographs. Secondary analysis, including content analysis, may suffer from researchers lacking control over the data because they were initially collected by someone other than the researchers.[42] In this case, since the researchers did not take the photographs themselves, they have no way of knowing the extent to which the photographs actually represent the complexion of the respondents under-study. Moreover, the arbitrary assignment of photographs as lighter or darker, even if the system is based on red and green, instead of black or white, is still somewhat subjective if not outright arbitrary.

The lack of understanding of the relationship between colorism and racism and the potential for bias in classifying subjects based upon a sociopolitical construct may point to the need to revisit the perspective and to develop more testable propositions to further understanding about this form of intragroup and intergroup discrimination, particularly as it relates to the world of sports, with athletes representing virtually every shade of the color spectrum.

Population and Structural Change Thesis

Missing from discussions about race and sports is an adequate treatment of the effects of population and structural change on various outcomes, including athletic destinations. On the one hand, it is apparent that certain racial groups are overrepresented in some sports and underrepresented in others. Beyond exploring events that have led to the integration of previously segregated sports, little scholarly attention has been devoted to understanding the impact of population and structural changes both within and outside the world of sports on players, spectators, owners, and the like. The few studies that give these matters due treatment are far too often descriptive in nature and seldom use proven demographic techniques and frameworks for understanding the complex linkages between race and sports. The population and structural change thesis is a valuable tool that should be widely used in sports studies, particularly for studies claiming to substantively address issues related to race.

It is difficult to tackle any subject matter involving race without accounting for population and structural changes. Changes in both the minority population and the social structure, according to Horton and Lundy, "interact to exacerbate racial inequality in society."[43] Looking at the effects of place and family structure on black family poverty, Horton and Lundy argued that the finding that the existence of and the persistence of race as a predictor of black family poverty supports the population and structural change thesis. Likewise, the existence and persistence of race as a predictor of a host of sport outcomes also provides support for the population and structural change thesis, which has yet to be adequately explored in sports and leisure studies. The significance of this is clear.

Beyond the social realities of the sports world, population changes and changes to the social structure matter. As the size and composition of the United States change, not just the size and composition of American athletic teams, and the social structure changes economically, politically, and culturally, the effects of race in virtually all areas of society become even more salient, and manifestations of racism become more overt. For example, as predictions that American racial and ethnic minorities will one day become the numerical majority occur at the same time as an economic downturn or a change in the political winds, efforts to re-establish the myth of group superiority become more dominant. This can be seen in many areas of social life, not just in sports.

As the racial and ethnic minority population has increased, efforts to exert more control and authority over matters of criminal justice and education have increased. This is due in part to unfounded fears on the part of some members of the dominant racial group, especially those in the lower and working class, that their historic position in society is being threatened. Draconian policies that have led to the overrepresentation of people of color in American prisons and in failing schools are just two examples. In the world of sports, population and structural changes have led to the institutionalization of white middle-class standards in the adoption of dress codes,[44] in the stacking of players in positions by color,[45] and by the existence of glass ceilings and glass walls when it comes to ownership and employment in decision-marking positions.[46] It has also led to the adoption of colorblind language,[47] a topic addressed later in this chapter.

Although the population and structural change thesis can inform research on race and sports, it does have some limitations. The population and structural change thesis does not fully account for variations within racial groups. Again, all blacks may not be equally disadvantaged.[48] Skin tone, ethnicity, and social class position are all factors that have been shown to have significant effects on a host of sociological outcomes.[49] Much like critical race theory and the colorism perspective, the population and structural thesis aids in our understanding of race and sports, but it is limited in the ways outlined.

Critical Demography

The critical demography paradigm addresses some of the identified shortcomings associated with critical race theory, colorism, and the population and structural change thesis in a manner that has yet to be explored. Established in 1999, the critical demography paradigm offers a critique of conventional demography.[50] The founder of the critical demography paradigm and co-author of this chapter, Dr. Hayward Derrick Horton, observed that demographers were reluctant to use racism as a concept of analysis, particularly those demographers conducting research on race. Racism is, after all, a primary component of the social structure and it is central to understanding population growth and development.[51]

The main strength of the critical demography paradigm is its ability to show how the social structure differentiates dominant and subordinate populations. To that end, the nature of power is an important part of the paradigm. Unlike in the case of critical race theory and colorism, *race* is not central; rather, *racism* is central to any analysis involving minority and majority group relations.[52]

Horton argues that much of the work conducted by American demographers is descriptive, but the critical demography paradigm calls for scholarly works that are both explanatory and predictive. Critical demography also calls for analyses that are theory, not data driven, and analyses that challenge the status quo. Furthermore, critical demography, unlike conventional demography, is reflexive and not assumptive.

An article published in *Perspectives* included a discussion about the civil rights movement by conventional demographers, and this is a discussion that scholars working in the area of sports and leisure studies should take note of.[53] The article observes that demographers treated this period of social change and upheaval as a historical event with little, if any, attention devoted to the demographic implications. The role of the civil rights movement in growing the black middle class was not anticipated and was not studied substantively by conventional demographers, though it could arguably have been predicted using a framework akin to the one developed by Horton.

Horton's article extols the use of the population and structural change thesis to aid in our understanding of the connection between changes in the population and in the social structure on the various sociological outcomes. In the world of sports and beyond, we have seen that as the composition of players and spectators change policy changes also. As the number of black players—particularly those from economically disadvantaged backgrounds—increased, the number of white fans decreased,[54] and policy changes such as the dress code were established. Recruitment efforts also changed. Greater efforts to obtain international players, particularly players from Europe, have increased over time,[55] and some contend it may be due —at least in part—to efforts to find the next Great White Hope for professional basketball.

The percentages of white players in the National Basketball Association (NBA), for example, decreased between the 1989/1990 season and the 2012/2013 season, while the percentage of black players had held relatively steady. The percentage of international players, many of them from European countries, also increased during this time period. During the 2003/2004 season, nearly 76 percent of NBA players were black. Just over 22 percent of players were white, and almost 17 percent were international players. By the 2012/2013 season, the percentage of black players remained at about 76 percent. The percentage of white players fell to 19 percent, and the percentage of foreign players was up to almost 19 percent.[56]

The most important contribution of the critical demography paradigm to the sociology of sports in general, and the sociology of race and sports in particular, is the centrality of racism, not merely race, and the call for the operationalization of the oft-used concept.

A Critical Demography of Athletic Destinations

Pulling together the elements that critical race theory, colorism, population structural change thesis, and critical demography have to offer studies about racism and sports, we introduce a framework called the critical demography of athletic destinations. This framework contributes to our understanding of why people of selected racial groups end up at particular athletic destinations. Population and structural changes are important contributing factors, though they are often neglected. Overt manifestations of racism increase as minority populations increase, and society undergoes various structural changes.

A critical demography approach to athletic destinations makes it clear that not only is race important, as in the case of critical race theory, but racism is at the core of all analyses. Using the newly introduced critical demography of athletic destinations approach, it can be shown that colorism is not understood as the latest iteration of racism; instead, colorism is itself a manifestation of racism. Population changes inside and outside sports matter, as do changes in the social structure such as increasing unemployment, political mistrust, or unrest. Critical demography, with its ability to account for power, is an important paradigm that can—and should—inform debates about the intersections between racism and sports, including how they relate to athletic destinations. More than many other variables in the study of sports, the over- and underrepresentation of certain racial groups at a particular athletic destination can be understood as a manifestation of racism in sports.

A critical demography of athletic destinations incorporates the following principles: (1) racism is a central feature of American social systems; (2) racism is institutional; (3) institutions, and the groups and individuals that make them up, reproduce these systems through social practices and policies; (4) members of the dominant group receive unmerited privileges, while members of subordinate racial minority groups receive unequal treatment; and (5) racism remains part of the our social system, changing in form but not function.

Using the critical demography of athletic destination perspective, we can see how racism was central in determining when, where, and how people participated in and consumed sports by race. We can see how federal officials and wealthy team owners were able to exert their will over society at large but particularly over the black population, despite opposition, which is the essence of power. This was case at the turn of the 20th century with boxing and in minor and major league baseball.

Boxing: A Case Study in the Critical Demography of Athletic Destinations

The latter part of the 19th century saw the nation attempt to come back together after a war that pitted brothers against brothers, the North against the South. It was a time of optimism and hope for many, including the formerly enslaved and their supporters, who thought they would finally have the freedom and liberty to pursue their life dreams without restrictions. Unfortunately, the century closed with a compromise deal that restored supporters of slavery to positions of authority and saw the rise of the Ku Klux Klan and the legal establishment of the separate but equal doctrine.[57]

Decades later, American society saw the rise of blacks in boxing, including Jack Johnson, at a time when the world was on the brink of a global conflict, race riots were dotting the American landscape, and economic distress was growing.[58] Blacks were trapped in the revolving system of debt commonly known as sharecropping, and many whites found themselves working for less than a livable wage.[59] At the same time, blacks were moving from the south to the north in numbers never before seen.[60] These population and structural changes created a perfect racial storm and one of the fronts, or fault lines, was in the boxing ring.

Because of the demographic and economic changes taking place in the early part of the 1900s, members of the dominant group saw it as their duty to try and maintain the status quo. They saw it as their obligation to be the gatekeepers of racial etiquette, to uphold the false doctrine of white supremacy and black inferiority. And they were buttressed by the claims of pseudoscientists purporting the intellectual inferiority and inhumanity of the black citizenry (eugenics, etc.). The mere fact that blacks were kept from fighting whites had an impact on their athletic destinations. Black boxers could either fight other black boxers or hang up their gloves.[61] White boxers could compete with other white boxers.

When black boxers like Jack Johnson were permitted to compete against whites—and win—their success became a curse for them personally and for blacks as a whole. Concerns that blacks would be confused about their place in society should a black boxer be permitted to go around violating miscegenation norms—and accumulating income and wealth—which characterized the way Jack Johnson lived his life, put blacks on the whole at risk for physical violence and discrimination. For example, it was reported that a white man who was displeased with Johnson's desire to be treated as a total person wanted to kill the champion. When the disgruntled man could not get close enough to Johnson, he killed another black man instead.[62]

One of the greatest manifestations of racism involving Jack Johnson concerned charges that violated the Mann Act, which

> made it a crime to transport women across state lines "for the purpose of prostitution or debauchery, or for any other immoral purpose." While designed to combat forced prostitution, the law was so broadly worded that courts held it to criminalize many forms of consensual sexual activity, and it was soon being used as a tool for political persecution of Jack Johnson and others, as well as a tool for blackmail.[63]
>
> The Mann Act itself was an example of a law based upon a racist ideology. It was born during the "white slavery" hysteria of the early 20th century. Along with other moral purity movements of the period, the white slavery craze had its roots in fears over the rapid changes that the Industrial Revolution had brought to American society: urbanization, immigration, the changing role of women, and evolving social mores. As young, single women moved to the city and entered the workforce they were no longer protected by the traditional family-centered system of courtship, and were subjected to what Jane Addams called the "grosser temptations" which now beset the young people who are living in its tenement houses and working in its factories.[64]

The Mann Act is also a great example of a response to population and structural changes based upon living within a racialized social system.

Accounts of Johnson's arrest and conviction, as told by historic black newspapers of the day, provide an interesting look at the relationship between what Johnson experienced and the overall treatment of blacks due to population and structural changes. For instance, on October 26, 1912, Cary B. Lewis, writing for *Freeman*, discusses Johnson's arrest and reactions to it. According to Lewis, no man—white or black—ever received as much attention in the Chicago press as Jack Jackson, and "a white woman in the case is the cause of it all."[65]

In Lewis's report we learn that an upcoming fight in Australia had been cancelled. The arrest cost Johnson his freedom and a lot of money. Johnson was expected to earn $50,000 for the bout, a purse of about $1 million when adjusted for inflation. The fight was cancelled because "sporting people over there were disgusted because of his relations with Cameron girl." The reporting by Lewis along with the brief history provided about the nature and development of the Mann Act make it clear that Johnson's trouble had little to do with boxing and a lot to do with racism and maintaining the status quo. Johnson's involvement with a white woman was seen as an affront to the established racial social order at home and abroad.[66]

An article in *Broad Ax*, published on November 9, 1912, described Johnson's arrest and indictment, noting he was charged "with bringing Belle Schreiber, a White lady, to this city, who at one time, according to the *Chicago Tribune*, resided at the Everleigh Sisters' Club." The article goes on to say, "Johnson is accused of bringing this highly cultured and refined lady from Pittsburgh, PA to Chicago to reside." Although the Everleigh Sisters' Club was a known place of prostitution, Schreiber was nonetheless characterized as "highly cultured" and "refined" until she crossed paths with Johnson and began to live a life of ill repute.

In the November 16, 1912, issue of *Broad Ax*, the deep-seeded hatred against Johnson was reported. Reverend Judson B. Thomas, pastor of the First Baptist Church of Austin was described as "one of the holy men of God declared, if Jack Johnson was swung up from a lamp post and his body riddled with bullets it would be light punishment for his sins." In the same article, the black newspaper writer called for blacks in the city to raise money "without delay, and make an effort to prosecute and punish the so-called holy man of God under the federal law for advocating mob and lynch law, murder and blood shed." Blacks across the nation "are wrought up to a high pitch of excitement over the cruel treatment he is receiving at the hands of the government," exclaimed the writer.[67]

The resources devoted to the prosecution of Johnson for the alleged violation of the Mann Act could have been put to better use. The government, reports the paper, "spent thousands of dollars of the peoples money which comes out of the pockets of the poor and not out of the pockets of the rich and high brows, in a vain effort to fasten some crime on Jack Johnson."

From the perspective of the writer at *Broad Ax*, who represented some segment of the larger black community, the government was committed to bringing Johnson down—some way, some how—and the Mann Act was selected as the means to get the job done. This was evidenced in the many attempts to apply the act to Johnson. When the charges did not hold in the case of Lucile Cameron, said the *Broad Ax*, government officials merely "turned the pages of the books two years containing the white slave and after spending a lot of more money belonging to the people, who are forced to work hard for a living, they learned that at about that time that Jack Johnson had permitted himself to come too close contact with Miss Bell Schreiber."[68]

Clearly, Johnson was being punished not only for his success in the boxing ring against white opponents, but also for his defiance of the social norms of the day. Great lengths were taken to ensure that not only was Johnson arrested, but his release would be difficult and come with a hefty price. Johnson was not permitted to post cash to secure his release. His mother was also forbidden from using property she owned in the city to get him out of custody.

A black newspaper report published on November 16, 1912, argued that Johnson was receiving unequal treatment. "Had Johnson mistreated girls of his own race in a similar manner the federal authorities would have considered it beneath their dignity to give it a moment's consideration." Despite the obvious differential treatment Johnson received, and despite claims of racial prejudice on the part of the government, the jurists handling the case rebuffed claims that the case had anything to do with race and said they were acting within the law.[69]

The oppression of people of color by the dominant group was overt during the life and times of Jack Johnson.[70] Blacks as a group were treated as second-class citizens at best.[71] The problem was so severe that scholar-activist W. E. B. Du Bois declared the issue of the color line as the defining issue of the decade.[72] Racism was a part of the day-to-day operations of many social institutions, including the white press, the criminal justice system, the economy, and sports. Whites enjoyed privileges that blacks did not.

Although blacks were no longer chained to one another on plantations, they still endured the indignity of unequal protection before the law, inadequate access to education, disenfranchisement, and the like.[73] Critical demography of athletic destinations allows us to understand the centrality of race and racism in the case of Jack Johnson within the broader context of population and structural changes, both internal and external, to the sport of boxing.

Through the prism of the critical demography of athletic destinations, we can gain a greater understanding of the impact of the integration of professional baseball in the modern era. It is a perspective that not only focuses squarely on racism, but also takes into account the importance of population and structural changes occurring within and external to the sport so many Americans have come to love.

Baseball: A Case Study in the Critical Demography of Athletic Destinations

Using the overarching framework that draws from critical race theory, colorism, the population and structural change thesis, and the critical demography paradigm, we have seen how the integration of baseball was not only a historical moment, as it is often treated in the media and in academic studies, but also an event with demographic implications, particularly in rural black communities where blacks owned the local Negro baseball teams and often the facilities where the teams played.

Minnie Forbes, a black female recently honored by the Obama administration, owned the Detroit Stars team, which she purchased from her uncle Ted Raspberry. Raspberry was already owner of the Kansas City Monarchs.[74] Other black owners included Abe Manley of the Newark Eagles.[75]

The Negro League eMuseum describes the league as multilayered with "Community teams, college teams, community economics, ownership, wealth consolidation," to name a few attributes.[76] The centrality of racism in American social life, and in the great American pastime of baseball, was particularly evident in the first few decades of the 20th century.

Although blacks had played baseball since the Civil War, they were not permitted to play against whites.[77] Racism and racist practices kept black and white players separated in different leagues.[78] The athletic destinations of players during this time period were determined not purely by performance on the diamond, but by the player's skin color.[79]

The official website for the Negro League's Baseball Museum reports the presence of some black players on teams with whites in the late 1800s.

However, within a few decades, "racism and Jim Crow laws would force them from these teams."[80] By 1920, a league for black players was formally organized. Andrew "Rube" Foster, himself a former player, manager, and owner, was the league's founder. Other leagues included the Southern Negro League, Eastern Colored League, Negro Southern League, American Negro League, East-West League, Negro National League, and Negro American League.

The *Advocate*, a historically black newspaper, covered the opening day of the National Negro Baseball League on April 27, 1923. The game featured the Kansas City Monarchs against the American Giants of Chicago. It was held in a venue formerly known as Association Baseball Park. Opening day was a community affair, the paper reported, with the usual "big auto parade," but this time over 300 automobiles participated, including one carrying Foster and several black police officers. Local elected officials were invited to participate, and for the first time, black umpires were to officiate. "Two of the best known race umpires have been selected to start the season."

Despite the excitement and optimism, it soon become clear that trouble was on the horizon for the league. In fact, the National Negro League and the Eastern Negro League met to discuss the mounting struggles. During the meeting, the leagues discussed a series of financial concerns that led to, among things, to an agreement to cap salaries. Attendees claimed, "The high salaries, for ball players, the enormous railroad and traveling expenses, the large cost of parks, has been the financial ruin of several cities." After careful deliberation, the leagues adopted a salary limit of $3,000 per month. In an earlier series of disputes, players left teams to join teams in the opposing league. The Negro Leagues simply did not have the resources or access to the human, social, economic, or cultural capital necessary to compete on equal footing with the white-owned major leagues. The wealth inequality exemplified in the ownership of black owned teams in the Negro League and white-owned teams in the major were indicative of the wealth inequality between blacks and whites in the society at large. Impacted players were, under the agreement reached by the league, to return to their team of origin or risk expulsion from both leagues for a period of five years.[81]

Not only was there evidence of wealth inequality between some of the owners in the Negro and in the major leagues, there was evidence of income inequality, too, which mirrored the income inequality that existed in society at large between the dominant racial groups of the day.[82] Black players, for example, earned much less than their white counterparts, even the star players. On average, whites in the minor league earned $500 compared to $466 for blacks in the minor league. In the decades that followed, similar patterns were observed.[83]

Research has shown that although "salaries varied from individual to individual, and teams differed in their methods of pay," player paychecks fluctuated with the economy. During the 1920s, "monthly salaries averaged about $230, but during the Depression-ridden 1930s, they fell to $170."[84] The researchers also found that "the average annual salary for blacks in the Negro League was probably about $5,000 to $6,000 in the 1920s and about $7,000 in the 1930s."[85]

Justice B. Hill, a writer for MLB.com, wrote about the legacy of the Negro League and the unequal treatment players received. In the article "Traveling Show: Barnstorming Was Common Place in the Negro Leagues," Hill wrote about how unwelcome the players were in hotels and how they were forced to live out of their suitcases or sleep on buses or in the stadiums where they played. Barnstorming was a way players made extra money by traveling around the countryside playing their favorite sport. Hill described what made these players willing to endure racial taunts and exclusion from areas of public accommodation. It was both economical and political: "Their incentive to barnstorm was for the extra money they earned from exhibition games against whites and other black teams. The games against whites were cash cows, often drawing thousands of fans to these small towns to watch the great Negro League players." The games gave an economic boost not only to the players, but to the towns. "On the meager salaries from the Negro Leagues," wrote Hill, "the players valued the extra pay. They had the added satisfaction of showing fans in these small towns how well blacks played the game." Hill sums up with the observation that "black players had to remain mindful of the color line. Not even money would let them cross it."

The Depression, mismanagement, and the death of Rube Foster have been cited as factors contributing to the decline of the Negro Leagues, but few events had the lasting impact of the integration of Major League Baseball in the modern era by Jackie Robinson. Luix Overbea wrote on this very subject on July 8, 1949, in the paper *Plaindealer*. Overbea described the many empty seats in the stadium where "the Giants, now the hottest team in Negro baseball," played. Across town, over 40,000 people went to see Jackie Robinson and the Brooklyn Dodgers take on the Cubs. "Of this massive crowd, at least one third was Negro." Blacks were cautioned against "killing the goose that lays the golden eggs." Negro baseball was the goose, and the players were the golden eggs. Journalists and others reminded fans that whites had refused to recognize black players for many years. One individual is quoted in Overbea's article as saying, "If Negro baseball dies there will be no other means to prepare Negro players for the majors." Perhaps the prediction was right, at least in part, and may help to explain blacks' disappearance from baseball.[86]

Black players and spectators had always hoped for the opportunity to prove that they were just as good as whites—both on and off the field. Racism kept this from happening for many years, and capitalist interests—not the desire to right historic wrongs—were the driving forces behind the integration of baseball.[87] The glass ceiling and the glass walls facing people of color in baseball at all levels, then and now, manifest the racism in the sport, as does the disappearance of the black players.

From these two examples provided in this chapter, it can be shown that population and structural changes in society, and in a given sport, affect athletic destinations on the basis of race. Manifestations of racism were evident in boxing and baseball in the first part of the 20th century, and manifestations of racism increased as the American population and social structure underwent profound changes, namely a larger minority population and economic peaks and valleys.

Even though separate black and white baseball leagues are no longer with us, and people of varying racial and ethnic groups may have their shot at a title fight, certain athletic destinations are still virtually off limits to some racial groups. The underrepresentation of people of color in certain field positions and certain front office positions, particularly those with decision-making authority, exemplify this today.[88] Coded words like "thug" and "hustler" conjure up black images in the white imagination, which often leads to discrimination in many areas of public life.[89] Just like in the larger society, overt expressions of racial discrimination and other manifestations of racism are less socially acceptable and are against the law. Consequently, new tactics have been employed to do the work Jim Crow laws used to do.[90]

Charles Hallman, writer for the *Minnesota Spokesman*, devoted an article to color-blind racism in sports today. He provided several powerful quotes from a contributor to this volume, Dr. David J. Leonard, who proclaimed the existence of color-blind racism.[91] He said, "It does exist. It is embedded into our language, our system and our institutions. When someone says, 'A player is a thug,' they don't need to be specific on which player they are referring to. Most of us know that 'thug' is code for black." While the term "thug" does not denote any particular race, "it still conveys racial meaning and has consequences. Terms like 'basketball IQ' is code for white," added Leonard.

"Team executives and marketing types also practice colorblind racism. 'Clearly the NBA is seeking a marketable, modifiable white player' to promote as a superstar," believes Leonard. "Marketing types blatantly push a white player with 'wholesome' looks over a Black player who's a superstar but his looks (i.e., tattooed from top to bottom) don't reach the white fan's comfort level," Leonard commented further.

Reflecting on Leonard's comments and his own observations about racism and sports in America, Hallman concluded, "Colorblind racism isn't just in the NBA but in all sports where blacks reside. Because a black player can dunk, catch, or run like the wind, it doesn't simply disappear; it's deeply embedded in our society."

Conclusion

Many theories, perspectives, and paradigms contribute to our understanding of the role of race in American society. Critical race theory, unlike many theories introduced before it, places the concept of race front and center. The colorism perspective not only places race in the forefront of analyses, it also provides a framework for understanding variations within a given population, namely variations based upon skin complexion. The population and structural change thesis, used primarily by demographers, is often used to explore links between race and mortality, fertility, and migration. Likewise, the critical demography paradigm links race and socio-demographic phenomenon and creates a framework for understanding race.

Of the theories and perspectives mentioned in this chapter, a couple found the way into discussions about sports and society, but in limited ways. Critical race theory and colorism are making inroads into studies about race and sports; however, racism is far too often not the focal point. Population and structure change thesis and the critical demography paradigm have yet to enter the scholarly discourse on racism and sports. As a result, as this chapter has shown, missing from existing research on racism and sports is a unifying overarching framework for understanding athletic destinations in relationship to population and structural changes in a way that makes racism, not race, as the focal point. The critical demography of athletic destination perspective introduced here provides researchers with a framework for explaining and predicting manifestations of racism in sports.

Notes

1. Sailes, G.A. (1991). The myth of black sports supremacy. *Journal of Black Studies* (4), 480.

2. Bejan, A., Jones, E.C., & Charles, J. (2010). The evolution of speed in athletics: Why the fastest runners are black and swimmers white. *International Journal of Design and Nature* 5(3), 199–211.

3. Brewster, Z.W., & Rusche, S.N. (2012). Quantitative evidence of the continuing significance of race: Tableside racism in full-service restaurants. *Journal of Black Studies* 43(5), 359–384; Feagin, J.R. (1991). The continuing significance of race: Antiblack discrimination in public places. *American Sociological Review* 56(1), 101–116; Warren, P.Y. (2010). The continuing significance of race: An analysis across two levels of policing. *Social Science Quarterly* 91(4), 1025–1042.

4. Forster-Scott, L. (2011). Understanding colorism and how it relates to sport and physical education. *Journal of Physical Education, Recreation & Dance* 82(2), 48–52; Hylton, K. (2010). How a turn to critical race theory can contribute to our understanding of "race," racism and anti-racism in sport. *International Review for the Sociology of Sport* 45(3), 335–354.

5. Bell, D.A. (1995). Who's afraid of critical race theory? *University of Illinois Law Review*, 893–910.

6. Herring, C., Keith, V., & Horton, H.D. (2004). Skin deep: How race and complexion matter in the "color-blind" era. Chicago: University of Illinois Press.

7. Horton, H.D. (2002). Rethinking American diversity: Conceptual and theoretical challenges for racial and ethnic demography. In *American diversity: A demographic challenge for the twenty-first century*, edited by Stewart Tolnay & Nancy Denton. Albany, NY: SUNY Press; Horton, H., & Allen, B. (1998). Race, family structure and rural poverty: An assessment of population and structural change. *Journal of Comparative Family Studies* 29(2), 397–406.

8. Horton, H. (1999). Critical demography: The paradigm of the future? *Sociological Forum* 14(3), 363; Horton, H.D., & Sykes, L.L. (2008); *Critical demography and the measurement of racism: A reproduction of wealth, status, and power. White logic, white methods: Racism and methodology.* Lanham, Maryland: Rowman & Littlefield Publishers; Massey, D.S. (1999). What critical demography means to me. *Sociological Forum* 14(3), 525.

9. Onwuachi-Willig, A. (2009). Celebrating critical race theory at 20. *Iowa Law Review* 94, 1497–1504.

10. Closson, R. (2010). Critical race theory and adult education. *Adult Education Quarterly* 60(3), 261–283; Fasching-Varner, K.J. (2009). No! The team ain't

alright! The institutional and individual problematics of race. *Social Identities: Journal for the Study of Race, Nation and Culture* 15(6), 811–829.

11. Burton, L.M., Bonilla-Silva, E., Ray, V., Buckelew, R., & Freeman, E. (2010). Critical race theories, colorism, and the decade's research on families of color. *Journal of Marriage & Family* 72(3), 440–459.

12. Romero, M. (2008). Crossing the immigration and race border: A critical race theory approach to immigration studies. *Contemporary Justice Review* 11(1), 23–37.

13. Ford, C.L., & Airhihenbuwa, C.O. (2010). Critical race theory, race equity, and public health: Toward antiracism praxis. *American Journal of Public Health* 100(S1), S30–S35; Graham, L., Brown-Jeffy, S., Aronson, R., & Stephens, C. (2011). Critical race theory as theoretical framework and analysis tool for population health research. *Critical Public Health* 21(1), 81–93.

14. Arai, S., & Kivel, B.D. (2009). Critical race theory and social justice perspectives on whiteness, difference(s), and (anti)racism: A fourth wave of race research. *Journal of Leisure Research* 41(4), 459–470; Carrington, B. (2013). The critical sociology of race and sport: The first fifty years. *Annual Review of Sociology* 39(1), 379–398; Hylton, K. (2010). How a turn to critical race theory can contribute to our understanding of "race," racism and anti-racism in sport. *International Review for the Sociology of Sport* 45(3), 335–354.

15. Bell, D.A. (1995). Who's afraid of critical race theory? *University of Illinois Law Review*, 893–910.

16. Burton, L.M., Bonilla-Silva, E., Ray, V., Buckelew, R., & Freeman, E. (2010). Critical race theories, colorism, and the decade's research on families of color. *Journal of Marriage & Family* 72(3), 440–459.

17. Bell, D.A. (1995). Who's afraid of critical race theory? *University of Illinois Law Review*, 893–910.

18. Zuberi, T. (2011). Critical race theory of society. *Connecticut Law Review* 43(5), 1573–1591.

19. Onwuachi-Willig, A. (2009). Celebrating critical race theory at 20. *Iowa Law Review*, 94, 1502.

20. Arai, S., & Kivel, B.D. (2009). Critical race theory and social justice perspectives on whiteness, difference(s), and (anti)racism: A fourth wave of race research. *Journal of Leisure Research*, 41(4), 459–470.

21. Bell, D.A. (1995). Who's afraid of critical race theory? *University of Illinois Law Review*, 893–910.

22. Treviño, A., Harris, M.A., & Wallace, D. (2008). What's so critical about critical race theory? *Contemporary Justice Review* 11(1), 7-10.

23. Onwuachi-Willig, A. (2009). Celebrating critical race theory at 20. *Iowa Law Review*, 94, 1502.

24. Hylton, K. (2008). *Race and sport*. New York: Routledge. http://www.bl.uk/sportandsociety/exploresocsci/sportsoc/sociology/articles/hylton.pdf, 3.

25. Ibid.

26. Ibid.

27. Ibid.

28. Treviño, A., Harris, M.A., & Wallace, D. (2008). What's so critical about critical race theory? *Contemporary Justice Review* 11(1), 7-10.

29. Ibid., 9.

30. Herring, C. (2004). Skin deep: Race and complexion in the "color-blind" era. In *Skin deep: How race and complexion matter in the "color-blind" era*, edited by C. Herring, V.M. Keith, & H.D. Horton. Champaign: University of Illinois Press, 3.

31. Ibid.

32. Edwards, K., Carter-Tellison & C. Herring. (2004). For richer, for poorer, whether dark or light: Skin tone, marital status, and spouse's earnings. In *Skin deep: How race and complexion matter in the "color-blind" era*, edited by C. Herring, V.M. Keith, & H.D. Horton. University of Illinois Press, 65–81; Herring, C. (2004). Skin deep: Race and complexion in the "color-blind" era. In *Skin deep: How race and complexion matter in the "color-blind" era*, edited by C. Herring, V.M. Keith, & H.D. Horton. University of Illinois Press, 1-21; Thompson, M.S., & Keith, V.M. (2004). Cooper brown and blue black: Colorism and self evaluation. In *Skin deep: How race and complexion matter in the "color-blind" era*, edited by C. Herring, V.M. Keith, & H.D. Horton. University of Illinois Press, 45–64.

33. Burton, L.M., Bonilla-Silva, E., Ray, V., Buckelew, R., & Freeman, E. (2010). Critical race theories, colorism, and the decade's research on families of color. *Journal of Marriage & Family* 72(3), 440–459.

34. Harris, A.P. (2008). From color line to color chart? Racism and colorism in the new century. *Berkeley Journal of African-American Law & Policy* 10(1), 54.

35. Ibid., 52–69.

36. Ibid.

37. Keith, V.M. (2009). A colorstruck world: Skin tone, achievement, and self-esteem among African American women." In *Shades of difference: Why skin color matters*, edited by in Evelyn Nakano Glenn. Los Altos, CA: Stanford University Press, 25–39.

38. Robst, J., VanGilder, J., Coates, C.E., & Berri, D.J. (2011). Skin tone and wages: Evidence from NBA free agents. *Journal of Sports Economics* 12(2), 143–156.

39. Hersch, J. (2008). Skin color discrimination and immigrant pay. *Emory Law Journal* 58(2), 357–377; Hunter, M. (2008). Teaching and learning guide for the persistent problem of colorism: Skin tone, status, and inequality. *Sociology Compass* 2(1), 366; Keith, V.M., & Herring, C. (1991). Skin color and stratification in the black community. *American Journal of Sociology*, 97, 760–778.

40. Robst, J., VanGilder, J., Coates, C.E., & Berri, D.J. (2011). Skin tone and wages: Evidence from NBA free agents. *Journal of Sports Economics* 12(2), 143–156.

41. Akee, R., & Yuksel, M. (2012). The decreasing effect of skin tone on women's full-time employment. *Industrial & Labor Relations Review* 65(2), 398–426.

42. Maconis, J. (2011). *Sociology*. Upper Saddle River, NJ: Pearson.

43. Horton, H., & Allen, B. (1998). Race, family structure and rural poverty: An assessment of population and structural change. *Journal of Comparative Family Studies* 29(2), 398.

44. Carter, R. (2005, November 17). NBA's new dress code: Racist or just smart business? *New York Amsterdam News*, 10–41.

45. Sack, A.L., Singh, P., & Thiel, R. (2005). Occupational segregation on the playing field: The case of Major League Baseball. *Journal of Sport Management* 19(3), 300–318.

46. Cashmore, E., & Cleland, J. (2011). Why aren't there more black football managers? *Ethnic & Racial Studies* 34(9), 1594–1607.

47. Hallman, C. (2012, June 27). Colorblind racism: Language of sports filled with barely disguised bigotry. *Minnesota-Spokesman Reporter*.

48. Martin, L.L. (2013). *Black asset poverty and the enduring racial divide*. Boulder, CO: First Forum.

49. Hunter, M. (2008). Teaching and learning guide for the persistent problem of colorism: Skin tone, status, and inequality. *Sociology Compass* 2(1), 366; Keith, V.M., & Herring, C. (1991). Skin color and stratification in the black community. *American Journal of Sociology* 97, 760–778; Martin, L. (2009). Black asset ownership: Does ethnicity matter? *Social Science Research* 38(2), 312–323.

50. Horton, H. (1999). Critical demography: The paradigm of the future? *Sociological Forum* 14(3), 363.

51. Ibid.

52. Ibid.

53. Horton, H.D. (n.d.). Critical demography and racism: The case of African Americans. *Perspectives*, http://www.rcgd.isr.umich.edu/prba/perspectives/springsummer2000/hhorton2.pdf, 1-6.

54. Fogarty, D. (2011, February 21). Are white people losing interest in the NBA because none of its superstars look like them? Retrieved from http://www.sportsgrid.com/nba/nba-white-people-interest/; Schneider-Mayerson, M. (2010). Too black: Race in the dark ages of the National Basketball Association. *International Journal of Sport and Society* 1(1), 223–233.

55. Wilbon, M. (June 25, 2011). The foreign flavor of this NBA draft. *ESPN*, http://sports.espn.go.com/espn/commentary/news/story?page=wilbon-110624.

56. Lapchick, R., Hippert, A., Rivera, S., & Robinson, J. (2013, June 25). The 2013 race and gender report card: National Basketball Association. http://www.tidesport.org/RGRC/2013/2013_NBA_RGRC.pdf.

57. Hine, D.C., Hine, W., & Harrold, S. (2011). *African American odyssey*. Upper Saddle River, NJ: Pearson.

58. Ibid.; Ward, G. (2006). *Unforgivable blackness: The rise and fall of Jack Johnson*. New York: Random House.

59. Hine, D.C., Hine, W., & Harrold, S. (2011). *African American odyssey*. Upper Saddle River, NJ: Pearson.

60. Eichenlaub, S.C., Tolnay, S.E., & Alexander, J. T. (2010). Moving out but not up: Economic outcomes in the great migration. *American Sociological Review* 75(1), 101–125.

61. Ward, G. (2006). *Unforgivable blackness: The rise and fall of Jack Johnson*. New York: Random House.

62. Ibid.

63. "The Mann Act." In *Knockout: Failing to Defeat Him in the Ring, His Enemies Take to the Courts*. Retrieved from http://www.pbs.org/unforgivable blackness/knockout/mann.html.

64. Ibid.

65. Lewis, C.B. (1912, October 26). Jack Johnson in bad! Champion pugilist roundly condemned by his own race for 19–year-old white girl. *Freeman*.

66. Ibid.

67. John Arthur Johnson the heavy weight prize fighting champion of the world. (1912, November 16). *Broad Ax*.

68. Ibid.

69. Attorneys William G. Anderson and Edward H. Wright are heartily congratulated on being able to secure the release of Jack Johnson from prison. (1912, November 23). *Broad Ax* (Salt Lake City, UT); *Chronicling America: Historic American Newspapers*. Lib. of Congress.

70. Ward, G. (2006). Unforgivable blackness: *The rise and fall of Jack Johnson*. New York: Random House.

71. Hine, D.C., Hine, W., & Harrold, S. (2011). *African American odyssey*. Upper Saddle River, NJ: Pearson.

72. Du Bois, W.E.B. (1903). *The souls of black folks*. New York: Penguin.

73. Kennedy, R. (1997). *Race, crime and the law*. New York: Routledge.

74. Gibbons, L. (2013, August 18). Former owner of Negro League baseball team honored by President Obama at White House. *MLive*, http://www.mlive.com/news/grand-rapids/index.ssf/2013/08/former_owner_of_negro_league_b.html.

75. Crawford, A. (n.d.). The first lady of black baseball: Manley was an innovator in the Negro Leagues. *MLB.com*, http://mlb.mlb.com/mlb/history/mlb_negro_leagues_story.jsp?story=effa_manley.

76. Negro Leagues baseball: A brief history. (n.d.). http://www.coe.ksu.edu/annex/nlbemuseum/history/overview.html.

77. Heaphy, L. (2011). *Baseball and the color line: From Negro Leagues to the Major Leagues*. In *The Cambridge companion to baseball*, edited by L. Cassuto & S. Partridge. New York: Cambridge University Press, 61–75.

78. Lumpkin, A. (2011). Negro Leagues: Black diamonds. *Phi Kappa Phi Forum* 91(2), 22.

79. Mathewson, A. (1998). Major League Baseball's monopoly power and the Negro Leagues. *American Business Law Journal* 35(2), 291.

80. "Negro Leagues History." http://www.nlbm.com.

81. National Negro Leagues meets in Philadelphia, Rube Foster presiding. (1926, January 15). *Kansas City Advocate* 12(25), 1.

82. Mathewson, A. (1998). Major League Baseball's monopoly power and the Negro Leagues. *American Business Law Journal* 35(2), 291.

83. Holway, John B. (2001). *The complete book of baseball's Negro Leagues: The other half of baseball history*. Fern Park, FL: Hastings House.

84. Gardner, R., & Shortelle, D. (1993). *The forgotten players: The story of black baseball in America*. New York: Walker and Company, 45.

85. Ibid.

86. Harris, M. (n.d). Blacks and baseball: Where have you gone, Jackie Robinson? *Nation*, 260(19), 674–676.

87. Mathewson, A. (1998). Major League Baseball's monopoly power and the Negro Leagues. *American Business Law Journal* 35(2), 291.

88. Volz, B. (2013). Race and the likelihood of managing in Major League Baseball. *Journal of Labor Research* 34(1), 30–51.

89. Bonilla-Silva, E. (2003). Racism without racists: Color-blind racism and the persistence of racial inequality in the United States. Lanham, MD: Rowman & Littlefield, 2003.

90. Ibid.

91. Hallman, C. (2012, June 27). Colorblind racism: Language of sports filled with barely disguised bigotry. *Minnesota Spokesman*, http://www.spokesman-recorder.com/2012/06/27/colorblind-racism-language-of-sports-filled-with-barely-disguised-bigotry/.

Bibliography

Akee, R., & Yuksel, M. (2012). The decreasing effect of skin tone on women's full-time employment. *Industrial & Labor Relations Review* 65(2), 398–426.

Arai, S., & Kivel, B. D. (2009). Critical race theory and social justice perspectives on whiteness, difference(s), and (anti)racism: A fourth wave of race research. *Journal of Leisure Research* 41(4), 459–470.

Bejan, A., Jones, E. C., & Charles, J. (2010). The evolution of speed in athletics: Why the fastest runners are black and swimmers white. *International Journal of Design and Nature* 5(3), 199–211.

Bell, D. A. (1995). Who's afraid of critical race theory? *University of Illinois Law Review*, 893–910.

Bonilla-Silva, E. (2003). *Racism without racists: Color-blind racism and the persistence of racial inequality in the United States.* Lanham, MD: Rowman & Littlefield, 2003.

Brewster, Z. W., & Rusche, S. N. (2012). Quantitative evidence of the continuing significance of race: Tableside racism in full-service restaurants. *Journal of Black Studies* 43(5), 359–384.

Burton, L. M., Bonilla-Silva, E., Ray, V., Buckelew, R., & Freeman, E. (2010). Critical race theories, colorism, and the decade's research on families of color. *Journal of Marriage & Family* 72(3), 440–459.

Carrington, B. (2013). The critical sociology of race and sport: The first fifty years. *Annual Review of Sociology* 39(1), 379–398.

Carter, R. (2005, November 17). NBA's new dress code: Racist or just smart business? *New York Amsterdam News*, 10–41.

Cashmore, E., & Cleland, J. (2011). Why aren't there more black football managers? *Ethnic & Racial Studies* 34(9), 1594–1607.

Closson, R. (2010). Critical race theory and adult education. *Adult Education Quarterly* 60(3), 261–283.

Crawford, A. (n.d.). The first lady of black baseball: Manley was an innovator in the Negro Leagues. MLB.com. http://mlb.mlb.com/mlb/history/mlb_negro _leagues_story.jsp?story=effa_manley.

Du Bois, W. E. B. (1903). *The souls of black folks.* New York: Penguin.

Edwards, K., Carter-Tellison, K. M. & Herring, C. (2004). For richer, for poorer, whether dark or light: Skin tone, marital status, and spouse's earnings. In *Skin deep: How race and complexion matter in the "color-blind" era,* edited by C. Herring, V. M. Keith, & H. D. Horton. Chanpaign: University of Illinois Press, 65–81.

Eichenlaub, S. C., Tolnay, S. E., & Alexander, J. T. (2010). Moving out but not up: Economic outcomes in the great migration. *American Sociological Review* 75 (1), 101–125.

Fasching-Varner, K. J. (2009). No! The team ain't alright! The institutional and individual problematics of race. *Social Identities: Journal for the Study of Race, Nation and Culture* 15(6), 811–829.

Feagin, J. R. (1991). The continuing significance of race: Antiblack discrimination in public places. *American Sociological Review* 56(1), 101–116.

Fogarty, D. (February 21, 2011). Are white people losing interest in the NBA because none of its superstars look like them? http://www.sportsgrid.com/ nba/nba-white-people-interest/.

Ford, C. L., & Airhihenbuwa, C. O. (2010). Critical race theory, race equity, and public health: Toward antiracism praxis. *American Journal of Public Health* 100(S1), S30–S35.

Forster-Scott, L. (2011). Understanding colorism and how it relates to sport and physical education. *Journal of Physical Education, Recreation & Dance* 82(2), 48–52.

Gardner, R., & Shortelle, D. (1993). *The forgotten players: The story of black base-ball in America*. New York: Walker and Company, 45.

Gibbons, L. (2013, August 18). Former owner of Negro League baseball team honored by President Obama at White House. MLive, http://www.mlive.com/news/grand-rapids/index.ssf/2013/08/former_owner_of_negro_league_b.html.

Graham, L., Brown-Jeffy, S., Aronson, R., & Stephens, C. (2011). Critical race theory as theoretical framework and analysis tool for population health research. *Critical Public Health* 21(1), 81–93.

Hallman, C. (June 27, 2012). Colorblind racism: Language of sports filled with barely disguised bigotry. *Minnesota Spokesman*, http://www.spokesman-recorder.com/2012/06/27/colorblind-racism-language-of-sports-filled-with-barely-disguised-bigotry/.

Harris, A. P. (2008). From color line to color chart? Racism and colorism in the new century. *Berkeley Journal of African-American Law & Policy* 10(1), 52–69.

Heaphy, L. (2011). *Baseball and the color line: From Negro Leagues to the major leagues*. In *The Cambridge companion to baseball*, edited by L. Cassuto & S. Partridge, 61–75. New York: Cambridge University Press.

Herring, C. (2004). Skin deep: Race and complexion in the "color-blind" era. In *Skin deep: How race and complexion matter in the "color-blind" era*, edited by C. Herring, V. M. Keith, & H. D. Horton. Champaign: University of Illinois Press, 1–21.

Hersch, J. (2008). Skin color discrimination and immigrant pay. *Emory Law Journal* 58(2), 357–377.

Hine, D. C., Hine, W., & Harrold, S. (2011). *African American odyssey*. Upper Saddle River, NJ: Pearson.

Holway, John B. (2001). *The complete book of baseball's Negro Leagues: The other half of baseball history*. Fern Park, FL: Hastings House.

Horton, H. (1999). Critical demography: The paradigm of the future? *Sociological Forum* 14(3), 363.

Horton, H., & Allen, B. (1998). Race, family structure and rural poverty: An assessment of population and structural change. *Journal of Comparative Family Studies* 29(2), 398.

Hunter, M. (2008). Teaching and learning guide for the persistent problem of colorism: skin tone, status, and inequality. *Sociology Compass* 2(1), 366.

Hylton, K. (2010). How a turn to critical race theory can contribute to our understanding of "race," racism and anti-racism in sport. *International Review for the Sociology of Sport* 45(3), 335–354.

Hylton, K. (2008). *Race and sport*. New York: Routledge. Available at http://www.bl.uk/sportandsociety/exploresocsci/sportsoc/sociology/articles/hylton.pdf.

Keith, V. M. (2009). A colorstruck world: Skin tone, achievement, and self-esteem among African American women. In *Shades of difference: Why skin color matters*, edited by Evelyn Nakano Glenn. Los Altos, CA: Stanford University Press, 25–39.

Keith, V. M., & Herring, C. (1991). Skin color and stratification in the black community. *American Journal of Sociology* 97, 760–778.

Kennedy, R. (1997). *Race, crime and the law*. New York: Vintage.

Lapchick, R., Hippert, A., Rivera, S., & Robinson, J. (2013, June 25). The 2013 race and gender report card: National Basketball Association. http://www .tidesport.org/RGRC/2013/2013_NBA_RGRC.pdf.

Lumpkin, A. (2011). Negro Leagues: Black diamonds. *Phi Kappa Phi Forum* 91(2), 22.

Maconis, J. (2011). *Sociology*. Upper Saddle River, NJ: Pearson.

Martin, L. (2009). Black asset ownership: Does ethnicity matter? *Social Science Research* 38(2), 312–323.

Martin, L. L. (2013). *Black asset poverty and the enduring racial divide*. Boulder, CO: First Forum.

Massey, D. S. (1999). What critical demography means to me. *Sociological Forum* 14(3), 525.

Mathewson, A. (1998). Major League Baseball's monopoly power and the Negro Leagues. *American Business Law Journal* 35(2), 291.

National Negro Leagues meets in Philadelphia, Rube Foster presiding. (1926, January 15). *Kansas City Advocate* 12(25), 1.

Negro Leagues baseball: A brief history. (n.d.). http://www.coe.ksu.edu/annex/ nlbemuseum/history/overview.html

Onwuachi-Willig, A. (2009). Celebrating critical race theory at 20. *Iowa Law Review* 94, 1502.

Robst, J., VanGilder, J., Coates, C. E., & Berri, D. J. (2011). Skin tone and wages: Evidence from NBA free agents. *Journal of Sports Economics* 12(2), 143–156.

Romero, M. (2008). Crossing the immigration and race border: A critical race theory approach to immigration studies. *Contemporary Justice Review* 11(1), 23–37.

Sack, A. L., Singh, P., & Thiel, R. (2005). Occupational segregation on the playing field: The case of Major League Baseball. *Journal of Sport Management* 19(3), 300–318.

Sailes, G. A. (1991). The myth of black sports supremacy. *Journal of Black Studies* 21 (4), 480.

Schneider-Mayerson, M. (2010). Too black: Race in the dark ages of the National Basketball Association. *International Journal of Sport and Society* 1(1), 223–233.

Thompson, M. S., & Keith, V. M. (2004). Cooper brown and blue black: Colorism and self-evaluation. In *Skin deep: How race and complexion matter in the "color-blind" era*, edited by C. Herring, V. M. Keith, & H. D. Horton. Champaign: University of Illinois Press, 45–64.

Treviño, A., Harris, M. A., & Wallace, D. (2008). What's so critical about critical race theory? *Contemporary Justice Review* 11(1), 7–10.

Volz, B. (2013). Race and the Likelihood of Managing in Major League Baseball. *Journal of Labor Research* 34(1), 30–51.

Ward, G. (2006). *Unforgivable blackness: The rise and fall of Jack Johnson.* New York: Random House.

Warren, P. Y. (2010). The continuing significance of race: An analysis across two levels of policing. *Social Science Quarterly* 91(4), 1025–1042.

Wilbon, M. (June 25, 2011). The foreign flavor of this NBA draft. *ESPN*, http://sports.espn.go.com/espn/commentary/news/story?page=wilbon-110624.

Zuberi, T. (2011). Critical race theory of society. *Connecticut Law Review* 43(5), 1573–1591.

Part II

Evidence of Racism in College and Professional Sports

Chapter 6

"Jackie Robinson Day": The Contemporary Legacy

David Naze

Jackie Robinson has been heralded in baseball circles as an iconic symbol of Major League Baseball's racial integration. With that iconic status comes both convenience and controversy as to how that status has been constructed and maintained over the course of the last half-century. There is convenience in how easy it is to point to Robinson's integration as a focal point in baseball's willingness to change its racist practices. There is controversy in how Robinson's legacy gets commemorated, particularly by Major League Baseball. This chapter looks at how Major League Baseball has commemorated Robinson's legacy. Major League Baseball's commemoration of Jackie Robinson excludes various aspects of Robinson's life, such as his political activity, his debates with other prominent members of the black community, and his criticism of Major League Baseball. Conversely, Major League Baseball's commemoration of Jackie Robinson contains primarily aspects that reflect a Major League Baseball that is inclusive, racially and culturally tolerant, and willing to correct its past injustices. In other words, Major League Baseball's commemoration of Jackie Robinson is one that stays away from the controversial Robinson and embraces the popular one. The commemoration ceremony analyzed in this chapter is representative of Jackie Robinson's popular, commemorative legacy.

At Shea Stadium, home of the New York Mets in Flushing, New York, 30,000 fans attended the first Jackie Robinson Day on April 15, 2004. I argue that this commemoration was an attempt by Major League Baseball to define the legacy of the man who broke baseball's color barrier over half a century earlier. In the week prior to this commemoration, Major League Baseball announced that April 15 would now serve as the annual tribute to Jackie Robinson's inclusion to professional baseball. This inaugural ceremony meant that every Major League Baseball organization would retire Robinson's number 42. No player will don this number on his jersey again, save those who were already wearing that number. This gesture was intended to preserve the legacy of an individual who made not only baseball history in 1947, but American history as well. Bud Selig, Major League Baseball commissioner, headed the ceremony with a presentation that illustrated Robinson's impact on the game and society as a whole. Included in the ceremony was a video montage that depicted Robinson from his days as a baseball player, with Robinson's widow and daughter watching the video while standing next to the commissioner. Jackie Robinson's memory and legacy, as well as his impact on the game, society, and history, were now "official."

Public memories help us understand our expression of values, myths, and cultural knowledge. Commemoration, as a specific from of public memory, allows us to see how such expressions seldom remain fixed or static but change over time.

In simplest terms, *Webster's* defines commemoration as "something that honors or preserves the memory of another." Marita Sturken argues that commemoration functions as "a narrative rather than a replica of an experience that can be retrieved and relived. It is thus an inquiry into how cultural memories are constructed as they are recollected and memory as a form of interpretation."[1] Stephen Browne addresses the interpretive aspect of commemoration: "When remembrance is organized into acts of ritual commemoration, it becomes identifiably rhetorical, thus a means to recreate symbolically a history otherwise distant and mute."[2] Studies on commemoration, Browne continues, "focus upon the processes of constituting the memory as well as the implications of the product for future audiences and uses."[3] For my purposes in this chapter, "commemoration" will refer to specific rhetorical practices that attempt to articulate cultural memory.

As Michael Kammen notes, "there is a powerful tendency in the United States to depoliticize traditions for the sake of 'reconciliation.' Consequently the politics of culture in this country has everything to do with the process of contestation *and* with the subsequent quest for reconciliation."[4] It would seem to follow, then, that *forgetting* is as important to public memory as *remembering*. Any particular public memory is based on the choices that are made about how to construct it, and this is perhaps especially true with regard to public memories that concern race in America. Consequently, a memory will inevitably exclude or eliminate any details that do not match the present narrative of said memory. In the case of Jackie Robinson Day, much of baseball's controversial past is eliminated. The narrative that Major League Baseball constructs is one that emphasizes the present-day status of baseball but fails to include the irreparable damage wrought on the Negro Leagues as a prosperous cultural institution.

This essay is a historical investigation into the political persona of Jackie Robinson and aims to explore how Robinson's legacy could indeed embrace a dramatic change. Ultimately, Jackie Robinson Day opens a critical space that invites us to question how a particular social group comes to own a specific public memory. In this case, Jackie Robinson Day puts an official stamp on this version of history. Major League Baseball's Jackie Robinson Day commemoration incorporates certain strategic choices that reflect a process that minimizes controversy, privileges white America's version of baseball's integration, and invokes a public amnesia about the social consequences Robinson's historic inclusion had on the Negro Leagues and the black community in general. Furthermore, this chapter explores the ways in which Jackie Robinson Day becomes a site that may impact not only our interpretation of the past, but also our subsequent behavior in the future. Major League Baseball's construction of Jackie Robinson's legacy has implications for the potential ownership of a piece of history. Ultimately, Major League Baseball's 2004 celebration of Jackie Robinson Day allows us to question how a particular memory becomes owned by an individual social group. In the case of Major League Baseball, Jackie Robinson Day is constructed as a tokenist rhetoric. My argument suggests that Jackie Robinson Day serves to justify a liberal meritocracy.[5] That is, Robinson's persona was appropriated by the ideology of liberalism once he achieved social prominence. Jackie Robinson Day represents a convenient symbol for racial equality by failing to include any of Robinson's political endeavors in the commemoration ceremony.

First, I will delve into the discourse of Jackie Robinson Day as it attempts to define a cultural persona of Jackie Robinson. Next, I will examine the political side of Robinson before finally considering some critical conclusions.

Major League Baseball: A Post-Racial Institution?

Before we get comfortable with Major League Baseball's construction of a cultural legacy, we need to know how this ceremonial context frames Major League Baseball as a postracial institution. By painting itself as a space that is free from any sort of racial bias, Major League Baseball makes its exclusionary past more palatable. Jackie Robinson, the remover of baseball's color line turned political figure, has long been represented as a revered cultural icon for racial equality. Robinson's inclusion in organized baseball in 1947 reinforces the belief that sport is a meritocracy—that is, rather than being judged on one's color, character, or class, one is judged on his or her merit. Selig's speeches, both in 1997 and 2004, put the lie to this myth of meritocracy because they recognized Robinson almost exclusively for breaking the color barrier. Thus, Major League Baseball's contemporary integration narrative frames baseball as a postracial institution. Furthermore, the memory of Robinson's legacy is deemed one that places racial inequality behind us and thus constitutes a more just America. However, because of the attempts to commemorate his legacy as a convenient symbol for racial equality, the collective memory of Jackie Robinson has become overly simplified.

Understanding the implications of the choices made in Major League Baseball's Jackie Robinson Day campaign, specifically Selig's commemoration speech, requires a brief examination of Major League Baseball's previous commemorative portrayals of Robinson's legacy. The 2004 commemoration had important continuities with, but also differences from, previous celebrations. Throughout, of course, the dominant portrayal of Robinson is that of resilient pioneer. While the legacy of Jackie Robinson has taken on myriad forms, the three commemorative events that depict Robinson as the most determined of American heroes came during the twenty-fifth, fiftieth, and fifty-seventh anniversaries of Robinson's rookie campaign with the Brooklyn Dodgers.

The first commemoration came on June 4, 1972, when Robinson was invited to Dodger stadium to celebrate the quarter-century that had passed since his rookie year in 1947. The celebration was primarily constructed to retire Robinson's number 42 within the Dodger organization. Spectators saw a determined yet broken down version of Robinson's former self—suffering from high blood pressure, diabetes, blindness in his right eye, and a limp—walking to the infield to accept his jersey retirement.[6] Robinson's number was retired that day alongside former teammates Sandy Koufax and Roy Campanella. Later that year, Major League Baseball commissioner Bowie Kuhn invited Robinson to appear in a pregame ceremony during game two of the World Series, which took place on October 15, 1972. After ending a self-imposed boycott of baseball, one in which Robinson had protested the sport's poor record of hiring minorities for managerial and front-office positions, Robinson agreed to attend. During the televised event, Robinson threw out the ceremonial first pitch then took to the microphone, voicing his disdain for Major League Baseball's unwillingness to employ black Americans in more capacities. As Robinson stated, "I'd like to live to see a black manager, I'd like to live to see the day when there's a black man coaching at third base."[7] Robinson never lived to see that day. The World Series would prove to be his final public appearance, as nine days later, Robinson passed away from heart failure.

In 1997, Robinson's legacy was marked with a big celebration that included invited dignitaries, but unlike in 1972, there was substantially more media coverage. The 1997 ceremony was similar to the 1972 commemoration in that Jackie Robinson's pioneering spirit was emphasized. Understanding the details of the 1972 ceremony is important because it tells us specifically two things about the 1997 event. First, the lack of media coverage of the 1972 ceremony suggests where we were in the racial landscape of American sports at that time. Perhaps Jackie Robinson's social impact still had not been felt broadly enough across the country that it warranted little media coverage. Second, Major League Baseball's lack of inclusion of minorities in front office and managerial positions as of 1972 was a glaring illustration of its exclusionary hiring practices, thus legitimizing Robinson's public critique. By the time the 1997 commemoration took place, Major League Baseball had at least made some strides in the hiring of minorities in positions of authority. With these two things in mind, we can look to the 1997 ceremony to see how the celebration was more robust and vigorous than the 1972 version.

The 1997 ceremony, which marked the fiftieth anniversary of Robinson's historic integration of the major leagues, included speeches by President Clinton, Major League Baseball commissioner Bud Selig, and Robinson's widow, Rachel Robinson. In addition to the speeches, there was musical entertainment, as singer Tevin Campbell performed first, singing "The Impossible Dream." While Campbell was performing, there was black-and-white footage of Robinson's career on and off the field shown on the stadium video screens in the outfield. After the performance and video footage, President Clinton and Jackie's widow Rachel Robinson, accompanied by Selig, took the field at Shea Stadium.[8] As the *Atlanta Journal and Constitution* reported,

Selig told the crowd that "no single person is bigger than the game—no single person other than Jackie Robinson." Then came Clinton, an avid sports fan, who said, "Today, I think every American should give special thanks to Jackie Robinson, to Branch Rickey and to all of Jackie's teammates with the Dodgers for what they did. This is a better, stronger and richer country when we all work together and give everybody a chance."[9]

Clinton also added, "Robinson's legacy didn't end with baseball. He knew that education, not sports, was the key to success in life."[10] Clinton then addressed how the racial barrier that Robinson broke on the field should be considered as a goal off the field as well. As Clinton stated, "Despite the gains made by the civil rights movement, Robinson's message of inclusion still applies to contemporary society. We can achieve equality on the playing field, but we need to establish it in the boardrooms of America."[11] Then Rachel Robinson spoke, adding that Robinson's legacy "is a great tribute to a more equitable society."[12]

The contrast between Selig's and Clinton's comments about Jackie Robinson's legacy bring the heroic arc of Major League Baseball's official narrative into focus. For instance, Selig mentioned that "no single person is bigger than that game ... other than Jackie Robinson."[13] These comments isolate Robinson at the top of the racial integration narrative. This is different than Clinton's final comments, noted earlier in this chapter, which bring attention to the collective efforts of all involved rather than highlighting Robinson's individual efforts. By stating that "this is a better, stronger and richer country when we all work together and give everybody a chance," Clinton suggests that no one, not even Jackie Robinson, can reach the top alone. It is only when given a chance by others that individual success stories can be achieved. Clinton's remarks, for instance, depict the white authority in the foreground with the memory of the African-American subject in the background. By doing so, there is an emphasis on the role that white authority continues to play in the narrative about race relations. Thus, in my analysis, Selig represents the voice of Major League Baseball, and his speech clearly shows, in contrast to Clinton's, an individualistic and heroic narrative. This is part of what compels me to focus primarily on Selig's statement in the 2004 commemoration.

2004: Analysis of a New Commemoration

Because the previous Jackie Robinson commemorations took place on significant anniversaries—in 1972 for the twenty-fifth anniversary of Robinson's first start with the Dodgers and in 1997 for the fiftieth anniversary—a special commemoration on the fifty-seventh anniversary seems not to fit the pattern. As we saw in 1972 and 1997, the anniversaries that were celebrated were those of the typical "round number" years, so the fifty-seventh anniversary almost seems arbitrary, if not puzzling. The commemoration did coincide with a moment of crisis for Major League Baseball's public image, however. I argue that the ceremony was concocted as a way to deflect attention from this crisis. In fact, Robinson's legacy is one that tends to privilege the benefits his integration had on the larger American landscape and neglects the dire consequences his integration had on the black community. Selig's similar neglect attempts to secure a rather limited and uncomplicated legacy of Jackie Robinson. Additionally, what was the impetus for this commemoration? Major League Baseball has never officially or publicly declared the motivation behind the timing of Jackie Robinson Day. The timing and of this celebration makes its purpose fuzzy and opens the door to speculation as to Major League Baseball's motivation. The dominant majority who control Major League Baseball—read white—may have had an ulterior motive. The ceremony primarily serves the needs of predominantly white Major League Baseball.

The 2004 commemoration came on the heels of the 10-year anniversary of Major League Baseball's 1994 lockout, and rumors of another player lockout were looming as baseball's collective bargaining agreement was being negotiated.[14] Rumors of league-wide steroid use were also emerging, with threats of potential investigations by Congress and the public threats from Senator John McCain. Thus, leading baseball officials and players were forced to confront these potential crises in their public image. Perhaps Major League Baseball felt the need to address the issue to forestall the possibility of waning interest in baseball from the fans. As columnist Filip Bondy wrote the following day:

> Jackie stepped to the plate in a major league game for the first time 57 years ago in Brooklyn. A new era had begun for the sport, and all the statistical achievements that came before that momentous date were rendered more or less irrelevant ... When we speak with justifiable skepticism about the home-run pace of today, when we worry how steroids are tearing apart bodies and skewing the record book, we should start speaking with less reverence about all the marks before 1947. That was a terrible, wrongful time as well. And maybe that era deserves a big, white asterisk of its own in the record books and at the Hall of Fame.[15]

Bondy's remarks suggest that an inevitable black eye was looming for Major League Baseball both socially and historically. Perhaps if the league could get out in front of the black eye by controlling and constructing its own social and cultural legacy regarding the praiseworthy racial integration of Jackie Robinson, a chapter in the history of Major League Baseball that almost everyone views positively, then the blow could be absorbed more easily. This strategy could be considered to have proven successful. For instance, the reaction to the ceremony was positive. The *Atlanta Journal-Constitution* the following day printed a story that was representative of the majority of the media responses:

> For all of Robinson's athletic success, he is remembered best for becoming the man who finally integrated baseball, and in the process helped set the stage for the civil rights movement ... Congratulations to Major League Baseball for recognizing such a special life, and for honoring it.[16]

Here we see that Major League Baseball is being commended and congratulated for celebrating the legacy of Robinson. Because of such public praise, the steroid controversy was ensured, at least for the short term, to be relegated to the background.

The broadcast of Selig's presentation began in the late morning, at approximately 11:00 a.m., an hour prior to the start of the New York Mets season opening game. Prior to the ceremony itself, Jackie's daughter Sharon rang the ceremonial opening bell at the New York Stock Exchange to honor Robinson's April 15 anniversary. Across the country, 13 Major League Baseball stadiums hosting a season opening game had ceremonies to commemorate the inaugural Jackie Robinson Day" Rachel Robinson, officials from the Major League Baseball foundation, and officials from the Jackie Robinson Foundation were present at the ceremony at New York Mets' Shea Stadium. At all 13 ballparks, Jackie Robinson Foundation scholars threw out the ceremonial first pitch. But the principal ceremony was in New York at Shea Stadium, which is where the visual nature of Robinson's memory is emphasized the most in the commemoration ceremony.[17] While Robinson passed away in 1972, the concept of a commemoration is to privilege the accomplishments and impact of an individual or event. Robinson's widow in the audience along with members of Robinson's immediate family, friends, colleagues, and former teammates clearly indicated that Selig valued Jackie Robinson's contribution and legacy: "Starting this season, we have proclaimed April 15th as 'Jackie Robinson Day' in an effort to bring more exposure to the life, values and accomplishments of Jackie Robinson." However, as we will see later in the chapter, Selig's valuing of Robinson's contributions and legacy are constructed in a way that, once again, provide further evidence that the controversial aspects of Robinson's legacy only disrupt the convenient legacy of an obedient Jackie Robinson. More specifically, there are three noticeable themes throughout the following analysis of Jackie Robinson Day. First, Commissioner Selig assumes his authority for Jackie Robinson's legacy. Second, there is no mention of the Negro Leagues or their subsequent demise because of Robinson's integration. Finally, the racial composition, particularly regarding African Americans, of Major League Baseball has not changed much in the 57 years since Robinson broke of the color line.

On April 15, 2004, Commissioner Selig stood before the media and 30,000 fans at Shea Stadium to commemorate Jackie Robinson's legacy. During his initial comments, Selig was paired up with Rachel Robinson, with both remarking on the journey Robinson and other athletes of color had to travel to make baseball what it is today.[18] Throughout his speech, there were images of Robinson juxtaposed with Selig's words. While Selig was talking, there were various points at which Selig's presence at the podium was supplemented with footage of Robinson during his playing days. As Selig's speech progressed, Rachel Robinson stepped aside. About 30 seconds into the speech, on the jumbo stadium screen, we saw footage of Robinson walking up the dugout steps and looking out onto the playing field, seemingly overwhelmed by the landscape. This image was immediately followed by footage of Robinson and Branch Rickey sitting next to each other signing Robinson's contract, laughing and smiling so as to suggest an always affable relationship between the owner and player. This was followed by a close-up of a newspaper headline: "Brooklyn Signs Jackie Robinson." Images of Robinson embraced by his white teammates as well as his induction into the Major League Baseball Hall of Fame were included. These images were shown while Selig urged the audience to "look back on the history of the game" so that we may remember what a powerful statement Robinson made. Selig's narration directed our interpretation of the images, providing only one version of history on which to reflect—the version that celebrates integration and leaves out other versions that question the political and economic motivations of Branch Rickey, including versions that make compelling arguments for Major League Baseball as the culprit in ruining a profitable and prosperous institution like the Negro Leagues.

Selig's role as Major League Baseball commissioner carried an authority throughout the speech, an authority that took ownership of Robinson's historical legacy, as it symbolized the relationship between those performing a public memory and the subject being remembered. As Selig proclaimed, "[Robinson's inclusion] should have happened decades earlier." Selig also positioned himself as an authority on how members of baseball circles felt about Robinson's impact, proclaiming that "baseball's proudest moment" was "when Jackie Robinson first set foot on a Major League Baseball field." Here Selig did not allow for discussion about the ambivalence that both black and white America felt regarding Robinson's inclusion in organized baseball, that is, Selig presented Robinson's integration as baseball's proudest moment, without equivocation. By not allowing for such discussion, Selig once again was able to take ownership of Robinson's historical legacy. Also, all that was shown was Selig by himself, not joined by anyone at the podium, with the official logo of Jackie Robinson Day on the wall behind him. This depicted the white authority in the foreground with the memory of the African-American subject in the background, emphasizing the role that white authority continues to play in the narrative about race relations. In this case, when whites speak out in support of a traditional and hegemonic narrative (the story of integration), there is seldom any controversy. When others invoke the sign of "race" to suggest that the narrative is something of a myth or fantasy, it is controversial. Selig presented himself as an authority on the social significance of the subject when he stated, "When you look back on the history of our game, there's no question in my mind that Jackie Robinson's coming to Major League Baseball on April 15, 1947 . . . was the most powerful moment in baseball history. It transcended baseball . . . It was a precursor to the civil rights movement by fifteen or sixteen years." Here Selig positioned himself as a retrospective authority, establishing the moment that the civil rights movement began. Selig was reinforcing his establishment as a racialized authority, pointing out to the audience that not only did he posit Robinson's legacy as historically important, but that he (Selig) had the power to denote precisely when the modern American civil rights movement began.

At worst, Selig ignored the political challenges that constantly emerged among the American people at that time as well as the apprehension from the black community.[19] It is important to notice the ambiguity of the pronoun "we" in this instance because the phrase "*We* are further ensuring" makes a multitude of assumptions about the audience. At best, Selig did not provide a space for potential political challenges to be discussed. This lack of space for potential political challenges is evident when Selig utilized the ambiguous pronoun "we" when addressing Robinson's legacy. For instance, Selig stated, "By establishing April 15 as 'Jackie Robinson Day' throughout Major League Baseball, *we* are further ensuring that the incredible contributions and sacrifices he made—for baseball and society—will not be forgotten." The pronoun "we" assumed that everyone in the audience wants to remember Robinson in this particular way; it presented Selig's efforts to invite everyone to remember Jackie Robinson in this way; it assumed that Selig could speak for everyone in the audience. Again, the phrase "We are further ensuring" assumed that everyone was on board with remembering Selig's illustration of Robinson's legacy. It assumed that everyone agreed that Robinson's integration was indeed the most powerful moment in baseball's history. It also assumed that the retiring of Robinson's number is a sufficient homage to his legacy. These assumptions further illustrate how a white authority, Selig in this case, attempted to take ownership of a particular historical narrative, especially when we can assume that the majority of the audience Selig was addressing was white.

Additionally, the notion of responsibility was foregrounded at the outset of the speech. As Selig reminded us early on: "All of you have heard me say from time to time that baseball is a social institution with what I regard as enormous social responsibilities." However, Selig did not follow this statement with any discussion about what those responsibilities might be. Consequently, there was no discussion about why or how the barriers to baseball's integration were created in the first place. Selig constructed Robinson's legacy as a reminder of a celebrated past that illustrates Major League Baseball's socially just response to racial discrimination. He did this, however, while simultaneously ignoring Major League Baseball's role in the invention of those socially unjust barriers in the first place. The social responsibility of which Selig vaguely spoke, then, was left for the audience to figure out—so long as the conclusion was one that privileges a just Major League Baseball rather than an unjust one. Selig's mention of baseball's social responsibility in the process of public memory thus unveiled the social function served by a specific commemorative representation. That is, Major League Baseball's commemoration of Robinson in this instance provided a narrative that painted Major League Baseball as a socially responsible institution.

In addition to Selig assuming his authority over Jackie Robinson's legacy, there is a second theme worth noting during the 2004 ceremony: the lack of reference to the Negro Leagues. In addition to Selig, others expressed interest in the legacy of Robinson's contribution to integration. Columnist Jim Litke of the Associated Press commented, "What no one could have known at the time was how much more lasting its effect would be on history than baseball. And perhaps Robinson's legacy will always be bigger outside the game than inside it."[20] The *Press Enterprise* had this to contribute: "Baseball has always been a metaphor for life in America. It's been about simple joy in a carefree setting, about individual opportunity and achievement. It has been a cross-cultural field of dreams."[21] Yet the alarming trend is that still no references to the Negro Leagues are being made. On ESPN's official website, there is a tribute to Jackie Robinson Day, with the lead article titled "Jackie Changed Face of Sports."[22] Major League Baseball included on its official website various perspectives on the 2004 commemoration, most of which focused on Robinson specifically. Again, there is sparse mention of the Negro Leagues in the text.[23] Consequently, a rhetoric of silence (of the Negro League legacy) is being foregrounded in the integration narrative. That is, Major League Baseball chooses to emphasize Robinson's legacy in an attempt to reinforce the notion that Major League Baseball is a just and invitational institution. To do so, Major League Baseball remains silent on the damage it did to the Negro Leagues through racial integration.

In addition to Selig's authority over Robinson's legacy and the erasure of the Negro Leagues from the narrative, there was a third prominent theme in the 2004 commemoration: that of baseball's stagnant racial composition regarding African-American baseball players in today's era. There was some concern expressed by critics about the impact Robinson's legacy may or may not have had on the game despite the impression that there is a racially equal playing field. The commentary from many members of the African-American community, including present and former players, journalists, and fans, expresses the fact that the alleged playing field is not so equal after all. Just after the celebration of Jackie Robinson Day had slowed down, the *Los Angeles Times* recognized that the alleged progress baseball claims to have made is not as evident as one might think: "At a time when baseball has again been celebrating the anniversary of Jackie Robinson's debut in breaking the color barrier, the numbers equate to the continuation of an alarming trend."[24] Dave Stewart, former four-time 20-game winner in the late 1980s and early 1990s, expressed great concern about Robinson's legacy, the state of baseball today, and the integration narrative that is passed off today. Stewart lamented, "In Bud's [Selig] words, the game is better today than it has ever been, but I think it has taken a drastic step backward. When you look at the numbers of blacks playing the game and the numbers in decision-making positions off the field, they're way down from even three years ago."[25] When asked about the celebrations that started in 1997 to honor Robinson, Stewart replied, "There was good progress and a feeling among black players I think that baseball was trying to do something positive. Now . . . it's as if there's been a quick turnaround . . . Why that's happened only the people internally know, but it's not good."[26] John Young, a veteran Major League Baseball scout, echoed a similar sentiment: "I think there [are] societal changes to which baseball was slow in responding."[27]

The concern did not stop there. The *New York Daily News* the following day was one of very few objectors to the way Robinson's legacy was constructed: "Robinson was allowed to change [the exclusion of blacks] to a degree, but he always knew he could not knock down all the barriers. To this day, disgracefully, New York baseball has never known a manager of color, despite the city's many teams and century-plus track record."[28] A week later, the *Seattle Times* pointed out a disturbing trend not mentioned in Selig's speech: "Only one team last season could field a pitcher and catcher who were both African-American. At those positions, the game looks about the same as it did before Jackie Robinson broke into the majors in 1947 . . . The overall number of African-American players was down to 10 percent as this season opened, and blacks comprised only 3.3 percent of all starters."[29]

Furthermore, the April 18, 2004, *San Francisco Chronicle* lamented baseball's alleged success as it stated, "What has changed since Robinson's arrival? Still no black owners. Only three black general managers, one currently. What appeared to be a progression in 1975 turned out to be a peak."[30] Something of which there is no mention in baseball's celebratory integration narrative is what the *San Francisco Chronicle* article brought to the fore: "The number of African-American big-leaguers is under 10 percent for the first time since full integration—that was 1959."[31] In Hank Aaron's editorial in the *New York Times*, the former Negro League star and Major League Baseball Hall of Fame inductee articulated the problem correctly when he stated, "Now, 50 years later, people are saying that Jackie Robinson was an icon, a pioneer, a hero. But that's all they want to do: say it . . . It is tragic to me that baseball has fallen so far behind . . . in terms of racial leadership. People question whether baseball is still the national pastime, and I have to wonder too."[32] Aaron continued to lament the concerns that are invisible in the integration narrative:

Here's hoping that . . . baseball will honor him [Robinson] in a way that really matters. It could start more youth programs, give tickets to kids who can't afford them, become a social presence in the cities it depends on. It could hire more black umpires, more black doctors, more black concessionaries, more black executives. It could hire a black commissioner.[33]

Consequently, there is a large portion of the integration legacy that does not match up with its mythical proclamations. In fact, Ralph Wiley, writing for ESPN.com, argued that even Robinson himself would be unsure of what to make about the state of the playing field in contemporary sport:

> If Jackie Robinson were around today, I get the uneasy feeling that he would take one look around at the wide, wide world of sports, at what's been done, and undone, and what's left to do, and for all his strength, power, versatility, and relentlessness, I believe he'd start to cry. What I don't know is whether they'd be tears of joy or pain.[34]

Even Rachel Robinson, Jackie's widow, perceives today's game as one that is in a state of ambiguity. When asked about how her husband would view baseball's present unrest, Rachel lamented, "Jack would be disappointed, obviously, and he would be fighting back, as he always did in his lifetime, and saying, 'Let's not forget what it took to get us to this point' . . . I think there is a perception that there is a level playing field now, and that things have progressed. That is not true."[35] The erasure of the Negro League legacy can be seen as a perpetuation of the decline in current African-American ballplayers. This conclusion is not definitive, but it is certainly a primary component in the integration narrative.

These three themes—Selig's authority of Robinson's legacy, the lack of reference to the Negro Leagues demise, and the lack of progress in African-American inclusion across baseball—tell us something about the 2004 celebration of Jackie Robinson Day. Primarily, Selig's authority over Robinson's legacy, and therefore the popular version of Robinson's legacy, carries much more weight when the public is not made aware of the lasting consequences Major League Baseball's endeavor in 1947 had on the black community. The mainstream narrative gains further traction as well when the celebration constructs a rosy image of baseball's equal playing field, despite statistics and a few objections to the contrary. These three themes do not work in isolation. Rather, they work together by offering a tidy, simple narrative that only reinforces the popular mainstream version of Jackie Robinson's legacy.

Conclusion

To this point, we have examined the ways in which the 2004 Jackie Robinson Day ceremony constructed the popular, uncontroversial version of Jackie Robinson's social impact. We have not only examined the 2004 ceremony alone, we have also looked at the 1972 and 1997 ceremonies to see how each commemoration was both similar and different in numerous ways. We will now discuss several implications of the 2004 ceremony, including a minimization of controversy, a perpetuation of the myth that baseball is a meritocracy, a public amnesia that results from public commemorations, a questioning of the motivation behind the construction of a public memory, an examination into the role identity politics plays on public commemorations, and a look into how public commemorations link the past to the present.

First, the choices made in Major League Baseball's Jackie Robinson Day commemoration reflect a process that minimizes controversy, privileges white America's version of baseball's integration, and invokes a public amnesia about the social consequences Robinson's historic inclusion had on the Negro Leagues and the black community in general. In most historical and popular circles, Jackie Robinson is depicted synechdochally for white America's pursuit of unity. Synecdoche is one particular trope that is useful for rhetorical critique, as "a metaphorical perspective entails other master tropes such as irony, metonymy, and synechdoche."[36] According to Kenneth Burke, synechdoche is a rhetorical trope that can be described as representing a "part for the whole," or "whole for the part."[37] In other words, Robinson is viewed as a symbol for unity, synecdochally reduced to serve as a sign for white America's willingness to excoriate outdated social barriers, ultimately constructing Robinson as courageous and Dodgers owner Branch Rickey as heroic.[38] Even when Robinson can symbolize the courageous nature of black Americans in the face of extreme racial adversity, his integration can still be questioned for bringing down the profitable black institution known as the Negro Leagues.[39] Yet the preference for the solemn, reserved, and patient image among predominantly white communities marks Robinson as a symbol of accommodation and reconciliation. Selig's speech further illuminates this depiction.

Consequently, the "Jackie Robinson" that was defined for the audience was one that portrayed a great athlete and a daring pioneer. Never once was there mention of Jackie Robinson as a prominent outspoken political advocate. The symbol of Jackie Robinson presented during this commemoration was incomplete, functioning more as a convenient, uncomplicated representation of racial equality in the American public landscape. Rather than complicate the ideal patriotic narrative that MLB has used Robinson to portray, Major League Baseball was content with a very limited construction of Jackie Robinson's legacy. This is not to say that the Jackie Robinson portrayed during this ceremony was a negative one. It was, however, at best narrow and apolitical.

Second, Jackie Robinson Day serves as a tokenist rhetoric for Major League Baseball to sustain the belief that baseball, as a significant cultural space, will always be remembered as a meritocracy. As a result, Major League Baseball's construction of Jackie Robinson's legacy has implications for the ownership of a bit of history. Consequently, the Jackie Robinson that was defined for the audience during Jackie Robinson Day in 2004 was one that portrayed a great athlete and a daring pioneer. Never once was there a mention of Jackie Robinson as a prominent outspoken political advocate. Never once did we hear mention of Robinson as a prominent political figure who testified in front of the House Un-American Activities Committee; as a political voice that publicly clashed with Malcolm X on the front pages of the *New York Post* and the *New York Amsterdam News*; as a controversial symbol for the inevitable destruction of the Negro Leagues; as Brooklyn Dodgers general manager Branch Rickey's third choice to integrate baseball; as someone who, by his own admission, began his career as a baseball player strictly for the money; nor as a critic of Major League Baseball's exclusion of blacks as baseball administrators during the 1972 commemoration ceremony. As we analyzed the ceremony throughout this chapter, we saw that these images or memories of Jackie Robinson are not included because they do not fit in the neat, uncomplicated, monovocal narrative that highlights not only Robinson's legacy, but Major League Baseball's trailblazing initiative to include blacks in the game.

From one perspective, Major League Baseball's creation of Jackie Robinson Day may be seen to serve nothing more than an epideictic function, celebrating the desire to remember an incomparable social icon. But if we examine the discourse more closely, we might begin to see that there is much more at stake here than the ways in which we preserve a figure from the past. As Marouf Hasian Jr. and Cheree Carlson argue, "collective memories are selectively chosen and highlighted to fit the needs of a particular social group."[40] In the case of Jackie Robinson Day as an instance of public memory, the question might be: Whose needs are being served?

Major League Baseball commissioner Bud Selig's presentation attempted to secure a rather limited and uncomplicated legacy of Jackie Robinson; most important for the present analysis, it failed to address the drastic impact that Robinson's integration had on the prosperous and profitable institution known as the Negro Leagues. The lack of an explicitly stated motivation for the 2004 commemoration might contribute to the suspicion that some ulterior purpose was in play.

Third, Jackie Robinson Day allows us to see the power of "forgetting" and the subsequent public amnesia that results from "remembering" the past. The power of forgetting can take full force in many of the contested meanings implanted in the process of public memory. In the case of Jackie Robinson Day, the elimination of Robinson's role as political advocate is significant because it further perpetuates white America's convenient symbol of racial equality. The same Robinson who was outspoken against the Vietnam War and who came to be portrayed as a political "agitator" later in his life is here presented as a relatively unproblematic symbol of America's alleged triumph over racial discrimination. It will be interesting to see if future celebrations of Jackie Robinson Day give voice to Robinson's role as a political actor. Understanding Robinson's role as a political actor also allows us to see the ways in which Robinson is possibly portrayed as a passive character, one who does not take such an active role breaking social barriers as was once thought.

Furthermore, memory both defines a culture and is the means by which its divisions and conflicting agendas are revealed. According to Cloud, "[B]ecause social systems and their prevailing ideological justifications ... are always contested, social stability depends on the ability of the ideology to absorb and re-frame challenges."[41] For Major League Baseball, any potential challenges to the integration narrative regarding Jackie Robinson must be either silenced or reframed so that the appearance of baseball as a just social institution can remain intact. Bud Selig's construction of this particular public memory speaks about the power struggle between white and black communities during Robinson's integration as well as today. However, Selig really only touches on how the white community (via Major League Baseball) utilized Robinson's integration as a way to showcase Major League Baseball's willingness to tolerate racial integration. Perhaps the most effective way for Major League Baseball to do that was to commemorate Robinson's legacy in a way that emphasized Robinson as a tolerated individual rather than as a capable, outspoken part of a collective movement.

Fourth, this particular public commemoration brings into question the true motivation behind the construction of a public memory. No one really knows why Major League Baseball decided to construct Jackie Robinson Day in 2004. When asked, Selig stated that it was to ensure that young people know who Jackie Robinson was. But that does not answer the question as to why he was commemorated in 2004 rather than any other year. The motivation behind a commemoration on the fifty-seventh anniversary remains ambiguous. This ambiguity, like the use of the ambiguous pronouns Selig used during his commemoration speech, is important because it opens up the discussion as to what Major League Baseball's true motivations for the ceremony were. The ceremony did not mark a significant anniversary of Robinson's integration like the twenty-fifth and fiftieth anniversaries did. It did, interestingly enough, however, coincide with off the field issues that baseball was facing at the time, issues that were gaining more and more national attention. Because of the rumors of steroid use and a looming player lockout mentioned earlier in the chapter, leading baseball officials and players were forced to confront fans' waning interest in baseball. With Major League Baseball confronting such adversity, what better solution than to divert attention from the negative publicity and celebrate the legacy of the remover of baseball's color line? In the midst of mayhem and division, Major League Baseball looked to the historical symbol of unity found in Robinson.

It would be easy to presume that Major League Baseball might consider the timing nothing more than a coincidence. But constructing a specific public memory requires planning and rhetorical strategy. The issues at stake were addressed by those in power, essentially the ones constructing the specific memory. Bud Selig's construction of this particular public memory speaks about the power struggle between white and black communities during Robinson's integration as well as today. Specifically, Major League Baseball—through Selig's address—articulated a simple narrative in an effort to cover or distract from more complex issues.[42] John Bodnar reminds us that while "public memory emerges from the intersection of official and vernacular expressions," it is the official expressions that "originate in the concerns of cultural leaders or authorities at all levels of society" that promote "interpretations of past and present reality that reduce the power of competing interests that threaten the attainment of their goals."[43] So official culture or official histories "stress the desirability of maintaining the social order . . . [and] the need to avoid disorder or dramatic change."[44] Major League Baseball's Jackie Robinson Day avoids such a dramatic change to the popular version of Robinson's legacy by constructing a monovocal historical narrative regarding Robinson's inclusion in organized baseball that fits very well with the narrative already established in popular or vernacular culture.[45] Investigating the rhetoric of this commemoration as an instance of how public memory can be understood as a space for competing social perspectives is a worthwhile endeavor for anyone interested in the ways in which a particular social discourse gets privileged over others. According to Roseann Mandziuk, "The examination of public memory as a rhetorical practice reveals how acts of memorializing are sites of contestation in culture."[46]

Fifth, this case study brings to the fore the role that identity politics play in public commemoration. In Robinson's case, the stakes in the politics of identity are high because supporters of his commemoration must struggle with the ways in which his legacy gets remembered. More specifically, Major League Baseball's ownership of Jackie Robinson's legacy is a microcosm of how U.S. race relations can be viewed. The destruction of the Negro Leagues is necessarily "forgotten" so that Major League Baseball can construct Robinson's legacy as a success story of U.S. race relations. Selig's version privileges the celebratory function of baseball's racial integration, resulting in a public amnesia of the damage Major League Baseball did to its black counterpart in 1947. As a result, certain representations of Robinson's impact are remembered while others are forgotten. The themes of imagery, authority, status, and responsibility are represented at the center of Selig's discourse, ensuring that these themes play a central role in the public memory of Jackie Robinson. The consequence is that the "official" version of Robinson's legacy could function to silence aspects of his history that could otherwise question dominant definitions of racial politics and black identity. Selig's Jackie Robinson Day speech follows the current trend of refusing to create a public space to commemorate the more radical images of Robinson, perhaps because at this moment in time we are not willing to publicize the "cultural scars of difference" that Robinson embodies.[47]

Finally, as social critics, we should not only articulate the impact public commemorations have on cultural values and meanings, but also articulate the ways in which public commemorations link the past to the present. As Hasian and Carlson argue, "We should subject every . . . narrative to an exacting analysis, revealing as many facets of a story as possible, thus enlarging the repository of memory from which to construct competing narratives. In this way, we might somewhat level the field of battle in the struggle to control the interpretation of the past."[48] When the author of a new discourse controls the way a historical event gets constructed in a contemporary context, critics should raise a red flag. This is not to say that Major League Baseball's commemoration of Jackie Robinson Day in 2004 is a revisionist account of Robinson's integration. However, the discourse of the 2004 ceremony does provide an account that makes us consider what is at stake when a public gets only a one-sided and privileged account of the narrative. To not question such a version of a commemorative narrative only allows that version to gain more traction and momentum in public circles.

Notes

1. Marita Sturken, *Tangled Memories: The Vietnam War, The AIDS Epidemic, and the Politics of Remembering* (Berkeley: University of California Press, 1997), 7.

2. Stephen Browne, "Remembering Crispus Attucks: Race, Rhetoric, and the Politics of Commemoration," *Quarterly Journal of Speech* 85 (1999): 169.

3. Ibid.

4. Michael Kammen, *Mystic Chords of Memory* (New York: Vintage, 1991), 13.

5. Dana Cloud, "Hegemony or Concordance? The Rhetoric of Tokenism in 'Oprah' Winfrey's Rags-to-Riches Biography," *Critical Studies in Mass Communication* 13 (1996): 124.

6. "Baseball Heroes: The Jackie Robinson Story," accessed February 6, 2012, http://www.wtv-zone.com/moe/moesboomerabilia/page16.html.

7. Rachel Robinson and Lee Daniels, *Jackie Robinson: An Intimate Portrait* (New York: Abrams, 1996), 216.

8. Mike Lupica, "Tribute to Hero in Jackie's Memory, No. 42 Lives Forever," *New York Daily News*, April 16, 1997, accessed March 14, 2010, http://articles.nydailynews.com/1997-04-16/sports/18039874_1_rachel-robinson-bud-selig-bill-clinton.

9. Terrence Moore, "Thanks, Jackie: Shea Becomes Center of National Attention," *Atlanta Journal-Constitution*, April 16, 1997, D1.

10. "Baseball Honors Jackie Robinson," last modified April 15, 1997, http://articles.cnn.com/1997-04-15/us/9704_15_robinson_1_robinsons-widow-jesse-sims-tribute?_s=PM:US.

11. Ibid.

12. Ibid.

13. Lupica, "Tribute to Hero."

14. The 1994 players' lockout resulted in only the second cancellation of the World Series and the first since 1904.

15. Filip Bondy, "History's Stats Add up to Doubt," *New York Daily News*, April 16, 2004, 91.

16. "He Conquered More Than a Game," *Atlanta Journal-Constitution*, April 16, 2004, 18A.

17. It should be noted that I am talking about the broadcast of the speech, not justthe printed transcript. The broadcast can be found online athttp://mlb.mlb .com/mlb/events/jrd/index.jsp?year=04.

18. Ibid.

19. There was much hesitation among the black community during Robinson's integration. Many owners of Negro League teams could foresee the consequences of integration regarding the future existence of black baseball. See Neil Lanctot, *Negro League Baseball: The Rise and Ruin of a Black Institution* (Philadelphia: University of Pennsylvania Press, 2004) for further discussion.

20. Jim Litke, "One Small Step in Baseball's Long Journey," *Daily Reporter*, April 17, 2004, B1.

21. "Jackie Robinson's Legacy," *Press Enterprise*, April 19, 2004, A08.

22. Larry Schwartz, "Jackie Changed Face of Sports," *ESPN: The Magazine*, accessed March 13, 2010, http://espn.go.com/classic/biography/s/Robinson _Jackie.html.

23. Mark Newman, "Robinson Honored with Special Day," accessed March 14, 2010, http://mlb.mlb.com/NASApp/mlb/mlb/news/mlb_news.jsp?ymd=20040415 &content_id=717876&vkey=news_mlb&fext=.jsp.

24. Ross Newhan, "On Baseball: This Problem Is More Than Skin Deep," *Los Angeles Times*, April 25, 2004, D6.

25. Ibid.

26. Ibid.

27. Ibid.

28. Bondy, "History's stats up to doubt," 91.

29. T. J. Quinn, "A 'Black QB' Mentality?" *Seattle Times*, April 23, 2004, E7.

30. John Shea, "Big Leagues a Black Hole for African Americans," *San Francisco Chronicle*, April 18, 2004, C7.

31. Ibid.

32. Hank Aaron, "When Baseball Mattered," *New York Times*, April 13, 1997, 15.

33. Ibid.

34. Ralph Wiley, "W.W.J.D.? [What Would Jackie Do?]," accessed March 14, 2010, http:espn.go.com/page2/s/wiley/030303.html.

35. Terence Moore, "Where Are Braves' Black Americans?" *Atlanta Journal-Constitution*, April 15, 2004, 1F.

36. Kenneth Burke, *A Grammar of Motives* (Berkeley: University of California Press, 1969), 507.

37. Ibid.

38. Branch Rickey was the owner of the Brooklyn Dodgers at the time and was responsible for signing Robinson of the Kansas City Monarchs of the now defunct Negro Leagues in 1945.

39. See Neil Lanctot, *Negro League Baseball: The Rise and Ruin of a Black Institution* (Philadelphia: University of Pennsylvania Press, 2004).

40. Marouf Hasian Jr. and Cheree Carlson, "Revisionism and Collective Memory: The Struggle for Meaning in the *Amistad* Affair," *Communication Monographs* 67 (2000): 42.

41. Cloud, "Hegemony or concordance," 118.

42. Major League Baseball in this case is considered to be represented by the words of Commissioner Bud Selig. This does not suggest that Selig's words are the only representation of Major League Baseball's viewpoint, but his words offer the most visible and concrete representation of how Major League Baseball addresses Robinson's historical legacy.

43. John Bodnar, *Remaking America: Public Memory, Commemoration, and Patriotism in the Twentieth Century* (Princeton, NJ: Princeton University Press, 1992), 13.

44. Ibid., 246.

45. This is not to say that only one official version exists within contemporary popular culture. It does, however, suggest that the popular versions of Robinson's legacy manifest themselves in ways that are easily digested by the mainstream public.

46. Roseann M. Mandziuk, "Commemorating Sojourner Truth: Negotiating the Politics of Race and Gender in the Spaces of Public Memory," *Western Journal of Communication* 67 (2003): 273.

47. Mandziuk, "Commemorating Sojourner Truth," 289.

48. Hasian and Carlson, "Revisionism," 60.

Bibliography

Aaron, Hank. "When Baseball Mattered." *New York Times*, April 13, 1997, final edition.

"Baseball Heroes: The Jackie Robinson Story." Last accessed February 6, 2012. http://www.wtv-zone.com/moe/moesboomerabilia/page16.html.

"Baseball Honors Jackie Robinson." Last modified April 15, 1997. http://articles.cnn.com/1997-04-15/us/9704_15_robinson_1_robinsons-widow-jesse-sims-tribute?_s=PM:US.

Bodnar, John. *Remaking America: Public Memory, Commemoration, and Patriotism in the Twentieth Century*. Princeton, NJ: Princeton University Press, 1992.

Bondy, Filip. "History's Stats Add up to Doubt." *New York Daily News*, April 16, 2004, 91.

Browne, Stephen. "Reading, Rhetoric, and the Texture of Public Memory." *Quarterly Journal of Speech* 81 (1995): 237–265.

Browne, Stephen. "Remembering Crispus Attucks: Race, Rhetoric, and the Politics of Commemoration." *Quarterly Journal of Speech* 85 (1999): 169–187.

Burke, Kenneth. *A Grammar of Motives*. Berkeley: University of California Press, 1969.

Cloud, Dana. "Hegemony or Concordance? The Rhetoric of Tokenism in 'Oprah' Winfrey's Rags-to-Riches Biography." *Critical Studies in Mass Communication* 13 (1996): 115–137.

Dyson, Michael Eric. *I May Not Get There with You*. New York: Free Press, 2000.

Hasian, Marouf, Jr. "Nostalgic Longings, Memories of the 'Good War,' and Cinematic Representations in *Saving Private Ryan*." *Critical Studies in Media Communication* 18 (2001): 338–358.

Hasian, Marouf, Jr., and Cheree Carlson. "Revisionism and Collective Memory: The Struggle for Meaning in the *Amistad* Affair." *Communication Monographs* 67 (2000): 42–62.

"He Conquered More Than a Game." *Atlanta Journal-Constitution*, April 16, 2004, 18A.

"Jackie Robinson's Legacy." *Press Enterprise*, April 19, 2004, A8.

Kammen, Michael. *Mystic Chords of Memory*. New York: Vintage, 1991.

Lanctot, Neil. *Negro League Baseball: The Rise and Ruin of a Black Institution*. Philadelphia: University of Pennsylvania Press, 2004.

Litke, Jim. "One Small Step in Baseball's Long Journey." *Daily Reporter*, April 17, 2004, B1.

Lupica, Mike. "Tribute to Hero in Jackie's Memory, No. 42 Lives Forever." *New York Daily News*, April 16, 1997. http://articles.nydailynews.com/1997-04 -16/sports/18039874_1_rachel-robinson-bud-selig-bill-clinton.

Mandziuk, Roseann. "Commemorating Sojourner Truth: Negotiating the Politics of Race and Gender in the Spaces of Public Memory." *Western Journal of Communication* 67 (2003): 271–291.

Moore, Terrence. "Thanks, Jackie: Shea Becomes Center of National Attention." *Atlanta Journal-Constitution*, April 16, 1997, D1.

Moore, Terrence. "Where Are Braves' Black Americans?" *Atlanta Journal-Constitution*, April 15, 2004, 1F.

Newhan, Ross. "On Baseball; This Problem Is More Than Skin Deep." *Los Angeles Times*, April 25, 2004, D6.

Newman, Mark. "Robinson Honored with Special Day." Last accessed March 14, 2010. http://mlb.mlb.com/NASApp/mlb/mlb/news/mlb_news.jsp?ymd=2004 0415&content_id=717876&vkey=news_mlb&fext=.jsp.

Quinn, T. J. "A 'Black QB' Mentality?" *Seattle Times*, April 23, 2004, E7.

Robinson, Rachel, and Lee Daniels. *Jackie Robinson: An Intimate Portrait* (New York: Abrams, 1996), 216.

Schwartz, Larry. "Jackie Changed Face of Sports." *ESPN: The Magazine*. Last accessed March 13, 2010. http://espn.go.com/classic/biography/s/Robinson _Jackie.html.

Shea, John. "Big Leagues a Black Hole for African Americans," *San Francisco Chronicle*, April 18, 2004, C7.

Sturken, Marita. *Tangled Memories: The Vietnam War, The AIDS Epidemic, and the Politics of Remembering*. Berkeley: University of California Press, 1997.

Wiley, Ralph. "W.W.J.D.? [What Would Jackie Do?]." Last accessed March 14, 2010. http:espn.go.com/page2/s/wiley/030303.html.

Chapter 7

Intentional Foul?: Sports Card Values and the (De)valuation of Black Athletes in the NBA, 1989–2009

Wade P. Smith, Eric Primm, and Valerie R. Stackman

Simply stated, "skin color mattered in the past and it matters today."[1] In contemporary U.S. society, a uniquely Eurocentric history has produced a white-black distinction that not only establishes oppositional categories, but functions metaphorically as well. As Pfeifer observes, "the undialectical opposition of white-black, light-dark, good-bad, clean-dirty results in the color *white* being perceived as good and *black* as evil."[2] Following from such distinctions, in contemporary society, one's skin color has the capacity to serve as a signifier of social worth. Analyzing this process of valuation in the context of sports is a growing body of research exploring customer racial discrimination in secondary markets for sports memorabilia. Findings from these studies are informative, as they often expose the more subtle and covert ways that race persists as a socially influential categorical system at the same time that overt forms of racism seem to be giving way and a postracial narrative is gaining in popularity.[3]

The institution of sport is "typically accorded an image of racial transcendence where race is insignificant and athletes are judged by their athletic abilities rather than their skin color."[4] Contradicting this popular image, however, scholars continue to observe the significant degree to which race influences, among other things, the on-the-field/court experience of athletes and the perceptions and judgments of spectators and consumers.[5] While similar observations are made across sporting contexts, it is notable that in the context of basketball, race, and more specifically the white-black distinction discussed here, "is a critical issue."[6]

When compared to other professional sport leagues (including Major League Baseball, Major League Soccer, the National Football League, and the Women's National Basketball Association) the National Basketball Association (NBA) has the highest proportion of black athletes.[7] With a largely white, middle-class consumer base, scholars and journalists alike have observed the ongoing and contentious process through which, as Hughes summarizes, "the NBA is marketed and managed with a specific, if often tacit, goal of making black men safe for (white) consumers."[8] While this foregrounding of race by the NBA (even if only tacitly) demonstrates the fallacy of the assumption that athletes are judged purely by their athletic abilities, we extend the line of inquiry that has analyzed in detail marketing and league management practices to explore consumer judgments more directly.[9] The general question we are interested in is whether consumers judge NBA players by their athletic abilities, by their skin color, or some combination thereof. To answer this question, we analyze the relationship between player race and basketball card values across a 20-year period.

Race and Sports Card Collecting

Collections and collecting behaviors are sociologically informative, as they "instruct us about the nature of the world."[10] In an effort to unpack the nature and consequences of a categorical system of race, some social scientists have systematically analyzed the relationship between race and sports card values. The focus of these studies is on the secondary market in which values are assigned for individual cards that feature a specific player. In the first word on the topic, Nardinelli and Simon found evidence of consumer racial discrimination as the cards of white baseball players were found to have significantly higher secondary market values than those of black and Hispanic players with comparable performance levels.[11] The growing body of research that has followed this initial investigation has in some instances found evidence of consumer racial discrimination and in others not.[12] With the majority of the literature on the topic focusing on the contexts of baseball and football, basketball card values have been relatively underanalyzed.

In the earliest analysis of basketball card values, Stone and Warren found no evidence of racial discrimination.[13] In the years following, the research efforts of Broyles and Keen corroborated this finding.[14] Acknowledging that in economic terms, such analyses should focus on those factors "affecting the 'demand' side of the equation," as that side "is driven by *consumers*, that is, collectors," Regoli, Smith, and Primm called into question the sampling strategies relied on in each of these prior studies.[15] Notably, these studies analyze an entire card set from a single year.[16] As acknowledged by Broyles and Keen, most of the cards in a single set such as the one they analyzed "sell at the 'common player' price, which is the minimum value of a card and is not related to performance of a player."[17] In response, Regoli and colleagues posed the following question: "If the objective of research is to ascertain the possibility of racial discrimination in the secondary sports card market based on the behavior of collectors, why rely on a source of data populated primarily by cards that by definition, collectors do not collect?"[18] Addressing this issue, Smith and colleagues recently analyzed NBA players' rookie card values and found that race does influence the demand side of the equation.[19]

In their analysis of rookie card values (collected in 2009) for 215 retired players who are identified as "stars" to one degree or another, Smith and colleagues found no direct effect of race.[20] They did observe, however, that the significant predictors of rookie card price differed for blacks and whites. Most notably, while induction into the Naismith Memorial Basketball Hall of Fame (BHOF) significantly increased the value of black players' cards, the increase in price associated with BHOF status for whites was not significant. Further exploring this interaction between race and BHOF status, the researchers found that controlling for other factors—including career performance, position, and card availability—black BHOF member cards were worth significantly more than the cards of white BHOF members and non-BHOF members of both races, with black non-BHOF members having the least valuable cards. One of the possible explanations considered by the researchers for this finding was that black members of the BHOF, in direct contrast to non-BHOF members of the same race, "have arguably demonstrated, at least to some extent, an ability to adapt to white, middle-class behavioral norms and values ... [and] may be perceived as valuable in the minds of white card collectors not only for their sporting performance, but their ability to adhere to white-defined ideals."[21] In support of this explanation, these scholars highlighted the BHOF enshrinement process, which includes the following statement: "should it be determined by the Board of Trustees that an individual has damaged the integrity of the game of basketball, he or she shall be deemed not worthy of Enshrinement and removed from consideration."[22] Notably, numerous researchers have suggested that the "integrity of the game" is defined by white middle-class standards of behavior.[23] Smith and colleagues thus suggest that black players in the NBA are judged by the color of their skin.[24] More specifically, the white-black, good-bad association seems to play a significant role, as only "good" blacks, as defined by adherence to white (read "good") values and norms, are valuable. Smith and colleagues carefully note, however, that because race is always in the process of "being *made*," studying 2009 price data provides only a snapshot of how race matters at a single point in time.[25]

In the same year for which Smith and colleagues collected price data for their study, Cunningham observed that "[o]ver the course of the past two decades, the image of the black athlete has been tarnished . . . result[ing] in a fusion of the black athlete with the black criminal."[26] The observations made by Smith and colleagues thus take place at a social-historical moment that follows the active construction of black athletes in the NBA as unruly, ungrateful, violent, dangerous, and menacing.[27] As Eberhardt and colleagues observe, associations such as these influence individual judgments, decisions, and actions not simply because they exist, but because over time they become automatic.[28] The findings of Smith and colleagues may thus be representative of once contentious but now automatic associations based on race that influence the (de)valuation of professional athletes, behaviors of basketball card collectors, and thus card values in the secondary sports card market.[29] Acknowledging this historical contingency, we expand here on the recent work of Smith and colleagues to determine the extent to which a changing social backdrop influences the valuation of players over time.

To date, longitudinal analyses of race and sports card values are rare and confined to the sport of baseball.[30] In the most expansive longitudinal analysis, Scahill tracks baseball card values from 1979 to 2001, finding that race variables are uniquely significant from 1984 to 1991.[31] In light of such findings and the scholarly observations discussed earlier in this chapter, we do not assume that the interaction effect observed by Smith and colleagues holds true for prior eras, but rather seek to extend their analysis to explore the possibility that race matters differently over time.[32] Specifically, we analyze the same data to track the observed interaction of race and BHOF status from 1989 to 2009. In the sections that follow, we describe our research design, report on our results, and inductively turn to literature on race and the NBA to unpack and explain our findings.

Setting the Stage

For their study, Smith and colleagues collected data for players who started their career no earlier than 1950 (the year the NBA was racially integrated), retired by 2009 (the year for which price data were collected for their study), and met one or more of the following criteria: induction to the BHOF as a player, selection for at least one NBA all-star game during their playing career, or inclusion in *Total Basketball*'s "One Hundred to Remember" list.[33] Because rookie cards are generally the most valuable and most sought after card issued for any given player throughout his career, the price data collected were for each player's rookie card.[34] In total, 215 players' cards were included in their analysis.[35] Based on our interest, the analysis herein includes the rookie cards of players in the original dataset that were retired by 1989. Our decision to focus on this subset is influenced by both scholarly observation and methodological considerations.

Numerous studies have observed the extent to which the image of black athletes in the NBA changed over the course of the last decade of the 20th and first decade of the 21st centuries.[36] Therefore, we expand Smith and colleagues' original dataset, adding price data that spans the 20-year period from 1989 to 2009.[37] Acknowledging the complex set of factors that influences collecting behavior and, in turn, card value, we agree with Broyles and Keen's suggestion that analyses should focus on the cards of retired players to eliminate the unpredictable contribution of any subjective "speculation on future performance."[38] For these reasons, we analyze here rookie card values for players who meet Smith and colleagues' original criteria for inclusion, yet were retired by 1989 ($n = 155$).[39]

To address our research question, we collected data on the dependent variable, card price, in five-year increments from 1989 to 2009. To expand Smith and colleagues' research, we include six independent variables that have been found in prior research to influence card price: race, card age, career performance, playoff appearances, position, and BHOF status. These variables and specific data collection processes are described later in this chapter.[40]

Data on card price were collected from Beckett's annual price guides published in 1989, 1994, 1999, 2004, and 2009. Applying an intricate analytical process to establish secondary market values "Beckett's ... has set the standard for price guides in the [card collecting] hobby" and is commonly the source of price data in studies of race and sports card values.[41] The price data we collected are for cards in near-mint or higher condition, reported in U.S. dollars, and standardized to 2009 dollars using an inflation calculator from the U.S. Department of Labor's Bureau of Labor Statistics.[42] Notably, this variable has a skewed distribution; however, when log-transformed (base e), the price variable for each year of interest is normally distributed.

Assessed by multiple researchers, player race was identified by visually inspecting photographic representations of players (predominantly via the "Historical Player Search" option on NBA.com, the NBA's official website). It is notable that first, such visual assessments reflect the process through which sports card collectors assess player race, and second, there were no discrepancies in the coding of race among the three researchers working independently. Through this process, of the 155 players who retired by 1989, 88 were identified as black (coded 1) and 67 as white (coded 0).[43]

Because researchers consistently find that older cards are more valuable than more recently produced ones, as is the case with many different collectibles, we include card age in our analysis. Furthermore, researchers consistently find, as would be expected, that on-the-field/court performance affects card value. While performance on the basketball court includes a variety of offensive and defensive measures that are individually difficult to compare, the points created per minute (PCM) value provided in *Total Basketball* has proven to be successful in capturing the complex nature of basketball performance.[44] Incorporating both offensive and defensive performance statistics, the PCM value represents the points created by a player for each minute he is on the court. Furthermore, and of significance for our interests here in which NBA players of different eras are being compared, an annual measure of league efficiency is included in the statistic's calculation, rendering an individual's PCM relative to the league as a whole.[45] In their study, Broyles and Keen found that the number of postseason appearances significantly increased a player's card value.[46] Therefore, we include here a measure of playoff appearances relative to a player's number of seasons played. Specifically, we include a variable that is the percentage of the total seasons played for which the player was a member of a team that made the NBA playoffs. In addition to these variables, it is notable that different positions on the court afford players different offensive and defensive opportunities and rely on different skill sets. With prior research indicating an influence of position on card value, we thus include the player's primary position recorded for the majority of his career coded as dichotomous variables for the following positions: point guard, shooting guard, small forward, power forward, and center.

TABLE 7.1 Unstandardized Regression Coefficients of Player Race and (Standard Errors) Predicting Natural Log of Rookie Card Prices, 1989–2009[1]

	1989	1994	1999	2004	2009
(Constant)	2.016***	3.671***	3.561***	3.408***	3.23***
	(.192)	(.194)	(.206)	(.198)	(.194)
Race[a]	−.736**	−.646*	−.702*	−.660*	−.685**
	(.255)	(.258)	(.273)	(.263)	(.257)
R^2	.051	.039	.041	.040	.044

[1]Reference categories:
[a] Whites
* $p < .05$
** $p < .01$
*** $p < .001$
Source: Compiled from Beckett, James. (1989, 1994, 1999, 2004, 2009). *The official price guide to baseball cards*. New York: House of Collectibles.

Neither the performance-related variables (PCM and percentage of play-off appearances) nor the position of the players change across time. However, players are inducted into the BHOF years after they retire, and in some instances with our data, after 1989. Therefore, the variable representing BHOF status changes over time, reflecting the induction of new members. In the section that follows, we describe the results of our analysis tracking the interaction between race and BHOF status from 1989 to 2009.

What We Found

Similar to Smith and colleagues, a series of baseline models were estimated to examine the effect of race on rookie card prices (see Table 7.1).[47] In all of these models, the race of a player has a statistically significant effect, with the cards of black players worth less than those of whites. This effect, however, is rather small, explaining between 3.9 percent (1994) and 5.1 percent (1989) of the variance in card prices.

Next, we estimated a series of models in which the logged card price for each year was regressed onto the six independent variables: race, BHOF status, card age, the percentage of playoff appearances, performance, and position. An examination of Table 7.2 shows the variance explained in these models increased dramatically, ranging from 76.6 percent (1989) to 79 percent (1999). The variable with the most influence in each model was card age. As expected, older cards were more valuable than newer ones. The next most prominent variables in each model were player performance

TABLE 7.2   Unstandardized Regression Coefficients and (Standard Errors) Predicting Natural Log of Rookie Card Prices, 1989–2009[1]

	1989	1994	1999	2004	2009
(Constant)	−4.728***	−3.929***	−4.760***	−5.026***	−6.008***
	(.504)	(.538)	(.598)	(.631)	(.656)
Card age	.147***	.137***	.150***	.144***	.149***
	(.011)	(.011)	(.011)	(.011)	(.011)
PCM	5.048***	5.864***	4.964***	4.164***	4.142***
	(.845)	(.896)	(.960)	(.956)	(.936)
PCT Playoff	.006†	.005†	.005	.005	.004
	(.003)	(.003)	(.003)	(.003)	(.003)
Point guard[a]	.104	.076	.020	−.003	−.074
	(.213)	(.214)	(.215)	(.211)	(.206)
Small forward[a]	−.174	−.160	−.239	−.228	−.344†
	(.194)	(.195)	(.197)	(.193)	(.189)
Power forward[a]	−.400†	−.452*	−.449*	−.385†	−.469*
	(.203)	(.203)	(.208)	(.205)	(.200)
Center[a]	−.078	−.314	−.208	−.253	−.355†
	(.218)	(.217)	(.222)	(.216)	(.211)
Race[b]	.019	.034	.073	.076	.065
	(.144)	(.144)	(.146)	(.143)	(.139)
BHOF status	.927***	1.014***	1.206***	1.219***	1.075***
	(.198)	(.177)	(.185)	(.183)	(.179)
R^2	.766	.768	.790	.782	.783

[1]Reference categories:
[a] Shooting guard
[b] Whites
† $p < .1$
* $p < .05$
** $p < .01$
*** $p < .001$
Source: Compiled from Beckett, James. (1989, 1994, 1999, 2004, 2009). *The official price guide to baseball cards*. New York: House of Collectibles.

and BHOF status, both affecting card price as expected: card price increased as performance levels increased, and BHOF members had more valuable cards than non-BHOF members. Interestingly, an examination of standardized coefficients revealed that player performance had a greater influence over card prices than BHOF status in 1989 and 1994, but in the remaining years, BHOF status had the stronger influence. Player position also had an effect on card prices. Specifically, when controlling for the other variables in the models, the cards of shooting guards (the reference category) were significantly more valuable than those of power forwards in three of the five models. Additionally, this difference approaches significance in 1989 ($p = .051$) and is marginally significant in 2004 ($p = .062$). No other positions in any of the models had significantly different card price than shooting guards, though the card values of small forwards ($p = .07$) and centers ($p = .095$) were marginally significant in 2009. While the percentage of playoff appearances approached significance as a contributor to card value in 1989 ($p = .054$) and was marginally significant in 1994 ($p = .084$) it did not have a statistically significant influence in any of the other models. Finally, the coefficients for race were positive across all models, indicating the cards of black players were more valuable than those of their white counterparts (the opposite direction of the baseline models). However, none of these coefficients were statistically significant when controlling for the other variables in the models.

These results are consistent with those of Smith and colleagues in that the race of a player has no direct impact on the value of his rookie card in any of the models.[48] To more carefully examine potential indirect effects of race via the interaction between race and BHOF status that Smith and colleagues reported, we next estimated models replacing race and BHOF status with a set of categorical variables representing the four groups of interest: black BHOF members, black non-BHOF members, white BHOF members, and white non-BHOF members (see Table 7.3).[49] As expected, the results of these regression models are very similar to those reported in Table 7.2, with the variance explained by the models ranging between 76.8 percent (1989) and 79.7 percent (1999). As with the models presented in Table 7.2, the variable that exerts the greatest influence on card prices in these models is the age of the card. Player performance is also a significant contributor to card value across all of these models. The percentage of playoff appearances does not have a significant influence on card value in any of the models, but it does approach significance in 1989 ($p = .052$) and is marginally significant in 1994 ($p = .076$) and 2004 ($p = .095$). Turning to player position, the cards of power forwards are worth significantly less than those of shooting guards in 1989 ($p = .043$), 1994 ($p = .036$), and 2009 ($p = .04$), and the difference is marginally significant in 1999 ($p = .057$). The only other marginally significant difference by position is

TABLE 7.3 Unstandardized Regression Coefficients and (Standard Errors) with Race and BHOF Dummy Variables Predicting Natural Log of Rookie Card Prices, 1989–2009[1]

	1989	1994	1999	2004	2009
(Constant)	−3.977***	−2.767***	−3.288***	−3.559***	−4.655***
	(.646)	(.640)	(.699)	(.727)	(.740)
Card age	.148***	.136***	.149***	.143***	.149***
	(.011)	(.011)	(.011)	(.011)	(.011)
PCM	5.057***	5.866***	4.923***	4.104***	4.069***
	(.845)	(.896)	(.949)	(.949)	(.923)
PCT Play-off	.006†	.005†	.005	.005†	.005
	(.003)	(.003)	(.003)	(.003)	(.003)
Point guard[a]	.120	.064	.006	−.014	−.088
	(.214)	(.214)	(.213)	(.209)	(.203)
Small forward[a]	−.197	−.137	−.167	−.165	−.268
	(.196)	(.196)	(.198)	(.195)	(.189)
Power forward[a]	−.415*	−.432*	−.397†	−.338	−.412*
	(.204)	(.204)	(.207)	(.205)	(.199)
Center[a]	−.067	−.306	−.189	−.250	−.351†
	(.219)	(.218)	(.219)	(.214)	(.208)
White BHOF[b]	.256	−.247	−.474†	−.414†	−.476*
	(.309)	(.252)	(.240)	(.233)	(.226)
White non-BHOF[b]	−.811**	−1.107***	−1.374***	−1.369***	−1.231***
	(.290)	(.246)	(.249)	(.243)	(.236)
Black non-BHOF[b]	−.724*	−1.163***	−1.494***	−1.464***	−1.373***
	(.282)	(.229)	(.229)	(.226)	(.219)
R^2	.768	.770	.797	.787	.790

[1]Reference categories:
[a] Shooting guard
[b] Black BHOF members
† $p < .1$
* $p < .05$
** $p < .01$
*** $p < .001$
Source: Compiled from Beckett, James. (1989, 1994, 1999, 2004, 2009). *The official price guide to baseball cards*. New York: House of Collectibles.

that of centers in 2009 ($p = .094$), whose cards are worth less than those of shooting guards.

Our examination of the categorical variables created to explore the interaction of race and BHOF membership produced noteworthy results. First, as expected considering BHOF status was a consistent contributor to card value in the models presented in Table 7.2, black BHOF members had cards that were significantly more valuable than those of black and white non-BHOF members across all models. Second, and again consistent with the findings of Smith and associates, the cards of black BHOF members were significantly more valuable than those of white BHOF members in 2009.[50] Finally, if we step back and look and the data in a broader context, a trend may have developed in relation to the card values of black and white BHOF members. In 1989, white BHOF members' cards are more valuable than those of black BHOF members, though this difference is not statistically significant ($p = .408$). In 1994, there is a shift in that the cards of black BHOF members are more valuable, but again the difference is not significant ($p = .328$). In 1999, black BHOF members again have more valuable cards, and this difference approaches significance ($p = .051$). The significance in the difference between black and white BHOF member card values wanes in 2004 ($p = .077$), but as stated earlier, reappears in 2009 ($p = .037$).

To illustrate the differing effects of BHOF status for black and white players over time, we computed the predicted natural log price of the cards of shooting guards (the largest position category in our sample) for each of the four categories. Using mean performance levels, percentage of playoff appearances, and card age for each model presented in Table 7.3, our prediction equations produced values for white non-BHOF members, black non-BHOF members, white BHOF members, and black BHOF members. Finally, to present the predicted values in more "intuitive" terms (most people do not think in terms of logarithms), dollar figures were calculated by taking the exponential function of the predicted y values ($e^{\hat{y}}$) for each model (see Figures 7.1 and 7.2).

Tracking the price differences of shooting guards across time, Figure 7.1 demonstrates the shift that occurred from 1989 to 1994 as well as the widening of the gap in value between black and white BHOF members that occurred between 1994 and 2009. Figure 7.2, which graphically represents rookie card price for shooting guards expressed as a percentage of black BHOF member card values, depicts the general trend that we observed. As shown, the cards of white shooting guards in the BHOF were worth

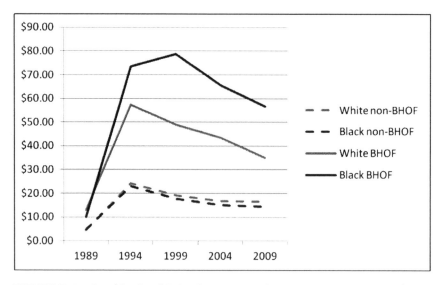

FIGURE 7.1   Rookie Card Price by Race and BHOF Status among Shooting Guards (in 2009 Dollars) by Group, 1989–2009. Compiled from Beckett, James. (1989, 1994, 1999, 2004, 2009). *The official price guide to baseball cards.* **New York: House of Collectibles.**

129.2 percent of their black peers' cards in 1989, 78.1 percent in 1994, 62.3 percent in 1999, 66.1 percent in 2004, and 62.1 percent in 2009. It is this general trend that is the focus of our discussion here.

What Does It Mean?

The impetus for this research was the observation that race matters differently at different points in time, as it is always in the process of "being *made*." To explain the trend in which black BHOF member rookie cards from 1989 to 2009 increasingly became more valuable than those of their white peers (as represented in Table 7.3 and Figures 7.1 and 7.2), we thus focus on how race was socially constructed in the NBA throughout this period. While the social constructions of interest were explicitly managed by NBA league officials, scholars have observed the degree to which the driving force behind the process was consumers.

It is notable that the consumer base and thus target audience of the NBA is largely the white middle and upper classes.[51] As such, the NBA works diligently "to create a product that is exciting but 'safe' for white, middle-class consumption."[52] Sports card collectors are primarily white middle-

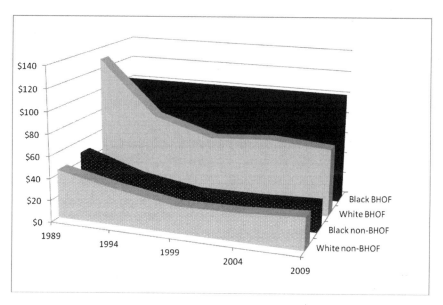

FIGURE 7.2 Rookie Card Price by Race and BHOF Status among Shooting Guards Expressed As a Percentage of Black BHOF Member Card Values, 1989–2009. Compiled from Beckett, James. (1989, 1994, 1999, 2004, 2009). *The official price guide to baseball cards.* New York: House of Collectibles.

class men, and we believe that the concerted efforts of the NBA and social acceptability of its "product" (as measured by white consuming behavior) are reflected in card collecting behavior, and in turn, basketball card values. It is worth mentioning, then, that in 1989, the only year in our analysis for which white BHOF member cards were worth more than those of black BHOF members, the league acknowledged a pressing need "to rehabilitate the perception of its [black] players" in an effort to regain its commercial footing.[53] While the 1989 difference in card value for BHOF members by race is not significant in our model, our review of the literature suggests that the change in direction of the relationship from 1989 to 1994 (see Table 7.3) is explainable by social circumstances that set the stage for later years in which the difference neared (1999, $p = .051$; 2004, $p = .077$) or reached a level of statistical significance (2009, $p = .037$).

Stated explicitly, "[a] central concern for the NBA leadership in the 1980s was the image of the league and its professional Black players whose behaviors were thought to alienate them from the White consumer majority."[54] This image was influenced by both broader social and local organizational factors. It is important to remember that 1980s, U.S. society was

shaped in various ways by a Reagan-era socio-political context characterized by a focus on individual responsibility accompanied by the unprecedented criminalization and mass imprisonment of black men.[55]
Furthermore, estimates in the early 1980s suggested that 75 percent of
NBA players were using drugs, and team hotels "became known as 'party
palaces' with marijuana and wall-to-wall hookers."[56] It was in this societal
and organizational context that the NBA appointed David Stern as league
commissioner in 1984. Recalling the focus of the league at that time, Stern
said, "sponsors were flocking out of the NBA because it was perceived as a
bunch of high-salaried, drug-sniffing back guys."[57] During the 1980s, then,
black men generally—and black players in the NBA specifically—came to
be viewed as criminally inclined and in turn, devalued.

According to Eberhardt and colleagues "crime . . . may trigger images of
those Black Americans who seem most physically representative of the
Black racial category (i.e., those who look highly stereotypical). Likewise,
highly stereotypical Blacks should be the most likely to trigger thoughts of
crime."[58] It takes little effort to find evidence that "stereotypical blacks" are
physical and aggressive, and thus athletic.[59] Associations of black professional
athletes with criminals are thus easily made in the minds of white consumers
via enduring stereotypes. It is precisely this association that we propose
explains our finding that in 1989 the cards of black BHOF members were
worth less than those of their white counterparts. The devaluation of blacks
in society more generally, we argue, correlates with the devaluation of black
NBA players (and thus their rookie card values) in 1989.

Remarkably, a shift occurred in 1994 as the value of black BHOF
member cards exceeded that of white BHOF member cards. As noted earlier in this chapter, social and organizational conditions of the 1980s
spurred attempts by NBA leadership to reestablish the public perception
of black players in the league. As David Stern recalled, "It was our conviction that if everything else went right, race would not be an abiding issue
to NBA fans, at least not as long as it was *handled correctly*."[60] Black players
and their public personas, it was suggested, were in need of careful control.
According to Maharaj, the provision of a product that was "safe" for white
consumers "depend[ed] on the recuperation of black players as model
citizens."[61]

As May suggests, deliberate efforts made by the NBA to market black
players as role models were explicit attempts to market black players as fol-
lowers of white middle-class standards of behavior.[62] Catering to a target
audience, after all, "means that athletes are carefully tailored to be attractive

to that group."[63] Perhaps the best and most socially influential example of this effort is the commodification of Michael Jordan's public persona.

Via a cautious and socially conscious process of identity management, Michael Jordan (whose storied career as an NBA player began in 1984 and ended in 2003) is one of the most widely marketed athletes of all time.[64] While his on-the-court physical accomplishments quickly vaulted him to worldwide fame, off the basketball court—and most notably in various and numerous commercial endorsements—Jordan was regularly portrayed "as an engaging, thoughtful, private family man," a depiction that countered "the socially constructed representations of African American men as dangerous, incompetent, and overtly hypersexualized."[65] In the words of Kellner, Michael Jordan was represented in the media as a "good black."[66] Perhaps best demonstrating the extent to which Jordan was accepted as "safe" for white consumption is Gatorade's advertising campaign slogan enticing the audience to "be like Mike," which was launched in 1991. It would be difficult to imagine a similar advertising campaign for NBA bad-boy and Jordan teammate Dennis Rodman, "who with his bleached and undisciplined hair, earring, fancy clothes, and regularly rebellious behavior represents the 'bad' Black figure."[67] Surely such a campaign would not be easily palatable to white middle- and upper-class consumers. When marketing Michael Jordan the engaging, thoughtful, private family man, however, the ad campaign "establish[es] Jordan as a role model, as the very icon of excellence and aspiration."[68] The campaign, it could thus be argued, renders Jordan, though black skinned, culturally white and in turn, "safe" for white middle-class consumers.

The commodification of "good" blacks such as Jordan accomplished much more than raising the social value of individual players, as it was not only in the realm of sports that "good" blacks assumed center stage (to a meaningful degree) during the 1980s and 1990s, but also in media representations more generally. As Andrews and Mower observe, popular representations of successful American statesman Colin Powell and Bill Cosby as Dr. Heathcliff Huxtable in The Cosby Show, for example, similarly suggested that an individual's race is socially irrelevant.[69] In turn, "the effective subsumption of Jordan et al.'s blackness by their over-determining association with the raced mythos of (white) Middle American values, reasserted whiteness as the 'natural default category against which others are raced.'"[70] The active construction of "good" blacks via media representations concurrently calls into being, then, "bad" blacks, or in the NBA, those who are distinctly not "like Mike."

The NBA's effort to revive the league by reinventing black players as role models appears to have worked by the mid-1990s. With David Stern at the helm, the league's annual revenues increased by 1,600 percent from 1984 to 1994.[71] Moreover, the results from our analysis suggest that public perceptions of black players in the NBA had indeed changed during this period. Though less valuable than cards of white BHOF members in 1989, the cards of black BHOF members were more valuable than those of their white peers just five years later in 1994. It appears, then, that the explanation posed by Smith and colleagues for their findings was beginning to take shape via media portrayals and public perceptions of "good" and "bad" blacks.[72] We must caution, however, that the difference in BHOF member card values by race is not statistically significant in 1994 and does not reach a level of significance until 2009 (though as stated previously, it approaches significance in the two prior years of observation, 1999 and 2004). In the discussion that follows, we leverage the narrative account provided thus far to explain the increasing significance in the difference between black and white BHOF member rookie card values across time.

As Boyd suggests, "the ideas that mediated sports produce are hammered home repeatedly."[73] As black sports role models such as Michael Jordan are consistently deracialized in media representations, whiteness is consistently reinstated and normalized as desirable. Concomitantly, "bad" blacks, defined by a lack of adherence to white defined ideals, are commonly racialized in media representations and depicted as "both natural athletes and natural thugs."[74] Demonstrating this argument is Boyd's characterization of publicized concerns with and reactions to Charles Barkley in the 1990s. As he suggests, "calls for Barkley to be a good role model are really calls for him to 'stop acting like a nigga' because too many impressionable white youth might try and imitate the behavior."[75] Through these contradictory practices of deracializing "good" blacks and racializing "bad" blacks in the NBA, media representations actively construct in the minds of the predominantly white middle-class audience the oppositional categories of "good" (read socially valuable) and "bad" (read "disposable") blacks.[76] Our interest here is in the lasting legacy such social constructions engender.

Following the NBA's explicit and successful attempt to market black role models (i.e., whiteness) under Commissioner David Stern's watch in the 1980s and 1990s, observers have begun to take note of an "ill-disciplined and disrespectful post-Jordan generation" of black players and the associated "'deteriorating' image of the NBA."[77] With the contemporary "fusion of the black athlete with the black criminal" fueled, for example, by the highly criticized actions of Allan Iverson who, known for his aggressive style of play, poor practice habits, and criminal allegations off the court (including aggravated assault and making terroristic threats), "has been labeled a thug since coming to the NBA in 1996" and has "become the face of a generation of basketball players who shun the ways of old ... [by] not conforming to any societal expectations," it would seem logical to assume that the trend we have been discussing would reverse itself.[78] Our results, however, reveal the opposite, as black BHOF member rookie cards become more valuable than those of white BHOF members over time.

"Amid a backlash against the influence of hip-hop within professional basketball," Leonard notes that numerous commentators have "called for action: reform to bring the league back to its glorious (White, and White controlled) past."[79] It is precisely this reference to a specific, and more important "glorious," past that we believe explains our findings. Without a Michael Jordan (i.e., "good" black), there is no "post-Jordan" (i.e., "post–good" black) era. Because, however, "Jordan's symbolic capital continues to inform the politics of racial representation and governance within the NBA," the deracialized "good" black (and thus whiteness) continues to serve as the reference point with which all contemporary black players are judged.[80] In an era characterized by a generation of players who are perceived to fail to conform to societal expectations, those who have demonstrated conformity are, we argue, exceptionally valuable.

In 2009, most NBA consumers could readily recall a time (the Jordan era) in which the NBA's product was characterized by "good" blacks." This is not to say that "bad" blacks were nowhere to be found, but rather that via comparative media portrayals such players served in the same capacity as "good" blacks by reinforcing the social value of whiteness. At the same time, however, 2009 consumers observed a league that was perceived, comparatively, to be saturated with "bad" blacks. "Good" blacks, it would seem, were few and far between. In result, "good" blacks, socially commendable for their adherence to white defined ideals, were exceptionally valuable in this context. As suggested by Smith and colleagues, black players who had been inducted into the BHOF had demonstrated, to one degree or another, an ability to be a "good" black by abiding by white middle-class standards of behavior.[81] The value of BHOF member cards in 2009 is thus influenced by a decades-long social construction of race in the NBA culminating in black BHOF member cards being worth significantly more than white BHOF member cards. We suggest, then, that it is not just the rarity of the rectangular piece of cardboard on which a player's image appears, but the perceived rarity of the player pictured that influences the value of NBA player sports cards.

Concluding Remarks

Through our analysis, we have exposed the extent to which social constructions of race in the past influence perceptions of social worth in the present. Because the social construction of race involves such a dynamic and complex process, we believe that more attention should be afforded the historical context in studies of race and sport. Studies of race and sports card values, for example, often ask the question "*does* race matter" but leave relatively unaddressed questions of *how* race matters, or perhaps even more important, *why* race does or does not matter. These latter questions, however, are of significant importance if we are to adequately understand the past, present, and future of race and ethnic relations in sporting contexts specifically and society more generally.

In the aptly titled volume *Making Race Matter*, Alexander and Knowles provide a collection of works that address pressing concerns about race in contemporary society. Accepting, as do the volume's editors, that race "is an ongoing *issue* for academic concern ... and that it carries consequences," we orient our concluding remarks toward two central questions that also serve as the focus of their book. First and foremost, the authors ask: "In this post-Millennial world of 'difference,' does race still matter?"[82] With whiteness providing the foundation upon which players are (de)valued in the NBA, as evidenced by our analysis of basketball card values, we most certainly acknowledge that it does. The institution of sport has observably not achieved racial transcendence as commonly suggested.[83] Of significant academic interest and social consequence, however, is not identifying *if* race still matters, but exposing *how* it matters in a "post-Millennial world of 'difference.'"

Addressing the *how* question, Alexander and Knowles ask: "In what ways is race *made* to matter, by whom and for whom?"[84] In the context of the NBA, the answer to this question is complicated and notably driven by the "for whom" portion of the question. With a predominantly white middle- and upper-class consumer base, "the NBA is marketed and managed with a specific ... goal of making Black men safe for (White) consumers."[85] Race is thus *made* in the image of whiteness by NBA league officials. In the pursuit of profit, race is actively *made* to matter in the NBA by first, socially constructing "good" blacks and "bad" blacks vis-à-vis whiteness, and second, as implied in NBA commissioner David Stern's own words, ensuring that bad blacks are "handled correctly."[86] In this process, "The rules, policies, and discourses regarding . . . representation engage in the labor of controlling and disciplining (i.e., commodifying) Black male bodies" in the image of whiteness "for the purpose of sale."[87] Following his analysis of such practices in the NBA, Leonard appropriately asks: "Wasn't slavery driven by both financial greed and White supremacy?"[88] We must ask, then, based on our findings herein, what are the social implications of 21st-century white middle-class consumers placing such a uniquely high value on "good" blacks?

Notes

1. Margaret L. Hunter, *Race, Gender, and the Politics of Skin Tone* (New York: Routledge, 2005), 112.

2. Emphasis in original. Theresa H. Pfeifer, "Deconstructing Cartesian Dualisms of Western Racialized Systems: A Study in the Colors Black and White," *Journal of Black Studies* 39 (2009): 533.

3. Joe R. Feagin, *Racist America: Roots, Current Realities, and Future Reparations* (New York: Routledge, 2000); Courtney Martin, "The Power of the 'Post-Racial Narrative,'" *American Prospect*, 2010, http://prospect.org/article/power-post-racial-narrative-0.

4. Rachel Alicia Griffin, "The Disgrace of Commodification and Shameful Convenience: A Critical Race Critique of the NBA," *Journal of Black Studies* 43 (2012): 161.

5. Jay Coakley, *Sports in Society: Issues and Controversies*, 10th ed. (New York: McGraw-Hill, 2008); Allen L. Sack, Parbudyal Singh, and Robert Thiel, "Occupational Segregation on the Playing Field: The Case of Major League Baseball," *Journal of Sport Management* 19 (2005), 300; Herbert D. Simons, "Race and Penalized Sports Behaviors," *International Review for the Sociology of Sport* 38 (2003), 5–22; David L. Andrews and Ron L. Mower, "Spectres of Jordan," *Ethnic and Racial Studies* 35 (2012), 1059–1077; Kevin Hylton, *"Race" and Sport: Critical Race Theory* (London: Routledge, 2009); Jonathan Markovitz, "Anatomy of a Spectacle: Race, Gender, and Memory in the Kobe Bryant Rape Case," *Sociology of Sport Journal* 23 (2006), 396–418.

6. Katherine L. Lavelle, "A Critical Discourse Analysis of Black Masculinity in NBA Game Commentary," *Howard Journal of Communications* 21 (2010): 297.

7. Richard E. Lapchick, *2011 Racial and Gender Report Card* (Orlando: University of Central Florida, 2011).

8. Lavelle, "Critical Discourse Analysis"; Glyn Hughes, "Managing Black Guys: Representation, Corporate Culture, and the NBA," *Sociology of Sport Journal* 21 (2004): 163.

9. Andrews and Mower, "Spectres of Jordan," 1059–1077; Griffin, "The Disgrace of Commodification"; David J. Leonard, "The Real Color of Money: Controlling Black Bodies in the NBA," *Journal of Sport & Social Issues* 30 (2006), 158–179.

10. Leah Dilworth, "Introduction," in *Acts of Possession: Collecting in America*, ed. Leah Dilworth (New Brunswick, NJ: Rutgers University Press, 2003), 6.

11. Clark Nardinelli and Curtis Simon, "Customer Racial Discrimination in the Market for Memorabilia: The Case of Baseball," *Quarterly Journal of Economics* 105 (1990), 575–595.

12. Torben Andersen and Sumner J. La Croix, "Customer Racial Discrimination in Major League Baseball," *Economic Inquiry* 29 (1991); Rodney Fort and Andrew Gill, "Race and Ethnicity Assessment in Baseball Card Markets," *Journal of Sports Economics* 1 (2000); Paul E. Gabriel, Curtis D. Johnson, and Timothy J. Stanton, "Customer Racial Discrimination for Baseball Memorabilia," *Applied Economics* 31 (1999); Eric Primm, Robert M. Regoli, and John D. Hewitt, "Does Membership Have Its Rewards? The Effects of Race and Hall of Fame Membership on Football Card Values," *Sociological Spectrum* 26 (2006); Philip Broyles and Bradley Keen, "Consumer Discrimination in the NBA Trading-Card Market," *Sport Journal* 8, no. 1 (2005), http://www.thesportjournal.org/article/consumer-discrimination -nba-trading-card-market; Joseph McGarrity, Harvey D. Palmer, and Marc Poitras, "Consumer Racial Discrimination: A Reassessment of the Market for Baseball Cards," *Journal of Labor Research* 20 (1999); Eric Primm et al., "The Role of Race in Football Card Prices," *Social Science Quarterly* 91 (2010): 129–142.

13. Eric W. Stone and Ronald S. Warren Jr., "Customer Discrimination in Professional Basketball: Evidence from the Trading-Card Market," *Applied Economics* 31 (1999).

14. Broyles and Keen, "Consumer Discrimination . . . Trading-Card Market"; Philip Broyles and Bradley Keen, "Consumer Discrimination in the NBA: An Examination of the Effect of Race on the Value of Basketball Trading Cards," *Social Science Journal* 47 (2010); Philip Broyles and Bradley Keen, "Consumer Discrimination in the NBA Revisited," *Social Science Journal* 47 (2010).

15. Emphasis in original. Primm, Regoli, and Hewitt, "Does Membership Have Its Rewards," 372; Robert M. Regoli, Wade P. Smith, and Eric Primm, "A Comment on Consumer Discrimination of Basketball Card Collectors," *Social Science Journal* 47 (2010).

16. Stone and Warren, "Customer Discrimination in Professional Basketball" (examined cards produced for the 1976–1977 season); Broyles and Keen, "Consumer Discrimination . . . Trading-Card Market" (examined the 1991–1992 Fleer card set); Broyles and Keen, "Consumer Discrimination Effect of Race"; Broyles and Keen."(examined the 1991–1992 Fleer card set); Consumer Discrimination Revisited." (examined the 1991–1992 Fleer card set).

17. Philip Broyles and Bradley Keen, "Consumer Discrimination in the NBA Trading-Card Market." *Sport Journal* 8, no. 1 (2005), 166.

18. Robert M. Regoli, Wade P. Smith, and Eric Primm. "A Comment on Consumer Discrimination of Basketball Card Collectors." *Social Science Journal* 47 (2010): 875–880, 877.

19. Wade P. Smith et al., "Does Race Matter? Assessing Consumer Discrimination in the Secondary Basketball Card Market," *Social Science Journal* 49 (2012).

20. Ibid.

21. Ibid., 80.

22. "Guidelines for Nomination and Election into the Naismith Memorial Basketball Hall of Fame," Naismith Memorial Basketball Hall of Fame, accessed March 2010, http://www.hoophall.com/enshrinement-process/.

23. Sarah Banet-Weiser, "Hoop Dreams: Professional Basketball and the Politics of Race and Gender," *Journal of Sport and Social Issues* 23 (1999); Phillip Lamarr Cunningham, " 'Please Don't Fine Me Again!!!!!' Black Athlete Defiance in the NBA and NFL," *Journal of Sport and Social Issues* 33 (2009); Hughes, "Managing Black Guys"; Simons, "Race and Penalized Sports Behaviors."

24. Wade P. Smith, Eric Primm, Nicole Leeper Piquero, Alex R. Piquero, and Robert M. Regoli, "Does Race Matter? Assessing Consumer Discrimination in the Secondary Basketball Card Market," *Social Science Journal* 49 (2012): 72–82.

25. Emphasis in original. Claire Alexander and Caroline Knowles, eds., *Making Race Matter: Bodies, Space and Identity* (New York: Palgrave Macmillan, 2005), 1; Smith et al., "Does Race Matter?"

26. Cunningham, " 'Please Don't Fine Me Again!!!!!' " 39–58, 39.

27. Banet-Weiser, "Hoop Dreams," 403–420.

28. Jennifer L. Eberhardt, Phillip Atiba Goff, Valerie J. Purdie, and Paul G. Davies, "Seeing Black: Race, Crime, and Visual Processing," *Journal of Personality and Social Psychology* 87 (2004).

29. Wade P. Smith, Eric Primm, Nicole Leeper Piquero, Alex R. Piquero, and Robert M. Regoli, "Does Race Matter? Assessing Consumer Discrimination in the Secondary Basketball Card Market," *Social Science Journal* 49 (2012): 72–82.

30. Johnson Gabriel and Stanton, "Customer Racial Discrimination"; Edward M. Scahill, "A Reinvestigation of Racial Discrimination and Baseball Cards," *Eastern Economic Journal* 31 (2005).

31. Edward M. Scahill, "A Reinvestigation of Racial Discrimination and Baseball Cards," *Eastern Economic Journal* 31 (2005): 537–550.

32. Wade P. Smith, Eric Primm, Nicole Leeper Piquero, Alex R. Piquero, and Robert M. Regoli, "Does Race Matter? Assessing Consumer Discrimination in the Secondary Basketball Card Market," *Social Science Journal* 49 (2012): 72–82.

33. Ibid.; Ken Shouler et al., eds., *Total Basketball: The Ultimate Basketball Encyclopedia* (Wilmington, DE: Sport Media Publishing, Inc., 2003).

34. Mike Bonner, *Collecting Basketball Cards: A Complete Guide with Prices* (San Jose, CA: toExcel Press, 1999).

35. For a more detailed description of the data, see Smith et al., "Does Race Matter?"

36. David L. Andrews and Ron L. Mower, "Spectres of Jordan," *Ethnic and Racial Studies* 35 (2012): 1059–1077; Sarah Banet-Weiser, "Hoop Dreams: Professional Basketball and the Politics of Race and Gender," *Journal of Sport and Social Issues* 23 (1999): 403–420; Phillip Lamarr Cunningham, " 'Please Don't Fine Me Again!!!!!' Black Athlete Defiance in the NBA and NFL," *Journal of Sport and Social Issues* 33 (2009): 39–58; Rachel Alicia Griffin, "The Disgrace of Commodification and Shameful Convenience: A Critical Race Critique of the NBA," *Journal of Black Studies* 43 (2012): 161–185; David J. Leonard, "The Real Color of Money: Controlling Black Bodies in the NBA," *Journal of Sport & Social Issues* 30 (2006): 158–179.

37. Wade P. Smith, Eric Primm, Nicole Leeper Piquero, Alex R. Piquero, and Robert M. Regoli, "Does Race Matter? Assessing Consumer Discrimination in the Secondary Basketball Card Market." *Social Science Journal* 49 (2012): 72–82.

38. Philip Broyles and Bradley Keen, "Consumer Discrimination in the NBA Trading-Card Market," *Sport Journal* 8, no. 1 (2005), 165.

39. Wade P. Smith, Eric Primm, Nicole Leeper Piquero, Alex R. Piquero, and Robert M. Regoli, "Does Race Matter? Assessing Consumer Discrimination in the Secondary Basketball Card Market." *Social Science Journal* 49 (2012): 72–82.

40. Ibid. (For a more detailed description of the data and data collection process.)

41. Beckett Media, "How We Price," Accessed March 22, 2011. http://www.beckett.com/estore/helpsys/viewarticle.aspx?ArticleId=319; Clark Nardinelli and Curtis Simon, "Customer Racial Discrimination in the Market for Memorabilia: The Case of Baseball," *Quarterly Journal of Economics* 105 (1990): 575–595, 578.

42. "BLS Inflation Calculator," U.S. Department of Labor, Bureau of Labor Statistics, accessed March 15, 2013, http://www.bls.gov/cpi/cpicalc.htm.

43. Eric Primm, Nicole Leeper Piquero, Robert M. Regoli, and Alex R. Piquero, "The Role of Race in Football Card Prices," *Social Science Quarterly* 91 (2010): 129–142.

44. Ken Shouler, Bob Ryan, Sam Smith, Leonard Koppett, and Bob Bellotti, eds., *Total Basketball: The Ultimate Basketball Encyclopedia* (Wilmington, DE: Sport Media Publishing, Inc., 2003).

45. Ibid. (For a detailed description of this statistic.)

46. Philip Broyles and Bradley Keen, "Consumer Discrimination in the NBA Trading-Card Market," *Sport Journal* 8, no. 1 (2005).

47. Wade P. Smith, Eric Primm, Nicole Leeper Piquero, Alex R. Piquero, and Robert M. Regoli, "Does Race Matter? Assessing Consumer Discrimination in the Secondary Basketball Card Market," *Social Science Journal* 49 (2012): 72–82.

48. Ibid.

49. Ibid.

50. Ibid.

51. David L. Andrews and Ron L. Mower, "Spectres of Jordan," *Ethnic and Racial Studies* 35 (2012): 1059–1077; Rachel Alicia Griffin, "The Disgrace of Commodification and Shameful Convenience: A Critical Race Critique of the NBA," *Journal of Black Studies* 43 (2012): 161–185; Glyn Hughes, "Managing Black Guys: Representation, Corporate Culture, and the NBA," *Sociology of Sport Journal* 21 (2004): 163–184; Katherine L. Lavelle, "A Critical Discourse Analysis of Black Masculinity in NBA Game Commentary," *Howard Journal of Communications* 21 (2010): 294–314; David J. Leonard, "The Real Color of Money: Controlling Black Bodies in the NBA," *Journal of Sport & Social Issues* 30 (2006): 158–179; Maharaj, Gitanjali, "Talking Trash: Late Capitalism, Black (Re)productivity, and Professional Basketball," *Social Text* 15 (1997): 97–110.

52. Jeffrey Lane, *Under the Boards: The Cultural Revolution in Basketball* (Lincoln: University of Nebraska Press, 2007), 45.

53. John Bloom, *A House of Cards: Baseball Card Collecting and Popular Culture* (Minneapolis: University of Minnesota Press, 1997); Gitanjali Maharaj, "Talking Trash: Late Capitalism, Black (Re)productivity, and Professional Basketball," *Social Text* 15 (1997): 97–110.

54. Reuben A. Buford May, "The Good and Bad of It All: Professional Black Male Basketball Players as Role Models for Young Black Male Basketball Players," *Sociology of Sport Journal* 26 (2009), 444.

55. May, "Good and Bad"; Becky Pettit, and Bruce Western, "Mass Imprisonment and the Life Course: Race and Class Inequality in U.S. Incarceration," *American Sociological Review* 69 (2004).

56. As cited in Maharaj, "Talking Trash," 101.

57. As cited in Ibid.

58. Jennifer L. Eberhardt, Phillip Atiba Goff, Valerie J. Purdie, and Paul G. Davies, "Seeing Black: Race, Crime, and Visual Processing," *Journal of Personality and Social Psychology* 87 (2004): 876–893.

59. To illustrate the persistent nature of this stereotypical perception, see Roger L. Williams and Zakhour I. Youssef, "Division of Labor in College Football along Racial Lines," *International Journal of Sport Psychology* 6 (1975); Lettie Gonzalez, E. Newton Jackson, and Robert M. Regoli, "The Transmission of Racist Ideology in Sport: Using Photo-Elicitation to Gauge Success in Professional Baseball," *Journal of African American Studies* 10, no. 3 (2006).

60. Emphasis added. As cited in Maharaj, "Talking Trash," 101.

61. Ibid., 102.

62. Reuben A. Buford May, "The Good and Bad of It All: Professional Black Male Basketball Players as Role Models for Young Black Male Basketball Players," *Sociology of Sport Journal* 26 (2009): 443–461.

63. Katherine L. Lavelle, "A Critical Discourse Analysis of Black Masculinity in NBA Game Commentary," *Howard Journal of Communications* 21 (2010): 294–314.

64. David L. Andrews and Ron L. Mower, "Spectres of Jordan," *Ethnic and Racial Studies* 35 (2012): 1059–1077.

65. Mary G. McDonald, "Michael Jordan's Family Values: Marketing, Meaning, and Post-Reagan America," *Sociology of Sport Journal* 13 (1996), 345.

66. Douglas Kellner, "Sports, Media Culture, and Race: Some Reflections on Michael Jordan," *Sociology of Sport Journal* 13 (1996).

67. Ibid., 462.

68. Ibid., 461.

69. David L. Andrews, and Ron L. Mower, "Spectres of Jordan," *Ethnic and Racial Studies* 35 (2012): 1059–1077.

70. Ibid., 1063.

71. Gitanjali Maharaj, "Talking Trash: Late Capitalism, Black (Re)productivity, and Professional Basketball," *Social Text* 15 (1997): 97–110.

72. Wade P. Smith, Eric Primm, Nicole Leeper Piquero, Alex R. Piquero, and Robert M. Regoli, "Does Race Matter? Assessing Consumer Discrimination in the Secondary Basketball Card Market," *Social Science Journal* 49 (2012): 72–82.

73. Todd Boyd, "Preface: Anatomy of a Murder; O.J. and the Imperative of Sports in Cultural Studies," in *Out of Bounds: Sports, Media, and the Politics of Identity*, eds. A. Baker and T. Boyd (Bloomington: Indiana University Press, 1997a), viii.

74. Kevin Hylton, *"Race" and Sport: Critical Race Theory* (London: Routledge, 2009); Sarah Banet-Weiser, "Hoop Dreams: Professional Basketball and the Politics of Race and Gender," *Journal of Sport and Social Issues* 23 (1999): 403–420, 407.

75. Todd Boyd, "The Day the Niggaz Took Over: Basketball, Commodity Culture, and Black Masculinity," in *Out of Bounds: Sports, Media, and the Politics of Identity*, eds. A. Baker and T. Boyd (Bloomington: Indiana University Press, 1997), 140.

76. David L. Andrews and Ron L. Mower, "Spectres of Jordan," *Ethnic and Racial Studies* 35 (2012): 1059–1077.

77. Ibid.; Katherine L. Lavelle, "A Critical Discourse Analysis of Black Masculinity in NBA Game Commentary," *Howard Journal of Communications* 21 (2010): 294–314, 295.

78. Cunningham, " 'Please Don't Fine Me Again,' " 39; Todd Boyd, *Young, Black, Rich, and Famous: The Rise of the NBA, the Hip Hop Invasion, and the Transformation of American Culture* (New York: Double Day, 2003), 4, 7.

79. David J. Leonard, "The Real Color of Money: Controlling Black Bodies in the NBA," *Journal of Sport & Social Issues* 30 (2006): 158–179, 158.

80. David L. Andrews and Ron L. Mower. "Spectres of Jordan," *Ethnic and Racial Studies* 35 (2012): 1059–1077, 1067.

81. Wade P. Smith, Eric Primm, Nicole Leeper Piquero, Alex R. Piquero, and Robert M. Regoli, "Does Race Matter? Assessing Consumer Discrimination in the Secondary Basketball Card Market," *Social Science Journal* 49 (2012): 72–82.

82. Emphasis in original. Alexander, Claire, and Caroline Knowles, eds. *Making Race Matter: Bodies, Space and Identity* (New York: Palgrave Macmillan, 2005), 2.

83. Griffin, Rachel Alicia, "The Disgrace of Commodification and Shameful Convenience: A Critical Race Critique of the NBA," *Journal of Black Studies* 43 (2012): 161–185.

84. Emphasis in original. Claire Alexander and Caroline Knowles, eds. *Making Race Matter: Bodies, Space and Identity* (New York: Palgrave Macmillan, 2005), 285.

85. Glyn Hughes, "Managing Black Guys: Representation, Corporate Culture, and the NBA," *Sociology of Sport Journal* 21 (2004): 163–184, 163.

86. As cited in Gitanjali Maharaj, "Talking Trash: Late Capitalism, Black (Re)productivity, and Professional Basketball," *Social Text* 15 (1997): 97–110, 101.

87. Rachel Alicia Griffin, "The Disgrace of Commodification and Shameful Convenience: A Critical Race Critique of the NBA," *Journal of Black Studies* 43 (2012): 161–185, 166.

88. David J. Leonard, "The Real Color of Money: Controlling Black Bodies in the NBA," *Journal of Sport & Social Issues* 30 (2006): 158–179, 167.

Bibliography

Alexander, Claire, and Caroline Knowles, eds. *Making Race Matter: Bodies, Space and Identity*. New York: Palgrave Macmillan, 2005.

Andersen, Torben, and Sumner J. La Croix. "Customer Racial Discrimination in Major League Baseball." *Economic Inquiry* 29 (1991): 665–677.

Andrews, David L., and Ron L. Mower. "Spectres of Jordan." *Ethnic and Racial Studies* 35 (2012): 1059–1077.

Banet-Weiser, Sarah. "Hoop Dreams: Professional Basketball and the Politics of Race and Gender." *Journal of Sport and Social Issues* 23 (1999): 403–420.

Beckett Media. "How We Price." Accessed March 22, 2011. http://www.beckett.com/estore/helpsys/viewarticle.aspx?ArticleId=319.

Bloom, John. *A House of Cards: Baseball Card Collecting and Popular Culture*. Minneapolis: University of Minnesota Press, 1997.

Bonner, Mike. *Collecting Basketball Cards: A Complete Guide with Prices*. San Jose, CA: toExcel Press, 1999.

Boyd, Todd. "Preface: Anatomy of a Murder; O.J. and the Imperative of Sports in Cultural Studies." In *Out of Bounds: Sports, Media, and the Politics of Identity*, edited by A. Baker and T. Boyd, vii–ix. Bloomington: Indiana University Press, 1997.

Boyd, Todd. "The Day the Niggaz Took Over: Basketball, Commodity Culture, and Black Masculinity." In *Out of Bounds: Sports, Media, and the Politics of*

Identity, edited by A. Baker and T. Boyd, 123–142. Bloomington: Indiana University Press, 1997.

Boyd, Todd. *Young, Black, Rich, and Famous: The Rise of the NBA, the Hip Hop Invasion, and the Transformation of American Culture*. New York: Double Day, 2003.

Broyles, Philip, and Bradley Keen. "Consumer Discrimination in the NBA Trading-Card Market." *Sport Journal* 8, no. 1 (2005). http://www.thesport journal.org/article/consumer-discrimination-nba-trading-card-market.

Broyles, Philip, and Bradley Keen. "Consumer Discrimination in the NBA: An Examination of the Effect of Race on the Value of Basketball Trading Cards." *Social Science Journal* 47 (2010): 162–171.

Broyles, Philip, and Bradley Keen. "Consumer Discrimination in the NBA Revisited." *Social Science Journal* 47 (2010): 881–883.

Coakley, Jay. *Sports in Society: Issues and Controversies*. 10th ed. New York: McGraw-Hill, 2008.

Cunningham, Phillip Lamarr. " 'Please Don't Fine MeAagain!!!!!' Black Athlete Defiance in the NBA and NFL." *Journal of Sport and Social Issues* 33 (2009): 39–58.

Dilworth, Leah. "Introduction." In *Acts of Possession: Collecting in America*, edited by L. Dilworth, 3–15. New Brunswick, NJ: Rutgers University Press, 2003.

Eberhardt, Jennifer L., Phillip Atiba Goff, Valerie J. Purdie, and Paul G. Davies. "Seeing Black: Race, Crime, and Visual Processing." *Journal of Personality and Social Psychology* 87 (2004): 876–893.

Feagin, Joe R. *Racist America: Roots, Current Realities, and Future Reparations*. New York: Routledge, 2000.

Fort, Rodney, and Andrew Gill. "Race and Ethnicity Assessment in Baseball Card Markets." *Journal of Sports Economics* 1 (2000): 21–38.

Gabriel, Paul E., Curtis D. Johnson, and Timothy J. Stanton. "Customer Racial Discrimination for Baseball Memorabilia." *Applied Economics* 31 (1999): 1331–1335.

Gonzalez, Lettie, E. Newton Jackson, and Robert M. Regoli. "The Transmission of Racist Ideology in Sport: Using Photo-Elicitation to Gauge Success in Professional Baseball." *Journal of African American Studies* 10, no. 3 (2006): 46–54.

Griffin, Rachel Alicia. "The Disgrace of Commodification and Shameful Convenience: A Critical Race Critique of the NBA." *Journal of Black Studies* 43 (2012): 161–185.

Hughes, Glyn. "Managing Black Guys: Representation, Corporate Culture, and the NBA." *Sociology of Sport Journal* 21 (2004): 163–184.

Hunter, Margaret L. *Race, Gender, and the Politics of Skin Tone*. New York: Routledge, 2005.

Hylton, Kevin. *"Race" and Sport: Critical Race Theory*. London: Routledge, 2009.

Kellner, Douglas. "Sports, Media Culture, and Race: Some Reflections on Michael Jordan." *Sociology of Sport Journal* 13 (1996): 458–467.

Lane, Jeffrey. *Under the Boards: The Cultural Revolution in Basketball*. Lincoln: University of Nebraska Press, 2007.

Lapchick, Richard E. *2011 Racial and Gender Report Card*. Orlando: University of Central Florida, 2011.

Lavelle, Katherine L. "A Critical Discourse Analysis of Black Masculinity in NBA Game Commentary." *Howard Journal of Communications* 21 (2010): 294–314.

Leonard, David J. "The Real Color of Money: Controlling Black Bodies in the NBA." *Journal of Sport & Social Issues* 30 (2006): 158–179.

Maharaj, Gitanjali. "Talking Trash: Late Capitalism, Black (Re)productivity, and Professional Basketball." *Social Text* 15 (1997): 97–110.

Markovitz, Jonathan. "Anatomy of a Spectacle: Race, Gender, and Memory in the Kobe Bryant Rape Case." *Sociology of Sport Journal* 23 (2006): 396–418.

Martin, Courtney. "The Power of the 'Post-Racial Narrative." *American Prospect*, 2010. http://prospect.org/article/power-post-racial-narrative-0.

May, Reuben A. Buford. "The Good and Bad of It All: Professional Black Male Basketball Players as Role Models for Young Black Male Basketball Players." *Sociology of Sport Journal* 26 (2009): 443–461.

McDonald, Mary G. "Michael Jordan's Family Values: Marketing, Meaning, and Post-Reagan America." *Sociology of Sport Journal* 13 (1996): 344–365.

McGarrity, Joseph, Harvey D. Palmer, and Marc Poitras. "Consumer Racial Discrimination: A Reassessment of the Market for Baseball Cards." *Journal of Labor Research* 20 (1999): 247–258.

Naismith Memorial Basketball Hall of Fame. "Guidelines for Nomination and Election into the Naismith Memorial Basketball Hall of Fame." Accessed March 2010. http://www.hoophall.com/enshrinement-process/.

Nardinelli, Clark, and Curtis Simon. "Customer Racial Discrimination in the Market for Memorabilia: The Case of Baseball." *Quarterly Journal of Economics* 105 (1990): 575–595.

Pettit, Becky, and Bruce Western. "Mass Imprisonment and the Life Course: Race and Class Inequality in U.S. Incarceration." *American Sociological Review* 69 (2004): 151–169.

Pfeifer, Theresa H. "Deconstructing Cartesian Dualisms of Western Racialized Systems: A Study in the Colors Black and White." *Journal of Black Studies* 39 (2009): 528–547.

Primm, Eric, Nicole Leeper Piquero, Robert M. Regoli, and Alex R. Piquero. "The Role of Race in Football Card Prices." *Social Science Quarterly* 91 (2010): 129–142.

Primm, Eric, Robert M. Regoli, and John D. Hewitt. "Does Membership Have Its Rewards? The Effects of Race and Hall of Fame Membership on Football Card Values." *Sociological Spectrum* 26 (2006): 369–385.

Regoli, Robert M., Wade P. Smith, and Eric Primm. "A Comment on Consumer Discrimination of Basketball Card Collectors." *Social Science Journal* 47 (2010): 875–880.

Sack, Allen L., Parbudyal Singh, and Robert Thiel. "Occupational Segregation on the Playing Field: The Case of Major League Baseball." *Journal of Sport Management* 19 (2005): 300–318.

Scahill, Edward M. "A Reinvestigation of Racial Discrimination and Baseball Cards." *Eastern Economic Journal* 31 (2005): 537–550.

Shouler, Ken, Bob Ryan, Sam Smith, Leonard Koppett, and Bob Bellotti, eds. *Total Basketball: The Ultimate Basketball Encyclopedia*. Wilmington, DE: Sport Media Publishing, 2003.

Simons, Herbert D. "Race and Penalized Sports Behaviors." *International Review for the Sociology of Sport* 38 (2003): 5–22.

Smith, Wade P., Eric Primm, Nicole Leeper Piquero, Alex R. Piquero, and Robert M. Regoli. "Does Race Matter? Assessing Consumer Discrimination in the Secondary Basketball Card Market." *Social Science Journal* 49 (2012): 72–82.

Stone, Eric W., and Ronald S. Warren Jr. "Customer Discrimination in Professional Basketball: Evidence from the Trading-Card Market." *Applied Economics* 31 (1999): 679–685.

U.S. Department of Labor, Bureau of Labor Statistics. "BLS Inflation Calculator." Accessed March 15, 2013. http://www.bls.gov/cpi/cpicalc.htm.

Williams, Roger L., and Zakhour I. Youssef. "Division of Labor in College Football along Racial Lines." *International Journal of Sport Psychology* 6 (1975): 3–13.

Chapter 8

Black Issues in Higher Education's Arthur Ashe Awards, 1995–2000: Invisible Men and Women (Scholars and Ballers)

C. Keith Harrison

The debate over intercollegiate athletics as a viable means for matriculation and graduation in higher and postsecondary education has a long history of public and scholarly attention.[1] Typically, descriptions of the "dumb jock" phenomenon express variables of deficient primary and secondary school preparation,[2] an overemphasis of the individual's family on sport,[3] a corrupt intercollegiate structure,[4] and low graduation rates.[5] In addition, there is the racial dynamic of the stigma of dumb jock.

For the male African-American student-athlete, the dumb jock phenomenon reveals a skewed representation of race and ethnicity in the major revenue sports of football and basketball. While there are many other intercollegiate athletics teams that field members from diverse backgrounds, heritages, and geographical locations, African-American football and basketball players are literally the most visible players in the context as athletic commodities.

In addition, student retention in higher education is a timely research issue.[6] Social scientists have only recently begun to investigate the relationships between faculty and student-athletes[7] as well as the social welfare of student-athletes.[8] These studies typically begin with a foundation of the problems and pathologies of student-athletes in higher education. Few studies, however, initiate their analyses with the theoretical paradigm of the "scholar-baller," which expresses the fusion of priorities of academics and athletics in a balance that is both valued and considered "cool."[9] A more in-depth definition will be articulated in the theory section of this chapter.

This chapter explores and empirically assesses the reality where students can be assessed as athletes and athletes as students. A situation such as this involves the efforts of individuals and groups who engage with one another and value both academic and athletic prowess. Specifically, a case study and snapshot for this investigation examines the Ashe Sports Scholars, founded formally in 1995 by *Black Issues in Higher Education*. This chapter is part of a larger study, and the type of background from which participants come, high school grade point average (GPA), type of institution, whether the participants competed at the Division I, II, or III level, and so on are not the focus of this original study of scholar-athletes. The Ashe Sports Scholar title is awarded in recognition of academic excellence to honor the memory of Arthur Ashe, the former tennis icon, activist, and graduate of the University of California at Los Angeles. The synthesis of relevant research inquiries and theoretical perspectives are illustrated throughout this chapter and focus on two basic research questions: (1) What are the profiles and characteristics of student-athletes that excel academically? and (2) What are the theoretical and empirical findings from a "scholar-baller" data set? Part of the motivation for this study is that athletics in American higher education is a unique entity and different from most other collegiate athletic programs on college campuses. While considered amateur, major revenue is produced in sports such as football, basketball, and hockey. First, the theoretical framework that fits the general objectives and thesis of this chapter will be presented.

Theory

Howard Becker contributed to the theory of labeling in *Outsiders: Studies in the Sociology of Deviance*. A label is a definition that is externally applied to a person by an audience who creates this definition based on its perceptions of the person.[10] The process by which labels are created and applied to social actors by an audience is called the labeling process.[11] The label of "athlete" in relation to the issue of student-athlete retention is problematic because of the emphasis on athlete at the expense of student. Student-athletes are often referred to as athletes only and not recognized as much for their student status. This is perpetuated by student-athlete anti-intellectual behavior and the historical public perception of "dumb jocks" in American culture.[12] In other words, the term "athlete" has developed a meaning inferior to intellectual pursuits throughout history by the individuals who are labeled and by institutional forces such as sport, "society," and American higher education, which socialize a cultural bias toward athletics. This phenomenon is similar to Becker's study of musicians who are "conceived of as an artist who possesses a mysterious artistic gift setting him apart from all other people. Possessing the gift, he should be free from control by outsiders who lack it. The gift is something which cannot be acquired through education; the outsider, therefore, can never become a member of the group." Parallel to the plight of the musician or "artist," the inferiority of the term "athlete" also is part of the broader discourses that limit the perceptions of this particular identity. The musician and the athlete seldom receive credit for their cognitive abilities; instead, most of the attention the musician and the athlete receive pertains to the physical traits of the performers. Further complicating this "athlete" label is the term "baller," from popular music, sports, and entertainment culture.[13] The term can be a noun, adjective, or verb. The semantics of the "baller" label will be elaborated on further in the race, sport, and American higher education section. The "baller" label is highly promoted at the "amateur" level of intercollegiate athletics in terms of popularity on campus and recognition nationwide. This includes the selling of student-athletes' jerseys, television and radio exposure, and possible opportunities for playing professionally.

There are consequences of labels being applied. When someone is labeled and identified as "deviant" by an external audience, it may lead to negative reactions that may affect the emotional state of the alleged deviant and may intensify behaviors and activities of the labeled individual. In effect, the labeled become the label itself (i.e., athlete versus student, baller versus scholar-baller).

Labels are subjectively applied, and individuals may be inappropriately labeled even in the absence of guilt (scholar-ballers, academically invested student-athletes). Who individuals are can influence how they are labeled as much as what they do. An example would be the status on campus as a high-profile athlete or baller. In the labeling process, characteristics of the offender are more important than characteristics of the act.[14] If this is true, then the orientation for many student-athletes in college sports may hinder their academic performance. Examples include the recruiting of gifted athletes who gain social acceptance due to athletic status and television or other mass media coverage of their athletic identities.[15]

Age, race, sex, and social class are also important factors influencing the outcomes of labeling.[16] Later, this chapter examines related variables such as sport, college major, gender, and class rank to determine how they impact student-athletes' grade point averages. The environment of this labeled population will be examined throughout the following synthesis of relevant literature and critique of African-American student-athletes in higher education. This focus is on the estimation of over two-thirds of the sample being comprised of African-American student-athletes.[17]

Race, Labels, and Sport in American Higher Education

The Ashe Sports Scholars Program comprises student-athletes of color; therefore, I will briefly review the literature and scholarship on race and sport as it relates to African-American student-athletes. The focus of this synthesis is on African Americans because the research literature on intercollegiate athletics and education is channeled toward this pattern. In a so-called race-neutral and color-blind society, it is noteworthy that former college president, professor, and student-athlete James Duderstadt revealed the following insights about race, in particular its relation to the "level playing field of sport":

> One of the most sensitive issues in intercollegiate athletics concerns race. Basketball and increasingly football are dominated by talented black athletes, whose representation in these sports programs far exceeds their *presence* elsewhere in the university. To be sure, sports provide many minority students with opportunities to attend and benefit from a college education.

Because of social stratification and campus isolation, there is little social and intimate contact between African Americans and whites on a legitimate level versus a superficial/artificial bias.[18] Underlying this issue is a conservative agenda and dialogue for dealing with racism in general,[19] a legacy of segregation in the U.S. educational system,[20] and an intercollegiate and professional athletic structure that channels African-American males to revenue sports with little regard for their academic and intellectual development beyond eligibility.[21]

Isssues related to retention, matriculation, and career transition with African-American student-athletes (especially males) are complex.[22] Based upon a related study, which involved two examples of real-life experiences, one positive career transition and one negative, of African Americans who were on athletic scholarships in higher education, the following conclusion was reached:

> Unfortunately, we do not know which ending is most typical of the athletic experience of the African American athlete. Does participation in college athletics provide African American student-athletes with the opportunity for an education, or does it exploit their physical skills without providing fair compensation?[23]

While Sellers's research analyses articulate the dangers of making generalizations without traditional empirical evidence, I want to argue a different point of view based on another contribution of Sellers.

Prior to entering a university and during higher education, socialization structural mechanisms in society and sport hinder the academic achievement of student-athletes, especially those of color or individuals and groups with limited resources.[24] The researchers examine the data, controlling for a number of variables. The findings are consistent with prior research which found that male African-American student-athletes involved in revenue sports tend to be less prepared prior to college entry, come from lower-income families than the average college student at a predominantly white campus, and are clustered in academic majors that are less time consuming and demanding than other disciplines.[25] This implies that the ideology of big-time collegiate sports is based on surplus for athletic production versus demand for academic excellence.[26]

A more pertinent challenge is to question how race gets "coded" in revenue sports and perpetuated by both educational and athletic systems as well as the agents of change in these institutions. From the time revenue participants are recruited, they are branded the "big men" on campus.[27] Not all are inferior academically, there are structural inequities that do not yield or produce intellectual capital, offer few academic resources, and have minimal academic expectations.[28] Race, sport, and American higher education have systemic pre- and postsocialization problems, but many of the issues are institutionally biased and discriminatory against any athletic participant.

Skewed Priorities: Getting What We Market, Socialize and Value?

Student-athletes are frequently excused from classes and lectures based on athletic responsibilities. In revenue-generating sports such as men's football, basketball, hockey, and baseball, and increasingly women's volleyball, basketball, and softball, an enormous amount of on-campus and classroom time is missed. Student-athletes also receive social praise and acceptance based on their performance on the fields.

Athletically, student-athletes are visualized as superior beings and are admired and envied by the public and campus at large.[29] Bowl games during the holidays offer student-athletes per diem money, cars, and cell phones so that they can enjoy themselves. Families, boosters, fans, and students plan holiday trips to support their athletic team and organization. Clearly, the structural focus is on winning and the production of athleticism.[30]

The question then becomes, who are these dedicated student-athletes such as Ashe Sports Scholars, and what are the characteristics that are attached to their individual and group identities that lead to academic success? What follows is an investigation and interpretation of who these student-athletes are and what characteristics constitute their academic profiles.

Methodology and Research Design

Analytical Strategies

First, to answer some of the research questions empirically, a quantitative component was incorporated to assess the magnitude of student-athlete characteristics and the relationship of those characteristics to GPA. Second, while not the focus in this traditional empirical design, qualitative data aspects are part of each Arthur Ashe Sports Scholar Award in terms of quotations from the top academic performers and winners. Qualitative analysis involves an immersion in the details, and specifics of the data are also presented. Qualitative analysis involves an immersion in the details and specifics of the data to discover important categories, dimensions, and interrelationships. Such an exploration begins by asking genuinely open questions rather than by testing theoretically derived hypotheses.[31] The standard procedure is to conduct an interview with the top male and female awardees (two total each year).

Participants.   As a "snapshot," I examined the Arthur Ashe Sports Scholar Awards, which were founded in 1995 by *Black Issues in Higher Education*. The sample was made up of 2,174 student-athletes who received the Arthur Ashe athletic scholarship award. The sample was selected over a six-year period from 1995 to 2000, the formal existence of the Ashe Awards and celebration of his life. This selection parameter excludes only awardees from the year 2001. Descriptive data results indicate that the gender sample was equal for men and women overall. A noteworthy point on the parameters of data selection was that the researcher chose to examine only those sports that involved 50 or more participants. It is for this reason that men's football, basketball, track and cross-country, soccer, tennis, and baseball were included. For women's sports teams, basketball, volleyball, and tennis constituted subsets of the total number of student-athletes in the study published in *Black Issues of Higher Education*. In terms of school year and rank, the sample was made up of mostly seniors, followed by juniors and then sophomores. Based on the set criteria by the Ashe Sports Scholar Team, no first-year students participated in the study.

The recognition of academic excellence is a dedication to the memory of Arthur Ashe, former tennis icon, lecturer, activist, and graduate of the University of California at Los Angeles. The criteria for each award recipient includes being a person of color; a minimum 3.0 grade point average (GPA), which is a B average on a 4.0 scale; athletic participation; and community outreach initiatives. This GPA criterion is comparable to the general student body average on most U.S. campuses and well above the minimum requirement for student-athletes to participate in sports (2.0 is the required average for eligibility). Nominees are generally selected by academic advisors or faculty members from their home institutions. National flyers advertise the Ashe Sports Scholars. By some estimates there are hundreds, if not thousands, of outstanding scholar-athletes who do not receive Ashe Awards due to extreme volume, late applications, and a lack of awareness about the award.[32]

There were an equal number of males and females in the overall sample. Most of the participants were seniors, followed by juniors and then sophomores. The majority of students in the sample majored in nonscience areas. The next most popular majors were business studies majors, kinesiology students, and undecided majors. This preliminary finding questions the stereotype that student-athletes tend to be only in liberal arts or general studies degree tracks. It also questions the notion that practical laboratories for challenging science courses, which generally involve taking four or five credits, cannot be taken while one is committed to playing a varsity sport.

The mean grade point average was 3.3. Students in the original sample represented 38 different sports teams; however, this analysis included only the nine teams with the highest percentages of student-athlete participants

(N = 1427). In the men's sports, football was the highest percentage followed by basketball, track, soccer, tennis, and baseball. The women's distribution had the most students in basketball, followed by volleyball and tennis.

Data Analysis, Findings, and Results

A linear regression was run to examine the relationship between student characteristics and grade point average. The following predictor variables were entered into a regression equation: gender, academic major (science, nonscience, business, kinesiology, and undecided), sport (men's: football, basketball, track, soccer, tennis, and baseball; women's: basketball, volleyball, and tennis). Since all of the predictor variables are nominal, they were dummy-coded before entering them into the regression equation. GPA was the outcome variable (dependent variable).

Female student-athletes earned significantly higher GPAs (M = 3.5, SD = .22) than their male counterparts (M = 3.4, SD = .21), and science majors reported higher GPAs (M = 3.5, SD = .23) than any other major (M = 3.4, SD = .21). Although these GPA differences are statistically significant, one could question their practical significance. With respect to sport, the following groups received significantly higher grades, on average, than other student-athletes: women's tennis (M = 3.5, SD = .24) and men's tennis (M = 3.5, SD = .23), men's football (M = 3.5, SD = .22), and men's track (M = 3.5, SD = .21). Men's soccer players received significantly lower grades (M = 3.3, SD = .21), on average, than male players from other sports (M = 3.4, SD = .21) (The variables that did not enter into the equation are the following majors: nonscience, business, kinesiology, and undecided; sports: men's basketball and baseball, women's basketball and volleyball).

An examination of the beta coefficients at the final step indicated that being a science major was positively related to grade point average and was the strongest predictor variable for a high GPA (r = .10, p < .05)[33]. The regression also indicated that playing soccer was the strongest inversely related variable to GPA (r = −.10, p < .05). In the final step of the regression, men's tennis and track demonstrated the least ability to predict GPA but still remained statistically significant (r = .05, p < .05; see Table 8.2). Using the previously mentioned variables, this model explains approximately 3 percent of the variance in grade point average. This means that 97.1 percent of the variations in grade point average can be explained with other variables such as high school grade point average and socio-economic status that were not measured.

Discussion

Approximately 3 percent of student-athletes' grade point average can be explained by the type of sport in which they participate. These results counter society's continued assumptions that relate student-athletes' GPAs to the sport that they play (e.g., soccer players get higher grades than football players). These results raise questions of why stereotypes continue to persist in public and private discourses about student-athletes in terms of their intellectual capabilities and capacities. Despite the minimal level of variance to explain GPA (3 percent), an entire culture of scholar-ballers exists that receives few external or commercial awards for its academic prowess. How are those stereotypes brought to campus? How are nonathletes informed of student-athletes' stereotypical behavior, both in the classroom and on the field? How does media ideology inform public discourse about those stereotyped in certain athletic teams? While evidence has been found that student-athletes tend to be clustered in certain majors (e.g., kinesiology, social science) these data indicate that a significant proportion of the student-athletes in this sample are science and business majors. Combined business and science majors composed over half of the sample (53.8 percent). This empirical finding questions the stereotype of dumb jock course placement and inferior academic abilities. This is an important finding when one considers the negative external perceptions of student-athletes, even while acknowledging that this sample population values its academic responsibilities.

In this sample, sports for men were mostly football, followed by basketball, track and cross-country, soccer, tennis, and baseball. Sports for women were basketball, volleyball, and tennis. Many people think of women's basketball as an African-American sport. Many people also believe African-American female basketball payers have relatively low college retention rates when compared with other women's sports. Empirical results also indicate some of the following: Gender is the most statistically significant variable. This suggests that sport is not necessarily the major barrier that hinders academic success; rather, apathetic mindsets and structural inequities may combine to cultivate inferior intellectual development for too many athletes on scholarship. Historically, the female sporting experience has not been co-opted by the lure of professional sport aspirations as in men's sports. Perhaps this is because of the glaring differences in pay, popularity, and notoriety between men's and women's sports.

It is also a myth that tennis players have high retention rates. Underclass tennis players often leave college early for the professional ranks, a situation often found in sports like baseball, hockey, and—more recently— basketball. The data in this sample indicate that playing tennis is a moderate predictor of high GPA.

The data in this sample break popular gender stereotypes of football players as hypermasculine and intellectually inferior. This has positive implications for the expectations of students who participate in athletes and struggle at the individual level to balance and athletic duties.

In terms of the quotations from the Ashe Sports Scholars top performers, the student-athlete responses summarize the demands and priorities of academic, athletic, and social life. The perspective of the scholar-baller is most important because this type of student-athlete is not rewarded at the level of ballers that receive audience praise and fan consumption based on athleticism and physical talents.

Implications and Limitations

This study has no direct control group. This does not pose methodological problems because the goal is to examine characteristics that predict GPA among student-athletes of color and how these characteristics might differ from public perception of student-athletes of color. For an indirect control group, it may be worthwhile to consider and interpret the extensive research conducted by Edwards.[34] These findings, along with other investigations,[35] illuminate that the control group to the Ashe Sports Scholars may be composed of the following underachievers in terms of academic and athletic balance:

- 65–75 percent of black athletes who are awarded athletic scholarships and may never graduate
- An estimated 75 percent of black athletes who do graduate with physical education degrees or majors that are generally held in low repute

The focus of this study was not too high in external validity. That is, I was not trying to generalize the results to the entire population. Furthermore, affiliations with Division I, II, III, and other sport ranking systems were not distinguished. Finally, it was not determined how many student-athletes were on partial athletic scholarship, received financial aid, or were walk-ons (players that are not highly recruited and offered an athletic scholarship).

With these limitations articulated, these data suggest that a highly intellectual and athletically talented group of people are excelling in a culture where "winning is everything." Student-athletes are systematically rewarded in extrinsic ways, whereas academics are intrinsically rewarded, without systematic and glamorous recognition from external sources. In other words, these conceptualizations of intrinsic and extrinsic rewards are often misleading. For example, academicians/scholars are extrinsically rewarded later in their careers, and many believe they will get this reward if they work hard, that is, if they personally invest in deferred rewards. The empirical analysis of relevant variables suggests the potential for this study as a conduit for examining other scholar-athlete populations at any level of participation. Based on a dedication to academics and athletics, the scholar-athlete culture in this study may believe it will be rewarded in the future for its long-term investments in various educational opportunities.

These data also warrant critical re-evaluation of typical perceptions and beliefs about student-athletes, with particular attention to those who play high-revenue sports such as football and basketball. Instead of further investigations that discuss whether student-athletes fit into typical deviant profiles of low academic achievement, it would be more valuable to examine policies, structural strengths, and weaknesses that enhance the academic experiences of students on athletic teams. The stereotypes of African-American participants and other groups of color as student-athletes should also be rethought, re-examined, and reanalyzed in the context of this selected and counterstereotypical group.

Conclusions and Recommendations

Deviancy Labels and College Athletics

The tenets of social deviancy and basic labeling theory can be used to expose the complexity of identity construction of the participants in college athletics. The major issue based on the deviancy literature[36] illustrates the structural and cultural context that simultaneously disempowers student-athletes through systematic labels and stigmas that are removed from intellectualism. As mentioned earlier, this process further exploits their athletic prowess for profit. This duality specifically fits Becker's synthesis of the term "outsiders," which Becker refers to as a double-barreled term. The duality of academic and athletic identities is comparable to outsiders like the musician and the dancer who also face the construct of square (academics) and artist (athlete).

Future research needs to replicate this study and expand the study of the variables of ethnicity and social class. While this particular data set is based on all student-athletes of color, future studies should be explicitly analyzed and qualified in terms of quantifying how many African Americans, Asians Americans, Latino/as Americans, Pacific Islanders, Native Americans, and others are in each selected sport. Qualitative inquiry would also provide richness to the individual stories from each of the awardees. These stories will enable researchers and practitioners to build on their experiences in an informative and effective way for healthy student development and positive career transition after exiting from the sport.

Using both qualitative and quantitative methods would also bring researchers closer to the experiences and navigation of the identity of a scholar and a baller. Social scientists also need a more empirical, systematic way of chronicling student-athletes who perform well in the classroom and on the field and who gravitate to occupations that do not require physical activity as the basis for employment. This would include those who persist to graduation into professional academic programs while still maintaining athletic eligibility. Chronicling their academic majors and future aspirations once again allows scholars and administrators of athletic programs to build on the knowledge base of this paradigm of academic and athletic balance. One structure and system of athletics in higher education that may be worth examining is also in North America. This would be Canada, which has competitive athletics but is truly amateur. Student-athletes are not awarded full athletic scholarships and are admitted to university based on their academic prowess.

In the broader society, capitalism, commercialism, and commodity culture can be exploited as a vehicle to create a new label. The term "scholar-baller" was coined to appeal to the masses of student-athletes that consume popular culture terms such as "baller" and "ballplayer" in hopes that the term will ignite interest in the concept and lead to research focusing on the student and that athlete.[37] It is significant to have a group of student-athletes dedicated to educational pursuits, considering the economic and visual realities of gate receipts, commercial advertising, and athletic victories. This researcher hopes that when discourse and scholarly investigation of the modern student-athlete occurs, perceptions include discussion of individuals like the Ashe Sport Scholars. These data are important element of inclusion when academic and athletic myths are constructed through public discourse. Student affairs professionals can benefit from the current study in several ways. First, Ashe Sports Scholars inform negative assumptions about student-athletes in higher education. Second, leaders in student affairs can use data from the Ashe Sports Scholars to promote and praise the *academic* side of those involved in athletics. This can be executed visually with the promotion of class valedictorians and other scholarly performers.

Notes

1. Sperber, M. (2000). *Beer and circus: How big-time college sports is crippling undergraduate education.* New York. Henry Holt and Company; Zimbalist, A. (1999). *Unpaid professionals: Commercialism and conflict in big-time college sports.* Princeton, NJ: Princeton University Press.

2. Sellers, Robert M. (2000). *Racism in College Athletics: African American student-athletes; Opportunity or exploitation?* edited by Dana Brooks, Ronald Althouse. Morgantown, WV: Fitness Information Technology.

3. Lapchick, Richard. (1991). *Five Minutes to Midnight.* New York: Madison Books,

4. Sack, A., & Ellen Staurowsky. (1998). *College athletics for hire: The Evolution and legacy of the NCAA's amateur myth.* Westport, CT: Praeger.

5. Anderson, A., & South, D. (2000). Racial differences in collegiate recruitment, retention, and graduation. In D. Brooks and R. Althouse (eds.), *Racism in college athletics: The African American Athlete's Experience*, 155–169.

6. Astin, A. (1984). Student involvement: A developmental theory for higher education. *Journal of College Student Personnel*, 25, 297–308; Astin, A. (1985). *Achieving educational excellence.* San Francisco: Jossey-Bass; Astin, A. (1993). *What matters in college?* New York: Jossey-Bass.

7. Allen, C. (1995). The relationship between athletic identity, peer and faculty socialization, and college student development. *Journal of College Student Development*, 36, 560–573; Baucom, C., & Lantz, C. (2001). Faculty attitudes toward male Division II student-athletes. *Journal of Sport Behavior* 24(3), 265–276; Coakley, J. (2000). *Sport in society.* Boston: McGraw Hill. Comeaux, E., & Harrison, C.K. (2001). Faculty (research one) and student-athlete (revenue sports) interactions: An organizational priority collision? Paper presented at the North American Society for the Sociology of Sport Annual Meeting in San Antonio, TX; Engstrom, C., Sedlacek, W., & McEwen, M. (1995). Faculty attitudes toward male revenue and nonrevenue student-athletes. *Journal of College Student Development* 36, 217–227; Suggs, W. (1999). Faculty study at Amherst questions academic qualifications of some athletes. *Chronicle of Higher Education* 46(13), A68.

8. Harrison, C. K. (2000a). Black athletes at the millennium. *Society* 27, 35–39; Sellers, Robert M. (1997). Goal discrepancy in African American male student-athletes' unrealistic expectations for careers in professional sports. *Journal of Black Psychology* 23(1), 6–23. Sellers, R., & Chavous, T. (1997). The African American student athlete: Motivation versus structure. *African American Research Perspectives* 3(1), 12–20.

9. Harrison, C.K., Holmes, S., & Moore, D. (2000). The effects of media ads on intercollegiate student-athletes: Exposure to athletic and professional occupational imagery. Paper presented at the North American Society for the Sociology of Sport Annual Meeting in Colorado Springs, CO.

10. Becker, Howard. (1963). *Outsiders: Studies in sociology and deviance.* New York: Free Press.

11. Goffman, Erving. (1959). *The presentation of self in everyday life.* New York: Anchor Books DoubleDay.

12. Sailes, G. (1993). An investigation of campus stereotypes: The myth of black athletic superiority and the dumb jock stereotype. *Sociology of Sport Journal* 10, 88–97.

13. Comeaux, E., & Harrison, C.K. (2004). *Labels of African-American ballers: A historical and contemporary investigation of African-American male youth's depletion from America's favorite pastime, 1885–2000.*

14. Becker, Howard. (1963). *Outsiders: Studies in Sociology and Deviance.* New York: Free Press. Goffman, Erving. (1959). *The Presentation of Self in Everyday Life.* New York: Anchor Books DoubleDay.

15. Sperber, M. (1990). *College sports Inc. The athletic department vs. The university.* New York. Henry Holt and Company.

16. Becker, 1963; Goffman, 1959

17. Matthews, F. (1999). Personal communication and interview; Roach, R. (2002). Personal communication and interview.

18. Allport, G. (1954). *The nature of prejudice.* Reading: MA: Basic Books. Chang, M. (2000). Improving campus racial dynamics: A balancing act among competing interests. *Review of Higher Education* 23(2), 153–175; Chang, M. (2001). Is it more than about getting along? The broader educational relevance of reducing students' racial biases. *Journal of College Student Development* 42(2), 93–105.

19. King, R.C., & Springwood, C.F. (2001). *Beyond the cheers: Race as a spectacle in college sport in college sport.* New York: State University of New York Press.

20. Edwards, H. (1996). The black athlete on the traditionally white college campus: Issues of access and diversity. Keynote address and paper presented at the Different perspectives on majority rules: Students and faculty of color in predominately white institutions inaugural conference at the University of Nebraska, Lincoln.

21. King & Springwood, 2001.

22. Sellers, 2000.

23. Sellers, 2000, p. 135.

24. Sellers and Chavous, 1997.

25. Purdy, Eitzen, and Hufnagel, 1982.

26. Edwards, 1996.

27. Howard, C. (1997). Big man on campus: Black man on campus, black athletes today. Unpublished paper; Morris, W. (1992). *The courting of Marcus Dupree*. Jackson: University Press of Mississippi; Sparks, D. (1999). *Lessons of the game: The betrayal of an All-American football star*. Los Angeles: Game Time.

28. Sellers, 1991, 1992 and 1997.

29. Coakley, J. (2000). *Sport in society*. Boston: McGraw Hill.

30. Bristol-Myers, L. (2000). *Collegiate athletic reform movements: Past and present* (Discussant). Paper presented at the North American Society for the Sociology of Sport Annual Meeting in Colorado Spring, CO; Sack, A. (2000). Attacking the NCAA where it hurts: The case of the Center for the Athletes rights and education. Paper presented at the North American Society for the Sociology of Sport; Sperber, M. (1990). *College sports Inc.: The athletic department vs. the university*. New York. Henry Holt and Company.

31. Patton, M.Q. (1990). *Qualitative evaluation and research methods*. New born Park, CA: Sage Publications, p. 40.

32. Matthews, 1999.

33. Harrison C. K., Holmes S. and Moore, D. (2000). The effects of media ads on intercollegiate student-athletes. Paper presented at the North American Society for Sociology of Sport Annual Meeting. Colorado Springs, Colorado.

34. Lapchick, Richard. (1991). *Five minutes to midnight*. New York: Madison Books.

35. Sellers, R.M., Kupermine, G.P., & Waddell, A.S. (1991, Fall). Life experiences of African American student-athletes in revenue producing sports: A descriptive empirical analysis. *Academic Athletic Journal*, 21–38; Sellers, R.M. (1992). Racial differences in the predictors for academic achievement of student-athletes in Division I revenue producing sports. *Sociology of Sport Journal* 9(1), 48–60; Sellers, Robert M. (1997). Goal discrepancy in African American male student-athletes' unrealistic expectations for careers in professional sports. *Journal of Black Psychology* 23(1), 6–23; Sellers, R., & Chavous, T. (1997). The African American student athlete: Motivation versus structure. *African American Research Perspectives* 3(1), 12–20.

36. Becker, 1963; Goffman, 1959.

37. Comeaux, E., & Harrison, C.K. (2004). *Labels of African-American Ballers: A historical and contemporary investigation of African-American male youth's depletion from America's favorite pastime, 1885–2000*.

Bibliography

Adler, P. and Adler, O. (1991). *Backboards and blackboards: College athletics and role engulfment*. New York: Columbia University Press.

Allen, C. (1995). The relationship between athletic identity, peer and faculty socialization, and college student development. *Journal of College Student Development* 36, 560–73.

Allport, G. (1954). *The nature of prejudice.* Reading, MA: Basic Books.

Anderson, A., & South, D. (2000). Racial differences in collegiate recruitment, retention, and graduation. In D. Brooks and R. Althouse (eds.), *Racism in college athletics: The African American Athlete's Experience,* West Virginia: Fitness Information Technology, 155–169.

Astin, A. (1984). Student involvement: A developmental theory for higher education. *Journal of College Student Personnel* 25, 297–308.

Astin, A. (1985). *Achieving educational excellence.* San Francisco: Jossey-Bass.

Astin, A. (1993). *What matters in college?* New York: Jossey-Bass.

Axtell, J. (1998). *The pleasures of academe: A celebration and defense of higher education.* Lincoln: University of Nebraska Press.

Baucom, C., & Lantz, C. (2001). Faculty attitudes toward male Division II student-athletes. *Journal of Sport Behavior* 24(3), 265–276.

Bensel-Myers, L. (2000). *Collegiate athletic reform movements: Past and present* (Discussant). Paper presented at the North American Society for the Sociology of Sport Annual Meeting in Colorado Spring, CO.

Benson, K. (2000). Constructing academic inadequacy; African-American athlete's stories of schooling. *Journal of Higher Education* 71(2), 223–246.

Blockston, C. (1998). *Damn rare: The memoirs of an African-American bibliophile.* Tracy, CA: Quantum Leap.

Brewer, B., Van Raalte, J., & Linder, D. (1993). Athletic identity: Hercules muscles or Achilles heel? *International Journal of Sport Psychology* 24, 237–254.

Brown, L. (1997). *The young Robeson: On my journey now.* Boulder, CO: Westview.

Chang, M. (2000). Improving campus racial dynamics: A balancing act among competing interests. *Review of Higher Education* 23(2), 153–175.

Chang, M. (2001). It is more than about getting along? The broader educational relevance of reducing students' racial biases. *Journal of College Student Development* 42(2), 93–105.

Coakley, J. (2000). *Sport in society.* Boston: McGraw Hill.

Comeaux, E., & Harrison, C. K. (2001). Faculty (research one) and student-athlete (revenue sports) interactions: An organizational priority collision? Paper presented at the North American Society for the Sociology of Sport Annual Meeting in San Antonio, TX.

Comeaux, E., & Harrison, C. K. (2004). *Labels of African-American Ballers: A historical and contemporary investigation of African-American male youth's depletion from America's favorite pastime, 1885–2000.*

Corenelius, A. (1995). The relationship between athletic identity, peer, faculty socialization, and college student development. *Journal of College Student Development* 36(6), 560–573.

Duderstadt, J. (2000). *Intercollegiate athletics and the American university: A University president's perspective.* Ann Arbor: University of Michigan Press.

Edwards, H. (1976). Paul Robeson's meaning to the twenty-first-century gladiator. In *Paul Robeson: The great forerunner.* New York: International Publishers.

Edwards, H. (1984). The collegiate athletic arms race: Origins and implications of the "Rule 48" controversy. *Journal of Sport and Social Issues* 8, 4–22.

Edwards, H. (1989). Racism, education, and sport. Paper presented at the University of Michigan, Ann Arbor.

Edwards, H. (1996). The black athlete on the traditionally white college campus: Issues of access and diversity. Keynote address and paper presented at the Different perspectives on majority rules: Students and faculty of color in predominately white institutions inaugural conference at the University of Nebraska, Lincoln.

Engstrom, C., Sedlacek, W., & McEwen, M. (1995). Faculty attitudes toward male revenue and nonrevenue student-athletes. *Journal of College Student Development* 36, 217–27.

Gerdy, J. (1997). *The successful college athletic program.* Phoenix: American Council on Education Oryx Press.

Harrison, C. K. (1998). Themes that thread through society: Racism and athletic manifestation in the African American community. *Race Ethnicity, Education* 1(1), 63–74.

Harrison, C. K. (2000). Black athletes at the millennium. *Society* 27 35–39.

Harrison, C. K. *Paving the way: Early African-American male scholar-athletes.* Working manuscript.

Harrison, C. K., Hamilton, P., & Richardson, Q. (2001). *You're blind: The African American athlete in advertising.* [Documentary]. Ann Arbor, MI.

Harrison, C. K., Holmes, S., & Moore, D. (2000). The effects of media ads on intercollegiate student-athletes: Exposure to athletic and professional occupational imagery. Paper presented at the North American Society for the Sociology of Sport Annual Meeting in Colorado Springs, CO.

Honea, M. (1987). No pass, no play . . . a counterproductive and dysfunctional policy. *Texas Coach*, 32–34.

Howard, C. (1997). Big man on campus: Black man on campus, black athletes today. Unpublished paper.

James, C. (2001). Interview and personal communication.

Kiger, G., & Lorentzen, D. (1986). The relative effect of gender, race, and sport on university academic performance. *Sociology of Sport Journal* 3, 160–167.

King, R. C., & Springwood, C. F. (2001). *Beyond the cheers: Race as a spectacle in college sport in college sport.* New York: State University of New York Press.

Lawrence, M. (2001). The African-American athlete's experience with race: An existential-phenomenological Investigation. Paper presented at the North American Society for Sport Sociology Annual Meeting in San Antonio, TX.

Matthews, F. (1999). Personal communication and interview.

Morris. W. (1992). *The courting of Marcus Dupree*. Jackson: University Press of Mississippi.

NCAA Workgroup data set. James Jackson and associates. University of Michigan.

Patton, M. Q. (1990). *Qualitative evaluation and research methods*. Thousand Oaks, CA: Sage.

Purdy, D., Eitzen, D. S., & Hufnagel, R. (1982). Are athletes also students? The educational attainment of college athletes. *Social Problems* 29(4), 439–448.

Roach, R. (2002). Personal communication and interview.

Sack, A. (2000). Attacking the NCAA where it hurts: The case of the Center for the Athletes rights and education. Paper presented at the North American Society for the Sociology of Sport. Colorado Springs, Colorado.

Sack, A., & Ellen Staurowsky. (1998). *College athletics for hire: TheeEvolution and legacy of the NCAA's amateur myth*. Westport, CT: Praeger.

Sailes, G. (1993). An investigation of campus stereotypes: The myth of black athletic superiority and the dumb jock stereotype. *Sociology of Sport Journal* 10, 88–97.

Saunders, E. L., Gillis, S. A., & Hogrebe, M. C. (1985). Academic performance of student athletes in revenue-producing sports. *Journal of College Student Personnel 26*, 119–124.

Sellers, R., & Chavous, T. (1997). The African American student athlete. Motivation versus structure. *African American Research Perspectives* 3(1), 12–20.

Sellers, R. M. (1992). Racial differences in the predictors for academic achievement of student-athletes in Division I revenue producing sports. *Sociology of Sport Journal* 9(1), 48–60.

Sellers, R. M., Kupermine, G. P., & Waddell, A. S. (1991, Fall). Life experiences of African American student-athletes in revenue producing sports: A descriptive empirical analysis. *Academic Athletic Journal*, 21–38.

Sellers, Robert M. (1997). Goal discrepancy in African American male student-athletes' unrealistic expectations for careers in professional sports. *Journal of Black Psychology* 23(1), 6–23.

Shriberg, A., & Brodzinski, F. (2001). *Rethinking services for college athletes*. San Francisco: Jossey-Bass nc.

Shropshire, Kenneth L. (1996). *In black and white: Race and sports in America*. New York: New York University Press.

Shulman, J. L., & Bowen, W. G. (2001). *The game of life: College sports and educational values*. Princeton, NJ and Oxford: Princeton University Press.

Sowa, C., & Gressard, C. (1983). Athletic participation: Its relationship to student development. *Journal of College Student Development* 22, 236–239.

Sparks, D. (1999). *Lessons of the game: The betrayal of an All-American football star*. Los Angeles: Game Time.

Sperber, M. (1990). *College Sports Inc.: The athletic department vs. the university.* New York: Henry Holt and Company.

Sperber, M. (2000). *Beer and circus: How big-time college sports is crippling undergraduate education.* New York. Henry Holt and Company.

Staurowsky, E. (2000). Faculty and their role in college athletic reform. Paper presented at the North American Society for the Sociology of Sport. Colorado Springs, Colorado.

Stone, J. (2000). Stereotype threat effects on the performance of black and white athletes. Paper presented at the North American Society for the Sociology of Sport Annual Meeting in Colorado Springs, CO.

Suggs, W. (1999). Faculty study at Amherst questions academic qualifications of some athletes. *Chronicle of Higher Education* (46)13, A68.

Thelin, J. (1994). *Games colleges play: Scandal and reform in the intercollegiate athletics.* Baltimore: Johns Hopkins University Press.

Thelin, J. R., & L. L. Wiseman. (1989). *The old college try: Balancing athletics and academics in higher education*, Washington, D.C.: George Washington University Press.

Walter, T., Smith, D. E. P., Hoey, G., & Wilhelm, R. (1987). Predicting the academic success of college athletes. *Research Quarterly for Exercise and Sport* 58(2), 273–279.

Waterson, J. (2000). *College football: History, spectacle, controversy.* Baltimore: John Hopkins University Press.

Wiggins, D. (1991). Prized performers but frequently overlooked students: The involvement of black athletes in intercollegiate sports on predominantly white campuses, 1890–1972. *Research Quarterly for Exercise and Sport* 62(2), 164–177.

Zimbalist, A. (1999). *Unpaid professionals: Commercialism and conflict in big-time college sports.* Princeton, NJ: Princeton University Press.

Part III

Race, Gender, and Media Representations

Chapter 9

Dilemmas and Contradictions: Black Female Athletes

David J. Leonard

One does not have to go very far to understand the place of black female athletes within contemporary culture. Whether typing in "female athletes" or "sexy female athletes" on Google, one will find an endless supply of "lists" (and pictures) of the sexiest or most attractive female athletes. For example, *Men's Health* offers a list of 38 female athletes and provides readers with the opportunity to judge the quality of beauty and sexiness of those who have "made it."[1] Of the 38, only four are African American, one being Lolo Jones, whose mixed background often results in debates about her identity and efforts to identify her as Creole, mixed, white, or otherwise not black. The Bleacher Report gives readers a list of 15 female athletes, none of whom are black. This list, like many others, offers a global focus, albeit through the "sexy women" of tennis, golf, surfing, and skiing. The description of Allison Stoke, a track athlete from Berkeley, California, encapsulates the tone and level of commodity eroticism that guides the consumption of female sports:

> Seriously, Allison Stokke needs to cash in on her Internet fame. The few and far between pictures we have of her are nice, but we're going to need more for 2010. I'm talking magazine articles, some sexy photo-spreads, or at the very least some more information on who she is. Now going into her junior year at Cal, Stokke remains one of the most sought after female athletes on the planet, so here's hoping that she'll let herself be found this next year.[2]

Another slide show list on the Bleacher Report provides a list of the "25 Hottest Elite Female Athletes." Serena Williams appears on this list, although the author works hard to deny her the beauty, femininity, and sexiness afforded to the others who are deemed worthy of inclusion.

> *Sigh* . . .
>
> I didn't want it to come to this, but after being alerted about a mistake I made about Laisa Andrioli, I am forced to put Serena Williams on here.
>
> Her resume is a stunner, having won 27 Grand Slam titles. 13 of those are in singles play.
>
> She also has two Olympic golds to her name. One in Sydney and the other in Beijing.
>
> Personally, she isn't my cup of tea, but I do know that many find her stunningly attractive.
>
> So those of you who think Serena is hot, thank the a-holes on the internet who wrongfully claimed Andrioli was a striker for the Brazilian national team. And thank me for being a gullible loser who believes sites like these. Because now Serena is on here.[3]

Concluding that she is not worthy of inclusion despite the strange tastes of some men, the author acknowledges her athletic resume, celebrating her athleticism while denying her the accepted trappings of femininity and beauty. Even ESPN, the supposed establishment sports media enterprise, offers its readers a "Hottest Female Athletes" list.[4] It does, however, offer one of the more diverse lists—two out of the 10 women celebrated are African American.

The hyperfocus on sexy, hot, and otherwise beautiful female athletes illustrates the ways in which sexism operates within contemporary sports media. Title IX and the increased opportunities for women to participate in sports have not generated equality and transformative possibilities. Yet the hyperfocus on white women reveals the ways in which black women are rendered undesirable and therefore invisible within a sports media context.[5] Despite the many sports media outlets in the U.S., there are few places for female athletes, much less black female athletes. "Studies have demonstrated that less than 10%" (3–8 percent) of all sports coverage within national and local highlight packages focuses on women's sports.[6]

Whereas white women are accepted and promoted within sports media only as sexual objects, black women have difficulty entering into the sporting world, as the few spots of celebration and visibility are those seen as sexually desirable, a process defined through whiteness.

To understand the history of representations of black women within sporting cultures is to understand the complex interface between race, class, and gender. At one level, the participation of black women within sports, a world defined and dominated not only by men, but a hegemonic definition of masculinity, challenges dominant understandings of femininity. McKay and Johnson, citing the work of K. Rowe, highlights the many ways in which women athletes challenge, or undermine the assumptions about femininity and the established hierarchies surrounding gender. Whenever woman are seen as being "too fat, too mouthy, too old, too dirty, too pregnant, too sexual (or not sexual enough) for the norms of conventional gender representation,"[7] the norms associated with the gender hierarchy are put into question. Laurie Schulze similarly argues that muscularity, a signifier associated with masculinity within the dominant imagination, in woman complicates, if not undermines, the traditional definitions of femininity and masculinity: "The deliberately muscular woman disturbs dominant notions of sex, gender, and sexuality, and any discursive field that includes her risks opening up a site of contest and conflict, anxiety and ambiguity."[8] At this level, we see how the increased visibility of female athletes holds the potential to challenge the hegemonic equating of strength, muscularity, power, and athleticism with manhood.

Yet the definitions embedded in the assumed links between masculinity and sports cultures, and incompatibility of heterosexual females to sports culture, operate through a lens of whiteness. In other words, as womanhood as long been defined through whiteness, the visibility and presence of black women within a sport context does not necessary undermine these traditional gender hierarchies. At this level, we see how the presence of black female athletes is not as jarring to hegemonic gender definitions because those definitions operate through whiteness. Black women are able to be athletes within the hegemonic imagination precisely because black woman have been historically denied femininity and womanhood within the white imagination. We see this in the celebration (and commodification) of athletes such as Diana Taursi, Anna Kournakova, Maria Sharapova, Brandi Chastain, and countless other white female athletes whose entry into the public sports discourse emanates from consumption of their sexualized bodies. For example, Matthew Syed argues, "There has always been a soft-porn dimension to women's tennis, but with the progression of Maria Sharapova, Ana Ivanovic, Jelena Jankovic and Daniela Hantuchova to the semi-finals of the Australian Open, this has been into the realms of adolescent (and non-adolescent) male fantasy." Attempting to elevate women's sports by telling readers that it is okay to view female athletes as sexual objects, he laments how Western culture has not "reached a place where heterosexual men can acknowledge the occasionally erotic dimension of watching women's sport without being dismissed as deviant."[9]

The commodification of black female bodies within so many hip-hop videos (as well as films, video games, government photo opportunities, and corporations) is not merely a reinforcement of long-standing racist inscriptions (stereotypes) of black femininity, but reflects a contradiction in the positioning of black women as sexual objects (women) and as the Other who is consistently conceived of as outside the bounds of whiteness.

This chapter looks at the complex interface between sports, gender, sexuality, and race, highlighting the ways in which media narratives and representations highlight the complex place black women sit within America's racial and gender hierarchy. "Representations of Black women athletes in mass media also replicate and contest power relations of race, class, gender, and sexuality," writes Patricia Hill Collins in *Black Sexual Politics*. "Because aggressiveness is needed to win, Black female athletes have more leeway in reclaiming assertiveness without enduring the ridicule routinely targeted toward the bitch."[10] In denying the existence of black femininity, dominant discourses allow for black female athletes to exist apart from the stereotypical images that deny the sexuality, femininity, and heterosexuality of women in sports. Allowed to be athletes yet denied femininity or womanhood, black woman are situated at the outskirts of the dominant frames and discursive articulations of female athletes.

> The stereotype of women athletes as "manly" and as being lesbians and for Black women as being more "masculine" than White women converge to provide a very different interpretive context for Black female athletes. In essence, the same qualities that are uncritically celebrated Black male athletes can become stumbling blocks for their Black female counterparts. Corporate profits depend on representations and images and those of black female athletes must be carefully managed in order to win endorsements and guarantee profitability.[11]

In other words, dominant representations commodify and celebrate female athletes who embody a heterosexual beauty and appeal. At the same time, the characteristics of blackness (physicality, athletic superiority, aggressiveness, toughness, strength) within the white imagination that result in hypercommodification of black male bodies precludes black female athletes from both the category of woman athlete and the category of "hot" athlete.

In this regard, this chapter explores the ways in which race, gender, sexuality, and body operate within the sporting politic. One the one hand, I argue that black woman athletes, who are seen as potential commodities, as crossover stars, become commodities or cross-over stars through a sexualizing process. Following the paths taken by many white female athletes, black female athletes who cross over must do so through both sexuality and a clear heterosexual body. Beyond replicating and fulfilling the accepted identities available to all contemporary female athletes, the process of becoming a sexy (female) athlete confers and is the result of their identification with whiteness. To become a popular female athlete requires sex appeal, and sex appeal has long been reserved for white women, so much so that when black female athletes "make it," they do not just make it as sexualized black female athletes, but rather as sexualized female athletes. Those discourses that sexualize erase race within the white imagination, fulfilling not simply a sexual fantasy but one of postracial fantasy. To put it simply, a desirable female athlete is a heterosexual and sexy woman. And as heterosexual and sexually appealing femininity is defined through whiteness, those black female athletes who are able to transcend, who are able to cash their athletic talents into commodity status, are imagined outside the margins of blackness. Of course, a corollary exists for those black female athletes who do not enter the marketplace as sexual icons, as sexually appealing athletes, and degree to which female athletes are defined by their blackness. With this in mind, this article explores the ways in which race, gender, and sexuality define the consumption of Candace Parker and the Williams sisters, arguing that while Parker is imagined through narratives of heterosexuality, sex appeal, beauty, a patriarchal family structure, marketability, and postracialness, the Williams sisters are constructed as black and therefore sexually unappealing, which leads to demonization and hypersurveillance.

Selling Sex: The Story of Candace Parker

As part of a 2011 special issue on sports in the *Nation*, Mary Jo Kane, in an article titled "Sex Sells Sex, Not Women's Sports," explains this marginalization, debunking the idea that sex can sell women's sports. Rather, she notes, "Sex sells sex, not women's sports," leaving little doubt about why women's sports continue to struggle within the marketplace. "Millions of fans around the globe just witnessed such media images and narratives during coverage of the Women's World Cup in Germany. Perhaps such coverage will start a trend whereby those who cover women's sports will simply turn on the camera and let us see the reality—not the sexualized caricature—of today's female athletes. If and when that happens, sportswomen will receive the respect and admiration they so richly deserve."[12] Patricia Hill Collins offers similar insights, arguing that contemporary sports media work to simultaneously celebrate and feminize their athleticism by showing women in action and showing their navels.[13] Reflecting on a past Women's National Basketball Association (WNBA) marketing campaign, she notes that WNBA "ads all shared another feature—unlike their basketball uniforms that provide more than adequate coverage for their breasts and buttocks, each woman was dressed in fitted sweat pants and in a form-fitting top that, for some, exposed a hint of their midriffs, an occasional naval."[14] To reflect on these dynamics and the continued struggles of the WNBA to transcend (or even undermine) the sexist grips of American sports, I want to discuss a feature on Candace Parker.

In 2009, *ESPN: The Magazine,* as part of its women in sports issue, featured an article on Candace Parker. This one story encapsulates the persistent sexism that detracts from and inhibits the development of women's sports within American culture. Reducing women athletes to sexual objects and potentially profitable spokeswomen, the article—entitled "The Selling of Candace Parker"—does little to introduce and celebrate the contributions of women's sports, but rather elucidates the systemic problems of American sports culture.

The emphasis on selling sex, rather than athletics and sport, is evident from moment one of the piece: "Candace Parker is beautiful. Breathtaking, really, with flawless skin, endless legs and a C cup she is proud of but never flaunts," writes Alison Glock. "She is also the best at what she does, a record-setter, a rule-breaker, a redefiner."[15] Eliciting some criticism about the references to her body, and the reduction of her body to its sexualized parts, *ESPN: The Magazine* brushed off accusations of sexism, identifying the article as sensible given the demographics of the magazine. According to Gary Belsky, editor-in-chief, "It's not the worst thing in the world in a men's magazine to talk about things like that."[16]

The sexualization of Parker and the focus on her body, at the expense of a narrative highlighting her athletic talents, does not end with this initial introduction of readers to her physical attributes. Glock continues this treatise on Parker's body before moving to a discussion of her "feminine charm":

She is a woman who plays like a man, one of the boys, if the boys had C cups and flawless skin. She's nice, too. Sweet, even. Kind to animals and children, she is the sort of woman who worries about others more than about herself, a saint in high-tops.

It is this unprecedented combination of game, generosity and gorgeous that has Team Parker seeing miracles. They believe with all their collective heart that their 22-year-old, 6'4" stunner with the easy smile and perfect, white teeth will soon be the most recognized woman in American sports.[17]

In other words, Parker represents an ideal femininity—nurturing, sexy, and heterosexual (the article make this clear though various rhetorical phrases; references to her husband, basketball player Sheldon Williams; and of course, its discussion/visual presentation of Parker's pregnancy). She is the perfect woman who happens to play basketball. In this regard, ESPN is selling Parker as a sexy and attractive woman whose job is to play basketball, a professional choice that in no way compromises her role as mother, wife, and sexual object to be consumed by male fans.

Yet Glock does not seem to limit Parker's immense potential as the Michael Jordan of women's sports because of her "flawless skin" and breast size (despite multiple references to it), rather arguing that Parker can transcend women's sports and break down commercial barriers to become "a one namer" because she is not like so many of today's (black) athletes, whose brash and hypermasculine demeanor alienates fans. She is "nice," humble, and likable. She "is the total package, an advertiser's dream: attractive yet benign enough to reflect any fantasy projected upon her. Like Jordan before her, Parker is a cipher of sorts, nothing outsize or off-putting. Nothing edgy. Nothing Iverson. Aside from being an athletic freak, she's normal. You could imagine her hanging out at your family barbecue. This matters; if Parker seems like a down-home gal, a possible friend, then it's a short step to trust, and with trust comes a willingness to buy what Team Parker is selling."

The racial text here is revealing in that Parker is positioned not only against the long-standing stereotype of the sexually undesirable (and likely lesbian) female athlete, but as a point of departure from the modern black male athlete. Parker, like Tiger Woods, is "characterized as a breath of fresh air." Her appeal was based on the fact that many Americans were getting tired of "trash talking, spit-hurling, head-butting millionaire." athletes[18] She can be both a sexual and postracial fantasy.

Yet Glock undercuts the commercial and iconic possibilities for Parker because she is a woman who chose to get pregnant. And choice is key here as the article positions Parker as someone who made a choice, likely against the will and advice of those inside Team Parker, within the WNBA, and elsewhere. Following the opening paragraphs, all of which highlight the profit potential resulting from her identity and sex appeal, Glock seems to walk back this same argument, noting that getting pregnant was not part of the plan. Parker's pregnancy "was a shock to her, her sponsors, and her WNBA team" because it would put the plans of so many counting on her on hold. Two years later, with Parker yet to fulfill this potential as WNBA star and marketing sensation, in part because of the time taken off with her pregnancy and then an injury, you can almost hear the skeptics saying, "We told you so."[19]

The implications of the article are striking in that they leave readers with a troubling message that Parker's appeal and her Achilles heel emanate from her female sexuality. That is, had she used her feminine appeal to attract male sports fans otherwise disillusioned by "thug" black males athletes and sexually undesirable female athletes, the sky was limitless. Yet her decision to put family first, to fulfill the hegemonic patriarchal expectations of society, undermines her sporting appeal.

Interestingly, Glock, in an effort to highlight both the marketing strategies embraced by Team Parker and her commercial appeal, reflects on the sexualizing demands placed upon contemporary female athletes. Noting that "there are avenues available to women athletes . . . that involve waxing," Glock laments that the once class acts of sports are now "nuding it up" in *Playboy*. Candace Parker is thus presented as a throwback within women's sports, more like Michael Phelps and Yao Ming (interesting choices to highlight the ideal athlete), who embody something different from those morally objectionable women.

"Women athletes are more likely to be marketed as sexy than as competent," notes Mary Jo Kane, who is quoted in Glock's article. "And many women go for it. These athletes are smart. They know what sponsors want. . . . It is the best and the worst of times. People like Candace are getting more coverage. But they are also forced to be sexy babes."[20] The feature article on Candace Parker is in fact exhibit A (and B, C, and D) for Kane's argument that the visibility afforded to Parker and women's sport is delivered by an article about her body, beauty, bust, femininity, and sex appeal. Inclusion in mainstream sports culture is the result of this sexualizing process. ESPN, like the broader sports culture, is not selling women's sports. Rather, it is selling sex. In this instance, as with the public recognition afforded to skier Lindsey Vonn, soccer star Hope Solo, and race-car driver Danica Patrick, sex and sexuality are the primary vehicles for both the commodification and consumption of contemporary female athletes.

In a summer (2011) that saw lockouts in the National Basketball Association and National Football League (not to mention labor strife within some European soccer leagues), that has seen waning interest in Major League Baseball and dissipating support for professional golf given the struggles of Tiger Woods, and that has not had to compete with international competitions such as the Olympics, the WNBA had a chance to increase its cultural and market share. With only a slight increase in attendance, the cultural relevance and broader appeal of the game saw little movement during a virtually sports-free summer. It missed an opportunity because of the continued efforts to sell women's sports through sex and sexual appeal rather than the beauty and brilliance of the game. As noted by Dave Zirin, "Every scrap of academic research shows that conditioning viewers to see women athletes as sex symbols comes at the expense of interest in the games themselves."[21] Or as Mary Jo Kane notes, "For a female athlete, stripping down might sell magazines, but it won't sell your sport." The peripheral place of the WNBA, a fact evident in and perpetuated by the sports media, the WNBA itself, and fans alike, demonstrates that the visibility afforded to women today (minimal at best) is not evidence of progress. Just ask Candace Parker!

Black Ain't Beautiful in the Sporting World: The Case of the Williams Sisters

Unlike Candace Parker, the Williams sisters have often been subjected to racist and sexist taunts about their bodies and physical looks. Compared to the idealized and authentically rendered femininity inside and outside of sports, the Williams sisters are imagined as the opposite end of the spectrum. Whereas athletes like Parker, Kournakova, and Patrick are represented as athletic but girly, sexual, and able to exist in two worlds, the Williams sisters have been constructed as muscular, aggressive, and natural athletes—as men. "The embodiment of preferred femininity in U.S. culture, Kournikova has publically mocked the physiques of the Williams sisters." Remarking on the ways in which Kournakova juxtaposes herself and the Williams sisters, Schultz illustrates the ways in which whiteness and blackness, femininity and masculinity, heterosexuality and asexuality operate as binaries within the sporting world. "I hate my muscles. I'm not Venus

Williams. I'm not Serena Williams. I'm feminine. I don't want to look like they do. I'm not masculine like they are," commented Kournikova.[22] Female athletes are defined through beauty and sexual appeal. Sexual appeal has historically been defined from the perspective of white hetero- sexuals. The Williams sisters, as black women, are denied acceptance as female athletes. They are seen as black athletes who because of their black- ness, physicality, and strength are imagined apart from their athletic sisters and therefore positioned in relationship to black male athletes. Ridicule of the Williams sisters though sexualizing tropes and those based on Western standards of beauty have been commonplace.

Jim Rome, a nationally syndicated talk show host, has consistently referred to them as Predator 1 and Predator 2. Likewise, during an appear- ance on the Don Imus radio show, radio personality Sid Rosenberg described the Williams sisters as unattractive: "I can't even watch them play anymore. I find it disgusting. I find both of those, what do you want to call them—they're just too muscular. They're boys," he announced. "One time my friend he goes, 'Listen, one of these days you're going to find Venus and Serena Williams in *Playboy.*' I said, 'You got a better shot at *National Geographic.*'" The rhetoric here has an important larger context (as does the hypersexualization of Parker) within American white supremacy:

> The dominant male, white culture drew a direct correspondence between stereotyped depictions of black womanhood and "manly" athletic and physi- cally gifted females. Their racialized notions of the virile or mannish black female athlete stemmed from a number of persistent historical myths: the linking of African American women's work history as slaves, their suppos- edly "natural" brute strength and endurance inherited from their African ori- gins, and the notion that vigorous or competitive sport masculinized women physically and sexually.[23]

The focus on their bodies and physical beauty, the ubiquitous criticisms directed at both Serena and Venus by fans and commentators alike, and the constant questioning of their attitude, work ethic, commitment, intelli- gence, and fortitude demonstrate the ways in which the Williams sisters enter into a public discourse through *both* race and gender.

"The public reacts to the Williams sisters not as African Americans or as women, but as African American women," writes Schultz. "Marked by the 'logic of coupling,'[24] Venus and Serena Williams are locked within a double bind."[25] In other words, the representations afforded to them reflect the inextricable combination of both racism and sexism, not to mention hetro-normative values.

Imagined as unattractive and undesirable—as black—the Williams sisters have faced a barrage of public criticism about their behavior. While both have been subjected to heightened levels of surveillance and demonization, Serena has faced far more public condemnation. In 2009 at the U.S. Open following a questionable foot-fault call, Serena lashed out at the land judge, prompting widespread denunciation of her poor sportsmanship. Her anger, her aggressiveness, and her "menacing tone" violated (just as her purported lack of physical attractiveness) the required demeanor of female athletes, particularly black female athletes who are required to distance themselves from the ways in which dominant discourse constructs the modern black male athlete. Two years later, during the 2011 finals, she once again found herself in the thick of controversy. Struggling in the match, Serena struck what appeared to be a momentum-changing winner, leading her to yell in an effort to pump herself up. Because the point was not over, the umpire ruled that her yell violated a rule prohibiting players from distracting their opponent, resulting in Williams losing the point and the game. Angered by the call, Serena challenged the ruling and the umpire as well:

> Are you the one that screwed me over the last time? You're a nobody. . . . If you ever see me walking down the hall, look the other way, because you're out of control. . . . You're totally out of control. You're a hater, unattractive inside. Who would do such a thing? And I never complain. Wow. What a loser.
>
> Give me a code violation because I expressed my emotion? We're in America last time I checked. Really, don't even look at me. I promise you. Don't look at me, because I'm not the one.

Following the match and in response to her confrontation with the match umpire, commentators have taken her task, deploying racialized and gendered criticism. Described as "petulant," "going bonkers," "a stereotypical Ugly American,"[26] and someone whose "ego"[27] led her to on a "tirade,"[28] the media's tone has rendered what appeared to be a tame and minor confrontation into a spectacle that rehashes long-standing stereotypes about black women as childish, emotional, lacking self-control, and otherwise angry. In other instances, Williams was demonized for an "outburst" and "menacing behavior,"[29] for "losing her cool" during an "ugly US Open meltdown,"[30] and the "the menacing tone of her remarks."[31] Mary Carillo, a well-known American sportscaster who regularly analyzes women's tennis matches and is also a former professional tennis player, referred to Serena's behavior as that of an "ass clown."[32]

Given the ways in which white supremacist discourse has pathologized and rendered African Americans as cultural, physical, and economic menaces, the references to her tone and demeanor as menacing are particularly revealing. "Racial logic has advanced a link between the legibility of black bodies, and a racial being," argues Delia D. Douglas. "If we consider that black bodies have historically been designated as the site and source of pathology, by extension, one's behavior and habits are seen as symptomatic of these racial distinctions" (Kawash, 1997). If the black body is the vessel through which one is able to identify and categorize difference, then by association, one's demeanor is seen as an extension of this racial being.[33]

The hyperbolic and racially and gendered rhetoric is encapsulated by a column from George Vecesey in the *New York Times*:

> "As she stormed at the chair umpire during a changeover, Williams was reverting to her vicious outburst at a line official that caused her to be disqualified at match point in a semifinal in 2009, the last time Williams was here." "But at what point does comportment, sportsmanship, become part of the measure of a great champion?" "The tantrum early in the second set caused many in the crowd to boo the decision, delaying the next point. Stosur kept her cool, and Williams never showed a trace of those couple of hard hits. She could have gone out with dignity on an evening when she did not have her best game. Instead, she called the chair umpire a hater, and later professed not to remember a word of it."[34]

The rhetoric offered by these commentators and others illustrates the ways in which race and gender rhetorical devices govern the analysis following the U.S. Open finals (2009); at the same time, it illustrates the ways in which a white racial frame or the sincere racial fictions[35] overdetermine the interpretations and analysis provided here in that Serena Williams's confrontation of the umpire was tame. While angry with a suspect call and unwilling to capitulate to authority merely because of custom, she was clearly composed, calm, and collective. There was no "outburst," she did not "lose her cool," and nothing about her behavior was "menacing."

Even the United States Tennis Association (USTA) concluded that the "controversy" was much ado about nothing and fined Williams $2,000. Explaining the fine, it announced:

> US Open Tournament Referee Brian Earley has fined Serena Williams $2,000 following the code violation issued for verbal abuse during the women's singles final. This fine is consistent with similar offenses at Grand Slam events. As with all fines at the US Open, the monies levied are provided to the Grand Slam Development Fund which develops tennis programs around the world.
>
> After independently reviewing the incident which served as the basis for the code violation, and taking into account the level of fine imposed by the US Open referee, the Grand Slam Committee Director has determined that Ms. Williams' conduct, while verbally abusive, does not rise to the level of a major offense under the Grand Slam Code of Conduct.[36]

Noting the existence of "similar offenses" during the course of all Grand Slam events, the USTA acknowledges the banality of the behavior from Serena Williams. Yet commentators and fans alike have continued their assault on her character.

At a certain level, I agree with the commentary offered on *The Crunk Feminist Collective* that her reaction was understandable: "And frankly, I see Serena's outburst as understandable and amusing. Call me a Williams' fan [sic] if you want to. It's true. But this is not about simple loyalty."[37] Yet I do not think it was an outburst but merely a moment where Serena voiced her displeasure for and anger about an absurd call from an umpire who chose to put herself and her authority above the game.

The umpire was determining the outcome of the game more than the player themselves, something that should give all of us pause. Yet the focus has not been on the call or an umpire determining the outcome of a game, but Serena's behavior not as a snapshot of a moment, but as a window into her soul. Williams has been positioned as yet another black athlete who may have the athletic talent but lacks the mental toughness and commitment needed to excel on the biggest stages. More significantly, the postmatch commentaries reveal the powerful ways that race operates within American culture. Her blackness and femininity, especially in the context of the white world of tennis, overdetermine her positioning within a sporting context. This moment illustrates the profound impact of *both* race and gender on Serena Williams, a fact often erased by both popular and academic discourses. According to Delia Douglas, "The failure to consider the ways in which sport is both an engendering and racializing institution has lead to myriad distortions, as well as the marginalization and oversimplification of black women's experiences in sport." As such, her stardom, her success, and the specifics of the incident do not insulate her from criticism and condemnation, but in fact contribute to the acceptability of fans and commentators alike shouting and, "Shut up and play."[38]

To understand the reaction is to understand a larger history involving Serena Williams. Two days before the finals, in a video commentary entitled "Embracing Serena," William C. Rhoden argued that Serena has not been accepted as "a great American story."[39] Citing a certain level of "ambivalence" and a refusal to celebrate the "resilience" and the "will" exhibited by the Williams sisters, Rhoden highlighted the ways in which cultural citizenship has been denied to the Williams sister; better said, he pointed to the racial double standards and the ways in which race and gender overdetermine the manner in which the Williams sisters are positioned and confined within the national landscape. On cue, commenters provided evidence of Rhoden's argument. Take Lewis, who used the moment to assail Serena's character, to demonize the parenting skills of Richard Williams, and to deny her work ethic and dedication through a reference to steroids:

> I've never been a fan of the Williams sisters, though through the years, I've warmed to Venus because of her low-key personality off the court.
>
> Serena, however, I'll never embrace. I can admire her tennis ability, but she has been for virtually all her career, a sore-loser and bad sport. This, I believe stems from her father from years past, and what a piece of work he is.
>
> Another thing, take a look at the massive size difference between Serena and Venus. Early on, Serena was quite a bit smaller all around. Her muscles are huge! Don't suppose that can be the result of steroids, now could it? was 'roid rage behind the incident with the lineswoman?[40]

Andrew agreed with Lewis on all counts, offering the following:

> 100% agree with Lewis on all counts. Surly, nasty personality for the most part, stingy in her graciousness towards opponents. The main thing you feel off of her in victory is narcissism. Very difficult person to root for, and I have long felt a steroid/HGH investigation is warranted. Are we so stupid to ignore the obvious?? She is ENORMOUS . . .
>
> p.s. other surly brats like Mac were hard to like but somehow you warmed to them over time because of some recognizable humanity . . . Serena just leaves me stone cold.[41]

Others follow suited (before and after the match), referring to Serena Williams as a "psychopath," immature, a "poor sport," an "embarrassment," a "hater," "out-of-control," "unattractive inside," "disgraceful" and a "poor loser," illustrating not only the vitriol, but the double standards and the ways in which race and gender overdetermine her placement in the sports world. It was evident after the 2009 U.S. Open.

We can see it with the constant references to her body (Jason Whitlock once referred to her as an "unsightly layer of thick, muscled blubber, a by-product of her unwillingness to commit to a training regimen and diet that would have her at the top of her game year-round")[42] and the ubiquitous references to her physicality, strength and power. "Black bodies have long been objects of scrutiny, the recipients of inordinate attention and discussion for over a century. Black bodies were seen as the site and source of black pathology, as boundaries against which one could determine acceptable sexuality, femininity and morality,"[43] writes Douglas. "Historically, white supremacist racial logic has long relied on 'the use of a dichotomous code that creates a chain of correspondences both between the physical and the cultural, and between intellectual and cognitive characteristics.'[44] In this context, blacks were understood as more body than mind."[45] The rhetorical descriptors long reserved for the Williams sisters and the hyperfocus on her "menacing" body following her 2009 final match of the U.S. Open illustrate the ways in which race and gender operate through the dissection and demonization of Serena's body. We see it the dissection, commentary, and surveillance of both Venus's and Serena's clothing and hair choices. We see it with the narrative choices that depict the Williams sisters as "ghetto Cinderellas" as worthy of celebration because tennis (whiteness) saved them from the "cradle of crack dealers and grunge courts" and led them to compete for championships and millions of dollars. We also can see it with the treatment Venus received at Indian Wells and with the overall cultural resistance to and demonization of the Williams sisters. We see it media coverage, fan reactions, and in so many places that there have been countless articles highlighting the ways in which "sport both reinforces and reproduces the 'persistent,' 'resurgent,' and 'veiled' forms of white power that permeate society."[46] What happened at the U.S. Open and in the hours that followed were another chapter of this larger history.

James McCay and Helen Johnson begin their article "Pornographic Eroticism and Sexual Grotesquerie in Representations of African American

Sportswomen" by citing a historic parallel in the treatment of Althea Gibson and Serena Williams:

> "Go Back To The Cotten [sic] Plantation Nigger." (Banner in the stands when Althea Gibson walked on court to defend her US Open title in 1958)
>
> "That's the way to do it! Hit the net like any Negro would!" (Racist male heckling Serena Williams before she served at the 2007 Sony Ericsson Championships in Miami)[47]

While illustrating the continuity of white supremacy and the fallacy of those postracial celebrations, the shared experience between Gibson and Williams encapsulates the dehumanizing and violent conditions that both endured and challenged during their careers. While acknowledging differences, it points to the powerful force of racism and sexism within America life. It also points to the ways in which Althea Gibson and Serena Williams (as well as Venus Williams) disrupt the hegemonic whiteness of the tennis world. To understand Serena's place within the history of tennis, including during the events surrounding the 2009 U.S. Open, is to understand her willingness to challenge authority and the culture of a normalized whiteness within (and beyond) tennis. As powerfully noted by Brittney Cooper, Serena Williams refuses to accept to be confined and controlled by the overdetermining logics of racism and sexism:

> Yes, I'm aware of all the ways in which her acts in this moment reinforce stereotypes of the Angry Black Woman. However, we cannot use our investment in a respectability politic which demands that Black women never show anger or emotion in the face of injustice to demand Serena's silence. Resistance is often impolite, and frequently it demands that we skirt the rules. . . . Serena continues to disrupt tennis spaces with her dark-skinned, powerful body, her flamboyant sartorial choices, her refusal to conform to the professional tennis obstacle course, and her willingness to get angry and show it. That disruption is necessary—because however "right" or "wrong" it may technically be—it demonstrates that all is not well racially in tennis. Black folks—men and women—are still largely understood within a narrative of brute, undisciplined physical strength—rather than as athletes who bring both physical and intellectual skills to their game. As long as these issues remain, tennis will continue to be "unattractive" from the inside out.[48]

And while others use this moment to "hate" Serena Williams, it is a reminder of how my love of sports is so often polluted by the racism, sexism, and "unattractive" realities of American culture.

Conclusion

On April 4, 2007, following a hotly contested champion game between Rutgers University and the University of Tennessee, Don Imus took to the air and disparaged, demonized, and otherwise ridiculed the women of Rutgers, referring to them as "nappy-headed hoes" during the following exchange. McGuirk was the show's executive producer. Charles McCord was Don's sidekick on the show. Rosenberg was on the phone. He was a sportscaster for 790 The Ticket. Lou Ruffino was the program engineer.

IMUS: So, I watched the basketball game last night between—a little bit of Rutgers and Tennessee, the women's final.

ROSENBERG: Yeah, Tennessee won last night—seventh championship for [Tennessee coach] Pat Summitt, I-Man. They beat Rutgers by 13 points.

IMUS: That's some rough girls from Rutgers. Man, they got tattoos and—

McGUIRK: Some hard-core hos.

IMUS: That's some nappy-headed hos there. I'm gonna tell you that now, man, that's some—woo. And the girls from Tennessee, they all look cute, you know, so, like—kinda like—I don't know.

McGUIRK: A Spike Lee thing.

IMUS: Yeah.

McGUIRK: The Jigaboos vs. the Wannabes—that movie that he had.

IMUS: Yeah, it was a tough—

McCORD: Do The Right Thing.

McGUIRK: Yeah, yeah, yeah.

IMUS: I don't know if I'd have wanted to beat Rutgers or not, but they did, right?

ROSENBERG: It was a tough watch. The more I look at Rutgers, they look exactly like the Toronto Raptors.

IMUS: Well, I guess, yeah.

RUFFINO: Only tougher.

McGUIRK: The [Memphis] Grizzlies would be more appropriate.[49]

Given the treatment of the Williams sisters and other black athletes through history, Imus's comments should be of little surprise. Throughout history, white newspapers have "trivialized African-American women's participation in sport, either by failing to cover the accomplishments of the athletes or by framing the athletes as masculine."[50] The efforts to demean and disparage the women of Rutgers through both racial and gendered language are illustrative of a larger history of black female athletes. Those who are able to fulfill the dominant white imagination regarding female athletes (to mimic a white aesthetic; to fulfill white sexual fantasies) enter into the public sphere as sexual objects, yet those who do not embody the sexualized aesthetics of white male pleasure find themselves ostracized. This is the case with Rutgers and with the Williams sisters, as opposed to the experiences of Candace Parker.

In totality, their experiences highlight the contradictory and difficult negotiation process placed upon black female athletes who have to deal with the heterosexist and misogynistic culture that demands sex appeal for female athletes while dealing with "controlling" images associated with black female bodies. "Thus, the negotiation of the contradictions in women's sport participation differs qualitatively for African-American female athletes given the ways in which African-American women have long been portrayed in the media, and specifically sports media, as both hypersexualized and less feminine," write Cookey, Wachs, Messner and Dworkin. "As a result, African-American female athletes are subject to particular 'controlling images' in the media."[51] In *Sister Citizen: Shame, Stereotypes, and Black Women in America*, Melissa Harris Perry expands our collective understanding of politics beyond legislation, voting, and campaigns, arguing that "the internal, psychological, emotional and personal experiences of black women are inherently politics." She goes on: "They are political because black women in America have always had to wrestle with the derogatory assumptions about their character and identity. These assumptions shape the social world that black women must accommodate or resist in an effort to preserve their authentic selves and to secure recognition as citizens."[52] The demonization, the contestation, the struggles and dilemmas, and the question for full citizenship (cultural and otherwise) are not limited to a particular venue, as we can see from the experiences of Candace Parker, the Williams sisters, the Rutgers women's basketball team, and countless others whose presence on and off the course continues to be defined but yet not contained by the hegemonic assumptions of race, gender, and sexuality.

Notes

1. "The Hottest Female Athletes: 2011," *Men's Health*, accessed October 5, 2011, from http://www.menshealth.com/hottest-female-athletes/

2. Mike McD, "The 15 Sexiest Female Athletes to Watch: 2010 Edition," *Bleacher* Report, December 23, 2009, accessed October 5, 2011 from http://bleacherreport.com/articles/313545-the-15-sexiest-athletes-to-watch-for-in-2010/page/16

3. Kyle Boberg, "25 Hottest Elite Female Athletes," *Bleacher* Report, June 6, 2011, accessed October 5, 2011 from http://bleacherreport.com/articles/735455-25-hottest-elite-female-athletes/page/2

4. "Hottest Female Athletes: 2011," accessed October 5, 2011 from http://sports.espn.go.com/espn/page2/features/hottestWomen?num=2

5. Faye L. Wachs, Cheryl Cooky, Michael A. Messner, and Shari L. Dworkin, "Media frames and displacement of blame in the Don Imus incident: Sincere fictions and frenetic inactivity," *Critical Studies in Media Communication*, 29 (2012): 421–438; Delia D. Douglas, "Venus, Serena and the Women's Tennis Association: When and where race enters." *Sociology of Sport Journal*, 22 (2005): 256–282; James McKay and Helen Johnson, "Pornographic eroticism and sexual grotesquerie in representations of African-American sportswomen," *Social Identities*, 14 (2008): 491–504: Tara McPherson, "Who's got next? Gender, race and the mediation of the WNBA," In *Basketball Jones: America above the rim*, edited by Todd Boyd and Kenneth Shropshire (New York: New York University Press, 2010): 184–197; Jaime Schultz, "Reading the catsuit: Serena Williams and the production of blackness at the 2002 U. S. Open," *Journal of Sport and Social Issues*, 29 (2005): 338–357.

6. Cooky, Wachs, Messner, and Dworkin, 2012, 142.

7. McKay and Johnson, 2008, 492.

8. Quoted in McKay and Johnson, 2008, 492.

9. Quoted in McKay and Johnson, 2008, 492

10. Patricia Hill Collins, *Black sexual politics: African Americans, gender, and the new racism,* (New York: Routledge, 2004): 134.

11. Ibid., 136.

12. Mary Jo Kane, "Sex Sells Sex, Not Women's Sports." *Nation*, July 27, 2011, accessed September 23, 2011 from http://www.thenation.com/article/162390/sex-sells-sex-not-womens-sports

13. Hill Collins, *Black sexual politics*, 136.

14. Ibid., 136.

15. Allison Glock, "The Selling of Candace Parker," *ESPN: The Magazine*, 2009, accessed September 23, 2011 from http://sports.espn.go.com/espnmag/story?id=3967891

16. Quoted in Q. Salazar-Moreno, "Pregnant Candace Parker Graces Cover of ESPN Magazine," March 13, 2009, accessed September 2011 from http://www.bvonsports.com/2009/03/13/pregnant-candace-parker-graces-cover-of-espn-magazine/

17. Glock, "The Selling of Candace Parker."

18. Stodghill quoted in C.L. Cole and David L. Andrews, "America's new son: Tiger Woods and America's multiculturalism," in *Sports stars: The cultural politics of sporting celebrity*, edited by David L. Andrews and Steven J. Jackson (New York: Routledge, 2001): 70–86.

19. Glock, "The Selling of Candace Parker."

20. Kane, "Sex Sells Sex."

21. Dave Zirin, "Athletic Excellence Competes with Raunch Culture at Women's World Cup," July 18, 2011, accessed September 23, 2009 from http://www.edgeofsports.com/2011-07-18-636/index.html

22. K. Giles, 2001 in Schultz, "Reading the catsuit," 346.

23. Vertinsky and Captain in Schultz, "Reading the catsuit," 347.

24. Stuart Hall, "What is this 'black' in black popular culture?" in *Stuart Hall: Critical dialogues in cultural studies*, edited by Huan-Sing Chen and David Morley, pp. 465–475 (London: Routledge), 472.

25. Schultz, "Reading the catsuit," 342.

26. Jeff Blair, "Petulant Serena goes bonkers again at U.S. Open," *Globe and Mail*, September 11, 2011, accessed October 5, 2011 from http://www.theglobeandmail.com/sports/jeff-blair/petulant-serena-goes-bonkers-again-at-us-open/article2161811/

27. Eric Ball, "Serena Williams: Enormous ego dooms Serena at US Open Final," *Bleacher Report*, September 12, 2011, accessed October 5, 2011 from http://bleacherreport.com/articles/845506-serena-williams-enormous-ego-dooms-serena-at-us-open-final

28. Matt Conner, "U.S. Open 2011: The disgraceful Serena Williams should heed her own words," *SB Nation*, September 11, 2011, accessed October 5, 2011 from http://kansascity.sbnation.com/2011/9/12/2420002/u-s-open-2011-the-disgraceful-serena-williams-should-heed-her-own/in/2184047

29. Karen Crouse, "Stosur captures the title after a Williams outburst," *New York Times*, September 11, 2011, accessed October 5, 2011 from http://www.nytimes.com/2011/09/12/sports/tennis/stosur-wins-us-open-womens-title.html?_r=2

30. Craig Dixon, " 'We're in America!' Williams loses her cool, and the US Open," *Sunday Morning Herald*, September 12, 2011, accessed October 5, 2011 from http://www.smh.com.au/sport/tennis/were-in-america-williams-loses-her-cool—and-the-us-open-20110912-1k4tj.html#ixzz1Zw2CYZaW

31. Martyn Herman, "Analysis: Serena rant leaves WTA with tough decision," *Reuters*, September 12, 2011, accessed October 5, 2011 from http://www.reuters.com/article/2011/09/12/us-tennis-serena-idUSTRE78B2G420110912

32. "Mary Carillo: Serena acted like an ass clown," accessed October 5, 2011 from http://www.yahoosportsradio.com/shows/mary-carillo-serena-acted-like-an-ass-clown-7089/

33. Delia D. Douglas, "To be young, gifted, black and female: A meditation on the cultural politics at play in representations of Venus and Serena Williams," *Sociology of Sport: Online*, accessed August 29, 2013 from http://physed.otago.ac.nz/sosol/v5i2/v5i2_3.html

34. George Vecessey, "From a voice to a roar, again," *New York Times*, September 11, 2011, accessed October 5, 2011 from http://www.nytimes.com/2011/09/12/sports/tennis/from-a-voice-to-a-roar-again.html

35. Joe Feagin, *The White Racial Frame: Centuries of Racial Framing and Counter-Framing* (New York, NY: Routledge, 2009); Nancy Spencer, "Sister act VI: Venus and Serena Williams at Indian Wells: 'Sincere Fictions' and white racism," *Journal of Sport and Social Issues*, 28 (2004): 115–135.

36. Steve Busfield, "Serena Williams fined $2,000 for US Open final outburst," *Guardian*, September 12, 2011, accessed from http://www.guardian.co.uk/sport/2011/sep/12/serena-williams-us-open-tennis-fine

37. Brittney Cooper, "Refereeing Serena: Racism, anger, and U.S. (Women's) Tennis," *Crunk Feminist* Collective, September 12, 2011, accessed October 5, 2011 from http://www.crunkfeministcollective.com/2011/09/12/refereeing-serena-racism-anger-and-u-s-womens-tennis/

38. Delia D. Douglas, "To be young, gifted, black and female."

39. William C. Rhoden, "Embracing Serena," *New York Times*, September 9, 2011, accessed October 5, 2011 from http://straightsets.blogs.nytimes.com/2011/09/09/sports-of-the-times-embracing-serena/

40. Lewis comment on Rhoden, "Embracing Serena."

41. Andrew comment on Rhoden, "Embracing Serena."

42. Dave Milz, "Serena Williams is a slacker, Jason Whitlock says: It's easy to agree," *Bleacher Report*, July 7, 2009, accessed October 5, 2011 from http://bleacherreport.com/articles/213700-jason-whitlock-thinks-serena-williams-is-a-slacker-its-easy-to-agree

43. Paula Giddings, *When and where I enter: The impact of black women on race and sex in America* (New York: William Morrow, 1984); Sander Gilman, "Black bodies, white bodies: Toward an iconography of female sexuality in late nineteenth-century art, medicine, and literature," *Critical Inquiry*, 12 (1984), 205–243.

44. Stuart Hall, *Minimal selves* (London: ICA, 1997), 290.

45. Douglas, "To be young, gifted, black and female."

46. C. Richard King, David Leonard, and Kyle Kusz, "White power: An introduction," *Journal of Sport and Social Issues*, 31 (2007): 5.

47. McKay and Johnson, 2008.

48. Wachs, F. L., Cooky, C., Messner, M. A., & Dworkin, S. L. (2012). "Media frames and displacement of blame in the Don Imus incident: Sincere fictions and frenetic inactivity." *Critical Studies in Media Communication*, 29 (5), 421–438.

230 Out of Bounds

49. Wachs, F. L., Cooky, C., Messner, M. A., & Dworkin, S. L. (2012). "Media frames and displacement of blame in the Don Imus incident: Sincere fictions and frenetic inactivity. Critical Studies in Media Communication." 29 (5), 421–438.

50. Ibid., 142.

51. Ibid., 152.

52. Melissa Harris-Perry, *Sister citizen: Shame, stereotypes, and black women in America* (New York: Harper & Row, 2011), 5.

Chapter 10

William Pope.L's *Budapest Crawl* and Black Male Sports Bodies in Advertising in the 1990s

Tiffany E. Barber

Major sports apparel corporations Nike, Reebok, Adidas, and Puma experienced unprecedented market growth through the success of large-scale television advertising campaigns in the 1980s and 1990s.[1] Nike and Reebok vied for the top market spot in the United States, while Adidas and Puma, strands of the same German-based company founded in 1924 by the Dassler brothers, battled over the top spot in the European market.[2] With national campaigns featuring iconic sports heroes, namely Michael Jordan, Charles Barkley, Carl Lewis, and Bo Jackson, Nike soon edged out Reebok and sought to expand to the European market, putting pressure on Adidas and Puma.[3] Between 1980 and 1999, Nike pumped billions of dollars into international marketing schemes. These highly developed media campaigns included print ads and television commercials, featured mostly male athletes of color, and boosted Nike's sales revenue.[4] Adidas responded with its own marketing ploy, the Adidas Streetball Challenge, a large-scale amateur competition built around the urban phenomenon streetball.[5] In 1999, U.S.-based contemporary artist William Pope.L staged *The Black Body and Sport,*[6] iterations of which were performed in Budapest, Berlin, Prague, and Madrid, four of the Adidas Streetball Challenge sites between 1992 and 1996.

Scholar Matthew Soar notes in his discussion of a recognizable Nike ad from 1980, "one ad from 1980—the first Nike ad in this survey actually to feature people—is a portrait of 17 men (two of whom are white) ... The headline reads 'The Supreme Court.' "[7] The advertisement's headline is particularly provocative given the sea of brown bodies represented in an advertisement promoting an industry historically relegated to the exclusive participation of white males. The headline's text recalls the historical specificity of the U.S. Supreme Court, the only court specially established by the Constitution of the United States in 1789, a little over a decade after the United States declared independence from Great Britain. The U.S. Supreme Court elected its first male justice of color, Thurgood Marshall, in 1967; its first woman, Sandra Day O'Connor, in 1981; and its first woman of color, Sonia Sotomayor, in 2009. Indeed, there are parallels between the historical make-ups of both "supreme courts"—the real and the figurative courts of law and basketball—as largely white male enterprises. However, the constructed image of nonwhite male bodies in Nike's supreme court advertisement differs drastically from the actual white male–predominated U.S. Supreme Court. The advertisement's image challenges the historical narrative of the Supreme Court and suggests that the highest rulers of the basketball and tennis court were no longer white males but male athletes of color. The advertisement's sea of brown bodies disrupts the normalcy of whiteness within the U.S. sports industry; the supreme court ad effectively announces that the majority and minority had been officially inverted.

Soar further describes Nike's shift in advertising strategies, saying, "Apart from two ads featuring John McEnroe ... [and] André Agassi ... [and] another featuring an unidentified white celebrity ... and one international ad from 1994 involving England's rugby team, there are no recognizably white sports stars in *any* of the ads from 1984 to 1995 inclusive."[8] Soar not only points out a shift from products to people, and their conflation, but also a shift from white athletes to nonwhite athletes in Nike's advertising strategies during the 1980s and 1990s. In fact, the athletes that dominated Nike's ad campaigns during this time were mostly black male athletes—Jordan, Lewis, Barkley, and Jackson, among others—thus visualizing an intricate relationship between black male bodies and contemporary consumer culture. As such, this essay examines how William Pope.L's artistic intervention responds to the co-option of black sports bodies and streetball in national and international sports advertising campaigns in the 1990s by focusing on constructions of blackness, masculinity, and the black sports body as a site of desire and consumption.

Turf Wars: A Brief History

Sports culture was on the rise in the 1990s, due to multimillion-dollar corporate marketing campaigns employed by companies such as Nike and Adidas. According to the official corporate website for Nike and its affiliate brands, by 1980, Nike had attained huge shares in the U.S. athletic shoe market.[9] Nike went public in December of that year, marking a period of transition for the company.[10] J. B. Strasser, Nike's first advertising manager, and sports journalist Laurie Becklund sum up Nike's position in the global sports market in the early 1980s:

> In America, Nike's volume came from people wearing athletic shoes to supermarkets and bars. In Europe, life was more formal, and athletic shoes weren't street fashion. Nike was trying to make a dent in the serious sport shoe market. But Adidas' products were better or perceived as better, they owned the soccer market, their prices were cheaper, [they were the] image of European quality, and they had dominated the most recent Olympics in Moscow, where the U.S. hadn't even competed.[11]

During the 1980s, Nike shifted its market focus. The company partnered with Oregon-based advertising agency Wieden & Kennedy to air its first national television commercials in October 1982, catapulting Nike into a global brand. Starting in 1984, Nike clutched a spot in the running shoe market as a result of the brand's performance during the Los Angeles Olympics and signed rookie Michael Jordan, arguably the greatest basketball player of all time, as a brand spokesperson.[12] Nike launched his signature basketball shoe, Air Jordan, in 1985. By this time, Nike had slipped from its position as the industry leader, in part because the company underestimated the aerobics boom; however, the debut of Jordan's signature shoe significantly bolstered Nike's bottom line.[13] Nike's 1989 "Bo Knows" advertising campaign featuring football and baseball star Bo Jackson cemented the ubiquity of the company's "Just Do It" slogan and iconic swoosh logo.[14] By the time Jordan led the Chicago Bulls to their first of six National Basketball Association (NBA) championships in 1991, Nike had regained its position as the industry leader; shoe and apparel sales soared.[15] Nike had cornered the U.S. athletic shoes and apparel market, with only minor competition from Reebok.[16] J. B. Strasser and Laurie Becklund note, "Nike was number one in America, but in Europe the Swoosh was either unknown of else known and dismissed as a poor alternative to Adidas."[17]

Nike soon set its sights on the international market, hoping to expand its reach to Europe and later Asia, Africa, and other global markets.

The 1992 Olympic Games in Barcelona, Spain, marked a prime advertising opportunity for Nike as basketball was quickly becoming an international sport due to the remarkable talent and media visibility of basketball superstars like Michael Jordan and Charles Barkley,[18] not to mention the heavily reported controversy that Jordan and Barkley sparked with their infamous refusal to wear Reebok apparel during the Games.[19] Both athletes, part of the 1992 U.S. Olympic Dream Team, were featured in Nike ad campaigns in the 1990s, including Jordan's partnership with up-and-coming film director Spike Lee as the consummate basketball and sneakers fan Mars Blackmon, and Barkley's controversial "Not a Role Model" commercials. Journalist Donald Katz remarks, "Three months before the Olympics, an interviewer from the *Harvard Business Review* asked (co-founder and chairman of Nike, Inc.) Phil Knight why Nike used so many athletes to support company initiatives. 'Because it saves a lot of time,' Knight said. 'You can't explain much in sixty seconds, but when you show Michael Jordan, you don't have to.' "[20] Knight's statements mark the company's transition from traditional advertising to a significant expansion in sports marketing that featured celebrity athletes, on which its success relied. But the European market proved to be a harder egg to crack despite Nike's multimillion-dollar allocations to European advertising and promotion in 1993. According to a brand identity comparative analysis by marketing expert Jean-Noël Kapferer, the European market resisted Nike's aggressive marketing strategies.[21] Nike's campaigns largely focused on individual performance and a competitive winning attitude evidenced by its use of solitary iconic figures like Steve Prefontaine, Ilie Nastase,[22] John McEnroe, Jordan, Jackson, Barkley, and Tiger Woods (who signed an endorsement deal with Nike in 1996). Nike's two-pronged approach to advertising campaigns between the late 1980s and the mid-1990s featured an irreverent attitude toward commodity culture and constructed the brand "as the vehicle of an ethos that integrates themes of personal transcendence, achievement, and authenticity."[23] Prime competitors Adidas and Puma promoted collective values, focusing on the team sport dynamic, community, and healthy competition by sponsoring whole teams and sports events. German-based Adidas, with its historical connection to the Olympics, had long held the leading European market position in sports apparel. However, Nike's European marketing strategies made the move to team sports when the company sponsored Brazil in the 1994

U.S.-hosted World Cup, confirming Nike as a viable opponent to Adidas's European market position. Additionally, in 1996, Nike signed an endorsement deal with Brazil's national soccer team as an initial foray into Latin America's emerging consumer market.[24]

Despite Nike's interest in soccer, basketball remained the company's preferred team sport. Donald Katz writes:

> Basketball, the Nike strategists believed, was on its way to dislodging soccer as the world game, and the Dream Team at the Olympics would be the best chance to show power basketball to the world. A year earlier, Michael Jordan was part of a Nike marketing caravan that had traveled through Europe. Several months later, it was difficult to find a wall or street lamp in Munich that failed to announce the imminent arrival of Nike stars Charles Barkley and Scottie Pippen for a colorful pre-Olympic festival of slam dunks and exhibition basketball.[25]

The Dream Team solidified the sporting power of basketball and its celebrity players. As a result, Europe became the next big market to fall to Nike's inscrutable conquests, adding to the company's rising global presence. Adidas answered Nike's mounting advertising challenge with a grassroots, youth culture–centered three-on-three basketball event: Adidas Streetball Challenge.[26] The first challenge was held in August 1992 in front of the Palast der Republik in Berlin.[27] Madrid, Paris, Stockholm, Zurich, and Vein also hosted challenges in 1992. During the next four years, the challenge expanded to include 23 cities in the former Soviet Union, as well as Prague. Budapest hosted the challenge's second world championship event in 1996.

Imaging Blackness

Nike's 1990s advertising campaigns, featuring a sizable number of black male athletes, revolutionized the media sphere and earned the company its first Emmy as well as the Cannes Advertising Festival's Advertiser of the Year award in 1994. As discussed, Nike's 1980 supreme court ad marked a shift in the company's advertising strategy from products to people. Until 1980, Nike had relied on word-of-mouth and print advertisements to sell athletic shoes and apparel.[28] With advancements in televisual communication, Nike maintained its competitive edge through mainstream media campaigns. Television commercials required more than catch phrases, slogans, and product knowledge; they needed images. Images of actual products sufficed for a time, but Nike soon used the relationship between mass media and image circulation to its advantage. After 1980, Nike's advertisements were designed to sell more than just products.[29] Black athletes became the central feature of Nike's U.S. advertising program during the 1990s, enacting a discursive relation between race, advertising, and brand recognition.[30] The overwhelming number of black male bodies used in Nike and other corporate ads subsequently promoted black bodies as sites of racialized sexual desire, a desire that reduced black bodies to consumable objects.

According to cultural critic Michael Eric Dyson, the culture of sports reinforced American values such as individuality, aggressive competition, and superiority for white male athletes. He writes, "For much of its history, American sports activity has reflected white patriarchal privilege, and it has been rigidly defined and socially shaped by rules that restricted the equitable participation of women and people of color."[31] Because basketball and other sports were relegated to white participation, whiteness became representative of and discursively linked to Americanness, an Americanness founded on and shored up by the institution of slavery during which black bodies were festishized and black men were reduced to both an assumedly inherent possession of exaggerated physical abilities and a mythic possession of sexual prowess. In other words, black men were bigger, stronger, more virile, and more sexually potent. Just as black male slaves were socially and politically marginalized, black males were excluded from the white male–dominated U.S. sports industry because of fears of black physical performance and virility to appease anxieties around white masculinity and American identity. This parallels with the proliferation of white faces and narratives in the television industry; until shows such as *Roots* (1977) and *The Cosby Show* (1984–1992), central black characters were largely held outside of representation in mainstream media. But even these examples are unable to escape the grips of racial essentialism and elitism. Despite spaces of visibility that these shows opened up in popular culture and in the national public imagination, *Roots*, *The Cosby Show*, and other representations of black culture in popular media have been criticized for assimilationist tendencies that serve to manage a particular trope of black subjectivity within dominant culture.[32] These shows, along with the history of sports culture in the United States and other sites of popular culture production, underscore the discourse of the visual that Pope.L's *Budapest Crawl* targets.

Soar's 2001 article recalls Michael Eric Dyson's 1993 essay on the heroic symbolism, cultural capital, and commodity fetishism represented by black athletes in American media, namely basketball icon Michael Jordan. Air Jordan's successful sales and "Be Like Mike" slogans contributed to making Michael Jordan into a spectacle by promoting his mythic abilities to fly—his logo consists of the player in silhouette, suspended in the air in mid-flight, reaching upward and defying gravity. Jordan became an icon with supernatural heroic talents, a mythic image of blackness, and a consumable object. The shoe, the symbol, the slogan, the very brand of Michael Jordan contributed to equating the man with the product. Sociologists Robert Goldman and Stephen Papson describe the relationship between Jordan, Nike advertising, and the brand's sign value: "In Nike's case ... joining images of Michael Jordan with the meaning of Nike shoes ... lends value to the meaning of the swoosh ... Michael Jordan himself has long been transformed into a global iconic presence in the media, so much so that in 1996 Nike introduced a 'Brand Jordan' line of shoes and apparel."[33] And according to Strasser and Becklund, "By the close of 1986, Nike and Jordan were so closely linked in the public eye that Jordan's teammate Orlando Woolridge quipped to *Sports Illustrated* that they should call the company 'Mikey.' "[34] Jordan was not only transformed into—or more accurately, reduced—to a commodity, his image and brand became synonymous with Nike, reinforced by Nike's global advertising regime. Soar asserts, "Advertising, and Nike's productions in particular, [have] ultimately led to the valorization of a particular, mediated notion of urban black maleness."[35] Soar's poignant characterization of Nike's advertising campaigns as *productions* returns us to the discursive poetics and politics of performance and identity construction. Here, it is a particular type of black masculinity being not only produced, but also idolized and consumed vis-à-vis the black male athletic subject in Nike advertising. Black male bodies are reduced to sites of desire and commodity, the ultimate fetish object. Pope.L's *The Black Body and Sport* series directly responds to this problematic mode of representation.

Budapest Crawl: William Pope.L and Black Masculinity

On a grey overcast day in July 1999, a man with a disheveled afro and scruffy beard dressed in a white AND 1 sports jersey, white athletic shorts, Nike sneakers, and elbow and kneepads steadily crawls along a highway, largely unnoticed. When pedestrians encounter the scene, they pause and stare, relatively unaware that they are witnessing a previously rehearsed performance. Using his limbs to pull his body along the street's gravel surface, the man's horizontality and determined crawl resemble a military training exercise, mobilizing a politics of submission and power that runs through the piece. The man is artist William Pope.L, known for his performative crawl interventions in the United States and abroad. A two-hour endurance action, *Budapest Crawl* took place between the Danube River and Hungary's parliament building.

The video documenting the artist's crawl begins with Pope.L preparing, adjusting his gloves and glasses. After affixing a flashlight to an inflated globe, he stretches briefly and descends into a crawl along the cement embankment of the river. Pope.L holds the globe in one hand and a half-empty bottle of cologne in the other hand for the duration of the performance. Next, the camera pans and captures the skyline, a river ferry, a police officer, and other onlookers. The artist switches to crawling alongside the highway's guardrail, increasing his encounters with the dangers of the street; cars race past and truck drivers issue loud, cautionary honks. Pope.L's steady, calculated crawling becomes almost meditative, methodic even, until the crawl's physical duress begins to take its effect. The artist's face tenses; his sweat increases and drips from his cheeks and chin; he grunts with every motion, indicating the physical (and perhaps mental) fatigue brought on by his performance. Here, Pope.L turns onto his back and uses a back crawl to combat the fatigue that his body experiences while performing his intervention. As the sun sets, Pope.L submits as he reaches the concrete steps rising out of the Danube River toward the highway. As the artist sits upright on the steps, he takes a few moments to gather himself, resting over the illuminated globe in his lap. Against a dusky sky, his head hangs as his torso rises and falls with each breath. In the last frame of the video, Pope.L stands and changes into a clean pair of clothes, marking the end of the performance. The camera pans a beautifully illuminated cityscape and fades to black with the well-lit monumental facade of Hungary's parliament building in the background.

Pope.L's larger series *The Black Body and Sport* critiques how the black athlete has been commodified and consumed in the United States and Europe. Following Pope.L, the black male sports body can be read as a marketing device in the public sphere, moving through various media sites—on billboards, in magazine advertisements, in commercials. As previously discussed, both Nike and Adidas were competing for top market spots in the sports apparel industry in the 1990s. As Nike jockeyed to dethrone Adidas, Adidas looked to the U.S. market for brand expansion. Nike coupled the use of iconic celebrity figures with the collective spirit in popular team sports in Europe, namely soccer and basketball, while Adidas launched its Streetball Challenge. By performing similar crawls in Berlin, Madrid, and Prague in 1999, Pope.L explicitly attended to the proliferation of images of black male sports bodies in Nike and Adidas's global sports product campaigns during the 1990s. The artist's AND 1 jersey and Nike sneakers remind us of the commingling of black athletic bodies with national sports, corporate brands, products and endorsements, and large-scale media campaigns. Like Nike, AND 1 is heavily associated with the sport of basketball, and more specifically streetball. The AND 1 brand launched in Philadelphia in 1993, just one year after Adidas launched its Adidas Streetball Challenge in efforts to compete in the American market.[36]

Streetball, also referred to as black basketball, emerged in both New York City and Washington, D.C., around the turn of the 20th century.[37] In streetball, regulations are relaxed to encourage unique showmanship, slam dunks, and trick plays. With increased popularity after World War I, largely attributed to postwar population growths in inner cities, streetball players formed teams, most notably the Harlem Renaissance, or "Rens."[38] Amateur leagues such as the Interscholastic Athletic Association and the Black Basketball League were also established. In 1946, New York City Parks and Recreation employee Holcombe Rucker started what is arguably the oldest and most famous streetball basketball tournament, the Rucker League.[39] Rucker Park in Harlem was established in 1956 and lawfully named after Rucker in 1974. After World War II, the Rens and other streetball teams toured the country, taking on all-white teams. Many streetball players enrolled in black colleges and played collegiate basketball. Their enrollment prompted the creation of the Colored Intercollegiate Athletic Association, later renamed the Central Intercollegiate Athletic Association.[40] In the late 1970s, the National Collegiate Athletic Association (NCAA) exposed mainstream America to collegiate streetball players through televised coverage of games. Televised NCAA basketball tournaments along with NBA stars such as Wilt Chamberlain, Patrick Ewing, Kareem Abdul-Jabbar, and others associated with streetball culture made streetball a global phenomenon, ripe for consumption. Through the popularity of Rucker's Park, NCAA telecasts, and the spectacle of the NBA, streetball offered a viable inroad to American youth culture.

Adidas and AND 1 both capitalized on the urban phenomenon of streetball and the niche gold mine of youth culture. Pope.L's AND 1 costume jersey expressly references this exchange. As Adidas co-opted streetball to gain a foothold in the U.S. sports apparel market and to counter Nike's mounting assault on the European market, more and more images of black male sports bodies cycled through the mass media. This hypervisibility of black masculinity in popular media sharply contrasts with stereotypical representations of blackness as abject, disenfranchised, and invisible in everyday life. Pope.L's *The Black Body and Sport* directly engages these preconceptions along with the idealization and idolization of black male sports bodies. As Franz Fanon declared in his definitive text *Black Skin, White Masks*, published 20 years after the Rucker League was established, "There is one expression that through time has become singularly eroticized: the black athlete."[41] Scholar Ben Carrington applies Fanon's theorizing of the black sports body and its relationship to white masculinity and commodity culture in *Race, Sport and Politics: The Sporting Black Diaspora*. He states, " 'The black athlete' as object and fetish thus serves as a boundary marker for white masculinity."[42] Carrington continues:

> Thus, the black athlete is seen to be the embodiment of hyper-masculinity; ultraviolent and the ultimate manifestation of phallic power . . . Fanon continues to suggest that blackness comes to signify biology itself . . . The logical conclusion to this sexualized discourse is that, via the processes of visual objectification and white mythological discourses (scientific, filmic and literary), the black man is effectively reduced to the phallus . . . The black athlete (as the quintessence of blackness) assumes the pre-eminent position as *the* "penis-symbol" and becomes a fantasmatic trope through which anxieties concerning the fragility of western (male) sexuality are played out. The black athlete is thus positioned as a site for voyeuristic admiration—the black is idolized for its sheer super-human physicality.[43]

Carrington's reading of Fanon sutures the black sports body to libidinal masculinity signified by phallic power, illustrating how the black sports body is constructed through a lens of Western male sexuality and marked as a site of both sexual and racial desire. Pope.L enacts a relationship between black masculinity and phallic power by negating the phallic verticality oft associated with black male sports bodies as erect, aggressive, physically superior, and hypermasculine. Here, the artist's performative spectacle is explicitly agitative; Pope.L's horizontality becomes a political act, an affronting destabilization of the black male sports body as a site of desire and consumption. The title of Pope.L's European crawl tour; his branded sports jersey, shorts, and sneakers; and his own black male body as medium situate the artist's performance within the discourse signaled by Fanon and Carrington. This spectacle of racial consumption and desire is at the center of Pope.L's larger artistic practice.

The Spectacle of Race in William Pope.L's Artistic Practice

Over the past four decades, Pope.L has explored racial categories in his carnivalesque performance interventions, theater productions, drawings, and installations. He is particularly interested in binary constructions of whiteness and blackness, and how blackness operates as a commodity. Pope.L first saw minimalist painter Robert Ryman's white-on-white monochromes in the early 1970s.[44] These paintings profoundly influenced Pope.L's conceptual practice, changing his understandings of whiteness and of painting as an artistic medium. Pope.L transposed his experience of Ryman's work into explorations of the discursive work of racial categories in the United States and abroad. Pope.L's meditations on the symbolism of whiteness emerged from the artist's formidable encounters with Ryman's monochromes. Pope.L's encounters signal both a certain racialization of Ryman's white-on-white monochromes and a focus on how the artist's formal engagement with Ryman's work has informed his larger practice of thinking binary oppositions like whiteness and blackness as social constructions.

In his temporary street performance *Milk Pour* (1999), performed the same year as *The Black Body and Sport*, Pope.L poured a gallon of milk into a street gutter, creating a fluid yet opaque stream of whiteness, thereby critiquing the complexities and materiality of whiteness and race at large. In *Sweet Desire* (1998), another performance piece, Pope.L was buried in a hole in the ground in 98-degree heat with a bowl of white (vanilla) ice cream slowly melting in front of him just beyond his reach. In his text-based *White Drawings* (2000), an ongoing series of mixed media works on paper, Pope.L takes whiteness as a point of departure in exploring the spectacularization and commodification of blackness. *White Drawings* visualize whiteness as a system of laws, behaviors, and institutions that privilege the visibility of whiteness as a racial category within the United States—a system that produces whiteness as hierarchically superior and forecloses the presence of blackness, of difference, of anything "other."

White Drawings are comprised of simple yet confounding text phrases rendered in sketched all-capital block letters. The use of all capital letters signals power, verticality, uniformity, and superiority. The angular block letters symbolize the rigid, absolute nature of ideological systems.

For Pope.L, the power of exclusion represented in his articulations of the discursive system of racialization—the very tyranny of whiteness—is what relegates blackness to the realm of invisibility. In *White Drawings*, Pope.L articulates power relations inherent to the color line, the opposition between whiteness and blackness that W. E. B. Du Bois proclaimed as the United States' most enduring problem in the 20th century. Pope.L's drawing series sardonically reifies binary constructions of whiteness and blackness within racial discourse through short, absurd, text-based compositions that image and imagine definitions of status and hierarchy. For Pope.L, whiteness and blackness are interdependent; whiteness—as superiority and power—is shored up by blackness. Alternately, blackness—in vying for visibility—is contingent upon whiteness. These works, each produced around the same time as *The Black Body and Sport*, foreground Pope.L's employment of restricted mobility, blackness as desire and commodity, and the symbolic value of the hole (as lack) in his crawl interventions.

Blackness as Desire and Lack

In the catalog for the artist's 2002–2003 traveling retrospective *eRacism*, Pope.L characterizes blackness as "a lack worth having,"[45] a lack fashioned in opposition to whiteness and predicated on a duality of inferiority and superiority. Pope.L further describes blackness as a desirable lack specific to masculinity: "This is the dilemma for the [black male body]. On the one hand, being male connotes a certain privilege and presence. On the other hand, being black connotes a certain subordination and lack."[46] For Pope.L, race, gender, and sexuality intersect and contingently inform one another. The privilege of black masculinity is centered on the myth of phallic power and physical and sexual prowess that situates black masculinity as a site of desire. Conversely, black masculinity as desirous is always undermined by the presence of blackness as racially signifying inferiority and lack. The tension between presence and absence here is made visible in the bottle of cologne that Pope.L holds in his hand for the duration of *Budapest Crawl*. The half-empty, half-full dialectic represented in the bottle of cologne echoes philosopher Martin Heidegger's ontological postulate of oscillation; that is, simultaneously "half being, half not being."[47] For Pope.L, blackness is articulated in this oscillation, in the simultaneity of being and not being, of visible yet invisible, as both desire *and* absence.

Performance studies scholar André Lepecki locates Pope.L's crawls within the context of theorist Henri Lefèbvre's writings on the production of space and social relations. Following Lefèbvre, Lepecki declares Pope.L's "performance of horizontality as a critique of verticality as phallic erectility, how the vertical 'bestows a special status to the perpendicular, proclaiming phallocracy as the orientation of space,' " and how the spatialization of the vertical represents the "brutality of political power, of the means of constraint: police, army, bureaucracy."[48] While I agree with Lepecki's association, I would like to suggest that there is more at play in Pope.L's crawl interventions. Pope.L explodes the myth of the black phallus by negating the metaphor of phallic erectility that Lepecki identifies with verticality by *choosing* to crawl, by choosing to submit to and temporarily inhabit horizontality, by *performing* abjection.

Horizontal and Vertical Axes in *Budapest Crawl*

Many critics have described Pope.L's performance of horizontality as a deliberate negation of verticality. Martha Wilson, artist and founding director of Franklin Furnace, says Pope.L's crawl interventions "literally place his body in the position of homeless people, taking [his body] out of the vertical posture representing power, forcing him and his unwitting audience to look at bodies that have been rendered invisible."[49] In many of his crawl interventions, Pope.L confronts notions of privilege by manipulating signs like verticality, business suits, and a capeless superman costume. In *Tompkins Square Crawl* (1991), Pope.L wore a business suit symbolic of upward mobility and desire for the fictive "better life" harbored in the American dream, thus highlighting the tenuous relation between race and class in the United States. For *The Great White Way: 22 Miles, 5 Years, 1 Street* (2001), performed in New York City along 22 miles of Broadway Avenue from the base of the Statue of Liberty to Pope.L's mother's house in the Bronx, the artist donned a capeless superman suit that signified a grounded heroism, particularly provocative in the wake of the September 11, 2001, attacks on the World Trade Center.

For Pope.L, verticality is a distinct characteristic, an uprightness that signals privilege, power, and mobility. In a 1996 *BOMB* magazine interview with Martha Wilson, three years prior to *Budapest Crawl*, Pope.L details his early fascinations with the symbolism that horizontality elicits:

> By treating your body in a certain way, by putting your body in a certain physiognomic situation, you can force it to experience in ways it normally wouldn't. In New York, in most cities, if you can remain vertical and moving

you deal with the world; this is urban power. But people who are forced to give up their verticality are prey to all kinds of dangers.[50]

Pope.L's statement returns us to the center of his practice: a politics of submission and power. Fanon's scholarship again resonates here: "I move slowly in the world, accustomed now to seek no longer for upheaval. I progress by crawling."[51] For Pope.L, crawling is bound mobility. Crawling, the very act of submitting to horizontality, to danger, and to powerlessness enacts struggle *performed*, negotiated, and made visible directly on the body. This performance of the politics of identity is made even more complex by Pope.L's assertion of his own raced, gendered body in public space. For Pope.L, verticality represents constructions of visibility, presence, being, unified subjectivity; horizontality represents constructions of invisibility, absence, lack, dispossession.[52] Verticality and horizontality function as metaphors that, like whiteness and blackness, are based in binary oppositions. In submitting to horizontality in his crawling interventions, the metaphor of invisibility is not solely about homelessness or raced bodies as invisible, but also the pervasiveness and the normalization of race as an ordering system that Pope.L responds to in his practice.

Tension between horizontal and vertical states of being is also amplified by editing techniques used in the video documentation of *Budapest Crawl*. Frictional horizontal and vertical axes are rendered through edited juxtapositions of modern transportation technologies, such as bridges and highways, with high-rise apartment buildings with glass façades, and the vertical monumentality and iconicity of Hungary's parliament building. One such apparatus, the Széchenyi Chain Bridge, is captured in the background as the camera pans the Budapest skyline between close-up shots of Pope.L's crawling body. The Széchenyi Chain Bridge opened in 1849 and was the first permanent bridge to connect the eastern bank Buda with the western bank Pest across the Danube River. Pest, Buda, and Óbuda were each separate cities until 1873, when they were united as the present Hungarian capital Budapest. The Széchenyi suspension bridge, with its balance of wrought iron and stone, represents a central European modern engineering icon as well as a national symbol and the linkage between east and west sides of the city. Margaret Bridge, the second oldest permanent bridge connecting Buda and Pest, is captured in the video frame as well, indicating the artist's two-hour crawl route between the bridges alongside the Hungary's parliament building. These two bridges accelerated flows of automobile traffic, trade, and commerce, creating economic growth along with a globalizing intercultural and intracultural metropolis.

While the encompassing panorama of the city is disrupted by the specificity and locality of the street, the rationalization and ordering of space through architectural verticality is complicated by both the horizontality of the bridges as well as Pope.L's derationalizing performance of horizontality. The mythos of verticality and aspiration expressed in the high-rising skyscrapers, the all-glass modernist condominiums, and the towering Gothic Revival style of the Hungary's parliament building along the Danube River is poignantly undercut by Pope.L's slow crawling body under duress. Pope.L's site-specific performance of horizontality here both interrupts this mythos of verticality and comments on symptoms of globalization—as a system of accelerated flows of information, products, and people as well as the global circulation of images that inform the construction of black masculinity vis-à-vis the black male sports body. Just as Pope.L's Nike sneakers specifically reference how Nike constructed images of black masculinity in its 1990s sports ads, subsequently producing dominant cultures of desire and consumption, Pope.L's globe illuminates the discursive power of globalization and how the world is imagined and constructed through the circulation and consumption of images. Here, the inflatable illuminated globe that Pope.L holds in his hand reads as a metaphor for mass media as a site for world making.

Pope.L's horizontal crawl also raises critical questions about the physical action of crawling itself. Crawling on all fours is typically associated with infancy or animalism, and as Ben Carrington argues about the sports industry as a site of racial construction:

> Blacks became creatures of the body and the body alone, helping to further consolidate colonial myths that sought to connect black Africans to the animal world rather than with emerging human civilizations. Second, the idea of the black athlete becomes a very powerful trope enabling a whole range of beliefs about primitive and savage blackness—violence, hyper-sexuality, aggression and so on—to be reproduced in a seemingly benign form, that is in the lauding of black athleticism.[53]

Following Carrington, Pope.L's choosing to crawl becomes a project of recovery and resistance. It is the very act of choosing, along with Pope.L's intervention and performance of the black male athlete as a trope of blackness, that bestows power and deconstructs ideological myths of racial hierarchies.

Exploded Myths

Pope.L often describes his work as rubbing myths together. In *Budapest Crawl*, Pope.L rubs together myths of blackness and masculinity, highlighting absurdist connotations of hypervisibility assigned to black male sports bodies through the metaphors of horizontality and verticality. Within the institution of racial slavery, black males were rendered subhuman. Conversely, black males became *hyper*masculine, *super*human through the sports industry, unable to ever inhabit a "normal" subjecthood. Pope.L's physically grounded body and laborious act of crawling candidly intervenes and dethrones these illusions of verticality and phallic erectility. In *Budapest Crawl*, Pope.L slithers along the street, subordinate to the vertical architectural structures that surround him. Pope.L further intensifies the tension between vertical and horizontal by deflating the myth of the black phallus. The artist's *performance* of a *construction*—the black male sports body as sign and trope—highlights the illusion, myth, and artifice of black masculinity, stripping it of its so-called phallic power. Pope.L's horizontal, sullied, fatigued body starkly contracts the mythic virility and verticality of black male athletes, particularly towering basketball players that are often reduced to sites of entertainment, titillation, spectacle, and consumption. *Budapest Crawl* complicates the larger subliminal implications of invisibility, not only through the performance of horizontality as a critique of phallic erectility, but also through the artist's nuanced attention to a politics of site, belonging, identity and space.

Pope.L's subversive performance strategy is made more complex through the spectacle of a history of consumption, desire, and fetishization of black male celebrity sports bodies in both U.S. and European advertising campaigns. By placing his own body in the public sphere, literally in the street, Pope.L directly engages and invites viewers' gazes, effectively luring spectators into consuming him. Here, Pope.L subverts advertising as an institution of power by making spectators complicit in the very act of consumption. Pope.L issues a double gesture by reducing his own body, his own image to that of an object to be consumed while simultaneously performing the commodified image of black masculinity through sports advertising. The artist's filming of *Budapest Crawl* adds another lens through which to consider the image of blackness that Pope.L performs.[54] Pope. L's *Budapest Crawl* doubles as both a video work and performance documentation. The video features filmic techniques—cuts that condense the two-hour performance into an eight-minute piece, panning shots, canted angles, and close-ups—qualifying the video as an independent document, a work in itself. Pope.L's video production amplifies the artist's investments in the carnivalesque and spectacular as well as his interrogation of problematic representations of black bodies in the media sphere. Pope.L delivers another double gesture by co-opting and employing a mechanism through which consumption is enacted in advertising: the camera. Pope.L's *Budapest Crawl* and larger series *The Black Body and Sport* explode racial and sexual myths by using consumption as a mocking metaphor. By interrogating how the sports advertising industry, with Nike and Adidas at its helm, constructed and promoted sensationalized and essentialist images of black masculinity during the 1990s, Pope.L demonstrates how the sports industry itself serves as a site of knowledge production wherein racial formation and racism occurs.

Notes

1. Robert Goldman and Stephen Papson, *Nike Culture: The Sign of the Swoosh* (London: Sage, 1998): 4. For an overview of the history of competition between Nike, Adidas, Puma, and Reebok, see Barbara Smit's *Sneaker Wars: The Enemy Brothers Who Founded Adidas and Puma and the Family Feud That Forever Changed the Business of Sport* (New York: Ecco, 2008). For more information on Adidas's branding strategies from the 1920s to present, see the Adidas Group's company document "At a Glance: The Story of the Adidas Group." The document is available online at http://www.adidas-group.com/en/ourgroup/assets/history/pdfs/history-e.pdf.

2. Ibid.

3. See J.B. Strasser and Laurie Becklund's *Swoosh: The Unauthorized Story of Nike and the Men Who Played There* (New York: Harcourt Brace Jovanovich, 1991) for this history.

4. Ibid.

5. Jan Runau, "20 Years of Adidas Streeball: A Success Story," Adidas Group, August 22, 2012, Blog post, Accessed at various times between October 2011 and December 2012, http://blog.adidas-group.com/2012/08/20-years-of-adidas-streetball-a-success-story/#more-7616. Runau was head of public relations (PR) for Adidas Germany and led all PR activities in Adidas's home market for four years from 1994 to 1998. At the time this essay was written, Runau was chief corporate communication officer for the Adidas Group. Besides this blog post, little has been written about the history of the Adidas Streetball Challenge. Consequently, in researching this chapter, I conducted an ethnographic study of various social media pages, blogs, and amateur websites devoted to documenting and archiving the history of the Adidas Streetball Challenge in various cities.

6. Note that the use of the phrase "*the* black sports body" throughout this text is deliberate to demonstrate how Nike's and Adidas's sports advertising strategies during the 1990s were collapsing and essentializing in their construction of black male athletes. Pope.L's *The Black Body and Sport* predates artist Hank Willis Thomas's responses to representations of black male sports bodies and advertising.

7. Matthew Soar, "Engines and Acolytes of Consumption: Black Male Bodies, Advertising and the Laws of Thermodynamics," *Body & Society* 7, no. 4 (2001): 49.

8. Soar 50. Emphasis in original.

9. "History & Heritage," Nike, Inc., n.d. Web. Accessed November 2011. http://www.nikeinc.com/pages/history-heritage.

10. Ibid. In *Swoosh: The Unauthorized Story of Nike and the Men Who Played There*, Strasser and Becklund report, "By 1981, [Nike] had become a public company with $458 million in revenues, 8,000 retail accounts, 140 shoe models, 130 sales reps, 2,700 employees, thousands of shareholders, and a value for everyone to see in the newspaper each day" (433).

11. J.B. Strasser and Laurie Becklund, *Swoosh: The Unauthorized Story of Nike and the Men Who Played There* (New York: Harcourt Brace Jovanovich, 1991), 445.

12. Barbara Smit, *Sneaker Wars: The Enemy Brothers Who Founded Adidas and Puma and the Family Feud That Forever Changed the Business of Sport* (New York: Ecco, 2008), 191–193.

13. Ibid. Barbara Smit states that "in the first year, [the Air Jordan] generated sales of more than $100 million for Nike."

14. Donald Katz, *Just Do It: The Nike Spirit in the Corporate World* (New York: Random House, 1994), 22. For an in-depth discussion of the branding power of Nike's swoosh logo and "Just Do It" slogan, see Robert Goldman and Stephen Papson's *Nike Culture: The Sign of the Swoosh* (London: Sage, 1998).

15. "History & Heritage," Nike, Inc., n.d. Web. Accessed November 2011. http://www.nikeinc.com/pages/history-heritage.

16. In 1987, Reebok led Nike with a score of 30.1 percent to 18.2 percent in market shares. By 1997, Nike brands accounted for almost 60 percent of shoes stocked by major retail chains such as Foot Locker and Finish Line. See Goldman and Papson's *Nike Culture: The Sign of the Swoosh*, p. 4, and Jennifer Steinhauer's "Nike Is in a League of Its Own, with No Big Rival, It Calls the Shots in Athletic Shoes," *New York Times*, June 7, 1997, 21.

17. J.B. Strasser and Laurie Becklund, *Swoosh: The Unauthorized Story of Nike and the Men Who Played There* (New York: Harcourt Brace Jovanovich, 1991), 445.

18. Donald R. Katz, *Just Do It: The Nike Spirit in the Corporate World* (New York: Random House, 1994), 29.

19. Ibid., 21. See Katz's chapter "Barcelona" for a full discussion of the media events at the 1992 Olympic Games.

20. Ibid., 25.

21. For detailed brand comparisons between Nike and Adidas, and how each company leveraged advertising campaigns and brand language to garner leading positions in the athletic shoe and apparel industries, see Katz's *Just Do It*; and Jean-Noël Kapferer's *Strategic Brand Management: New Approaches to Creating and Evaluating Brand Equity* (New York: Free Press, 1992) and *Reinventing the Brand: Can Top Brands Survive the New Market Realities?* (London: Kogan Page, 2001).

22. Romanian tennis player Ilie Nastase became the first professional athlete to sign an endorsement deal with Nike in 1972. However, Barbara Smit writes that Nastase switched to Adidas after signing a four-year contract with the company (*Sneaker Wars*, 212). The endorsement deal with Adidas marked the beginning of Nastase's long-time friendship with and Adidas heir Horst Dassler.

23. Robert Goldman and Stephen Papson, *Nike Culture: The Sign of the Swoosh* (London: Sage, 1998), 3.

24. Jeff Manning, "Goal! Nike Signs on Brazil's Soccer Team," *Oregonian*, December 6, 1996, C1, C6.

25. Donald R. Katz, *Just Do It: The Nike Spirit in the Corporate World* (New York: Random House, 1994), 29.

26. For a brief history of the Adidas Streetball Challenge in Hungary between 1993 and 2002, see http://www.streetballnet.hu/tortenet.html. Accessed at various times between October 2011 and December 2012. At the time this chapter was written, the latest Adidas Streetball Challenge in Budapest had taken place on September 22, 2012.

27. Runau, "20 Years of Adidas Streetball: A Success Story," Adidas Group, August 22, 2012, Blog post, Accessed at various times between October 2011 and December 2012, http://blog.adidas-group.com/2012/08/20-years-of-adidas -streetball-a-success-story/#more-7616.

28. For an in-depth discussion of Nike's advertising and corporate branding histories from the mid-1960s to 1994, see Strasser and Becklund's *Swoosh: The Unauthorized Story of Nike and the Men Who Played There* and Donald Katz's *Just Do It: The Nike Spirit in the Corporate World*.

29. Goldman and Papson note, "The shoe vanished from Nike TV ads some time ago. Then in the mid 1990s the Nike name ... quietly disappeared, leaving only the swoosh logo to mark the ads" (1); Robert Goldman and Stephen Papson, *Nike Culture: The Sign of the Swoosh* (London: Sage, 1998).

30. In "Engines and Acolytes of Consumption: Black Male Bodies, Advertising and the Laws of Thermodynamics," Matthew Soar investigates the historical development of Nike's award-winning advertising campaigns in the United States during the 1990s, revealing that African-American athletes had become a primary focus; Matthew Soar, "Engines and Acolytes of Consumption: Black Male Bodies, Advertising and the Laws of Thermodynamics," *Body & Society* 7, no. 4 (2001): 37–55.

31. Michael Eric Dyson, "Michael Jordan and the Pedagogy of Desire," in *The Michael Eric Dyson Reader* (New York: Basic Civitas, 1993), 462.

32. Alex Haley's 1970s miniseries *Roots* and the graphic imagery that circulated in mainstream television had a profound impact on a collective consciousness around slavery in the United States. However, many critics have positioned popular culture as a site where the management of difference occurs and progresses an assimilationist, regulatory, or tolerant narrative. Furthermore, popular culture since the 1960s, particularly literature, television, and film, have offered representations of black life that align with my argument, that is, *Roots, Amistad, Beloved*. There are a number of criticisms around these representations as iconic, reconciliatory, domesticating, and complicit in a liberalist ideology of inclusion and harmony. See Herman Gray's *Watching Race: Television and the Struggle for Blackness* (Minneapolis: University of Minnesota Press, 1995) and Wendy Brown's *Regulating Aversion: Tolerance in the Age of Identity and Empire* (Princeton, NJ: Princeton University Press, 2006).

33. Robert Goldman and Stephen Papson, *Nike Culture: The Sign of the Swoosh* (London: Sage, 1998), 2.

34. J.B. Strasser and Laurie Becklund, *Swoosh: The Unauthorized Story of Nike and the Men Who Played There* (New York: Harcourt Brace Jovanovich, 1991), 629.

35. Matthew Soar, "Engines and Acolytes of Consumption: Black Male Bodies, Advertising and the Laws of Thermodynamics," *Body & Society* 7, no. 4 (2001): 37–55, 51.

36. Adidas Streetball Challenges included specially designed shoes, on-site autograph sessions with featured athletes, and album compilations by some of the most popular and current hip-hop artists, such as Easy E, Shaquille O'Neal, and others. Given the multimedia presence of the Adidas Streetball Challenge, its popularity, and its target youth audience, coupled with the lack of scholarly literature on the subject, I consulted a number of Facebook pages, blogs, and amateur websites devoted to documenting and archiving the history of the Adidas Streetball Challenge in various cities. For Moscow 1999, see http://www.tci.ru/modx/?id=651> and <http://www.tci.ru/modx/?id=652. For Sao Paulo 1995, see https://www.facebook.com/pages/Trials-X-adidas-Streetball-Challenge-1995/250782838327299 for archived photos. For Bremen, Germany, 1998, see http://blog.adidas-group.com/2012/08/20-years-of-adidas-streetball-a-success-story/streetballcrowd/. All websites were accessed frequently between October 2011 and December 2012.

37. For an in-depth study of streetball's origins and its major players, see Lars Anderson and Chad Millman's *Pickup Artists: Street Basketball in America* (London: Verso, 1998).

38. Ibid., 62.

39. Ibid., 66.

40. For this history, see *Pickup Artists: Street Basketball in America* and John Huet, Jimmy Smith, and John C. Jay's *Soul of the Game: Images and Voices of Street Basketball* (New York: Melcher Media/Workman, 1997). John Huet is an award-winning sports and advertising photographer. At the time *Soul of the Game* was published, Jimmy Smith was a senior copywriter for the Nike account at Wieden & Kennedy, and John C. Jay was a partner and creative director at Wieden & Kennedy.

41. Franz Fanon, *Black Skin, White Masks* (New York: Grove, 1967), 136.

42. Ben Carrington, *Race, Sport and Politics: The Sporting Black Diaspora* (London; Los Angeles: Sage, 2010), 87.

43. Ben Carrington, *Race, Sport and Politics: The Sporting Black Diaspora* (London: Sage, 2010), 88.

44. William Pope.L retrospectively notes his experience of Ryman's mono-chromes, "I could never see myself throwing that much white (weight) around . . . He must think he's some kind of super-hero who only eats white food and only helps white people by making only white culture . . . [H]is was a sociology of painting (whether he was hip to it or not)" (39). For a larger discussion of Pope.L's career, see the exhibition catalog *William Pope.L: The Friendliest Black Artist in America* (Cambridge, MA: MIT Press, 2002).

45. Mark Bessire, ed. *William Pope.L: The Friendliest Black Artist in America* (Cambridge, MA: MIT Press, 2002), 62.

46. Ibid.

47. Martin Heidegger, *Introduction to Metaphysics* (London; New Haven, CT: Yale University Press, 1987), 28. Pope.L often references Heidegger, Nietzsche, and other European philosophers as influences for his practice and thought.

48. Henri Lefèbvre, *The Production of Space* (Oxford; Cambridge: Wiley-Blackwell, 1991), 287 in André Lepecki's *Exhausting Dance: Performance and the Politics of Movement* (New York; London: Routledge, 2006), 93.

49. Martha Wilson, "Limited Warranty," *William Pope.L: Friendliest Black Artist in America*, 45.

50. Martha Wilson, "William Pope.L," *BOMB* 55 (Spring 1996) Web, Accessed November 2011. http://bombsite.com/issues/55/articles/1957.

51. Fanon, "The Fact of Blackness," in *Black Skin, White Masks*, 116.

52. For an in-depth discussion of Pope.L's crawl practice and the idea of dispossession, see Darby English's chapter on Pope.L in *How to See a Work of Art in Total Darkness* (Cambridge, MA: MIT Press, 2007).

53. Ben Carrington in an interview with Simon Dawes, "Interview with Ben Carrington," *Theory, Culture and Society*, June 20, 2011, Blog post, accessed November 2011. http://theoryculturesociety.blogspot.com/2011/06/interview-with-ben-carrington.html.

54. Pope.L often films and exhibits his crawls as both performance documentation and independent video works.

Bibliography

Aaker, David A., and Erich Joachimsthaler. *Brand Leadership*. New York: Free Press, 2000.

Anderson, Lars, and Chad Millman. *Pickup Artists: Street Basketball in America*. Brooklyn, NY: Verso, 1998.

Bessire, Mark, ed. *William Pope.L: The Friendliest Black Artist in America*. Cambridge, MA: MIT Press, 2002.

Bird, Beverly. "The History of Streetball." http://www.livestrong.com/article/351452-the-history-of-streetball/.

Brown, Wendy. *Regulating Aversion: Tolerance in the Age of Identity and Empire*. Princeton, NJ: Princeton University Press, 2006.

Carrington, Ben. *Race, Sport and Politics: The Sporting Black Diaspora*. London: Sage, 2010.

Carrington, Ben, with Simon Dawes. "Interview with Ben Carrington." *Theory, Culture and Society* (June 20, 2011). Accessed November 2011. http://theoryculturesociety.blogspot.com/2011/06/interview-with-ben-carrington.html.

Dailey, Meghan. "William Pope.L: Artists Space/The Project/Mason Gross Art Galleries at Rutgers University." *Artforum International* (April 2004): 162.

Dyson, Michael Eric. *The Michael Eric Dyson Reader*. New York: Basic Civitas, 2004.

Dyson, Michael Eric. "Michael Jordan and the Pedagogy of Desire," *The Michael Eric Dyson Reader*. New York: Basic Civitas, 1993.

English, Darby. *How to See a Work of Art in Total Darkness*. Cambridge, MA: MIT Press, 2007.

Fanon, Franz. *Black Skin, White Masks*. New York: Grove, 1967.

Goldman, Robert, and Stephen Papson, *Nike Culture: The Sign of the Swoosh*. London: Sage, 1998.

Gray, Herman. *Watching Race: Television and the Struggle for "Blackness."* Minneapolis: University of Minnesota Press, 1995.

Heidegger, Martin. *Introduction to Metaphysics*. London; New Haven, CT: Yale University Press, 1987.

"Holcombe Rucker Park," *City of New York Parks and Recreation*. http://www.nycgovparks.org/parks/M216/highlights/8727.

Huet, John, Jimmy Smith, and John C. Jay. *Soul of the Game: Images & Voices of Street Basketball*. New York: Melcher Media/Workman, 1997.

Kapferer, Jean-Noël. *Reinventing the Brand: Can Top Brands Survive the New Market Realities?* London: Kogan Page, 2001.

Kapferer, Jean-Noël. *Strategic Brand Management: New Approaches to Creating and Evaluating Brand Equity*. New York: Free Press, 1992.

Kapferer, Jean-Noël, and Philip Gibbs. *Strategic Brand Management: New Approaches to Creating and Evaluating Brand Equity.* New York: Free Press, 1992.

Katz, Donald R. *Just Do It: The Nike Spirit in the Corporate World.* New York: Random House, 1994.

Lefèbvre, Henri. *The Production of Space,* Oxford; Cambridge: Wiley-Blackwell, 1991.

Lepecki, André. *Exhausting Dance: Performance and the Politics of Movement.* New York: Routledge, 2006.

Manning, Jeff. "Goal! Nike Signs on Brazil's Soccer Team." *Oregonian,* December 6, 1996, C1, C6.

Pollack, Barbara. "The Art of Public Disturbance: William Pope.L's Street Performance Work Titled 'eRacism.'" *Art in America* (May 2003): 120.

Pope.L, William, and Chris Thompson. "America's Friendliest Black Artist." *PAJ: A Journal of Performance and Art* 24, no. 3 (2002): 68–72.

Smit, Barbara. *Pitch Invasion: Three Stripes, Two Brothers, One Feud: Adidas and the Making of Modern Sport.* London: Allen Lane, 2006.

Smit, Barbara. *Sneaker Wars: The Enemy Brothers Who Founded Adidas and Puma and the Family Feud That Forever Changed the Business of Sport.* New York: Ecco, 2008.

Soar, Matthew. "Engines and Acolytes of Consumption: Black Male Bodies, Advertising and the Laws of Thermodynamics." *Body & Society* 7, no. 4 (2001): 37–55.

Soar, Matthew. "Engines and Acolytes of Consumption: Black Male Bodies, Advertising and the Laws of Thermodynamics." Body & Society 7, no. 4 (2001): 49.

Strasser, J. B., and Laurie Becklund. *Swoosh: The Unauthorized Story of Nike and the Men Who Played There.* New York: Harcourt Brace Jovanovich, 1991.

Thompson, Carlyle Van. *Eating the Black Body: Miscegenation as Sexual Consumption in African American Literature and Culture.* New York: Peter Lang, 2006.

Thompson, Chris. "Afterbirth of a Nation: William Pope.L's Great White Way." *Women & Performance: A Journal of Feminist Theory* 14, no. 1 (2004): 63–90.

Three Pieces: Video Compilation. Dir. William Pope.L., ed. James Pruznick. Informative Media, Inc. 2001.

Tompkins Square Park Crawl. Dir. William Pope.L. Ed. James Pruznick. Informative Media, Inc. 1991.

Wilson, Martha. "Limited Warranty." *William Pope.L: Friendliest Black Artist in America,* 45 (Summer 2003).

Wilson, Martha. "William Pope.L." *BOMB* 55 (Spring 1996) Web, Accessed November 2011. http://bombsite.com/issues/55/articles/1957.

Chapter 11

Armstrong, Bonds, and PEDs: Racial Framing in U.S. Newspapers, 1999–2006

Jennifer Greer and Christopher Murray

Two world-class athletes making their assaults on sports history at the turn of the 21st century are forever linked. One was a baseball slugger often referred to as one of the greatest living players in the history of the game. The other was a cyclist known as much for his courageous triumph over testicular cancer as his amazing athletic ability. One was an African-American man with a quick temper and an even quicker bat. The other was a white man with a warming smile and a welcoming handshake. Despite their differences, Barry Bonds and Lance Armstrong were both athletic wunderkinds who set records thought to be unbreakable—Bonds by crushing 73 home runs in a single season and Armstrong by winning seven Tours de France. And by 2013, both had admitted what had been rumored, and been denied, for years.[1] They had doped during their competitive years.

Bonds, in grand jury testimony that was later confirmed by his attorney, admitted in 2003 to taking steroids but insisted that he was tricked by his personal trainer into doing so. *Sports Illustrated* reported the sealed testimony in 2006, quoting Bonds as saying, "When he (the trainer) said it was flaxseed oil, I just said, 'Whatever.' It was in the ballpark, in front of everybody ... I didn't hide it."[2] Armstrong, after years of denying using performance-enhancing drugs (PEDs), detailed in a January 2013 Oprah Winfrey interview an elaborate doping regimen. In 1999, when the French newspaper *Le Monde* first printed stories on Armstrong's drug use, he accused the paper of committing "vulture journalism."[3] By June 2013, he gave the paper an exclusive on the eve of the 100th Tour de France, arguing that his "life has been ruined by the U.S. Anti-Doping Agency investigation that exposed as lies his years of denials that he and his teammates doped."[4]

Throughout the 2000s, the narratives of these two athletes and their use of PEDs were remarkably similar, yet public opinion of the men was markedly different. A 2006 AP/AOL poll found 48 percent of Americans were rooting for Bonds to fall short of Hank Aaron's all-time home run record.[5] In contrast, until Armstrong admitted to using PEDs in 2013, he was seen as "Saint Lance." A columnist for FoxSports.com wrote in 2011: "Bonds, Armstrong. Armstrong, Bonds. Let's face it. Same story. Same guy. What?! But one is an American hero! And the other is a sleazeball . . . But close your eyes when told the particulars of their stories, and see if you can tell me which is which."[6] Even as early as 2005, *San Francisco Chronicle* columnist Gwen Knapp argued: "Bonds and Armstrong have too much in common for them to be treated so differently. Either both should be presumed clean and accorded full admiration for their athletic accomplishments, or both should be presumed highly suspicious superstars in a doped-up sports world."[7]

Media critics contend the men were perceived differently at the peak of their games because they were portrayed differently. Some contend that the color of their skin cannot be overlooked in making that assessment. Bonds argued that the Major League Baseball steroids coverage focused on him in the 2000s because he is African American. *San Francisco Chronicle* columnist Glenn Dickey agreed, writing in 2004 that Bonds was treated differently than slugger Mark McGwire, who also later admitted to doping. "I think media and fans do view blacks and Latinos differently from white players."[8] Political columnist Dave Zirin (2006) was blunt in his assessment of the role raced played in media coverage of Bonds's steroid use: "The fact is that racism smears this entire story like rancid cream cheese on a stale bialy."[9]

Although coverage has been criticized, no empirical study has formally analyzed media portrayals of the two men during the height of their careers. This chapter aims to do just that through a content analysis of coverage in six major U.S. newspapers between 1999 and 2006. The study compares stories about Bonds and Armstrong and performance-enhancing drugs (PEDs) on the amount, tone, framing, and stereotyping present in coverage.

Background

Racial Framing and Stereotypes in Sports Coverage

Frames are the "the process by which a communication source, such as a news organization, defines and constructs a ... public controversy."[10] Frames guide how audiences think about an issue and can cause them to make different conclusions and judgments about that issue.[11] Frames shape and activate racial attitudes and can reinforce popular stereotypes, especially about race.[12] Further, the aspirations of young people, especially African Americans, are significantly linked with media coverage.[13] The media's overrepresentation of African Americans in professional sports and the underrepresentation of African Americans in other high-profile jobs, such as doctors and lawyers, increases young African-Americans' aspirations to become professional athletes.[14]

Minority athletes have long been covered differently than white athletes.[15] The exclusion of minorities during most of the 20th century created a white male hegemony in sports, or a form of "white power" in which minority athletes are trivialized.[16] For example, African-American college football and basketball players received significantly less coverage and significantly less positive coverage than white players in the *Washington Post* in the 1970s.[17]

One meta-analysis of past studies found that minority groups in any profession are likely to be framed differently than the majority group.[18] As the minority group becomes more integrated and prevalent in the profession, these differences fade. In recent decades, U.S. sports pages are one area in which African Americans are prominently featured, and the amount of coverage has been seen as equitable.[19] "The story of Black men who matter in America is more and more being told in the sports pages," wrote Lawrence Wenner, who argued that the trend as troubling because it limits how citizens think about race and leads to stereotypical views.[20]

Indeed, research has found that racial stereotypes are alive and well in text and images on sports pages.[21] Stereotypes oversimplify issues and are "subtle, yet powerful mechanisms which maintain the status quo, and thereby reaffirm existing prejudices."[22] One 1977 study found that football announcers credited the success of African-American players to innate physical ability and the success of white players to cognitive skills, perseverance, and hard work.[23] This finding was reinforced in a similar study in 1994 that examined assessments of National Football League (NFL) quarterbacks.[24] These portrayals have been linked to fan opinion that

African-American athletes are more physically gifted, and white athletes are more intellectually gifted.[25]

One general stereotype of African-American males, one of the brute, has been found in sports coverage. The brute stereotype characterizes African-American males as primitive, temperamental, overreactive, violent, and sexually powerful.[26] One study found that sports pages paid more attention to the unsportsmanlike behaviors of African-American athletes than they did to the unsportsmanlike behaviors of white athletes.[27] A content analysis of U.S. newspaper coverage of NFL quarterback showed that critical comments were made about African-American quarterbacks at a slightly higher rate than those directed at white quarterbacks.[28] In short, most of the racial stereotypes connected to black athletes have been negative; stereotypes connected with white athletes are typically positive.

Even commercials shown during sports programming rarely feature African Americans, and when they are shown, African Americans are framed as inferior to whites with techniques such as improper grammar.[29] Researcher Pamela Wonsek wrote: "If racial discrimination persists in the U.S. today, the role that the media plays in perpetuating racial stereotypes and preserving the white dominant culture must be considered."[30]

Lawrence Wenner argues that "sports stories are quite formulaic" and often paint athletes as heroes or goats with no middle ground.[31] The romanticization of sports heroes dates back nearly a century when early sportswriters gave players nicknames like "The Great Bambino" (Babe Ruth) and "The Galloping Ghost of the Gridiron" (Red Grange). These iconic frames helped turn sports heroes into God-like figures and popularize sports as a whole. The hero frame goes hand in hand with the "damaged hero" frame brought on by "growing media intrusion."[32] The male sports celebrity can now exemplify "contemporary laddishness, drunken exploits, wife and girlfriend beatings and gay relationships, all of which influence the image of the modern day sports hero," wrote Gill Lines.[33] African-American athletes, in particular, feel the brunt of this. For example, media portrayed National Basketball Association (NBA) superstar Michael Jordan as a *good black* and boxer Mike Tyson as a *bad black*. These fallen hero narratives can affect public perception of a race.

Episodic Framing and Thematic Framing

Shanto Iyengar identified two main types of frames for political news stories: episodic and thematic.[34] Thematic framing tends to attribute problems to a macro level (societal problems), while episodic frames attribute problems to a micro level (flaws within an individual). Iyengar found that episodic framing was used almost 80 percent of the time in the stories he analyzed. Applying this to the sports coverage, stories about PEDs could be framed in a thematic nature (blaming the sport's culture) or an episodic nature (blaming the individual accused of doping).

The frame in a story can effectively shift the blame from an organization to an individual or vice versa. Episodic frames can breed stereotypes, while thematic frames can help create a greater understanding of the problem at hand.[35] By "framing issues more broadly," journalists can help encourage the "true deliberation" necessary to "revitalize public life," argued Davis Merritt.[36] Conversely, episodic framing tends to shrink the focus of the problem and stymie the development of a broader understanding of the issue at hand.

This problem of stereotyping can be magnified by the use of exemplars, which two researchers defined as "case studies about individuals whose circumstances illustrate the phenomenon in question."[37] Exemplars are commonly used in episodic framing, and celebrities often play the role of an exemplar because their sensationalistic nature can amplify the issue. Research has shown that people rely on these exemplars when forming judgments about social issues and often ignore specific evidence if an exemplar is present.[38] After reviewing coverage of Kobe Bryant's rape case, David Leonard concluded that "media culture is only too happy to use Black figures to represent transgressive behavior and project society's sins onto Black figures." In this case, he argued, the focus was on Bryant's individual sins rather than the larger problem of rape in society.[39]

Questions Investigated in This Study

We seek to answer six questions about coverage of the two athletes. Based on previous works pointing out that African-American athletes are covered in a more negative manner than white athletes, each question contains an assumption of directionality against Bonds. The questions we ask are:

- Is the percentage of stories mentioning Barry Bonds and illegal performance-enhancing drugs (PEDs) greater than the percentage of stories mentioning Lance Armstrong and illegal PEDs?
- Do stories about Barry Bonds contain a larger percentage of information and more prominent mentions linking him to illegal PEDs than stories about Lance Armstrong and PEDs?

- Are stories mentioning Barry Bonds and illegal PEDs more prominent than stories mentioning Lance Armstrong and illegal PEDs?
- Are stories mentioning Barry Bonds and illegal PEDs more negative in tone than stories mentioning Lance Armstrong and illegal PEDs?
- Do stories mentioning Barry Bonds and illegal PEDs use more episodic framing than thematic framing in comparison to stories mentioning Lance Armstrong and illegal PEDs?
- Is coverage of Barry Bonds and Lance Armstrong framed in racially stereotypical terms?

For each question, we investigate whether the different newspapers we examined differed in their approaches to covering the two athletes.

The Study

We investigated stories in six newspapers: (1) *Boston Globe*, (2) *Denver Post*, (3) *Houston Chronicle*, (4) *New York Times*, (5) *San Francisco Chronicle*, and (6) *USA Today*. As of 2013, each newspaper had a Sunday circulation in excess of 300,000, according to the Alliance for Audited Media. Further, all were among the nation's 30 largest newspapers, meaning their coverage often can set the agenda for other media outlets. Their influence is further amplified by the wire service distribution of the stories they produce. In addition, each newspaper has a well-established online presence, indicating a potential national and international audience. Houston and San Francisco are studied here because these papers are in states the two athletes called home during the period of coverage examined.

To be included in this study, a story has to mention either Bonds or Armstrong *and* illegal performance-enhancing drugs (PEDS). Only stories that include one of the athletes' names and a reference to doping are included.

Stories that ran from January 1, 1999, to December 31, 2006, were analyzed. This time frame was chosen for a variety of reasons. In 1999, Armstrong began his string of seven consecutive Tour de France titles, and the French newspaper *L'Equipe* reported that he used the illegal drug EPO. In addition, according to the book *Game of Shadows*, Bonds began using steroids after the 1998 season, meaning 1999 was the first season that coverage of his alleged doping could have emerged. Both athletes rose to the peak of their fame during this time frame through their athletic feats and off-the-field controversies. Armstrong won a record seven straight Tours de France, and Bonds added four Most Valuable Player awards to his record seven, while breaking the single-season home run record. Both were dogged by allegations of abusing illegal performance-enhancing drugs throughout this period. The ending point was set at 2006 because both men had fallen off the peak of their careers at this point. Although 2006 was the year after Armstrong retired the first time (before he came back to competitive cycling briefly in 2009), it was the year in which Bonds broke Babe Ruth's home run record. Therefore, the researchers ended their study period with eight full years of coverage to analyze.

During the time frame, the papers published a combined 7,117 stories about Bonds and 2,152 stories about Armstrong. Of the Bonds stories, 1,661 mentioned PEDs, and an even 400 of the Armstrong stories mentioned PEDs. These stories mentioned both the athlete and illegal PEDs but did not necessarily link the athlete to the PEDs. For some of the questions, a random sample of 360 stories was drawn (180 for each athlete). Stories were retrieved from the LexisNexis newspaper database.

Three coders examined the stories. Sixty stories (almost 17 percent of the 360-story sample) were examined by more than one coder. Cohen's Kappas for all variables ranged from 0.79 to 1.00, indicating excellent agreement.

Findings

Stories in the sample ($N = 360$) ranged from 221 words to 4,176 words, with an average of 857.27 words per story ($SD = 459.92$). The word count of the stories linking the key athlete to PEDs ranged from 0 words to 1,743 words, with an average of 149.73 words per story ($SD = 216.46$). The number of stories/graphics that accompanied the stories ranged from zero to nine, with an average of 0.92 photos per story ($SD = 1.17$). The most common story type was a straight news story (67.2 percent, $N = 242$), followed by columns (30.8 percent, $N = 111$) and a few editorials (1.9 percent, $N = 7$).

Number of stories. We first looked at the overall number of stories written about the key athlete and compared that figure with the number of stories that mentioned both the athlete and PEDs. As Table 11.1 shows, stories mentioning Bonds and PEDs appeared almost four times as often as stories mentioning Armstrong and PEDs. This is driven, in part, by the greater number of stories about Bonds. However, PEDs were mentioned in a much higher percentage of stories about Bonds (23.34 percent) than in stories about Armstrong (18.59 percent).

The remaining results are based on a sample of 360 of the stories that mentioned one of the athletes and PEDs (180 for each athlete).

TABLE 11.1   Number of Total Stories and PED Stories on Athlete

Newspaper	Bonds Stories	Bonds and PEDS	Armstrong Stories	Armstrong and PEDS
Boston Globe	363	153 (42.15%)	251	63 (25.10%)
Denver Post	467	120 (25.69%)	170	28 (16.47%)
Houston Chronicle	1,106	202 (18.26%)	718	105 (14.62%)
New York Times	1,016	353 (34.74%)	500	118 (23.60%)
S.F. Chronicle	3,289	599 (18.21%)	117	18 (15.38%)
USA Today	876	234 (26.71%)	396	68 (17.17%)
Total	7,117	1,661 (23.34%)	2,152	400 (18.59%)

Note: Total Bonds stories labeled as "Bonds Stories" and total Bonds stories and mentions of PEDs labeled as "Bonds and PEDs." Percentage of total Bonds stories mentioning PEDs is in parentheses under "Bonds and PEDs" column. The same format is used for Armstrong stories.

Prominence of PED coverage within stories. We examined prominence of coverage about the athletes and PEDs by looking first at word count and placement of the portion of the stories mentioning PEDs, whether this part of the story directly linked the athlete to drugs or not. Based on independent sample t tests, no statistically significant differences were found between Bonds and Armstrong in the word count of the stories mentioning PEDs or the percentage of stories that mentioned PEDs. For Armstrong, on average, 20.86 percent of each story was about PEDs compared with an average of 17.61 percent of each story for Bonds. PEDs, however, were mentioned significantly higher in the Bonds stories ($M = 3.37$) than in the Armstrong stories ($M = 2.98$, t [339] $= 2.95$, $p < .003$).

The differences appear clearly when stories mentioned a *specific link* between one of the athletes PEDs. As Table 11.2 shows, Armstrong was significantly less likely to be linked to PEDs in stories than was Bonds (χ^2 [5] $=$ 76.52, $p < .001$). In fact, nearly 40 percent of the Armstrong stories in the sample did not link the cyclist to illegal or banned substances. In these stories, PEDs were mentioned in general or were linked to another athlete. In contrast, nearly 90 percent of the stories that mentioned Bonds and PEDs linked Bonds directly to drugs. Links of Bonds to drugs were significantly more likely to be concentrated in the lead or first third of the story (69.4 percent of the time) in comparison to Armstrong (49.1 percent of the stories). Although Armstrong escaped the direct link to PEDs in more

TABLE 11.2   Placement of First Reference Linking Athlete to Illegal PEDs

Athlete	Entire Story	Lead	First Third	Second Third	Final Third	Not Linked
Bonds	2 (1.1%)	33 (18.3%)	92 (51.1%)	25 (13.9%)	8 (4.4%)	20 (11.1%)
Armstrong	20 (6.1%)	15 (8.3%)	37 (20.6%)	21 (11.7%)	16 (8.9%)	71 (39.4%)

Note: Percentages represent those across the rows, so the total for all percentages combine to equal 100% for each athlete.

than three times as many stories as Bonds (71 to 20), his ties with PEDs were the focus of the entire story 20 times, compared with Bonds's two times.

Prominence of stories overall. Next, prominence of the stories mentioning the athletes and PEDs were examined by looking at placement of the stories, total word count, and the number of photos/graphics used, as these visuals often draw readers' eyes to a story. The word count of Bonds stories ($M = 862.37$) and Armstrong stories ($M = 852.18$) did not differ significantly. However, Armstrong stories had significantly more visuals on average ($M = 1.13$, $p < .001$) than did Bonds stories ($M = 0.72$). Further, as Table 11.3 shows, Bonds stories with mentions of PEDs were significantly more likely to be given a higher prominence placement in the newspaper ($\chi^2 [3] = 14.40$, $p < .002$).

Both athletes had 15 of 180 in the sample make the front page and roughly the same number inside the first section of the paper. However,

TABLE 11.3   Placement of First Reference Linking Athlete to Illegal PEDs

Athlete	Front Page (A Section)	Inside Section Cover	Inside A Section	Inside an Inside Section	Totals
Bonds	15 (8.3%)	70 (38.9%)	10 (5.6%)	85 (47.2%)	180 (100%)
Armstrong	15 (8.3%)	39 (21.7%)	8 (4.4%)	118 (65.6%)	180 (100%)

Note: Percentage of stories on athlete are listed in parentheses next to the total number in each row.

Bonds's stories were significantly more likely to be placed on another section front (usually the sports section) than were Armstrong's stories, which were more likely to be placed inside of the section.

By newspaper title, the *Houston Chronicle* gave Bonds higher prominence than the other papers (χ^2 [3] = 18.106, $p < .0001$). The *Chronicle* placed Bonds stories on a section front 56.7 percent of the time, compared to 13.9 percent of the time for Armstrong. This represented the most unbalanced coverage of any newspaper and was especially noteworthy because Armstrong was living in Texas at the time.

Tone. Next, we examined the tone of the stories and the portion of the each story linking the athlete to PEDs. Each paragraph was coded as positive, negative, mixed, or neutral. Summing that data, the story or the portion of the story was scored on a (1) entirely negative to (5) entirely positive scale, so higher numbers indicated more positive coverage. Brief neutral mentions of the athlete were removed from the analysis on this question. There were only 11 of these, three for Bonds and eight for Armstrong. Also, tone of the athlete-PED link could be computed only in stories that directly linked the athlete to PEDs. As shown earlier, 40 percent of Armstrong stories did not contain such a link.

Significant differences were found in both the overall tone of the stories and the tone toward the athlete in relation to PEDs. The overall tone of Bonds stories ($M = 2.08$) was significantly more negative than the tone of Armstrong stories ($M = 4.27$, $p < .001$). In addition, the tone of the portion of the story linking Bonds to PEDs was significantly more negative ($M = 1.71$) than it was for Armstrong ($M = 3.70$, $p < .001$). Also of note was that Bonds fell on the negative end of the scale in both overall tone and PED tone, while Armstrong fell on the positive end on both variables. Therefore, not only was there a significant difference in the tone of coverage between the two athletes, it is clear that Bonds was framed as a negative figure, and Armstrong was framed as a positive figure.

Episodic and thematic frames. Each story was coded for mentions of the key athlete's ties with PEDs, other athletes' ties with PEDs, and the sport's (or other sports') ties with PEDs. These were coded to see if the problem of doping was being framed as an individual problem (episodic) or an institutional problem (thematic). Four categories were created to examine episodic and thematic framing: (1) thematic frame (mentions of sports' tie with doping), (2) individual episodic frame (mentions of individual athletes' tie with doping, excluding the key athlete), (3) key athlete episodic frame (mentions of key athlete's tie with doping) and (4) overall

TABLE 11.4   Kinds of Frames Used in Bonds and Armstrong Stories

Athlete	Thematic Frame Score	Episodic Frame Average	Episodic Frame toward Others	Episodic Frame toward Key Athlete
Bonds	0.79	1.17***	0.86	1.48***
Armstrong	0.73	0.86	0.71	1.01**

Note: * $p < .05$, ** $p < .01$; *** $p < .001$ for differences between thematic frame score and specific episodic frame score.

episodic frame (the mean of measure 2 and 3). For each category, the story was given a 0 (frame not present), a 1 (frame present in one sentence), or a 2 (frame present in two or more sentences).

As shown in Table 11.4, episodic framing was significantly more common than thematic framing in Bonds stories. Also, episodic framing was based around Bonds more than other athletes. Armstrong stories were also more episodic than thematic. An independent sample t test, however, showed that Bonds' coverage was significantly more episodic in nature than Armstrong's coverage, meaning these stories framed Bonds' issues as an individual, rather than a systemic issue.

All six newspapers framed Bonds in episodic terms significantly more than thematic terms ($p < .01$). However, coverage for Armstrong was balanced between episodic and thematic in four newspapers. That means that although Armstrong's issues were covered in a more episodic frame overall, this phenomenon was really driven by two newspapers (the *San Francisco Chronicle* and *USA Today*).

Racial frames. The final research question examined how much the coverage relied on racially driven frames. To examine whether racial framing was present, we looked for the presence of five common *African-American stereotypes* and five common *white stereotypes*. The African-American stereotypes were the athlete (1) having superior physical strength; (2) having superior natural athletic ability; (3) being a threat and/or outsider; (4) being violent, over reactive, and/or temperamental; and (5) having problems with the judicial system. The white stereotypes were the athlete: (1) having a superior work ethic; (2) having superior heart and/or courage; (3) having superior intellect; (4) doing good deeds; and (5) having financial success. These frames were taken from past studies.[40] Each stereotype was scored as being not present (0), present briefly (1), or

TABLE 11.5   Kinds of Frames by Newspaper in Armstrong Stories

Newspaper	Thematic Frame Score	Episodic Frame toward Key Athlete	T Value
Boston Globe	0.73	0.83	n/s
Denver Post	0.89	0.93	n/s
Houston Chronicle	0.64	1.08	n/s
New York Times	0.97	1.00	n/s
San Francisco Chronicle	0.63	1.31	2.11*
USA Today	0.49	1.03	3.12**

Note: * $p < .05$, ** $p < .01$; *** $p < .001$ for differences between thematic frame score and specific episodic frame score; N/S - not significant.

present in two or more sentences (2). Additionally, we examined whether the athlete's race is mentioned in the story, a more overt framing device.

As Table 11.5 illustrates, Bonds and Armstrong were framed in racially stereotypical terms on several fronts. Bonds was framed significantly more often through three of the five stereotypical African-American frames (physical strength, criminal activity, athletes as a threat). Armstrong was framed significantly more often through four of the five stereotypically white frames (work ethic, heart/courage, good deeds, economic success). Additionally, the race of Bonds was overtly mentioned significantly more than the race of Armstrong. In fact, Bonds's race was mentioned in 15 stories, while Armstrong's race was not mentioned at all.

Interestingly, while few differences were found by newspaper title throughout the study, several differences were found on racial framing. Differences by newspaper were discovered on four of the variables—mention of race (F [5, 354] = 2.98, $p < .012$), mention of crime (F [5, 147] = 5.41, $p < .001$), mention of heart of courage; (F [5, 147] = 3.21, $p < .01$) and total African-American frame score (F [5, 147] = 5.15, $p < .002$). Therefore, these were investigated further.

The *San Francisco Chronicle* mentioned race more than any other paper ($M = 0.22$), compared to the average score for mention of race of .07 for all six papers combined. Because race was not mentioned in any Armstrong story, the *San Francisco Chronicle*, therefore, was significantly more likely to frame the Bonds stories in racial terms than were the other papers.

USA Today used the stereotype of heart or courage significantly more than any other paper except the *New York Times*. *USA Today* had a score of 0.19 compared with scores of 0.00 for the four other papers that never used this stereotype. The *New York Times* used it sparingly ($M = 0.04$). Because Bonds was never linked with the heart or courage stereotype, *USA Today* was found to be significantly more likely than most other papers to frame Armstrong as courageous.

Because both Bonds and Armstrong were framed in terms of crime and with the total African-American frame, a factorial analysis of variance was run comparing newspaper title and athlete on these two variables. For mention of crime, main effects emerged for newspaper title ($F [5, 153] = 3.54, p < .005$) and for athlete ($F [1, 153] = 40.35, p < .001$), but no interaction effect was found for newspaper and athlete together, indicating that in all newspapers, mentions of crime were more likely to appear in the Bonds stories. The *San Francisco Chronicle* stories were most likely to contain mention of crime in relation to Bonds.

For total African-American framing, main effects emerged for newspaper title ($F [5, 153] = 3.35, p < .005$) and for athlete ($F [1, 153] = 39.16, p < .001$), but no interaction effect was found for newspaper and athlete together, indicating that in all newspapers, African-American framing was more likely to appear in the Bonds stories. Again, the *Chronicle* was most likely to include African-American frames in its coverage overall.

Discussion

Prominence

Nearly a quarter of the Bonds stories that appeared in the seven years in these six newspapers mentioned both Bonds and PEDs, compared with less than 20 percent for Armstrong. These repeated mentions of Bonds and PEDs in the same stories can pair Bonds and PEDs in the reader's mind, even if Bonds is not linked directly to PEDs in the story. Thus, Bonds becomes synonymous with PED use and becomes a face of the problem of doping in professional sports.

Interestingly, while a higher percentage of stories about Bonds mentioned PEDs, when the stories made a direct link between the key athlete and PEDs, there was no significant difference in the percentage of the story devoted to this link. There also were no significant differences in the placement of the first mention of that link. However, when all the stories in the sample were examined, Bonds was more likely than Armstrong to be directly linked to doping. Bonds was identified as a potential doper in nearly 90 percent of the stories that mentioned both him and PEDs, but Armstrong was identified as a potential doper in only 60 percent of his stories. In addition, the first reference to PEDs was higher in the Bonds stories than it was in the Armstrong stories. This could strengthen the connection that readers make between Bonds and PEDs.

Bonds and PEDs stories were more prominently placed in the newspaper than stories mentioning Armstrong and PEDs, a further signal to readers that Bonds's ties with PEDs are more important than Armstrong's ties with PEDs.

Differences in Tone

As the bulk of the anecdotal and empirical evidence suggested, tone toward Bonds was significantly more negative than toward Armstrong both overall and in the portion of the stories linking them directly to PEDs. Bonds was portrayed as a negative figure, while Armstrong was a positive figure. There were no significant differences by newspaper title, meaning all six of these publications framed Bonds as more negative in tone and conceptualized him a negative figure.

As Braddock and Wonsek found in their studies, African-American athletes are generally depicted in more negative terms than white athletes. While Braddock found that African-American athletes receive significantly less positive coverage, Wonsek found that African-American athletes are typically described as inferior to white athletes.[41] Kellner found that some African-American athletes (Michael Jordan, for example) have become so prominent in the sports media that they can transcend race and not be depicted in stereotypically negative terms.[42] This study reaffirmed the findings of Braddock and Wonsek but was inconsistent with the findings of Kellner such that Bonds received significantly less positive coverage than Armstrong.

Funneling the majority of the negative coverage toward Bonds and shielding Armstrong from negative coverage should not come as a surprise. After reviewing media coverage of basketball star Kobe Bryant, Leonard concluded that "media culture is only too happy to use Black figures to represent transgressive behavior and project society's sins onto Black figures."[43] In many ways, that is exactly what is happening with steroid abuse in sports as Bonds has become the face of what is a bigger societal problem. Many argue that the amount of evidence that links Bonds to

PEDs is similar to the evidence linking Armstrong to PEDs, but in most cases, Bonds is the problem in the stories while Armstrong stories equally portray PEDs as a personal issue and a sport-wide issue.

Episodic/Thematic Framing

Bonds stories mentioning PEDs were significantly more likely to use episodic framing than thematic framing both for him individually and other athletes. Bonds was more likely to be tied to doping than all the other athletes combined, meaning that Bonds was the face of doping in these stories. Armstrong stories mentioning PEDs also were significantly more likely to use episodic framing than thematic framing, but only for him individually. But Bonds was framed episodically significantly more often than Armstrong. While we already knew from the second research question that Bonds's ties with doping were mentioned significantly more often than Armstrong's, this analysis showed that in Bonds's stories, the link to doping was more likely to be driven by his individual narrative rather than a narrative involving others or sport in general.

All six newspapers covered Bonds in a more episodic nature than thematic nature, but the *San Francisco Chronicle* and *USA Today* drove the overall trend that showed Armstrong being covered in a more episodic nature. This means that only two papers made Armstrong the face of doping in the stories, while the others tended to link the sport to doping almost as frequently as they did Armstrong.

Episodic framing focuses the attention of the story on one person, and thematic framing widens the story lens by providing greater context and spreads the focus of the story to a larger variety of sources.[44] So while Bonds became the centerpiece of coverage about steroid use in Major League Baseball, the focus of doping in cycling was more balanced and attributed to more sources than solely Armstrong. This is one of the most important findings of this study because Bonds and Armstrong are more than just athletes. They are representatives of their sports and, more important for this study, representatives of their ethnicities. The public has a general impression of these two athletes that is driven, in part, by media coverage. So when Bonds is covered in a more negative tone, the ramifications can go beyond simply vilifying Bonds. In many ways, Bonds's race is also pinned with his sins. This problem is exacerbated by the fact that racial stereotypes are commonly used in covering these athletes. Further, episodic framing, which fosters stereotypes, is commonplace.

This is not to say that every African American is being portrayed as a criminal or a negative figure because of Bonds, but research has shown that media depictions of minorities, especially one of Bonds's prominence, can have a lasting effect on the audience for better or worse. "Media images of minorities have been shown to have a considerable impact on white audiences. The portrayal of a lazy, incompetent, rebellious or violent person of color is an enduring mental image. Subsequent stereotypes on the part of the white viewer have been found to occur," argued one team of media effects researchers when summarizing findings to date.[45]

Racial Stereotypes

Overall, Bonds and Armstrong were racially stereotyped at an equal rate. The only difference was the kind of stereotypes they fell into—Bonds as African American, Armstrong as white. Bonds was significantly more likely to be portrayed as a criminal and a threat/outsider, and to be defined by his physical strength. Armstrong, in contrast, was described in terms of work ethic, heart/courage, good deeds, and economic success.

These findings are disheartening because they suggest that newspapers have made little progress in dispelling long-held stereotypes. The role the media play in enabling these stereotypes must be considered. Sports writers must be made aware of these trends so that they can see when stereotypes are slipping into their coverage. Hiring more minority sports writers also could help increase sensitivity to these pitfalls in coverage.

Two findings on racial stereotyping were somewhat surprising. The first was that both Bonds and Armstrong were equally likely to be framed as violent, temperamental, and overreactive. This is an important finding because it shows that Bonds's surly personality is likely not the reason for the differences in coverage found between the two athletes. The second unexpected finding was that Armstrong was significantly more likely to be framed in terms of economic success, despite Bonds being one of the richest athletes in world, making on average $15 million per season since 1999. Armstrong was portrayed as a business owner and someone with great economic clout. Bonds, meanwhile, was often described as an outsider when it came to business, with many stories mentioning how he broke away from the players' union so that he could have complete ownership of his name brand.

Finally, given Niven's argument that media are not comfortable discussing race and would rather criticize those who bring up race than "appraise the state of racial fairness in sports media coverage," it is not surprising that race was mentioned in so few stories.[46] The *San Francisco Chronicle* mentioned race more than all of the other newspapers combined, but only for Bonds. A few *Chronicle* columns offered race as a possible factor in differential coverage. However, the majority of the *Chronicle*'s overt mentions of race were there because Bonds brought up race. Writers often simply wrote this off as Bonds playing the "race card." The validity of Bonds's claims was not explored.

Differences by Newspaper

The *Houston Chronicle* was significantly more likely than the other newspapers to give high placement to stories mentioning Bonds and PEDs. Both athletes' home area newspapers—the *San Francisco Chronicle* for Bonds and *Houston Chronicle* for Armstrong—were the least likely by percentage to mention PEDs in stories mentioning their respective local athlete. Additionally, the *San Francisco Chronicle* was significantly more likely to mention crime, mention race, use stereotypical African-American frames, and frame Armstrong in an episodic nature than most other newspapers. The San Francisco paper also offered the most even coverage among athletes, as Armstrong drew as much scrutiny as Bonds, which in turn boosted the use of stereotypical African-American frames and episodic framing. The *Houston Chronicle* was significantly more likely to use stereotypical African-American frames than some other newspapers. Meanwhile, coverage among the other four newspapers in this study was strikingly similar. In short, coverage by *local* newspapers showed significant differences from the *nonlocal* coverage, and the *nonlocal* newspapers differed little from each other.

These findings might be linked to the influences on media content. One model of news influence posits that content is shaped by factors at five distinct levels: (1) individual, (2) media routines, (3) organizational, (4) extramedia, and (5) ideological.[47] When it comes to local issues, individual differences might trump the other levels because journalists have personal contact with their sources. In nonlocal situations, the media routines, extramedia pressures, and ideological similarities might play a larger role.

Conclusion

This is the first study to systematically analyze the coverage of Bonds and Armstrong and their relationship to illegal performance-enhancing drugs.

This study shows that Bonds and Armstrong were both covered in a racially stereotypical nature. It also shows that they were framed in an episodic nature, which once again leads to stereotypes. The research shows Bonds was the target of more negative coverage as well as more scrutiny than Armstrong. By using stereotypes and a negative tone in covering Bonds, the media, either knowingly or unknowingly, could be sending subtle messages to readers about race.

Notes

1. Pierre Ballester and David Walsh, *L.A. Confidentiel: Les Secrets de Lance Armstrong* (Paris: La Martiniere, 2004); Mark Fainaru-Wada and Lance, *Game of Shadows: Barry Bonds, BALCO, and the Steroids Scandal That Rocked Professional Sports* (New York: Penguin, 2006); Jeff Pearlman, *Love Me, Hate Me: Barry Bonds and the Making of an Antihero* (New York: HarperCollins, 2006).

2. Mark Fainaru-Wada and Lance Williams, "The Truth about Barry Bonds and Steroids," *Sports Illustrated* (March 13, 2006), accessed March 23, 2012, http://sportsillustrated.cnn.com/vault/article/magazine/MAG1116081/12/index.htm.

3. "Lance Threatened LeMond," *Toronto Sun* (June 26, 2006), S9.

4. "Lance Armstrong: 'Impossible' to Win Tour de France without Doping," *USA Today* (June 28, 2013), accessed Aug. 4, 2013, http://www.usatoday.com/story/sports/cycling/2013/06/28/lance-armstrong-impossible-win-tour-de-france-doping/2471413/.

5. "Poll: Half of Fans Don't Want Bonds to Hit 755." *Associated Press* (Oct. 21, 2006), accessed June 13, 2012, http://sports.espn.go.com/mlb/news/story?id=2631763.

6. Kalani Simpson, "Bonds, Armstrong and Double Standards," *FoxSports* (Jan. 23, 2011) accessed Feb. 26, 2012, http://msn.foxsports.com/mlb/story/Why-are-Barry-Bonds-and-Lance-Armstrong-perceived-differently-012011.

7. Gwen Knapp, "Lance: Teflon Doper?" *San Francisco Chronicle* (Aug. 24, 2005), p. D1.

8. Glenn Dickey, "Return of the 'Race Card.'" *San Francisco Chronicle* (March 9, 2004), p. C2.

9. Dave Zirin, "You're Damn Right Race Matters: The Press Mob, Their Rope and Barry Bonds," *Counterpunch* (April 1-3, 2006), accessed June 19, 2012, http://www.counterpunch.org/2006/04/01/the-press-mob-their-rope-and-barry-bonds/.

10. Thomas Nelson, Rosalee Clawson, and Zoe Oxley, "Media Framing of a Civil Liberties Conflict and Its Effect on Tolerance," *American Political Science Review 91* (3, 1997): 567–583.

11. Robert M. Entman, "Framing: Toward Clarification of a Fractured Paradigm," *Journal of Communication 43* (4, 1993): 51–58.

12. John D. Richardson, "Switching Social Identities: The Influence of Editorial Framing on Reader Attitudes toward Affirmative Action and African Americans," *Communication Research 32* (4, 2005): 503–528; Clint C. Wilson II and Félix F. Gutiérrez, *Race, Multiculturalism, and the Media: From Mass to Class Communication* (Thousand Oaks, CA: Sage, 1995).

13. Jeffrey A. Bierman, "The Effect of Television Sports Media on Black Male Youth," *Sociological Inquiry 60* (4, 1990): 413–427.

14. Jomills H. Braddock, "Race, Sports, and Social Mobility: A Critical Review," *Sociological Symposium 30* (1, 1980): 18–38; Keith Andrew Strudler, "The Mass Mediated Sports Hero as a Role Model for Adolescent Males" (PhD diss., University of Florida, 2000).

15. Paul Martin Lester and Randy Miller, *African American Pictorial Coverage in Four U.S. Newspapers, 1995.* Presented at the Association for Education in Journalism and Mass Communication Annual Meeting, Anaheim, CA, 1996; Carolyn Martindale, "Changes in Newspaper Images of Black Americans," *Newspaper Research Journal 11* (1, 1990): 40–50; Audrey Murrell and Edward M. Curtis, "Causal Attributions of Performance for Black and White Quarterbacks in the NFL: A Look at the Sports Pages," *Journal of Sport & Social Issues 18* (3, 1994): 224–233; Raymond E. Rainville and Edward McCormick, "Extent of Covert Racial Prejudice in Pro Football Announcers' Speech," *Journalism & Mass Communication Quarterly 54* (1, 1977): 20–26.

16. Richard C. King, David J. Leonard, and Kyle W. Kusz, "White Power and Sport," *Journal of Sport & Social Issues 31* (1, 2007): 3–94.

17. Jomills H. Braddock, "Sports Pages: In Black & White," *Arena Review 2* (2, 1978): 17–25.

18. Alice H. Eagly, Mona G. Makhijani, and Bruce G. Klonsky, "Gender and the Evaluation of Leaders: A Meta-Analysis." *Psychological Bulletin 111* (1, 1992): 3-32.

19. Lester and Miller, *African American Pictorial Coverage;* Martindale, "Changes in Newspaper Images."

20. Lawrence A Wenner, "The Good, the Bad, and the Ugly: Race, Sport and the Public Eye," *Journal of Sport and Social Issues 19* (3, 1995): 227–231, 228.

21. Lester and Miller, *African American Pictorial Coverage;* Martindale, "Changes in Newspaper Images."

22. Ben Lombardo, "The Harlem Globetrotters and the Perception of the Black Stereotype," *Physical Educator 35* (2, 1978): 60–63, 60.

23. Rainville and McCormick, "Extent of Covert Racial Prejudice."

24. Murrell and Curtis, "Causal Attributions of Performance."

25. Jacco van Sterkenburg and Annelies Knoppers, "Dominant Discourses about Race/Ethnicity and Gender in Sport Practice and Performance," *International Review for the Sociology of Sport 39* (3, 2004): 301–321.

26. Joseph Boskin, *SAMBO: The Rise & Demise of an American Jester* (New York: Oxford University Press, 1986).

27. Vernon L. Andrews, "Black Bodies—White Control: The Contested Terrain of Sportsmanlike Conduct," *Journal of African American Men 2* (1, 1996): 33–59.

28. David Niven. "Race, Quarterbacks, and the Media: Testing the Rush Limbaugh Hypothesis," *Journal of Black Studies 35* (5, 2005): 684–694.

29. Pamela Wonsek, "College Basketball on Television: A Study of Racism in the Media," *Media Culture & Society 14* (3, 1992): 449–461.

30. Wonsek, "College Basketball," 450.

31. Wenner, "The Good, the Bad, and the Ugly," 228.

32. Gill Lines, "Villains, Fools or Heroes? Sports Stars as Role Models for Young People," *Leisure Studies 20* (4, 2001): 285–303.

33. Lines, "Villains, Fools or Heroes?" 287.

34. Shanto Iyengar, *Is Anyone Responsible? How Television Frames Political Issues* (Chicago: University of Chicago Press, 1991).

35. Renita Coleman and Esther Thorson. "The Effects of News Stories That Put Crime and Violence into Context: Testing the Public Health Model of Reporting," *Journal of Health Communication 7* (5, 2002): 401–425.

36. Davis Merritt. *Public Journalism and Public Life: Why Telling the News Is Not Enough* (Hillsdale, NJ: Lawrence Erlbaum, 1995), 74.

37. Coleman and Thorson, "The Effects of News Stories," 404.

38. Daniel Kahneman and Amos Tversky, "On the Psychology of Prediction," *Psychological Review 80* (4, 1973): 237–251.

39. David J. Leonard, "The Next MJ or the Next OJ? Kobe Bryant, Race, and the Absurdity of Colorblind Rhetoric," *Journal of Sport & Social Issues 28* (3, 2004): 284–313, 304.

40. Andrews, "Black Bodies—White Control"; Boskin, "SAMBO"; Lester and Miller, *African American Pictorial Coverage*; Martindale, "Changes in Newspaper Images"; Murrell and Curtis, "Causal Attributions of Performance"; Rainville and McCormick, "Extent of Covert Racial Prejudice"; Wilson and Gutiérrez, *Race, Multiculturalism, and the Media*.

41. Braddock, "Sports Pages"; Wonsek, "College Basketball."

42. Douglas Kellner, "Sports, Media Culture, and Race: Some Reflections on Michael Jordan," *Sociology of Sport Journal 13* (4, 1996): 458–467.

43. Leonard, "The Next MJ or the Next OJ?" 304.

44. Iyengar, *Is Anyone Responsible*.

45. Jennings Bryant and Susan Thompson, *Fundamentals of Media Effects* (New York: McGraw-Hill, 2001), 337.

46. Niven, "Race, Quarterbacks, and the Media," 692.

47. Pamela J. Shoemaker and Stephen D. Reese, *Mediating the Message* (White Plains, NY: Longman, 1996).

Bibliography

Andrews, V. (1996). Black bodies, white control: The contested terrain of sportsmanlike conduct. *Journal of African American Men, 2(1)*, 33–59.

Ballester, P., & Walsh, D. (2004). *L.A. Confidentiel: Les secrets de Lance Armstrong.* France: La Martiniere.

Bierman, J. A. (1990). The effect of television sports media on black male youth. *Sociological Inquiry, 60(4)*, 413–427.

Boskin, J. (1986). *SAMBO: The rise & demise of an American jester.* London: Oxford University Press.

Braddock, J. H. (1978). The sports page: In black and white. *Arena Review, 2(2)*, 17–25.

Braddock, J. H. (1980). Race, sports, and social mobility: A critical review. *Sociological Symposium, 30*, 18–38.

Bryant, J. & Thompson, S. (2002). *Fundamentals of media effects.* New York: McGraw-Hill.

Coleman, R., & Thorson, E. (2002). The effects of news stories that put crime and violence into context: Testing the public health model of reporting. *Journal of Health Communication, 7(5)*, 401–425.

Dickey, G. (2004, March 9). Return of the "race card." *San Francisco Chronicle*, C2.

Eagly, A., Makhijani, M., & Klonsky, B. (1992). Gender and the evaluation of leaders: A meta-analysis. *Psychological Bulletin, 111(1)*, 3–32.

Entman, R. M. (1993). Framing: Toward clarification of a fractured paradigm. *Journal of Communication, 43(4)*, 51.

Fainaru-Wada, M., & Williams, L. (2006). *Game of shadows: Barry Bonds, BALCO, and the steroids scandal that rocked professional sports.* New York: Penguin.

Gitlin, T. (1980). *The whole world is watching.* Berkeley: University of California Press.

Iyengar, S. (1991). *Is anyone responsible? How television frames political issues.* Chicago: University of Chicago Press.

Jacobs, R. N. (2000). *Race, media, and the crisis of civil society: From the Watts to Rodney King.* New York: Cambridge University Press.

Kahneman, D., & Tversky, A. (1973). On the psychology of prediction. *Psychological Review, 80(4)*, 237–251.

Kellner, D. (1996). Sports, media culture, and race: Some reflections on Michael Jordan. *Sociology of Sport Journal, 13(4)*, 458–467.

King, R., Leonard, D. J., & Kusz, K. W. (2007). White power and sport: An introduction. *Journal of Sport & Social Issues, 31(1)*, 3–10.

Knapp, Gwen. (2005, August 24). Lance: Teflon doper? *San Francisco Chronicle*, D1.

Lance Threatened LeMond. (2006, June 26). *Toronto Sun*, S9.

Leonard, D. J. (2004). The next M. J. or the next O. J.? Kobe Bryant, race, and the absurdity of color blind rhetoric. *Journal of Sport & Social Issues, 28(3),* 284–313.

Lester, P. M., & Miller, R. E. (1996). *African-American Pictorial Coverage in Four U.S. Newspapers, 1995.* Retrieved January 17, 2007, from California State University, Fullerton website at http://commfaculty.fullerton.edu/lester/writings/aastudy. html#bone

Lines, G. (2001). Villains, fools or heroes? Sports stars as role models for young people. *Leisure Studies, 20(4),* 285–303.

Lombardo, B. (1978). The Harlem globetrotters and the perception of the black stereotype. *Physical Educator, 35(2),* 60–63.

Lupica, M. (2006, May 29). Second thoughts find this guy is no Aaron. *New York Daily News,* 54.

Martindale, C. (1990). Changes in newspaper images of black Americans. *Newspaper Research Journal, 11(1),* 40–50.

Merritt, D. (1995). *Public journalism and public life: Why telling the news is not enough.* Hillsdale, NJ: Lawrence Erlbaum.

Murrell, A., & Curtis, E. (1994). Causal attributions of performance for black and white quarterbacks in the NFL: A look at the sports pages. *Journal of Sport and Social Issues, 18(3),* 224–233.

Nelson, N. E., Clawson, R. A., & Oxley, Z. M. (1997). Media framing of a civil liberties conflict and its effect on tolerance. *American Political Science Review, 91(3),* 567–583.

Niven, D. (2005). Race, quarterbacks, and the media: Testing the rush Limbaugh hypothesis. *Journal of Black Studies, 35(5),* 684–694.

Pearlman, J. (2006). *Love me, hate me: Barry Bonds and the making of an Antihero.* New York: HarperCollins.

Rainville, R., & McCormick, E. (1977). Extent of covert racial prejudice in pro football announcers' speech. *Journalism Quarterly, 54(1),* 20–26.

Richardson, J. D. (2005). Switching social identities: The influence of editorial framing on reader attitudes toward affirmative action and African Americans. *Communication Research, 32(4),* 503–528.

Strudler, K. (2000). *The mass mediated sports hero as a role model for adolescent males.* Unpublished Doctoral dissertation, University of Florida.

Van Sterkenburg, J., & Knoppers, A. (2004). Dominant discourses about race/ethnicity and gender in sport practice and performance. *International Review for the Sociology of Sport, 39(3),* 301–321.

Walker, B. (October 20, 2006). Poll: Half of fans don't want Bonds to hit 755. *Associated Press.*

Wenner, L. A. (1995). The good, the bad, and the ugly: Race, sport, and the public eye. *Journal of Sport and Social Issues, 19(3),* 227–231.

Williams, R. (2005, July 25). Armstrong rides into history with seventh tour win. *Guardian* (London), 1.

Wilson, C., & Gutierrez, F. (1995). *Race, multiculturalism, and the media: From mass to class communication.* Thousand Oaks, CA: Sage.

Wonsek, P. (1992). College basketball on television: A study of racism in the media. *Media, Culture & Society, 14(3),* 449–461.

Zirin, D. (2006). You're damn right race matters: The press mob, their rope and Barry Bonds. Retrieved February 11, 2007, from http://www.counterpunch .org/zirin04012006.html

Chapter 12

Racial Knowledge about Sport: A Mixed-Method Approach for Investigating Cultural Myths and Stereotypes about African-American Male Athleticism

C. Keith Harrison, Suzanne Malia Kirkland,
Louis Harrison, Larry Proctor, and Quentin G. Love

Natural selection is a more important factor determining human genetic variation than race or common ancestry.

—Livingstone, 1964

African Americans have contributed more intellectually to this country than they have athletically.

—Jim Brown, 2001, *For the Record*
(panel with Bob Costas, Jon Entine,
and John Edgar Wiedman)

There are more differences within the races than between the races.

—Vic Katch, 1998

The most talented part of Michael Jordan is his cerebellum, not his body.

—Marvin Boluyt, 2001

The failure of the scholarly community to seriously examine the history of Blacks in intercollegiate sports is a "missed opportunity" to understand an important dimension of African American intellectual history, the nature and development of the modern civil rights struggle, and the Black protest movement.

—Donald Spivey, 1983, cited in Raymond Winbush, 1987

After fifty years of trying to prove the genetic superiority of Blacks as athletes, science has proved little. Culture, class and environment still tell us the most. Instead of developing theories about why Black Americans excel in sports, perhaps more time will now be spent on the achievement of Black Americans in human rights, medicine, law, science, the arts and education who overcame the attitudes and institutions of whites to excel in fields where brains dictate the champions.

—Lapchick, 1991

Athletic ability has a certain property value in American culture, and in order to maintain the structures of white supremacy whites must control the logic *[emphasis added] of that ability. If Blacks are excelling in and dominating major revenue generating sports (i.e., basketball and football) then whites are losing on their property investment, which is the form of cultural capital. By writing off Black athleticism as an aberration whites effectively devalue athletic ability as cultural capital and maintain their hegemonic positioning as the real profiteers within the economy of US sports.*

—Jason Chang, 1999

Introduction

The poster reads, "What's superhuman to you comes second nature to them." Images of three African-American athletes in the National Basketball Association (NBA) are depicted next to the aforementioned narrative advertising "The world's greatest game of all." Messages such as these reinforce status quo and "commonsensical" beliefs and attitudes about African-American athleticism (image of poster based on field observation by the first author of this study at a suburban sports bar). With the overrepresentation of African-American male athletes in sprinting events, basketball, football, and boxing, who can blame the average observer for believing what they see? What they see is more complex than dominant and common beliefs by many but not all individuals and groups of people in the public domain. One would assume that with the visibility and success of African-American athletes, public opinion and popular myths would be systematically documented in relation to their talent expression, but this is not the case. Sailes empirically investigated this issue, however;

specifically, he focused on black and white athletic abilities. Sailes found African-American male student-athletes were perceived to be inferior academically but superior athletically.[1] The primary researchers in this study focused on these binary racial categories also, but also investigated other ethnic groups in terms of the sports they dominate and participate in.

While Hallinan investigated stereotypes using athletic pictures (with race as the major variable)[2] and Stone found racial stereotypes to be significant in terms of sport performances by black and white participants,[3] only one other published study was found that empirically assessed popular and public opinion of athletic ability with race as a major variable.[4] Hence, the scholarly journey begins within this extremely controversial territory.

Nature or Nurture

The debate of African-American excellence in sport is both a historic and contemporary debate.[5] In Entine's text titled *Taboo: Why Black Athletes Dominate Sports and Why We're Afraid to Talk about It*, he cultivated further debate on a timeless discussion of African-American athletic dominance in only a few sports.[6] The social science literature revealed findings and theories that educational, cultural, historical, economical, and institutional ideologies garner the most significant variables when raising questions about this issue.[7] Nonetheless, myths and stereotypes by the public at large illuminate genetic, musculature, and anatomical differences about African-American athletes.[8] Few research studies have indicated some differences that confirm on a very minuscule significant level these beliefs and attitudes.[9] These findings have limitations, which include methodological flaws, small sample sizes, and isolated elite athletic populations; more damaging is what Hallinan noted:

> Curricula and teaching must be anchored around concepts and variables that are valid. Enculturated forms of classification by "race" are pervasive and thus appear to be rational schema of naturally occurring biological units. To this end "race," as an unambiguous biological variable, should be refuted. It obfuscates the research questions, permits the formation of theories and explanations, which are antiscientific and, according to Hirsch (1973), confines us to an "intellectual cul-de-sac."[10]

In terms of public perception, many groups and individuals have internalized anecdotal myths, stereotypes, and fallacies about African-American athletic performance.[11] These stereotypes may serve to distort and shroud the grim reality African Americans must come to terms with, namely the high rates of physical inactivity and prevalence of obesity.[12]

Preliminary findings by Harrison[13] and Proctor and Harrison[14] correlated these perceptions to lack of education on this issue. In other words, empirical findings revealed a that higher number of scholarly articles read by participants in this area of race and athleticism can significantly decrease perceptions of inaccurate myths, stereotypes, and beliefs about African-American athletes. The expected outcome of investigating what the public believes and why they believe what they do is to assess the gap between fact and fiction and then to disseminate the realities and accurate research findings. The last goal is to educate both the public and the participants, with the data collected in this study, that will possibly cultivate perceptions that are healthy, respectful, and not born out of ignorance.[15] Presently, there are few systematic studies that examine public perceptions of race and athleticism.[16]

Theoretical Framework

Allport suggested that positive effects of intergroup contact occur only in situations marked by four key conditions: (1) equal group status within the situation; (2) common goals; (3) intergroup cooperation; and (4) the support of authorities, law, or custom.[17] Equal status within the situation is important because if the two groups are not on equal footing, a power dynamic will be created that prevents healthy and productive understanding.

Competition between the in-groups and out-groups leads to less understanding, so intergroup cooperation is a vital component of Allport's contact hypothesis.[18] The greatest evidence of the impact and power of cooperation comes from schools.[19] Children and adults (it is more difficult when they are older) show great improvement when they cooperate in groups. When people do things together, they have opportunities to judge people on their own merits rather than base feelings and attitudes on stereotypes.[20]

The contact hypothesis theory helps explain why various ethnic groups have biased assumptions about African-American athleticism. In other words, narrow views may result from a polarized United States, coupled with myopic imagery of African-American bodies on television in comic, athletic, and physical roles.[21] Conversely, Becker[22] and Goffman's[23] contributions to labeling theory may also apply in terms of deviant populations and the stigmas attached to populations such as musicians, entertainers, and athletes. To summarize and link to this study, the labeling phenomenon of both theorists, stigmas attached to the subordinates (athletes), coupled with a deviant mainstream structure of power (the public discourse of whiteness) may skew and negatively affect thought processes of various issues in society.

Through the sociology of sport lens, Coakley[24] contextualized the effects of "race logic" on many African Americans that participate and have participated in sport. Race logic is a train of thought based on biased beliefs about race and the U.S. racial classification system. In short, social Darwinism was internalized as law in earlier centuries, and the effects are inductive in relation to social relations and common thought about racial differences.

These laws led many to believe white-skinned people were superior beings who deserved to be in control and take ownership over all power positions in sport and society. Further, there are political and social implications of "seeing" sport performances in black and white terms.[25] Skewed and narrowed beliefs about human behavior maintain some of these historical notions of intellectual and athletic prowess and can lead to a misunderstood social expression such as African Americans in sport. This was a major theme for the primary researchers to conduct and report the findings in the current study. While citing various scholars who have studied the ethnographic and qualitative effects of race logic,[26] Coakley called for more research in terms of *race logic* and ways various people deconstruct and process behaviors in sport.[27]

Methods

Participants

A sample of 301 students was collected in the fall of 2000 from a midwestern university. Participants were enrolled in large introductory communications classes. The sample consisted of 211 (70 percent) females and 90 (30 percent) males. The ethnic distribution of the sample was as follows: 246 (81.7 percent) whites, 19 (6.2 percent) Asians, 18 (6 percent) African Americans, 12 (4 percent) Hispanics, and 6 (2.1 percent) others. The mean age of the students in the sample was 20. Each student received one point of extra credit from the instructor for their participation in the study. The data collection process took approximately 20 minutes for each introductory class to complete the *Athletic Ability, Achievement and Attitudes and Belief Instrument (AAAABI).*

Survey Instrument

There are few inventories to specifically examine the topic in this study, thus the need for *AAAABI*. The *AAAABI* was developed by experts in the field of sport science and logical content from related literature. The *AAAABI* contained 53 items. Forty-five items were measured using a five-point Likert scale. There were closed and open-ended questions. Reliabilities were run on the Likert scale items, and alphas were obtained. The items measured students' perceptions of athletes in terms of race on four general levels:

1. Athletes achieve at sports because of hard work (23 items, $r = .98$)
2. Athletes achieve at sports because of natural ability (12 items, $r = .97$)
3. Athletes achieve at sports because they are physically better than others (2 items, $r = .91$)
4. Athletes achieve at sports because they are mentally better than others (2 items, $r = .88$)

Quantitative Data Analysis

Using Statistical Package for the Social Sciences (SPSS) 19.0, data were entered for computation and tabulation. Next, regressions and cross tabs were computed in terms of white and black participants.

Qualitative Data Analysis

Participants were presented with two open-ended questions regarding African-American and white American athleticism and instructed to offer written responses to each question. After the written responses to the profile were collected, they were transcribed into a hard copy Word document for data analysis. An investigative team, which consisted of four individuals trained in qualitative research methodology (two were the primary researchers), was utilized throughout the data analysis process.

Hierarchical content analysis, as suggested by Patton,[28] was utilized in the analysis. Following transcription, each investigator read each of the participant's transcripts to get a sense of the students' perceptions. Each investigator independently identified raw-data themes, which characterized participants' responses. Raw-data themes are quotations that capture a concept provided by the participant. Then the investigative team met to discuss the transcripts. The primary purpose of this meeting was to interpret and identify major themes. Raw data themes were utilized in conducting an inductive analysis to identify common themes or patterns of greater generality. Themes were derived from all of the transcripts, and attempts were made to interpret commonalties among the experiences described in each of the transcripts.[29] Major themes and subthemes were identified across transcripts, and support for each theme was located in each of the transcripts.[30]

Finally, utilizing the major themes, transcripts were coded and categorized by two trained researchers. Meaning units associated with each theme were identified in each of the transcripts in order to determine the number and percentage of participants that responded within each of the major themes.

Quantitative Findings: General Overview

Current students agreed that athletes succeed at their particular sport because of hard work. Most students were unsure whether athletes of different races succeed because of natural ability. Current students disagreed with the idea that athletes of one race achieved because they were mentally or physically better than another race.

The primary researchers were interested in examining the differences in beliefs held about athletes by race. The sample was split into two categories: African-American students ($N = 18$) and white students ($N = 223$). An independent t-test was run on items to determine if there were differences based on race. White students were more likely to "agree," while black students were more likely to "strongly agree" with the following statements: (a) African Americans achieve at the following sports because of hard work: football, basketball, baseball, boxing, and golf; (b) African-American women achieve at basketball because of hard work; (c) Hispanic Americans achieve at baseball because of hard work; (d) Asian Americans achieve at baseball because of hard work; and (e) White Americans achieve at basketball and baseball because of hard work ($p < .05$, see Table 12.1). However, no differences were found between African Americans' and white Americans' perceptions about achievement and natural ability of athletes.

The amount of TV watched per day was examined by age and race. Younger students watched significantly more TV than older students ($t = -2.11$, $p < .05$). Compared to white students, African-American students watched significantly more hours of TV per day in high school ($t = 3.73$, $p < .05$). However, the difference in hours per day of TV watched in college

TABLE 12.1   Students' Perceptions of Athletes and Athletic Ability by Race

Item	Overall N = 301 Mean (SD)	Afric. Am n = 18 Mean (SD)	White Am n = 223 Mean (SD)	Significant Difference
Af Am achieve at football bc of hard work	2.11 (1.0)	1.61 (.85)	2.13 (.99)	$t = -2.14$, $p < .05$
Af Am achieve at basketball bc of hard work	2.04 (.97)	1.50 (.86)	2.09 (.98)	$t = -2.47$, $p < .05$
Af Am achieve at baseball bc of hard work	1.99 (.95)	1.56 (.86)	2.02 (.95)	$t = -2.01$, $p < .05$
Af Am achieve at boxing bc of hard work	1.96 (.98)	1.53 (.80)	2.00 (1.0)	$t = -1.91$, $p < .05$
Af Am achieve at golf bc of hard work	2.00 (1.0)	1.50 (.86)	2.09 (1.1)	$t = -2.05$, $p < .05$
Af Am women achieve at basketball bc of hard work	1.97 (1.0)	1.39 (.78)	2.09 (.98)	$t = -2.53$, $p < .05$
Hispanic Am achieve at baseball bc of hard work	2.01 (.94)	1.53 (.87)	2.04 (.95)	$t = -2.16$, $p < .05$
Asian Am achieve at baseball bc of hard work	2.10 (.97)	1.59 (.94)	2.14 (.97)	$t = -2.26$, $p < .05$
White Am achieve at basketball bc of hard work	2.00 (.98)	1.56 (.78)	2.04 (1.0)	$t = -1.99$, $p < .05$
White Am achieve at baseball bc of hard work	2.01 (.97)	1.56 (.86)	2.05 (.98)	$t = -2.07$, $p < .05$

Source: Authors' data set.

between white and African-American students was not significantly different (see Table 12.2).

An independent samples *t*-test was performed to determine the relationship of television on white students' beliefs about athletic achievement of African Americans. White students were divided into two groups based on their daily college TV watching habits: (a) students who watched one hour of TV or less per day (N = 81) and (b) students who watched three or more hours of TV per day (N = 71). White students who watched more TV were more likely to perceive basketball as a mostly African-American

TABLE 12.2 Students' Beliefs About African-American Athletic Ability and Achievement by Hours of Television Watched Per Day in College

Item	Overall N = 301 Mean (SD)	African Am n = 18 Mean (SD)	White Am n = 223 Mean (SD)	Significant Difference
Hours per day watching TV, high school	2.97 (1.4)	4.06 (1.6)	2.89 (1.3)	$t = 3.73$, $p < .05$
Hours per day watching TV, college	2.23 (1.3)	2.89 (1.5)	2.15 (1.2)	$t = 1.99$, $p > .05$

White Students Only

Daily College Television Habits

Item	1 hour or less n = 81 Mean (SD)	3 or more hours n = 70 Mean (SD)	Significant Difference
Age	19.53 (.68)	19.86 (1.1)	$t = -2.1$, $p < .05$
Basketball is mostly Af Am because they are physically better than whites	3.36 (1.3)	2.89 (1.1)	$t = 2.47$, $p < .05$
Af Am women achieve at track and field bc of hard work	2.79 (1.1)	2.39 (1.1)	$t = 2.24$, $p < .05$

Source: Authors' data set.
Note: Only 151 white participants answered these particular items; 72 participants failed to answer.

TABLE 12.3   White Students' Beliefs about African-American Athletic Ability and Achievement by Number of Articles Read about African-American "Natural" Athleticism

Item	Read No Articles $n = 177$ Mean (SD)	Read 3 or More Articles $n = 44$ Mean (SD)	Significant Difference
Af Am achieve at baseball bc of natural ability	2.72 (1.0)	2.34 (.94)	$t = 2.32$, $p < .05$
Af Am achieve at basketball bc of natural ability	2.55 (1.0)	2.20 (.95)	$t = 2.08$, $p < .05$

Source: Authors' data set.
Note: Only 221 white participants answered these particular items; two participants failed to answer.

sport because African Americans are physically better than whites ($t = 2.47$, $p < .05$). No significant differences were found among any other variables.

The primary researchers examined white students' ($N = 246$) perceptions of African-American athletes based on the number of articles they had read on the topic of natural athleticism (see Table 12.3). The majority of the students in the sample, 60 percent (148), had never read a scholarly article regarding the debate of "natural" athleticism of African-American athletes. Of the sample, 27 percent (66) reported reading one to two articles, 8 percent (17) reported reading three to four articles, and 5 percent (12) reported reading four or more articles.

The primary researchers were interested in the impact of reading these articles on white students' views of African-American athletes. What follows are the summaries of the t-tests by race. White students who read three or more articles were more likely to attribute African-American achievement in baseball and basketball to natural ability compared to white students who did not read any articles ($t = 1.97$, $p < .05$; $t = 2.08$, $p < .05$ respectively). No other variables differed significantly based on the number of articles read.

Regression Specificity

A series of regressions was run to examine the determinants of the number of articles a student read about nature athleticism. The same

TABLE 12.4   Impact of Demographic Variables on Number of Articles Read about Natural Athleticism among African Americans ($N = 287$): Beta[1] after Step

Step	R	Variable	r	1	2	3
1	.18	Age	.18	.18	.19	.16
2	.24	Hispanic	.15	.15	.15	.15
3	.27	Female	−.13	−.13	−.13	−.13

[1]The coefficient for any variable not yet entered in the equation shows the beta that variable would receive if it were entered into the equation at the next step.
Source: Authors' data set.
Note: All coefficients are significant, $p < .05$.
Variables not entering into the equation:
African American
Asian
Other ethnicities
Hours per day watching TV in high school
Hours per day watching TV in college

methodological strategy was used to determine student views about: natural ability, hard work, and physical ability of African Americans. Students' age was a significant predictor of how many articles they had read about the natural athleticism of African-American athletes; older students were significantly more likely to read more articles than younger students (r^{31} = .16, $p < .05$). Hispanic students were also more likely to have read more articles than non-Hispanic students ($r = .15$, $p < .05$). Finally, males were significantly more likely to have read more articles than females ($r = -.13$, $p < .05$, $R = .27$). The following variables were not significant: being white, African American, Asian, or another race and hours per day watching TV in high school and college (see Table 12.4).

The second regression used demographic characteristics as predictor variables and "African Americans achieve at football because of hard work" as the outcome variable. The only significant predictor of the "hard work" outcome variable was being African American ($r = .12$, $p < .05$, $R = .12$). Nonsignificant variables were as follows: (a) age; (b) gender, other races (white, Hispanic, Asian, and other); (c) hours of television watched in high school and college; and (d) number of articles read about natural athleticism in African Americans (see Table 12.5).

The next regression used "African Americans achieve at football because of natural ability" as the outcome variable and the demographic

TABLE 12.5   Impact of Demographic Variables by the Belief African Americans Achieve at Football Due to Hard Work ($N = 287$)

Step	r	Variable	r	1	2	3
1	.12	Black	.12	.18	.19	.16

Source: Authors' data set.
Note: All coefficients are significant, $p < .05$.
Variables not entering into the equation:
Age
Gender
White
Hispanic
Asian
Hours per day watching TV in high school
Hours per day watching TV in college
Number of articles read about natural athleticism by African Americans

characteristics as predictor variables. The only significant predictor of the belief in natural ability of African-American athletes was hours of television watched per day in college ($r = .12, p < .05, R = .12$). Nonsignificant variables were as follows: (a) age, (b) gender, (c) race (white, African American, Hispanic, and Asian), (d) hours of television watched in high school, and (e) number of articles read about natural athleticism in African Americans.

The final regression employed was run on the following statement: "Football is mostly African American because they are physically better than Whites" as the outcome variables, and the predictor variables remained demographic characteristics. Gender and Hispanic were significant predictors of the physical outcome variable. Females were significantly more likely than males and Hispanics more likely than non-Hispanics to believe that football is mostly African American because they are physically better than whites ($r = .25, p < .05$; $\beta = .17, p < .05$ respectively, Final $R = .30$).

Qualitative Results

Qualitative themes were derived from participants' responses to two open-ended questions about black and white athletic ability. The primary focus of the two questions was to assess participants' perceptions of the African-American athlete and their opinion as to whether white athletes are inferior to them. Due to the volume of data, the scope of this study examined only white and African-American participants' responses.

African-American Qualitative Themes

Four major themes emerged that are descriptive of the African-American participants' ($n = 18$) perceptions and thoughts concerning the debate of African-American athleticism: environment, natural ability, pure will to succeed, and media hype. The following section examines attitudes about African-American athleticism.

Environment.   The first theme, environment, involves participants' thoughts that African-American athleticism is due to environmental factors. This theme describes participants' recognition of lack of resources in certain lower-class neighborhoods. It also depicts the relevance of encouragement toward athletic participation. Consider this example from a participant:

> No: I think the prevalence of certain groups in certain sports can be explained by looking at the opportunities these groups had growing up and what they were encouraged to do. Sometimes, it has a lot to do with the neighborhoods people grow up in. Not every neighborhood has a golf course and not every neighborhood has a frozen pond or skating rink.

Nearly 40 percent of respondents attributed African-American athleticism to environmental factors: culture, upbringing, resources, and opportunity (see Table 12.6).

Natural Ability.   The second theme, natural ability, describes participants' responses that use genetics and natural ability to explain African-American athletes' dominance in certain sports (football, basketball, and track). Participants expressed the significance of God-given talent in regards to athleticism. One participant explained:

> Absolutely. People are afraid to say it because they think it will come off as racist but the key is Blacks are better athletes than Whites. It doesn't mean he does not work hard to develop his talents. It doesn't mean he is any less capable, mentally. What truly separates blacks from whites is their God-given physical abilities. The numbers don't lie. Many more black players are in the NBA than white players. The same can be said for the NFL. (157)

Thirty-three percent (6/18) of the African-American participants attributed African-American athleticism to natural physical ability (see Table 12.6).

Pure Will to Succeed.   Another reason given for African-American athleticism is the desire on the part of African-American athletes to succeed at all costs. Participants recognized African-American athletes' strong work ethic, as the following comment illustrates:

> I believe it's because of our history—we've never had anything delivered to us on a silver spoon. We work hard everyday in the struggle therefore there's more of a mean to strive for the "good life." (130)

Twenty-two percent (4/18) of the African-American participants mentioned work ethic and will to succeed in their explanation of the difference between white and African-American athletes' abilities (see Table 12.6).

Media Hype.   Media hype was the final theme that emerged from participant responses. This theme holds the media accountable for societal viewpoints concerning athleticism. Participants reported that the media is responsible for perpetuating stereotypes concerning African-American athleticism as described by one participant:

TABLE 12.6   African-American Participants' Qualitative Themes and Quotations: Descriptive Percentage of Transcripts: N = 18

Theme	Quote	N	Percent
Environment	African Americans achieve in these sports because they practice. These sports are a big part of their culture and they dedicate a lot of time playing and practicing these sports.	7	39%
Natural ability	People are afraid to say it because they think it will come off as racist but the key is Blacks are better athletes than Whites.	6	33%
Pure will to succeed	Maybe it is just that African Americans are expected to be better, which may make people think they are better than Whites. If someone wants something bad enough, however they can achieve it if they are willing to work hard.	4	22%
Media hype	I think minorities get more coverage in these sports.	1	6%

Source: Authors' data set.

I feel that the way society perpetuates these stereotypical viewpoints that one race is better than the next. Through this method, the people listening to the media have a higher chance to think these are true. However, I think that the physiognomy of particular individuals is better suited for a specific sport and therefore those who just don't have the same genetic physical make-up. (252)

Surprisingly, few African Americans identified the media as a determinant of African-American athleticism. In fact, only one African-American participant identified the media as a determining factor.

White American Qualitative Themes

The following seven major themes emerged that are descriptive of the white American participants' ($n = 223$) perceptions and thoughts concerning the debate of African-American athleticism: genetic/natural ability, cultural/socio-economic status, no edge, multiple factors, dedication, representation, and stereotypes. The following section outlines the specific themes and offers direct quotations from the white American participants.

Genetic/Natural Ability.   The first theme, genetic/natural ability, involves the participants' explanation of African-American athlete dominance in some sports. This theme describes the recognition on the part of at least some athletes, of biological and physiological differences between white and black athletes. It also depicts the thought that white athletes are inferior. Consider this example from a participant:

I totally feel they are biologically and physiologically inferior to Blacks on average in some physical activities. Different genetic profiles yield different abilities; it's not brain surgery. If Blacks generally have more muscle mass, or the ability to develop more muscle mass, or have more fast-twitch muscle fibers on average, then yea they can probably jump higher or faster. Whites sprint in track, why aren't they many or any Whites at the Olympic 100m finals, you think it's because Blacks work harder—hardly. Whites do the same amount of work; they are simply slower. (156)

White American participants expressed a belief in strong genetic differentiation of athletes among races. Twenty-eight percent (62/223) of them alluded to this explanation in some way (see Table 12.7).

Cultural/Socio-Economic Status.   The second theme, cultural/socio-economic status, describes participants' explanations that athletes play

TABLE 12.7 White American Participants' Qualitative Themes and Quotations: Descriptive Percentages of Transcripts: *N* = 223

Theme	Quote	*N*	Percent
Genetic/ natural ability	I think that "White men can't jump" is completely true with respect to African Americans. I went to an all Black school and I have to say that Blacks can just jump higher and run faster. This doesn't mean all can rather I think in general many more Blacks possess these talents versus Whites. So naturally this will help them in basketball and football and track and field.	62	28%
Cultural/ socio-economic status	Yes, I think that White people are generally inferior in basketball. Maybe it's because many Blacks live in urban areas and it's not only cheap to play basketball there, but it also doesn't take up that much space and is often encouraged. On the contrary, White kids who often grow up in suburban areas are not encouraged to pursue basketball as much. Also, these suburban White kids often don't play teams that are as good as the urban Black kids face; therefore, the inner–city kids face stronger competition, so they get better.	58	26%
No edge	No, I don't feel that White athletes are inferior in certain sports. There are many White athletes that possess just as much talent as Black athletes in particular sports like football, basketball and track and field and other sports.	40	18%
Multiple factors	I don't think White athletes are inferior to African-American athletes. I just think depending on how you were raised, how much work you put into the sport and many other factors are what makes you good at a sport.	25	11%
Dedication/ Motivation	I don't think they are naturally less capable than African Americans. I think that maybe African Americans just try harder and have more desire to succeed.	20	9%

TABLE 12.7   (Continued)

Theme	Quote	N	Percent
Representation	I think in certain sports such as basketball, football and baseball, African Americans do appear better than White Americans. This can be due to the large number of African Americans in these sports.	13	6%
Stereotypes	No, I do not feel White athletes are inferior in sports. I believe the reason people believe that they are is because of racial stereotyping. People have come to believe that Whites should be doctors/lawyers and that African Americans should excel at sports, neither one of these stereotypes reflect true facts.	5	2%

Source: Authors' data set.

certain sports based on their upbringing, culture, opportunity, and class level. Participants also attributed success in sports primarily to hard work and time commitment. One participant expressed opposition to the typical white athlete stereotype utilized in the question:

> I don't agree that there's some "White men's disease" that doesn't allow them to excel in sports. I think the differences come in the ways African Americans are raised versus how Whites are raised. In the African American community sports are seen as a way of achieving fame, success, prestige and money—probably more so than Whites view sports as just an extracurricular activity. I don't think there's anything in genes or "natural" ability that dictates how well you can play basketball (or any sport for that matter) it depends on how much time and effort you put into it. (177)

Twenty-six percent (58/223) of white American participants recognized the differences of how the various races are raised and cultural distinctions between the two (see Table 12.7).

No Edge.   The third theme, no edge, depicts participants' thoughts that there is no evident edge in sport based on race. Participants reported that such sayings as "White man's disease" cause racism in our society. Participants also expressed that African Americans do not have an advantage over white athletes based on race, as the following comment illustrates:

Notions like "White man's disease" just add to racism in our society and paint African Americans as savage beast capable of little more than athletics. This so-called disease is simply untrue. There are plenty of successful athletes of both races. (140)

Eighteen percent (40/223) of white American participants reported that there are excellent athletes in sport regardless of race (see Table 12.7).

Multiple Factors.   The fourth theme, multiple factors, involves participants' explanation of several reasons for athletic prowess between both races (whites and African Americans). Participants also recognized various factors that attribute to African-American dominance in certain sports (football, basketball, and track). For example, one participant stated:

There are more African American professional football, basketball, and track and field athletes than Caucasian. I believe this is a consequence of several factors including: natural physical ability, cultural expectations, the environment of one's youth (is it conductive to hours and hours of practice or schoolwork, chores, jobs, etc. take precedence?) and hard work. (241)

Some white American participants listed various explanations, 11 percent (25/223) of which attributed athletic success to natural ability, culture, opportunity, genetics, and neighborhoods, just to name a few (see Table 12.7).

Dedication/Motivation.   Dedication/motivation was another theme that emerged from the data. Black athletes' sheer determination and hard work was realized. One participant stated:

This label of Black athletes as "natural" athletes has partial validity. A lot of success, historically are attributed to dedication and hard work. While many Black athletes have come from under-privileged poor families. They have fought more racial barriers to be where they are today. For some Blacks, athletics isn't their gift. For others, it is a way of life, playing pickup games on concrete urban playgrounds. Much of Black progress has been in professional sports. Give credit to their hard work and perseverance. (247)

A few white American participants acknowledged the dedication and motivation of lack athletes (9 percent; 20/223) (see Table 12.7).

Representation.   The theme of representation consists of respondents' awareness of participation rates by race in specific sports. Participants acknowledged the high representation of African Americans in certain sports, as the following comment illustrates:

> African Americans dominate football, basketball, track and field. White people dominate golf, baseball and hockey. Its all involving a ball, and sweat. Let's move on to something that actually matters. (131)

Some white American participants simply stated that African-American athletes are overrepresented in some sports. Six percent (13/223) responded thus in response to the questions and failed to offer an explanation (see Table 12.7).

Stereotypes.   Stereotypes is a theme that emerged based on the tendency for society to label people of certain races. The following participant explained how racial stereotyping has influenced people's opinions and expectations:

> No, I do not feel White athletes are inferior in sports. I believe the reason people believe that they are is because of racial stereotyping. People have come to believe that Whites should be doctors/lawyers, and that African Americans should be excel at sports, neither one of these stereotypes reflect true facts. (291)

Some white American participants, 2 percent (5/223), acknowledged the common stereotypes associated with white and black athletes (see Table 12.7).

Discussion

On average, African-American students' agreement with the statement "African Americans succeed at sports because of hard work" is significantly stronger than White students'. It is possible these black participants more strongly agree because of their experiences as persons of color on a predominantly white campus and because of self-empowerment based on diligence and effort. There were no differences between black and white respondents with respect to how hard blacks work. The aforementioned statement does automatically lead to the conclusion then, that whites support the ideal that black athletes are innately superior to whites where athletics are concerned.

The primary researchers agree that some blacks develop superior achievement, athletic skills, and physical aptitudes in certain sports, but the analysis of the scientific evidence suggests this is not due to biology.[32]

The primary researchers also contend that other groups from all ethnic backgrounds are superior in other endeavors (e.g., education, law, medicine, and corporate leadership positions). Is superiority in one realm associated with inferiority in another? The answer to this question is still debated in American society, but these data suggest numerous citizens perceive racial superiority as a phenomenon peculiar to sport.

White students who watched three or more hours of TV per day in college were more likely to agree with the statement that basketball is mostly African American because blacks are physically better than whites. In terms of the contact hypothesis, whites in general are exposed to limited images of African Americans on television. This is well documented by ethnographic and historical analyses.[33] Furthermore, there are those who believe American culture is virtually created by television, films, and advertising.[34]

In terms of articles read on the natural athleticism of African Americans, white students who read three or more articles were more likely to attribute African-American achievement in basketball and baseball to natural ability compared to white students who read no articles. This suggests that racial science is historically ingrained and institutionalized in school and in formal and formal mechanisms of social control as well as in other subtle and overt forms of educating the public.[35] The academic and discipline history (and scholarship bias) of sport sociology, sport history, and cultural studies of sport (which did not formally begin in the academy until the early 1970s) no doubt plays a role in terms of what students read and have read about this issue of race and sport. Approximately 40 percent of the sample had read articles regarding natural athleticism of African Americans. That 40 percent was significantly more likely to be younger, male, and Hispanic. This is pertinent when considering these are college-educated students at a highly prestigious intellectual institution. Regardless of the lack of scholarship consumption (sport sociology) by the sample in terms of articles read, many had strong opinions, thoughts, stigmas, and beliefs about why African Americans exist and participate in certain sports.[36]

Being black was the only significant predictor of agreement with the following statement: "African Americans succeed at football because of hard work." These beliefs outside of the natural athlete myth and the stereotype suggest that African Americans in our sample may be biased, but not in terms of social desirability. I concur that their bias might be a phenomenon of race and auto-ethnography.[37] This suggests that while they are only a small number in this study (less than 20 African-American respondents), these participants see hard work as the major factor or variable for success in football.

Of the entire sample, the students who watched three or more hours of TV per day in college were more likely to agree with the statement "African Americans achieve at football because of natural ability" (this relationship may differ depending on the type of sport, for example, basketball, baseball). For whites, this relationship was different. White students who watched three or more hours of TV in college per day were more likely to agree with the statement that basketball is mostly African American because blacks are physically better than whites. This confirms a great body of literature in communication and mass media that suggests when whites and blacks are primed with limited imagery, biased and less-complex cognitive processes are often internalized.[38]

Qualitative Context

Due to the disparity in the number of participants that were African American ($n = 18$) and white Americans ($n = 223$), there was a difference between the numbers of themes that emerged for each race. African-American responses were categorized into four themes and white American responses into seven themes. The most common theme among African-American responses was environment. African-American participants attributed African-American athletes' dominance in certain sports (football, basketball, and track) to several factors such as culture, upbringing, opportunity, and neighborhoods. They also reported lack of resources as an integral explanation of why black athletes play sports like football, basketball, and track. Their responses reflect claims by noted scholars on race and sport.[39]

The most common theme among white American responses was genetic/natural ability. White American participants attributed African-American athletes' dominance in certain sports (football, basketball, and track) primarily to biological and physiological differences between races. Some even mentioned specific differences such as black athletes have an extra muscle, a longer tendon, a longer femur, and more fast-twitch muscles than their white counterparts. Most of these participants also reported that white athletes are inferior to black athletes. In comparing the most common themes from both groups (African Americans and white

Americans) of responses, the primary difference is that one group (African-American participants) believes that African-American athleticism is due to environmental factors, and the other group (white Americans) maintains that it is due to strong genetic differences of athletes among races. In contrast to other studies, what is interesting about these findings is the empirical consistency of some mainstream white Americans believing the locus of control for African-American athletes is external, not internal.[40]

The second most common themes among participants are also vital to understanding the differences between the two groups. Surprisingly, natural ability was the second most common theme (33 percent) among African-American responses. Thirty-three percent of African-American students attributed African-American athleticism to natural ability and genetics. They reported that some black athletes simply have God-given talent in regards to athleticism. The second most common theme of white American responses was cultural/socioeconomic status. About a quarter of participants attributed African-American athleticism to cultural and social factors. This white response coincides with the most common theme (39 percent) from the African-American participants termed environment. Basically, all participants had similar explanations for African-American athleticism; however, one factor/explanation such as cultural/environmental (39 percent) seems to be more common among African-American responses than whites. The other factor of genetics (28 percent) seems to be more important among white American responses than blacks. Another distinction involved participants' perceptions of white athletic inferiority. African-American participants from the two primary themes failed to state that white athletes are inferior. On the other hand, white American participants who consisted of the primary theme of genetic/natural ability clearly stated that white athletes are inferior.

Black participants reported that black athletes are superior in a few sports because of genetics. Many of these viewpoints based on genetics are simply myths (there is no conclusive evidence in the research). Another contrast between the two groups of respondents was that African-American results consisted of the theme media hype, and white American responses failed to mention the influence of media. Some similarities include a common mention of athletes having a strong work ethic.

Conclusions and Implications

This study examined public attitudes toward myths related to African-American athletic success and elite performance in certain sports.

Specifically, university students' perceptions were evaluated in the context of racial beliefs about sport abilities. Limited images of African Americans in mainstream media affect perceptions of how racial groups are seen and psychologically embraced in some instances.[41]

This phenomenon often leads to limited and damaging stereotypes and social categorization of diverse and complicated behaviors. Future research should examine the following: (a) public perceptions at various institutions such as historically black colleges and universities (HBCUs); (b) sports establishments such as sports bars and fans at athletic contests; (c) the athletes themselves at virtually all levels (e.g., elementary, high school, college, and professional); (d) residents in society (e.g., homes, common living arrangements, and apartments); (e) and in general more systematic data on how and why people perceive the superiority of racial and ethnic representation in various sports versus participation and achievement in other sports and also societal occupations.[42]

The primary researchers pose this question: *If African-American athletes are not respected for cognitive mastery and athletic industry in a few sports, what might this say about the public perception of African Americans and their presence in nonsporting realms?* The research quests are open for further questioning and interpretation.

Note: The primary researchers ran regression on the concept that white Americans achieve at football because of hard work, and none of the demographic variables (age, gender, races [black, white, Hispanic, Asian, and other], hours of television watched in high school and college, and number of articles read about natural athleticism in African Americans) were significant predictors.

Notes

1. G. Sailes, "The Myth of the Dumb Black Jock." *Sociology of Sport Journal* 10 (1993): 88–97.

2. C. Hallinan, "The Presentation of Human Biological Diversity in Sport and Exercise Science Textbooks: The Example of 'Race.'" *Journal of Sport Behavior* 17, no. 1 (1994): 3–12.

3. J. Stone, "Black and White Athletic Performances: Stereotype Threat." Paper Presented at the North American Society for the Sociology of Sport Annual Meeting in Colorado Springs, CO, 2000.

4. C. Keith Harrison and Suzanne M Lawrence, "College Students' Perceptions, Myths, and Stereotypes about African American Athleticism: A Qualitative Investigation." *Sport, Education and Society* 1 (2004).

5. J. Coakley, *Sport in Society; Issues and Controversy* (Boston: McGraw Hill, 2001); H. Edwards, "The Sources of the Black Athlete's Superiority." *Black Scholar* (1971): 33–41; C.K. Harrison, "Black Athletes' Success Transcends Biomechanics." *Biomechanics* 8, no. 2 (2001): 73–81; J. Hoberman, *Darwin's Athletes* (Boston: Houghton Mifflin, 1997); E. Smith, "The Genetically Superior Athlete: Myth or Reality," in *Black Studies: Theory, Method, and Cultural Perspectives*, ed. T. Anderson (Pullman: Washington State University Press, 1990).

6. J. Entine, *Taboo: Why Black Athletes Dominate Sport and Why We're Afraid to Talk about It* (New York: Public Affairs, 2000).

7. P. Gilroy, *Against Race: Imagining Political Culture beyond the Color Line* (Cambridge, MA: Belknap Press of Harvard University Press, 2000).

8. D. Wiggins, *Glory Bound: Black Athletes in White America* (New York: Syracuse University Press, 1997).

9. C. Bouchard, "Preface: Racial Differences in Performance." *Canadian Journal of Sport Sciences* 13, no. 2 (1988): 109–116.

10. C. Hallinan, "The Presentation of Human," 3–12.

11. H. Edwards, "Crisis of Black Athletes on the Eve of the 21st Century." *Society* 37, no. 3 (2000): 9–13.

12. C.K. Harrison, "Black Athletes' Success Transcends Biomechanics." *Biomechanics* 8, no. 2 (2001): 73–81.

13. C. K. Harrison, "The Myth of the 'Natural' Black Male Athlete: Rhetoric, Representation and Reality." Paper presented as a tutorial at the American College of Sports Medicine in Seattle, WA, 1999.

14. L. Proctor & C.K. Harrison, "African American Males and Their Game: Culture, Environment and Eugenics Propaganda," Paper presented at the North American Society for Sociology and Sport Annual Meeting in Cleveland, OH, 1999.

15. G. Sailes, "The Myth of the Dumb," 88–97.

16. C.K Harrison, "The Myth of the Natural"; C.K. Harrison, "Black Athletes at the Millenium." *Society* (2000): 35–39; C.K. Harrison, "Black Athletes' Success Transcends Biomechanics." *Biomechanics* 8, no. 2 (2001): 73–81; J. Stone, "Black and White Athletic Performances," 2000.

17. G. Allport, *The Nature of Prejudice* (Reading, PA: Addison-Wesley, 1954).

18. Ibid.

19. R. Nassau, "The Benefits of Racial Contract through Sport." Unpublished, 2001.

20. R. Nassau (2001); Romo, "Improving Ethnic and Racial Tensions in the Schools," *ERIC Digest*, 1997.

21. Bristor & Associates, "Race and Ideology: African Americans in Television Advertising." *Journal of Public Policy* 14 (1995): 48–59.

22. H. Becker, *Outsiders: Studies in the Sociology of Deviance* (New York: Free Press, 1963).

23. E. Goffman, *The Presentation of Self in Everyday Life* (Garden City, NJ: Doubleday Anchor, 1959).

24. J. Coakley, *Sport in Society: Issues and Controversy* (Boston: McGraw Hill, 2001).

25. J. Chang, "What's at Play? Sport Discourse and the Codification of Race." Unpublished graduate paper for the class Current Issues in Sport at the Rackham Graduate School, Ann Arbor, MI, 1999; J. Coakley, *Sport in Society*.

26. P. Adler and P. Adler, *Backboard and Blackboards: College Athletes and Role Engulfment* (New York: Columbia University Press, 1991); C.K. Harrison, "Themes That Thread through Society: Racism and Athletic Manifestation in the African American Community." *Race, Ethnicity, and Education* 1, no. 1 (1998): 63–74.

27. J. Coakley, *Sport in Society*.

28. M.Q. Patton, *Qualitative Evaluation and Research Methods* (Newborn Park, CA: Sage, 1990, 2001).

29. Ibid.

30. Ibid.

31. Beta are reported at the final step.

32. J. Coakley, *Sport in Society*; P. Miller, "The Anatomy of Scientific Racism: Racialist Responses to Black Athlete Achievement." *Journal of Sport History* 25 (1998): 199–151.

33. D. Bogle, *African Americans on Prime Time Blues: Network Television* (New York: Farrar, Straus, and Giroux, 2001); Bristor & Associates, "Race and Ideology," 48–59; S. Coltrane and M. Messineo, "The Perpetuation of Subtle Prejudice: Race and Gender Imagery in 1990's Television Advertising." *Sex Roles* 42, no. 5 & 6 (2000): 363–389.

34. V. Wikan, "The Self in a World of Urgency and Necessity." *Ethos* 23 (1995): 259–285.

35. K. Russel, *The Color of Crime* (New York: University Press, 1997).

36. C.K. Harrison, M. Plecha, and E. Comeaux. Unpublished raw data set (qualitative and quantitative empirical findings, 2001.

37. N. Denzin, *Qualitative Inquiry* (Thousand Oaks, CA: Sage, 1995).

38. N. Valentino, "Crime News and the Priming of Racial Attitudes during Evaluations of the President." *Public Opinion Quarterly* 63 (1999); 293–320.

39. H. Edwards, *Sociology of Sport* (Homewood, IL: Dorsey, 1973): H. Edwards, "Crisis of Black Athletes,"; R. Lapchick, *Five Minutes to Midnight: Race and Sport in the 1990s* (Lanham, MD: Madison Books, 1991); R. Lapchick, *Smashing Barriers* (Lanham, MD: Madison Books, 2001).

40. A. Murrell and E. Curtis, "Casual Attributions of Performance for Black and White Quarterbacks in the NFL: A Look at the Sports Pages." *Journal of Sport and Social Issues* 18, no. 3 (1994): 224–233; J. Rada, "Color Blind-Sided: Racial Bias in Network Television's Coverage of Professional Football Games," in *Facing*

Difference: Race, Gender, and Mass Media, ed. S. Biagi and M. Kern Foxworth (Thousand Oaks, CA: Pine Forge, 1996); R. Rainville and E. McCormick, "Extent of Covert Racial Prejudice in Pro Football Announcer's Speech." *Journalism Quarterly* 54 (1977): 20–26.

41. T. Dixon, "A Social and Cognitive Approach to Studying Racial Stereotyping in the Mass Media." *African American Research Perspectives* 6, no. 1 (2000): 60–68.

42. C. K. Harrison, "Black Athletes' Success . . . ," 2001.

Bibliography

Adler, P., & Adler, P. *Backboards and blackboards: College athletes and role engulfment.* New York: Columbia University Press, 1991.

Allport, G. *The nature of prejudice.* Reading, PA: Addison-Wesley, 1954.

Becker, H. *Outsiders: Studies in the sociology of deviance.* New York: Free Press, 1963.

Bogle, D. *African Americans on prime time blues: Network television.* New York: Farrar, Straus and Giroux, 2001.

Bouchard, C. "Preface: Racial differences in performance." *Canadian Journal of Sport Sciences* 13, no. 2 (1988): 109–116.

Bristor & Associates. "Race and ideology: African Americans in television advertising." *Journal of Public Policy* 14 (1995): 48–59.

Brown, J. *For the Record.* HBO, 2001.

Chang, J. "What's at play? Sport discourse and the codification of race." Unpublished graduate paper for the class Current Issues in Sport at the Rackham Graduate School, Ann Arbor, MI, 1999.

Coakley, J. *Sport in society: Issues and controversies.* Boston: McGraw Hill, 2009.

Coltrane, S., & Messineo, M. "The perpetuation of subtle prejudice: Race and gender imagery in 1990's television advertising." *Sex Roles* 42, no. 5 & 6 (2000): 363–389.

Denzin, N. *Qualitative inquiry.* Thousand Oaks, CA: Sage, 1995.

Dixon, T. "A social cognitive approach to studying racial stereotyping in the mass media." *African American Research Perspectives* 6, no. 1 (2000): 60–68.

Edwards, H. "The sources of the black athlete's superiority." *Black Scholar* (1971): 33–41.

Edwards, H. *Sociology of sport.* Homewood, IL: Dorsey, 1973.

Edwards, H. "Crisis of black athletes on the eve of the 21st Century." *Society* 37, no. 3 (2000): 9–13.

Entine, J. *Taboo: Why black athletes dominate sport and why we're afraid to talk about it.* New York: Public Affairs, 2000.

Gilroy, P. *Against race: Imagining political culture beyond the color line.* Cambridge, MA: Belknap Press of Harvard University Press, 2000.

Goffman, E. *The presentation of self in everyday life.* Garden City, NJ: Doubleday Anchor, 1959.

Hallinan, C. "The presentation of human biological diversity in sport and exercise science textbooks: The example of 'race.' " *Journal of Sport Behavior* 17, no.1 (1994): 3–12.

Harrison, C. K. "Themes that thread through society: Racism and athletic manifestation in the African American community." *Race, Ethnicity, and Education* 1, no.1 (1998): 63–74.

Harrison, C. K. "The myth of the 'natural' black male athlete: Rhetoric, representation and reality." Paper presented as a tutorial at the American College of Sports Medicine, Seattle, WA, 1999.

Harrison, C. K. "Black athletes at the millennium." *Society* (2000): 35–39.

Harrison, C. K. "Black athletes' success transcends biomechanics." *Biomechanics* 8, no. 2 (2001): 73–81.

Harrison, C. K., Plecha, M., & Comeaux, E. Unpublished raw data set (qualitative and quantitative empirical findings), 2001.

Harrison, C. Keith, and Suzanne M Lawrence. "College students' perceptions, myths, and stereotypes about African American athleticism: A qualitative investigation." *Sport, Education and Society* 1 (2004).

Harrison, L., Jr. "Understanding the influence of stereotypes: Implications for the African American in sport and physical activity." *Quest* 53, no. 1 (2001): 97–114.

Hoberman, J. *Darwin's athletes.* Boston: Houghton Mifflin, 1997.

Lapchick, R. *Five minutes to midnight: Race and sport in the 1990s.* Lanham, MD: Madison Books, 1991.

Lapchick, R. *Smashing barriers.* Lanham, MD: Madison Books, 2001.

Livingstone, F. B. "On the nonexistence of human races." In *The concept of race,* edited by A. Montagu. New York: Free Press of Glencoe, 1964.

Miller, P. "The anatomy of scientific racism: Racialist responses to black athletic achievement." *Journal of Sport History* 25 (1998): 199–151.

Murrell, A., & Curtis, E. "Causal attributions of performance for black and white quarterbacks in the NFL: A look at the sports pages." *Journal of Sport and Social Issues* 18, no. 3 (1994): 224–233.

Nassau, R. "The benefits of racial contact through sport." Unpublished paper, 2001.

Patton, M. Q. *Qualitative evaluation and research methods.* Newborn Park, CA: Sage, 2001.

Proctor, L., & Harrison, C. K. "Biological determinism: The crutch (MYTHS) supporting the attitudes of the socially privileged in our society." Paper presented at the North American Society for Sport History Annual Meeting in College Station, PA. 1999.

Proctor, L., & Harrison, C. K. "African American males and their game: Culture, environment and eugenics propaganda." Paper presented at the North American Society for Sociology of Sport Annual Meeting in Cleveland, OH, 1999.

Rada, J. "Color blind-sided: Racial bias in network television's coverage of professional football games." In *Facing difference: Race, gender and mass media*, edited by S. Biagi & M. Kern-Foxworth, 23–29. Thousand Oaks, CA: Pine Forge, 1996.

Rainville, R., & McCormick, E. (1977). "Extent of covert racial prejudice in pro football announcer's speech." *Journalism Quarterly* 54 (1977): 20–26.

Romo, Harriet. "Improving ethnic and racial tensions in the schools." *ERIC Digest*, 1997.

Russell. K. *The color of crime*. New York: University Press, 1998.

Sailes, G. "The myth of the dumb black jock." *Sociology of Sport Journal* 10 (1993): 88–97.

Schofield, J. W. "Improving intergroup relations among students." *Handbook of research on multicultural education*, 1995.

Smith. E. "The genetically superior athlete: Myth or reality." In *Black studies: Theory, method, and cultural perspectives*, edited by T. Anderson. Pullman, WA: Washington State University Press, 1990.

Stone, J. "Black and white athletic performances: Stereotype threat." Paper presented at the North American Society for the Sociology of Sport Annual Meeting in Colorado Springs, CA, 2000.

Valentino, N. "Crime news and the priming of racial attitudes during evaluations of the president." *Public Opinion Quarterly* 63 (1999): 293–320.

Wiggins, D. *Glory bound: Black athletes in White America*. New York: Syracuse University Press, 1997.

Wikan, V. "The self in a world of urgency and necessity." *Ethos* 23 (1995): 259–285.

Winbush, R. "The furious passage of the African-American intercollegiate athlete." *Journal of Sport and Social Issues* 11, no. 1 & 2 (1987): 97–103.

About the Editor and Contributors

LORI LATRICE MARTIN, PhD, is Associate Professor of Sociology and African & African American Studies at Louisiana State University. Her forthcoming published works include ABC-CLIO's *White Sports/Black Sports: Racial Socialization and Athletic Destinations*. Martin is also the author of *Black Asset Poverty and the Enduring Racial Divide* (First Forum Press, 2013). Dr. Martin holds a doctorate in sociology from University at Albany, State University of New York.

TIFFANY E. BARBER is a Doctoral Student at the University of Rochester. Her research interests include contemporary art with an emphasis on the expressions and theorizations of (post)blackness and afrofuturism, politics of identity performance, and public space, intersections between visual and literary practices, and histories of exhibition and curatorial practices.

AKILAH R. CARTER-FRANCIQUE, PhD, is Assistant Professor of Health and Kinesiology at Texas A&M University. Her research interests include black/African-American females and obesity; black/African-American females in sport and physical activity; diversity management in sport and recreation organizations; and sport and social justice. She is the author of numerous articles and book chapters.

JOSHUA B. DICKHAUS, PhD, is Assistant Professor of Communications at Bradley University. Dickhaus earned a BA in Mass Communication from Miami University in 2004 and a Master's in Speech Communication in 2006, also from Miami University. From 2006 to 2008, Dr. Dickhaus was a lecturer in the department of communication at Penn State

University, leaving to enter the mass communication PhD program at the University of Alabama. In August 2011, Dr. Dickhaus graduated with his PhD. Dr. Dickhaus teaches in the Sports Communication concentration.

JOE R. FEAGIN, PhD, is Professor of Sociology at Texas A&M University. He is one of the nation's foremost experts on race and racism. Recent examples of his work can be seen in *Racial and Ethnic Relations* (Sixth edition; Prentice-Hall, 1999; with Clairece Booher Feagin); *Living with Racism: The Black Middle Class Experience* (Beacon, 1994; with Mel Sikes); *White Racism: The Basics* (Routledge, 1995; with Hernan Vera); *Double Burden: Black Women and Everyday Racism* (M.E. Sharpe, 1998; with Yanick St. Jean); *The Agony of Education: Black Students at White Colleges and Universities* (Routledge, 1996; with Hernan Vera and Nikitah Imani); and *The New Urban Paradigm* (Rowman and Littlefield, 1998). His book with Harlan Hahn, *Ghetto Revolts* (Macmillan, 1973), was nominated for a Pulitzer Prize, and *Living with Racism* and *White Racism* have won the Gustavus Myers Center's Outstanding Human Rights Book Award. Feagin is past president of the American Sociological Association (ASA).

JOHN A. FORTUNATO, PhD, is a professor at Fordham University in the School of Business, Area of Communication and Media Management. He is also the author of four books, including *Commissioner: The Legacy of Pete Rozelle* and *Making Media Content* (Taylor Trade Publishing, 2006). He has published articles in *Public Relations Review, Journal of Interactive Advertising, Journal of Sports Media, Journal of Brand Strategy,* and multiple law reviews. Dr. Fortunato previously taught at the University of Texas at Austin in the Department of Advertising and Public Relations, and he received his PhD from Rutgers University in the School of Communication, Information, and Library Science.

JENNIFER GREER, PhD, is a Professor and Chair of the Department of Journalism at the University of Alabama. Before joining Alabama's faculty in 2007, Greer was an associate professor of journalism and social psychology at the University of Nevada, Reno. She has worked as a newspaper reporter for the *Kansas City Star* and other publications and was the managing editor of the online edition of the *Gainesville* (FL) *Sun*. Her research focuses on media effects and audience attitudes. Recent work has focused on media credibility and emerging delivery forms as well as gender and sport. She is on the editorial boards of *Mass Communication & Society*, *Journalism & Mass Communication Monographs*, and *Journalism & Mass Communication Educator*.

C. KEITH HARRISON, EdD, is Associate Professor in the DeVos Sports Business Management Program at University of Central Florida and Associate Director of The Institute for Diversity and Ethics in Sports (TIDES). He has extensive teaching and research experience in issues relating to leadership and race and diversity in sport. He has created and co-produced six educational documentaries or videos and has been the author and principal investigator for the annual *Black Coaches Association Hiring Report Card* since 2003.

LOUIS HARRISON, PhD, is an expert in race and culture in physical activity and sport and identity development in African Americans. An Associate Professor at University of Texas at Austin, Dr. Harrison has focused his research on the influences of race-related self-schemata and African-American racial identity on physical activity choices and performance. The purpose of this line of research is to investigate the factors that influence sport and physical activity participation, and identity developmental patterns of African Americans. Through his research, he hopes to gain a deeper understanding of the racial labels ascribed to particular sports and physical activities, and how these labels affect participation, persistence, effort expended, and performance. Additionally, he wishes to investigate ways physical educators and coaches can precipitate changes in the development of self-schemata for sport and physical activities in an effort to erase these racial labels and broaden the perceived physical activity choices of all students.

HAYWARD DERRICK HORTON, PhD, is Professor of Sociology and the School of Public Health at the State University of New York at Albany. Professor Horton specializes in demography, race/ethnicity, public sociology, and sociology of place. He has published over 30 articles on topics such as the demography of rural black families, differences in black-white levels of home ownership, the demography of black entrepreneurship, and the feminization of poverty. Professor Horton is co-editor of the book *Skin Deep: How Race and Complexion Matter in the "Color Blind" Era* (University of Illinois Press, 2004).

LANCE KINNEY, PhD, is Associate Professor in the Department of Advertising and Public Relations at the University of Alabama. Kinney's research interests include the impact of mood on advertising response, along with alternative marketing communication techniques, including corporate sponsorship of sports and other events. Kinney has presented original research at both national and international forums. He has also published research in professional journals, along with book chapters.

SUZANNE MALIA KIRKLAND, PhD, is a professor in the Graduate Physical Education Program at Azusa Pacific University (APU) in Azusa, California. Dr. Kirkland's research interests include the racial experiences of white/black athletes, career transitions of college athletes, stereotypes surrounding athleticism, academic achievement of college athletes, and the lived experience of her participants/students. She is an existentialist who values individual experience and the essence of perception. Dr. Kirkland encourages self-confidence, teamwork, and leadership in her students. In the last two years, she was awarded with the APU School of Education's Excellence in Research Award twice and won the Dean's Emerging Scholar and Dean's Accomplished Scholar Awards as well.

DAVID J. LEONARD, PhD, is Associate Professor and Chair in the Department of Critical Culture, Gender and Race Studies at Washington State University, Pullman. He is the author of *After Artest: Race and the Assault on Blackness* (SUNY Press, 2013) as well as several other works. Leonard is a regular contributor to *NewBlackMan,* Feminist Wire, *and Urban Cusp.* He blogs *@No Tsuris.* Follow him on Twitter *@drdavidjleonard.*

QUENTIN G. LOVE is a graduate of University of Michigan and Wayne State University, where he earned a Master's Degree in Business Administration. Quentin is the Founder and Chief Executive Officer (CEO) of AMC, a strategic firm that delivers marketing and consumer solutions. Quentin is a marketing and strategy veteran. He has worked with a number of organizations including a variety of Fortune 500 companies and/ or their established consumer brands such as Walmart, GM, Disney, Pepsi, Sony, Intel and events such as the ESPN the Weekend, Democratic National Convention (Denver 2008) and the Pan Arab Games (Doha, Qatar 2011).

CHRISTOPHER MURRAY is a reporter for the *Reno* (NV) *Gazette-Journal*. He is the newspaper's sports columnist and also has held roles as a designer, beat writer, and assistant sports editor at the paper. Murray has won several Nevada Press Association awards and has won honors from the Associated Press Sports Editors five times for project reporting, explanatory journalism, breaking news reporting, and overall beat writing. He earned his Bachelor's degree in journalism from the University of Nevada, Reno, in 2004 and received his Master's degree in journalism from the school in 2007. Murray is a voter in the Associated Press football poll and has covered high school, college, and minor and major league sports, as well as PGA Tour events.

DAVID NAZE, PhD, is Associate Professor of Communication at Prairie State College in Chicago Heights, Illinois. He received his PhD in Communication and Culture with an emphasis in Rhetorical Studies from Indiana University, Bloomington. His dissertation—"From Kansas City to Cooperstown: Re-Remembering the Cultural Legacy of Jackie Robinson"— focuses on the intersection of race, public memory, and sport.

ERIC PRIMM, PhD, is an Associate Professor of Sociology at the University of Pikeville. He received his PhD in sociology from the University of Colorado in Boulder. His research interests include race and sport, social class, class culture, and deviant subcultures.

LARRY PROCTOR, PhD, is CEO of BEAM, LLC. Balance, Empowerment, Accountability, Multiculturalism helps companies develop outstanding health and fitness programs tailored to each company's needs.

MICHAEL REGAN is a Doctoral Student in the Department of Sociology at Texas A&M University.

WADE P. SMITH is a Doctoral Candidate in the Department of Sociology at the University of Colorado. His research interests include organizational sociology with a focus on military and sport organizations.

VALERIE R. STACKMAN, PhD, is as an Assistant Professor of Sociology and Criminal Justice at the University of Pikeville. She received her PhD in Sociology from Howard University with specializations in Criminology and Medical Sociology. Both her courses and research take a critical approach to examining inequality in the criminal justice system on the basis of race/ethnicity, social class, gender, and other social demographic differences.

JEROME D. WILLIAMS, PhD, is the Prudential Chair in Business and Interim Director and Research Director of the Center for Urban Entrepreneurship & Economic Development, in the Department of Management and Global Business, Rutgers Business School–Newark and New Brunswick. His current research interests cover a number of areas in the consumer marketing domain, with an emphasis on multicultural marketing. He has conducted research on marketing communications and promotion strategies targeting multicultural market segments and consumer behavior of multicultural market segments related to public health communication issues. He was a member of the Institute of Medicine Committee on Food Marketing and Diets of Children and Youth that authored the book *Food Marketing to Children and Youth: Threat or Opportunity?* (National Academies Press). He is also co-editor of a book entitled *Advances in Communication Research to Reduce Childhood Obesity* (Springer).

Index